Microsoft® Office 6 in 1

Contributing Authors:
Peter Aitken
Sherry Kinkoph
Trudi Reisner
Faithe Wempen

Compiled by Faithe Wempen

A Division of Macmillan Computer Publishing
201 West 103rd Street, Indianapolis, Indiana 46290 USA

To Margaret and J.P., my family.   F.W.

Microsoft® Office 6 in 1

Library of Congress Catalog Card Number: 95-71448

International Standard Book Number: 0-7897-0559-1

98 97 96 95   8 7 6 5 4 3 2 1

Interpretation of the printing code: the rightmost double-digit number is the year of the book's first printing; the rightmost single-digit number is the number of the book's printing. For example, a printing code of 95-1 shows that this copy of the book was printed during the first printing of the book in 1995.

Screen reproductions in this book were created by means of the program Collage Plus from Inner Media, Inc., Hollis, NH.

Trademarks

All terms mentioned in this book that are known to be or are suspected of being trademarks or service marks have been appropriately capitalized. Que Corporation cannot attest to the accuracy of this information. Use of a term in this book should not be regarding as affecting the validity of any trademark or service mark.

Publisher
Marie Butler-Knight

Publishing Manager
Barry Pruett

Managing Editor
Elizabeth Keaffaber

Product Development Specialist
David Bradford

Editors
Mark Enochs
Audra Gable
Phil Kitchel
Rebecca Mayfield
Julie McNamee
Kelly Oliver
San Dee Phillips

Cover Designer
Jay Corpus

Designer
Barbara Kordesh

Indexers
Ginny Bess
Gina Brown

Production Team
Steve Adams
Brian Buschkill
Chad Dressler
Amy Gornik
Jason Hand
Damon Jordan
Daryl Kessler
Bob LaRoche
Michelle Lee
Kaylene Riemen
Bobbi Satterfield

Special thanks to C. Herbert Feltner for ensuring the technical accuracy of this book.

CONTENTS

vii

Part II: Word 123

Part III: Excel

229

Introduction

"There aren't enough hours in the day." It's a common complaint. Time is a commodity everyone can use more of. The Microsoft Corporation has packaged five of their most powerful and useful software products into one impressive package called Microsoft Office Professional. These programs run with the help of a sixth package, Microsoft Windows 95. With these software products, you can save time as you create impressive business documents, financial statements, and presentations, and manage your daily schedule.

Windows 95 is a graphical user interface (GUI) that allows you to organize and run your software packages in a graphical operating system, instead of using prompts and obscure commands (like you do with DOS). Windows 95 comes with several useful applications, including a word processor (Write), a graphics painting program (Paint), and a communications program (HyperTerminal). It also features many accessories, such as a clock, a calendar, and a phone dialer, that will help organize and simplify your work.

The five software packages in Microsoft Office are:

- **Word for Windows**   Arguably the best Windows-based word processing program on the market. Word has features to let you create a one-page memo, a newsletter with graphics, or even a 500-page report.

- **Excel**   A powerful yet easy-to-maneuver spreadsheet program. Excel can be used to generate impressive financial statements, charts and graphs, and databases, and to share the information with other software packages.

- **PowerPoint**   An easy-to-use presentation program that lets you create impressive slides and overheads or print out presentations.

- **Schedule+**   A daily planner, calendar, and to-do list that helps you get the most out of your day through careful schedule management.

- **Access**   A database program that's quickly become a leader in the industry because of its powerful capabilities and ease of use. Access is included only in the Professional edition of Office, not the Standard version.

Using This Book

Microsoft Office 6 in 1 is designed to help you learn these six programs (Office's five programs plus Windows 95) quickly and easily. You don't have to spend any time figuring out what to learn. All the most important tasks are covered in this book. There's no need for long classes or thick manuals. Learn the skills you need in short, easy-to-follow lessons.

The book is organized into seven parts—one for each of the six software packages, with 20-30 lessons in each part, and a final part that helps you integrate the various programs to work seamlessly together. Because each of these lessons takes 10 minutes or less to complete, you can quickly master the basic skills needed to navigate Windows, create documents, financial statements, or slide shows, or send and reply to mail messages.

If this is the first time you've ever used Windows 95 or a Windows 95 product, begin with the Windows 95 part of this book. What you learn in this part will help you navigate your way through the other software packages.

Conventions Used in This Book

Each of the short lessons in this book includes step-by-step instructions for performing specific tasks. The following icons are included to help you quickly identify particular types of information:

 Icons (small graphic symbols) indicate ways you can save time when you're using any of the Microsoft Office products.

 Icons offer easy-to-follow definitions that you'll need to know in order to understand how to use a software package.

 Icons help you avoid making mistakes.

In addition to the icons, the following conventions are also used:

On-screen text	On-screen text appears in boldface type.
What you type	Information you type appears in boldface type.
Items you select	Items you select or keys you press appear in boldface type.

Acknowledgments

Que Corporation would like to acknowledge the contributing authors of this book: Peter Aitken, Trudi Reisner, Sherry Kinkoph, and Faithe Wempen. Thanks also to Faithe Wempen for coordinating the third edition of this book.

And finally, thanks to our hard-working Que production team: Steve Adams, Ginny Bess, Gina Brown, Chad Dressler, Damon Jordan, Daryl Kessler, Bob LaRoche, Elizabeth Lewis, and Kaylene Riemen.

WINDOWS

Understanding Windows

In this lesson, you'll learn what Windows 95 is, and how to start it. You'll also learn the parts of the Windows 95 desktop and find out how to use a mouse to manipulate items on the desktop.

The What and Why of Windows

Microsoft Windows is a program that sets up an "environment" for you to work in at your computer, based on colorful pictures (called *icons*) and menus. This friendly environment is called a *Graphical User Interface (GUI)*.

Graphical User Interface A GUI (pronounced "GOO-ey") is a picture-based way of interacting with your computer. Instead of typing commands at a prompt, you select from menus and pictures to tell the computer what you want.

Windows comes with many useful accessory programs, including a no-frills word processor (WordPad), a graphics program (Paint), and a communication program (HyperTerminal). It also provides several handy tools such as a Calculator and a Notepad. Some users never need more features than these simple programs provide. However, those who do need more features often turn to the Microsoft Office suite of applications, which you'll learn about in later parts of this book.

Application Another word for a computer program that does something useful, like help you compose a letter (Word) or create a spreadsheet (Excel). Sometimes, the small accessory applications that come with Windows are called "applets."

Since this book is about Microsoft Office, we'll assume that you have purchased the more powerful Windows-based Microsoft Office applications, which do everything the simple programs do and more. That's why we won't attempt to cover applications like WordPad in this book; we'll assume you're using the Office products. If you are interested in learning more about WordPad, Paint, and the other free Windows applications, check out *The Complete Idiot's Guide to Windows 95* by Paul McFedries.

Starting Windows 95

Once Windows 95 is installed on your system (see the inside front cover of this book for instructions on how to do this), you go directly to the Windows 95 desktop each time you start your computer. There's no need to issue a special startup command. If you see a DOS prompt on the screen (something like **C:\>**), try typing **EXIT** and pressing **Enter**. If Windows 95 does not appear, turn your computer off and back on again. If Windows 95 still does not appear, the program is not yet installed.

Understanding the Windows Desktop

As you can see in Figure 1.1, the Windows 95 desktop is made up of several components. These components are used throughout Windows 95 and Windows applications to make it easy for you to get your work done.

The components of the desktop include the following:

Icons Icons are pictures that represent programs (Microsoft Excel, WordPerfect, and so on), files (documents, spreadsheets, graphics), printer information (setup options, installed fonts), and computer information (hard and floppy disk drives). Although when you first see the Windows 95 desktop, you have only two icons (My Computer and the Recycle Bin), icons are used throughout Windows 95 and Windows applications. Icons come in two sizes, large and small, and Windows 95 uses four types of icons: program, file, printer, and computer. I will point out each type of icon as it is introduced in the book.

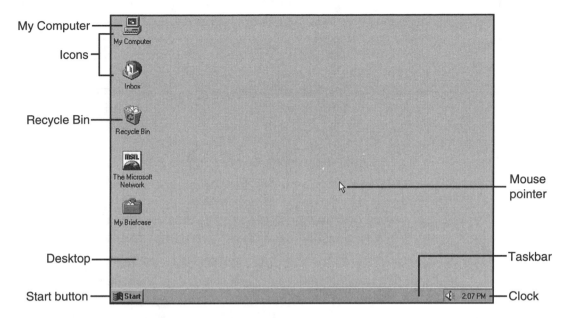

Figure 1.1   The Windows 95 Desktop.

Desktop   This is the area that takes up the entire background of the screen.

Mouse pointer   The on-screen pointer (usually an arrow) that you use to select items and choose commands. You move the pointer by moving the mouse across your desk or mouse pad. You'll learn how to use the mouse later in this lesson.

My Computer   The My Computer icon gives you access to a window in which you can browse through the contents of your computer or find out information about the disk drives, control panel, and printers that you have on your computer.

Recycle Bin   The Recycle Bin serves as your electronic trash can. You drag unwanted files, folders, or other icons to the Recycle Bin, and the Recycle Bin appears to have papers spilling over the top of it. To permanently delete the items, first double-click on the Recycle Bin icon to open its window. Select the items you want to delete, pull down the File menu, and choose Empty Recycle Bin. Windows asks you for your confirmation.

5

Start button   You click the Start button to display the Start menu, which contains a list of commands that enable you to get to work quickly and easily. The Start menu contains commands for launching programs, opening the most recently used files, changing settings, finding files or folders, accessing Help topics, running a program by entering a specific command line, and shutting down Windows 95.

Taskbar   Click a button on the taskbar to either launch a program or switch to a different task. For each application that you open, a button appears on the taskbar. When you use more than one application at a time, you can see the names of all the open applications on the taskbar. At any time, you can click the appropriate button on the taskbar to work with an open application.

Initially, the taskbar appears at the bottom of the screen. However, you can move it to the top, left, or right side of the screen to suit your needs. For example, if you were using the Microsoft Word for Windows program and the taskbar appeared above the status bar, you might want to drag the taskbar to the top of the screen and position it below the toolbars, where it is more convenient for use.

Clock   A clock at the right end of the taskbar displays the current time, and if you have a sound card, the Volume Control icon appears next to the clock. The Volume Control feature enables you to control the volume for sounds played through your computer speaker and multimedia devices.

Taskbar/Task List   Windows 95's taskbar is different from the Windows 3.1 task list because the taskbar is accessible at all times. In Windows 3.1, you had to press Ctrl+Esc to access the Task List and press Alt+Tab to switch to a different task.

Network Neighborhood   If your computer is on a network, you have another icon on the desktop called Network Neighborhood. Double-click the Network Neighborhood icon to browse through your network and see what it contains. This icon also provides information on mapped drives and interfaces. (This icon isn't shown in Figure 1.1.)

Inbox   If you installed Microsoft Exchange during setup, you have the Inbox icon on the desktop. The Inbox functions as a central place to get information from various information services, such as The Microsoft Network, electronic mail systems, and Microsoft Fax software. Double-click the Inbox icon to send and receive mail and faxes on your network.

My Briefcase   If you chose the Portable or Custom option to install Briefcase, you have the My Briefcase icon on your desktop. You can use Briefcase to keep copies of your files updated at home on your main computer or on the road on your portable computer.

Using the Mouse

You can use the mouse to quickly select any object on-screen, such as an icon or a window. (You'll learn about windows in the next lesson.) The process involves two steps: pointing and clicking.

To point to an object (icon, window title bar, and so on), move the mouse across your desk or mouse pad until the on-screen mouse pointer touches the object. You might have to pick up the mouse and reposition it if you run out of room on your desk.

To click, point the mouse pointer at the object you want to select, and then quickly press and release the left mouse button. If the object is an icon or window, it becomes highlighted.

When you're pointing at an object, you can also click the right mouse button (right-click) on it to bring up a menu of actions you can perform on the object (a shortcut menu). These shortcuts are mentioned throughout the book.

When you double-click on an item, you point to the item and press and release the left mouse button twice in rapid succession. Double-clicking takes action—if you double-click on an icon or a file, it opens.

You can also use the mouse to move an object (usually a window, dialog box, or icon) to a new position on-screen. You do this by dragging the object. To drag an object to a new location on-screen, point to the object, press and hold the left mouse button, move the mouse to a new location, and release the mouse button. The object moves with the mouse cursor.

In this lesson, you learned about the Windows 95 desktop, and you learned how to use the mouse to manipulate items on the desktop. In the next lesson, you'll learn how to work with windows, the main building blocks of the Windows 95 program.

Working with a Window

In this lesson, you will learn how to open a window, use scroll bars, resize a window, move a window, and close a window.

What Is a Window?

A window is a rectangular area of the screen in which you view program folders, files, or icons. The window is made up of several components (see Figure 2.1) that are the same for all windows in Windows 95 and Windows applications and make it easy for you to manage your work.

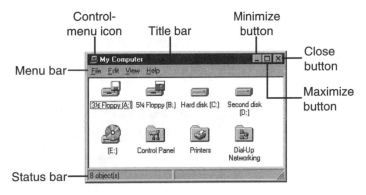

Figure 2.1 The My Computer window.

Same Controls, New Look For the most part, the components in the Windows 95 and Windows 3.1 windows are the same. The main difference is that the title bar, the Minimize, Maximize, and Restore buttons, and the Control menu have new looks in Windows 95. In addition, Windows 3.1 windows don't have Close buttons, and the Minimize command varies slightly in that it reduces the window to a button on the taskbar, while in Windows 3.1 it reduces the window to an icon on the desktop.

Opening Windows

To open a window from an icon, double-click the icon. For example, point at the My Computer icon on the desktop and double-click. If you do it correctly, the My Computer icon opens up to the My Computer window, as in Figure 2.1.

You can also use a shortcut menu to open a window. Just point to the icon and click the right mouse button, and a shortcut menu appears. Select Open on the shortcut menu, and the icon opens into a window.

Using Scroll Bars

Scroll bars appear along the bottom and right edges of a window when text, graphics, or icons in a window take up more space than the area shown. Using scroll bars, you can move up, down, left, or right in a window.

Figure 2.2 shows an example. Because this window's content is not fully visible in the window, scroll bars are present on the bottom and right sides of the window.

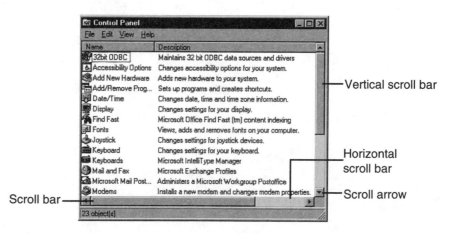

Figure 2.2   Scroll bars.

The following steps show you one way to use the scroll bars to view items outside the window:

1. To see an object that is down and to the right of the viewable area of the window, point at the down arrow located on the bottom of the vertical scroll bar.

2. Click on the arrow, and the window's contents scroll up.

3. Click on the scroll arrow on the right side of the horizontal scroll bar, and the window's contents move left.

By its size within the scroll bar, the scroll box depicts how much of a window is not visible. In Figure 2.2, the scroll bar size indicates that the portion visible in the window now is slightly more than half vertically and about one-quarter horizontally.

If you know approximately where something is in a window (maybe two-thirds of the way down, for example), you might want to drag the scroll box. To drag a scroll box and move quickly to a distant area of the window (top or bottom, left or right), use this technique:

1. Point to the scroll box in the scroll bar and hold down the left mouse button.

2. Drag the scroll box to the new location.

3. Release the mouse button.

Sometimes you might need to move slowly through a window. You can move the contents of a window one windowful at a time by clicking in the scroll bar on either side of the scroll box.

Sizing a Window with Maximize, Minimize, and Restore

You may want to increase the size of a window to see its full contents, or you may want to decrease a window's size (even down to button form on the taskbar) to make room for other windows. One way to resize a window is to use the Maximize, Minimize, and Restore commands. If you use the mouse, you will use the Maximize, Minimize, and Restore buttons located on the right side of the window's title bar. If you use the keyboard, you can use the Maximize, Minimize, and

Restore menu commands on the Control menu. The following list defines the purpose of each of these buttons and commands:

- Select the **Maximize** button or command to enlarge the window to its maximum size.

- Select the **Minimize** button or command to reduce the window to a button on the taskbar.

- Select the **Restore** button or command to return a window to the size it was before it was maximized. (The Restore button and command are available only after a window has been maximized.)

Figure 2.3 shows the My Computer window maximized to full-screen size. At full size, the Minimize and Restore buttons are available. At any other size, you see the Maximize button instead of the Restore button.

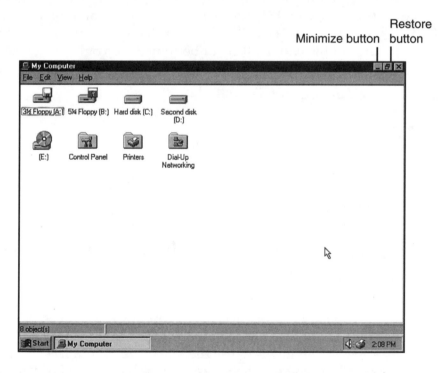

Figure 2.3 The My Computer window maximized to full-screen size.

To maximize, minimize, or restore a window with the mouse, click the appropriate button. To maximize, minimize, or restore a window with the keyboard, follow these steps:

1. Press **Alt+Spacebar** to open the window's Control menu.

2. Select the **Restore**, **Minimize**, or **Maximize** command from the menu.

Document Windows Are Different   Later in this book, when you are working with Office components, you will open documents within application windows. To access the control-menu for a document window, press Ctrl+– (minus sign).

Sizing a Window's Borders

At some point, you may need a window to be a particular size to suit your needs. If so, simply drag the window border to change the size of the window.

To use the mouse, follow these steps:

1. Place the mouse pointer on the portion of the border (vertical, horizontal, or corner) that you want to resize. When the mouse pointer is positioned correctly, it changes into one of the shapes described here:

   ↕   The vertical double-headed arrow appears when you position the mouse pointer over the top or bottom window border. It enables you to resize the window's height by dragging the border up or down.

   ↔   The horizontal double-headed arrow appears when you position the mouse pointer over either side of the window border. It enables you to resize the window's width by dragging the border left or right.

   ↗   The diagonal double-headed arrow appears when you position the mouse pointer over any of the four corners of the window border. It enables you to resize the window's height and width proportionally by dragging the corner diagonally.

2. Press the mouse button and drag the border. A faint line appears, indicating where the border will be when you release the mouse button.

3. Once the border is in the desired location, release the mouse button. The window is resized.

To resize a window using the keyboard, follow these steps:

1. Press **Alt+Spacebar** (or **Alt+–** for a document window in an application) to open the window's Control menu.

2. Press **S** to choose the Size command. The pointer becomes a four-headed arrow.

3. Use the arrow keys to move the pointer to the border or corner you want to resize. The mouse pointer turns into a different shape.

4. With the pointer on the border or corner, press the arrow keys to resize the window. A faint line appears showing the new border location.

5. When the faint line appears to be the size you want, press **Enter**. To cancel the operation, press **Esc**.

Moving a Window

When you start working with multiple windows, moving a window becomes as important as sizing one. For example, you may need to move one or more windows to make room for other work on your desktop.

You can move a window with the mouse or keyboard. To move a window using the mouse, point at the window's title bar, press and hold the left mouse button, and drag it to a new location. To use the keyboard, follow these steps:

1. Press **Alt+Spacebar** (or **Alt+–** for a document window in an application) to open the window's Control menu.

2. Press **M** to choose the Move command. The pointer changes to a four-headed arrow.

3. Use the arrow keys to move the window to a new location.

4. When the window is located where you want it, press **Enter**. To cancel the operation and return the window to its original location, press **Esc**.

Closing a Window

When you're finished working with a window you should close it. This can help speed up Windows, conserve memory, and keep your desktop from becoming cluttered.

To close a window with the mouse:

1. Click on the Control menu icon to display the Control menu.

2. Choose (click) the Close command to close the window.

 Quickie Close   To quickly close a window with the mouse, click on the Close button, or double-click the Control menu icon.

If you'd rather use the keyboard, select the window you want to close and press **Alt+F4**.

In this lesson, you learned how to use windows. In the next lesson, you'll learn how to use menus.

Using Menus

In this lesson, you learn how to select and open menus, choose menu commands, and read a menu.

What Is a Menu?

A menu is a group of related commands that tells Windows 95 what you want to do. Menu commands are organized in logical groups. For example, all the commands related to starting your work in Windows 95 are on the Start menu. The names of the available menus appear in the Start menu or on the menu bar in an application window.

In telling you to choose commands from a pull-down menu, this book uses the format *menu title, menu command*. For example, the statement "choose **File, Properties**" means to "open the File menu and select the Properties command."

 Pull-Down Menu   A menu that appears to "pull-down" from the menu bar. You access the menu by clicking on its name in the menu bar.

Choosing Menu Commands with the Mouse

To choose a menu command with the mouse, click on the menu title in the menu bar. The menu opens to display the available commands. To choose a particular command, simply click on it. For example, to see the Help options available for My Computer, click the **Help** menu title in the My Computer menu bar. The Help menu appears (see Figure 3.1). You can make the menu disappear by clicking anywhere outside it.

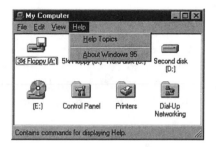

Figure 3.1   The Help menu.

To see the available topics from the Help facility, choose the **Help Topics** command, and a Help window appears. (Remember, to close this or any window, click the **Close** button.) For more information on using Help, refer to Lesson 5.

Choosing Menu Commands Using the Keyboard

You can also select menus and menu commands with the keyboard. To do so, press **Alt** to activate the menu bar of the active window. The first menu title becomes highlighted, indicating that the menu bar is active. With the menu bar active, you can select a menu using either of two methods:

- Use the arrow keys to highlight the menu title you want, and then press **Enter**.

- Press the key that corresponds to the underlined letter of the menu. For example, to open the Help menu, press **H**.

Once the menu is open, you select a command from the menu using the same techniques you used to open the menu. Highlight the command with the arrow keys and press **Enter**, or press the key that corresponds to the underlined letter to select the command you want.

To open the Control menu with the keyboard, press **Alt+Spacebar** in an application window (such as Microsoft Word or My Computer), or press **Alt+-** (hyphen) in a document. Then highlight your selection using the arrow keys and press Enter, or press the key that corresponds to the underlined letter of the command. To close the Control menu (or any menu for that matter), press **Esc**.

Commands, Options, or Selections?   Commands, menu options, and menu selections all refer to the same thing: items you choose from a menu. Further, commands may be "performed," "executed," or "selected." This simply means that the computer carries out the instructions associated with the command (whether it is to display another menu or perform an operation).

Reading a Menu

Windows 95's menus (and those of most other Windows applications) contain a number of common elements. For example, selection letters (letters that you press to choose a command) appear underlined. Some menu commands list shortcut keys that you can use to bypass the menus; shortcut keys are displayed to the right of their associated commands. (Shortcut keys aren't available for every menu option; generally, they are available for such common commands as Open, Save, and Print.) And some commands appear with a right-pointing arrow to the side, which indicates that if you choose the command, another menu will appear with more menu options.

Unavailable Commands   Some menu commands may appear grayed-out, which means that you cannot currently use them. These commands are only available for use under certain circumstances. For example, you cannot select the **Copy** command if you have not first selected an object to copy.

Another menu element that you will see often is the ellipsis (…). An ellipsis appears after a command to indicate that Windows 95 needs more information in order to complete the command. To get that information, Windows 95 displays a dialog box. For more on dialog boxes, see Lesson 4.

Figure 3.2 shows a number of these common menu elements.

You can press the underlined selection
letter to choose the command.

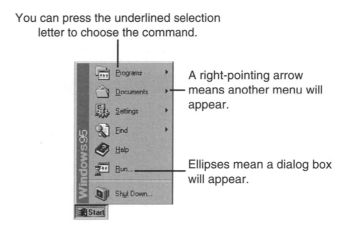

A right-pointing arrow
means another menu will
appear.

Ellipses mean a dialog box
will appear.

Figure 3.2   The Start menu.

Another common menu element is the check mark. The check
mark indicates that a menu option is currently active. Each time you
choose the menu command, the option is turned on or off (like a light
switch). When a check mark is present, the option is turned on.

To practice using menu commands, let's suppose you want to shut
down Windows 95. (Remember, you must shut down Windows before
you turn off or restart your computer.) Follow these steps:

1. Open the **Start** menu using either the mouse or the keyboard.

2. Choose **Shut Down** (notice the ellipsis following the Shut Down
command). A dialog box appears.

3. To shut down Windows 95, click the **Yes** command button or press
Enter. To abort the shut down process, click the No command
button or press **Esc**.

Using Shortcut Keys Instead of Menus

When you first get started, you'll need to use the menus to view and
select commands. However, once you become familiar with Windows
95, you'll probably want to use shortcut keys for commands you use
often. Shortcut keys enable you to select a command without using the

menus. Shortcut keys generally combine the Alt, Ctrl, or Shift key with a letter key (such as W). If a shortcut key is available, it is listed on the pull-down menu to the right of the command.

For example, Figure 3.3 shows the Edit menu from the My Computer window. Notice that you can choose **Edit, Select All** to select everything in the window, or you can press the shortcut key **Ctrl+A** to bypass the menu.

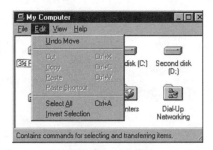

Figure 3.3   Use shortcut keys to bypass menus.

In this lesson, you learned how to use menus. In the next lesson, you'll learn how to use dialog boxes.

Using Dialog Boxes

In this lesson, you learn how to use the various dialog box components.

What Is a Dialog Box?

Windows 95 uses dialog boxes to exchange information with you. As you learned in Lesson 3, a menu command followed by an ellipsis (…) indicates that when you select the command, a dialog box will appear asking you for the information the program needs to complete the operation.

Windows 95 also displays dialog boxes to give you information. For example Windows 95 might display a dialog box to warn you about a problem (for example, to say File already exists, Overwrite?) or to confirm that an operation should take place (for example, to confirm that you're ready to shut down).

Using the Components of a Dialog Box

Dialog boxes vary in complexity. Some simply ask you to confirm an operation before it is executed (in which case you select OK to confirm the operation or Cancel to abort it). On the other hand, some dialog boxes are quite complex, asking you to specify several options.

The following list briefly explains the components of a dialog box, and the rest of the lesson describes the components and how to use them in greater detail.

Text box   A text box provides you with a place to type an entry, such as a name for a file you want to save or a path (drive and directory) you want to use to find a specific file.

List box   A list box presents a list of possible choices from which you can choose. Scroll bars often accompany a list box so that you can scroll through the list. In addition, a text box is sometimes associated with a list box: the list item that you select appears in the text box associated with the list.

Drop-down list box   This box is a single-line list box with a down-arrow button to the right of it. When you click on the arrow, the drop-down list box opens to display a list of choices.

Option buttons   Option buttons present a group of related choices from which you can choose only one. Simply click on the option button you want to select, and all others become deselected.

Check boxes   Check boxes present a single option or group of related options. A check mark appears in the box next to an option to indicate that it is active.

Command buttons   When selected, command buttons carry out the command displayed on the button (Open, Help, Quit, Cancel, OK, and so on). If there is an ellipsis on the button (such as Options...), choosing it will open another dialog box.

Tabs   Tabs represent multiple sections of a dialog box. Only one tab is displayed at a time, and each tab contains related options. Choosing a tab changes the options that appear in the dialog box.

Using Text Boxes

You use a text box to enter the information that Windows 95 needs to complete a command. This information is usually a file name or directory name. Figure 4.1 shows a text box and list boxes in the Open dialog box (accessed from the Windows 95 WordPad File menu).

To activate a text box by using the mouse, simply click in the text box. Notice that the insertion point (the flashing vertical line that indicates where the text you type will appear) appears in the active text box.

To activate a text box by using the keyboard, press **Alt+*selection letter***. For example, to activate the File Name text box shown in Figure 4.1, press **Alt+N**.

Figure 4.1   A text box and list boxes in the Open dialog box.

Once you have activated a text box and typed text into it, you can use several keys to edit the text. Table 4.1 outlines these keys.

Table 4.1   Editing Keys for Text Boxes

Key	*Description*
Delete	Deletes the character to the right of the insertion point.
Backspace	Erases the character to the left of the insertion point.
End	Moves the insertion point to the end of the line.
Home	Moves the insertion point to the beginning of the line.
Arrow keys	Move the insertion point one character in the direction of the arrow.
Shift+End	Selects the text from the insertion point to the end of the line.
Shift+Home	Selects the text from the insertion point to the beginning of the line.
Shift+Arrow key	Selects the next character in the direction of the arrow.
Ctrl+C	Copies selected text to the Clipboard.
Ctrl+V	Pastes selected text from the Clipboard.

Using List Boxes

You use a list box to make a selection from a list of available options. There are two kinds of list boxes: the kind where all the options are displayed at once, like the folders in Figure 4.1, and the drop-down kind, like the Look in box in Figure 4.1.

To select an item from a list box, click on the appropriate list item. If it's a drop-down list, you must click on the down arrow next to the box to open the list first.

To select an item from a list box using the keyboard:

1. Press **Alt+***selection letter* to activate the list box. For example, to activate the Look In list box displayed in Figure 4.1, press **Alt+I**. Press the **Tab** key to move to the list.

2. Press the up and down arrow keys or **PageUp** and **PageDown** to move through the list. Each list item appears highlighted as you come to it.

3. When the item you want is highlighted, press **Enter** to accept the selection and close the dialog box.

To select a drop-down list box item using the keyboard:

1. Press **Alt+***selection letter* to activate the list box.

2. Press the down arrow key to open the drop-down list box.

3. Press the up and down arrow keys or **PageUp** and **PageDown** to scroll through the list.

4. Press **Enter** to make your selection and close the dialog box.

Using Option Buttons

Option buttons enable you to make a single choice from a list of possible command options. For example, the Print Range options displayed in Figure 4.2 enable you to choose which pages of your document you want to print. The active option (the All option in Figure 4.2) is indicated by the small filled-in circle.

To select an option button with the mouse, click the circle for the option you want. To use the keyboard, press **Alt+***selection letter* for the option you want. For example, press **Alt+A** to activate the All option.

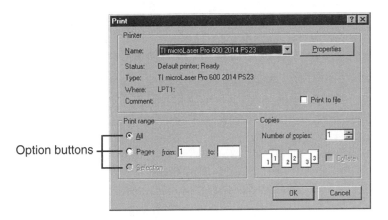

Figure 4.2   Option buttons in WordPad's Print dialog box.

Using Check Boxes

Command options that you can select (activate) or deselect (deactivate) are usually presented as check boxes. When a check box is selected, a check mark appears in the box, indicating the associated command option is active (see Figure 4.3).

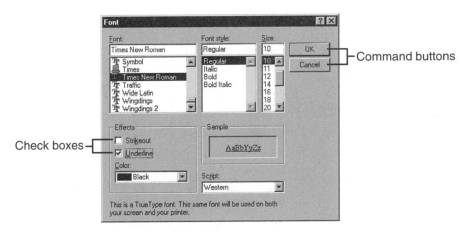

Figure 4.3   Check boxes in WordPad's Font dialog box.

To select or deselect a check box with the mouse, click on its box. Using the keyboard, press **Alt+***selection letter* to select or deselect a check box. For example, press **Alt+U** to activate the Underline option shown in Figure 4.3.

Using Command Buttons

You use command buttons to perform operations. To select command buttons with the mouse, simply click the appropriate command button. Figure 4.3 shows two common command buttons: OK and Cancel. Some dialog boxes, like the one in Figure 4.4, have additional command buttons for special features like Apply, Options, or Properties.

Select the **OK** button to accept the information you have entered or to verify an action and close the dialog box. (Pressing **Enter** is equivalent to selecting the **OK** button.) Select the **Cancel** button to leave the dialog box without executing the information you provided in the dialog box. (Pressing **Esc** is the keyboard equivalent to selecting the Cancel button.)

Accidents Happen   If you accidentally select the Cancel command button, don't worry. You can always reenter the dialog box and continue. Be careful when you select OK, however: the instructions you have entered in the dialog box will be executed.

Using Tabs

Windows 95 uses tabs to organize the options in a dialog box into categories (like a set of index dividers in a notebook). Tabs appear across the top of some dialog boxes, and each tabbed section contains a different set of options. Click on a tab to go to that area of the dialog box and access that tab's set of options. Figure 4.4 shows three tabs.

Tabs

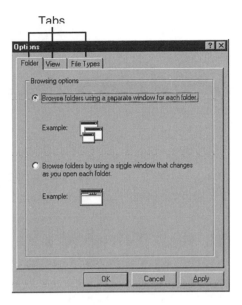

Figure 4.4   The Folder tab, the View tab, and the File Types tab in My Computer's Options dialog box.

In this lesson, you learned how to use the different components of dialog boxes. In the next lesson, you'll learn how to use Windows 95's Help system.

Using Windows Help

In this lesson, you learn how to get help, use Help's shortcut buttons, and use the What's This? feature.

Getting Help in Windows 95

Windows 95 offers several ways to get online help, instant on-screen help for menu commands or other tools. Online help is Help information that appears in its own window whenever you request it. The Help feature is organized like a reference book with three tabs: Contents, Index, and Find. The Contents and Index features show you step-by-step how to use commands and functions and how to perform operations in Windows 95's applications and accessories. The Find feature enables you to search for specific words and phrases in a Help topic. Whether you use the keyboard or the mouse to access Help, help information is always available at your fingertips. If you do not know or cannot remember how to perform some task, you can use Windows 95's Help system to tell you how.

Consistent Help Systems   You should take the time now to master the Windows help system, because the Help in all Microsoft Office products is very similar.

To get help on common tasks, follow these steps:

1. Click the **Start** button. The Start menu appears.

2. Choose **Help** from the Start menu. The Help Topics: Windows Help window appears, showing a list of Help topics.

3. Click the **Contents** tab to browse through the Help topics listed in the Help window, or click the **Index** tab to search for a specific Help topic. You can click the **Find** tab to search for specific words or phrases in a Help topic.

Fast Help   You can press **F1** at any time to access the Help system from within a program.

New and Improved Help   The Help systems in Windows 3.1 and Windows 95 are organized differently. Whereas Windows 3.1 is divided into the categories Contents, Search, and Glossary, Windows 95 is divided into the categories Contents, Index, and Find. In addition, you no longer have to scroll through the Help window to find a topic because the list of Help topics is short: they all fit on one small screen.

Using the Contents Feature

You can get help with common tasks using Help's Contents feature. The Contents feature displays the top level groups of information covered in Help, such as How To and Tips and Tricks. When you open a major group, a list of main topics appears. As you can see in Figure 5.1, both the major groups and the main topics in each group are represented by book icons, and subtopics are represented by page icons (with a question mark). You can simply select a book to see a list of the subtopics.

Follow these steps to use Help's Contents feature.

1. Click the main group that contains the Help topic you want to open. The group's name becomes highlighted.

2. Click the **Open** button to open the group. A list of chapters in that group appears.

3. Click the chapter that contains the Help topic you want to open. The chapter name becomes highlighted.

4. Click the **Open** button to open the chapter. A list of subtopics appears below the open chapter.

5. Click the subtopic you want to display and click the **Display** button that appears. A window appears, displaying the Help information.

6. After you read the explanation, click the **Close** button in the Help window's title bar to close the Windows Help window.

Double-click a book icon to display a list of topics.

Double-click a page icon to display a Help window.

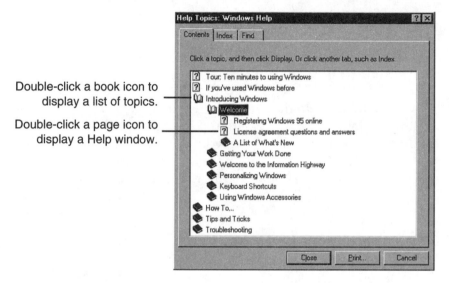

Figure 5.1   The Help Topics: Windows Help window.

If you want to print the list of Help topics in the Help Topics: Windows Help window, click the **Print** button at the bottom of the window. The Print dialog box appears. Click the **OK** button to print the list of help topics and subtopics.

Using the Index Feature

Help's Index feature provides a list of Help topics arranged alphabetically in the Index list box. In Figure 5.2, for example, the "copying" topic appears in the topic text box and is highlighted in the topic list. In some cases, Windows 95 displays more than one related topic in the topic list, and you can select which topic you need more information on. The Index is especially useful when you cannot find a particular Help topic in Help Contents' list of topics.

To use the Help Index, follow these steps:

1. Click the **Index** tab in the Windows Help window. The Index options are displayed.

2. Type a topic in the text box. This enters the topic for which you want to search and scrolls to the first entry that matches the word you typed. That topic appears highlighted in the topic list.

3. Click on a subtopic, if necessary. Then click the **Display** button, and Windows 95 displays the selected Help topic information in a Windows Help window.

4. When you are finished reading the Help information, click the **Close** button to close the Windows Help window.

Topic List   Instead of typing something in the text box, you can scroll through the topic list and select the topic you want from the list.

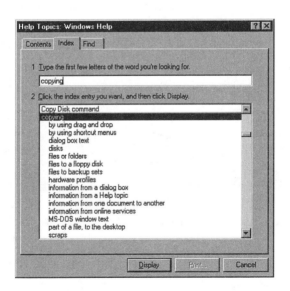

Figure 5.2   The Index tab in the Windows Help window.

Using the Find Feature

You can search for specific words and phrases in a Help topic instead of searching for a Help topic by category.

The first time you use the Find tab, you have to help Windows create a list that contains every word from your Help files. A special dialog box will guide you. Then you can search for words and phrases similar to existing words and phrases in a Help topic. The Find feature is especially useful when you cannot find a particular help topic in Help Contents' or Index's list of topics.

To build a word list (the first time only), follow these steps:

1. Click the **Find** tab in the Windows Help dialog box. The dialog box that appears gives an explanation of the Find feature and gives you these options: Minimize database size, Maximize search capabilities, and Customize search capabilities.

2. Choose the **Minimize database size** option to create a short word list, choose the Maximize Search Capabilities option to create a long word list, or choose the **Customize search capabilities** option to create a shorter word list if you have limited disk space.

3. Click the **Next** button to continue.

4. Click the **Finish** button to create the word list.

After Windows creates the word list, the Find tab contains a text box, a word list, and a topic list.

To search for words or a phrase in a Help topic:

1. Type the word you want to find in the first text box at the top of the dialog box. This enters the word for which you want to search and scrolls to the first entry that matches the word you typed. The word appears highlighted in the word list.

2. Click on another word in the word list to narrow the search if necessary.

3. Click on a topic in the topic list, and then click on the **Display** button. Windows 95 displays the selected Help topic information in a Windows Help window.

4. When you are finished reading the Help information, click the **Close** button to close the Windows Help window.

Topic List   Instead of typing something in the text box, you can scroll through the word list and select the word you want from the list. If you want to find words similar to the words in a Help topic, click the **Find Similar** button.

Accidents Happen   If you don't want to use the first list that Windows created, don't worry. You can rebuild that list to include more words or to exclude words. Simply click the **Rebuild** button and choose a word list option to re-create the word list.

Using Help Windows

When you display any Windows Help option, a button bar is displayed at the top of the Help window, and it always remains visible. This button bar includes three buttons: Help Topics, Back, and Options. Click the **Help Topics** button to return to Help's table of contents. Click the **Back** button to close the current Windows Help window and return to the preceding one. Click the **Options** button to display a menu with the following commands:

Annotate   Select this command if you want to add notes to the text in the Windows Help window. A dialog box appears, in which you can type and save your text. When you save the annotation, a green paper clip appears to the right of the Help topic to indicate that it has an annotation. Click the paper clip to view the annotation.

Copy   Select this command if you want to copy Help text to the Clipboard.

Print Topic   Select this command to display the Print dialog box. Then click the OK button to print the topic using the current printer settings, or click the Properties button to change printer settings.

Font   Select this command to change the size of the font displayed in the Windows Help window. When you select this command, another menu appears from which you can select Small, Normal, or Large. A check mark indicates the current size.

Keep Help on Top   Select this command if you want the Windows Help window to always be in the foreground of your screen. When you select this command, another menu appears from which you can select Default, On Top, or Not On Top. A check mark indicates the current selection.

Use System Colors   Select this command if you want Windows to use regular system colors for Help windows. When you select this command, a dialog box appears, informing you that you must restart Help for the color change to take effect. Choose Yes to close Help or choose No to return to the Windows Help window.

Help windows often display shortcut buttons as well. Using shortcut buttons, you can jump to the area of Windows 95 to which the Help information refers. For example, suppose you're reading a Help topic that contains information on how to change the wallpaper on the desktop (see Figure 5.3). You click the shortcut button (the button with an arrow that curves up and to the left) to jump to the Control Panel's Properties for Display dialog box from within Help. There you can make the necessary changes and get on with your work.

To use a shortcut button, simply click on it, and you're immediately taken to that area of Windows 95.

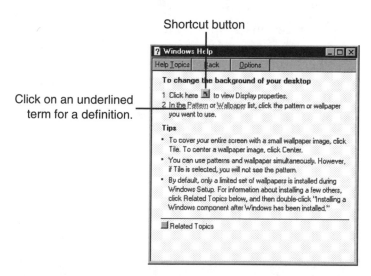

Figure 5.3   The shortcut button in the Help window.

Using the What's This? Feature

The What's This? feature provides a handy way of getting more information about dialog box options. You activate this feature by selecting the **?** icon, which appears on the right side of the title bar in most Windows 95 dialog boxes.

The following steps tell you how to use the What's This? feature to display a description of any option in a Windows 95 dialog box.

1. Click the **?** icon in the upper right corner of a Windows 95 dialog box. A large question mark appears next to the mouse pointer.

2. Click on any option in the dialog box. Windows 95 displays a box containing a short description of the item you selected.

3. When you are finished reading the Help information, click anywhere on the screen to close the Help box.

Quick Description   If you right-click on an option in a dialog box, a shortcut menu appears displaying one menu command: What's This?

Click on What's This? to view a description of the option.

In this lesson, you learned how to access Windows 95's Help system. In the next lesson, you'll learn how to shut down Windows 95.

Shutting Down Windows 95

In this lesson, you learn the various ways you can shut down and restart Windows 95.

You can shut down Windows 95 in one of three ways: you can shut down the computer, you can restart the computer, or you can restart the computer in MS-DOS mode. The following sections cover each of these methods.

Shutting Down the Computer

Before you shut down Windows 95, you should save any work you have in progress and close any open DOS applications so you won't lose any data. In most Windows applications, you choose **File, Save** to save a document, and then choose **File, Exit** to exit the application. If you don't save your data and close open applications, when you shut down, Windows closes each application for you and asks you to confirm saving each file.

To shut down the computer:

1. Click the **Start** button. The Start menu appears.

2. Choose **Shut Down** from the Start menu. The Shut Down Windows dialog box appears (see Figure 6.1), displaying a list of shut down options.

3. Choose the **Shut down the computer?** option and click **Yes**. Windows 95 prompts you to turn off your computer.

4. Turn off your computer.

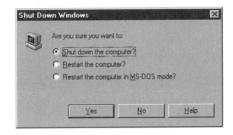

Figure 6.1   The Shut Down Windows dialog box.

Shutting Down   If you close all open documents and applications and return to the Windows 95 desktop, you can press **Alt+F4** to shut down the computer.

Because you can work with several documents and applications at one time, you may get carried away and forget to save a document before you shut down. Fear not: Windows 95 protects you from losing your data. For example, if you're working on a WordPad document and try to shut down Windows 95 without saving the document, the dialog box shown in Figure 6.2 appears, prompting you to save your changes.

Figure 6.2   WordPad prompts you to save changes before shutting down.

Select **Yes** to save the changes, select **No** to discard any changes you made, or select **Cancel** to cancel the shut down command altogether.

Forget to Save?   This message is your only warning. If you accidentally respond **No** to saving changes, the changes you made in the document are lost.

Restarting the Computer

When you experience system problems, you can restart the computer to clear up any problems you have encountered. To do so, follow these steps:

1. Click the **Start** button. The Start menu appears.

2. Choose **Shut Down** from the Start menu. The Shut Down Windows dialog box appears (see Figure 6.1), displaying a list of shut down options.

3. Choose the **Restart the computer?** option and click **Yes**. Windows 95 restarts your computer. If you're on a network, Windows asks you to log in.

 Restarting the Computer   Choosing the **Restart the computer?** option in Windows 95's Shut Down Windows dialog box is different from pressing **Ctrl+Alt+Delete**. If you press **Ctrl+Alt+Delete** in Windows 95, the Close Program dialog box appears, in which you can end selected tasks or choose the **Shut Down** option.

Restarting the Computer in MS-DOS Mode

You can run most DOS programs from within Windows, but occasionally you may find a program that performs poorly from within Windows. In most cases, you can fine-tune its properties to run correctly, but you might find it simpler to restart the computer in MS-DOS mode and run the program from there. Since Windows 95 does not load when the computer restarts, any conflicts with Windows 95 are eliminated.

Before restarting your computer, make sure you save your work and close any open applications. Then follow these steps:

1. Click the **Start** button. The Start menu appears.

2. Choose **Shut Down** from the Start menu. The Shut Down Windows dialog box appears (see Figure 6.1), displaying a list of shut down options.

3. Choose the **Restart the computer in MS-DOS mode** option and then choose **Yes**. Your computer is restarted, and the MS-DOS prompt appears on-screen.

4. To return to Windows, type **EXIT** at the MS-DOS prompt and press **Enter**. The computer restarts.

Closing All Programs and Logging On as a Different User

If you're on a network, you can log off the computer and let someone else sign in on your machine. This is useful if you have to share a computer with another user. To log off, choose the **Close all programs and log on as a different user** option in the Shut Down Windows dialog box. Choose **Yes**, and then enter your network password.

Logoff   The Logoff feature in Windows 95 is not available in Windows 3.1 unless you're running Windows for Workgroups.

In this lesson, you learned how to shut down Windows. In the next lesson, you'll learn how to start and exit applications.

Starting and Exiting Applications

In this lesson, you learn how to start Windows applications, use a document window, and exit Windows applications.

Starting Windows Applications

A Windows application is a program designed to take advantage of the graphical user interface (GUI) built into Windows 95. As you learned in Lesson 1, a GUI provides a common interface between you and your programs that enables you to use the same procedures to execute commands in most compatible applications. That means that you can start (and exit) most Windows applications using the same procedures. If you are using a non-Windows (DOS) application through Windows 95, you will need to consult that application's manual to learn how to start and exit.

There are several ways to start a Windows application. This lesson discusses four of those ways.

Using the Programs Menu

To start an application from the Programs menu using the mouse, follow these steps:

1. Click the **Start** button. The Start menu appears.

2. Choose **Programs** from the Start menu. The Programs menu appears.

3. Click the program folder that contains the program icon for the application you want to use. For example, if you want to use WordPad, open the Accessories folder to access the WordPad program icon (see Figure 7.1).

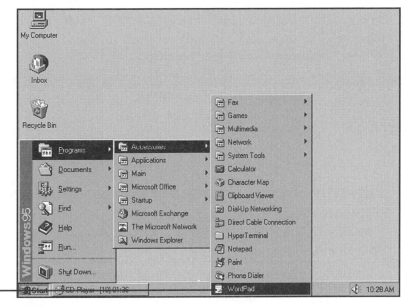

Click here to start
WordPad.

Figure 7.1 Program icons in the Accessories program folder.

4. Click the program icon for the application you want to start, and the application window appears.

To start an application from the Programs menu using the keyboard, follow these steps:

1. Press **Ctrl+Esc** to access the Start menu.

2. Press **P** to select Programs from the Start menu. The Programs menu appears.

3. Use the arrow keys to highlight the program folder that contains the program item for the application you want to use. Press **Enter** to select the folder.

4. Use the arrow keys to highlight the program icon for the application, and press **Enter** to start the application. The application window appears.

Starting an Application When You Start Windows

To view the applications in the Startup folder, click on the **Start** button, select **Programs**, and select **Startup**.

Startup   The Startup folder functions much the same way the Startup program group does in Windows 3.1's Program Manager.

Starting an Application from a Document

There are several ways that you can start an application from a document. You can start an application from the Documents list by following these steps:

1. Click the **Start** button. The Start menu appears.

2. Click on **Documents**, and the Documents list appears, displaying the names of the 15 documents you've used most recently.

3. Click on the document you want. Windows opens the application in which the document was created and then opens the document.

You can also open a document from the Explorer or My Computer by simply double-clicking on the document. Windows immediately starts the application in which the document was created and opens the document.

Using the Run Command

You can use the Run command to start applications that you use infrequently and that are not listed in the Programs menu. Or you might start a program with the Run command so you can enter command parameters or options that change the way the application starts. For example, in most word processing programs, if you start the program using the Run command, you can add a parameter that tells the application to open a specific file automatically upon startup.

What Are Your Options?   Check the documentation that comes with your software to find out about the available start-up options. You may want to jot down special start-up commands you plan to use often.

To use the Run command, follow these steps:

1. Click the **Start** Button. The Start menu appears.

2. Choose **Run** from the Start menu. The Run dialog box appears (see Figure 7.2).

3. Type the required command in the Open text box. Figure 7.2 displays the command that opens a setup program on a floppy disk in drive A.

4. When the command is complete, select **OK**. (If you decide not to use the Run command, select **Cancel**.)

 Can't Remember the Command?   If you don't remember the command that runs the application, click the **Browse** button in the Run dialog box. In the Browse dialog box that appears, choose the files you want to run.

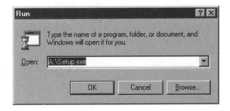

Figure 7.2   You can start any program with the Run command.

Working with Document Windows

When you use certain applications with Windows 95, you will create documents. For example, any letter you write in Word for Windows, or any drawing you create in Windows 95's Paint program, is contained in a document. These documents are sometimes called files or document files. When you are working on a document, it appears in a window.

When you start up an application, the application automatically creates a window for a new document. In most applications, you can create another document window by choosing the **File, New** command from that application's menu bar. The application creates a new window so you can start a new document, but any other document you might have been working on remains available. (If you're using WordPad, you can open only one document at a time. However, you can have multiple WordPad windows open simultaneously.)

When you are finished with a document, always save your changes by choosing **File, Save**, and then close the document window by choosing **File, Close** or simply by double-clicking on the document window's **Control menu** icon. This ensures that the document will not be lost or damaged accidentally. When you close a document window, the application remains open. The next section explains how to close the document window(s) and exit the application.

Exiting Windows Applications

Before you exit an application, be sure to save and close any documents you have worked on in that application (using the commands on the File menu).

Forget to Save Your Changes?   If you attempt to close a document window or exit an application without saving your changes, Windows 95 will ask you if you want to save before closing. To save any changes, click **Yes**; to exit without saving, click **No**; to remain in the application, click **Cancel**.

Once you have saved and closed all document files, you can exit a Windows application using any of the following four methods.

- To exit an application using its Control menu icon (the icon in the upper left corner of the application window), double-click the **Control menu** icon. If you prefer to use the keyboard, press **Alt+Spacebar** to open the application's Control menu and press **C** to choose the Close command.

- To exit an application using its Close button, click the **Close** button (the button with an X on the right end of the application's title bar).

- To exit an application using the menus, choose **File, Exit**. You can click on the commands with the mouse, or you can press **Alt+F** to open the File menu and press **X** to select Exit.

- The quickest way to exit is to use the shortcut key. Press **Alt+F4**, and you're on your way.

Exit Quickly   You can right-click on the application's button on the taskbar to display the shortcut menu. Then choose **Close** to close the application.

Exiting Windows Applications   Exiting Windows applications in Windows 95 and Windows 3.1 is handled the same way except that the Control menus look different, and application windows in Windows 3.1 do not have a Close button.

In this lesson, you learned how to start applications, use a document window, and exit applications. In the next lesson, you'll learn how to work with multiple windows.

Working with Multiple Windows

In this lesson, you learn how to arrange windows, move between windows in the same application, and move between applications.

In Windows 95, you can use more than one application at a time, and in each Windows application, you can work with multiple document windows. As you can imagine, opening multiple applications, each with its own windows, can make your desktop pretty cluttered. That's why it's important that you know how to manipulate and switch between windows. The following sections explain how to do just that.

Arranging Windows

When you have multiple windows open, some windows are inevitably hidden by others, which makes the screen confusing. You can use the commands on the taskbar's shortcut menu (which you access by right-clicking on the taskbar) to arrange windows.

Cascading Windows

A good way to get control of a confusing desktop is to right-click a blank area on the taskbar and choose the **Cascade** command from the shortcut menu. When you choose this command, Windows lays all the open windows on top of each other so that the title bar of each is visible. Figure 8.1 shows the resulting cascaded window arrangement. To access any window that's not on the top, simply click on its title bar.

Each title bar is
aligned in a —
cascading group.

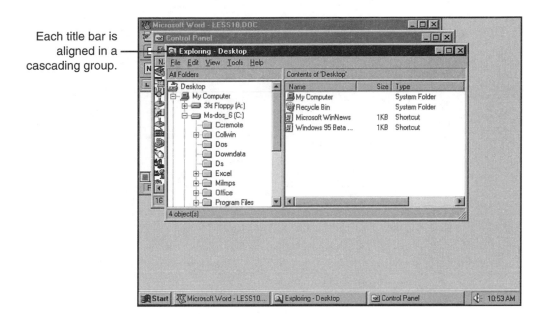

Figure 8.1   Cascaded windows.

Tiling Windows

If you need to see all of your open windows at the same time, use the
Tile command on the shortcut menu. When you choose this command,
Windows resizes and moves each open window so that they appear
side by side horizontally or vertically.

Right-click a blank area on the taskbar and choose the **Tile Horizontally** command from the shortcut menu to create an arrangement
similar to that shown in Figure 8.2. To arrange the windows in a vertically tiled arrangement (as shown in Figure 8.3), right-click a blank area
on the taskbar and choose the **Tile Vertically** command.

If you want to minimize all the windows at once, right-click a
blank area on the taskbar and choose **Minimize All Windows**. The
opened windows disappear from the desktop, but the application
buttons remain visible on the taskbar.

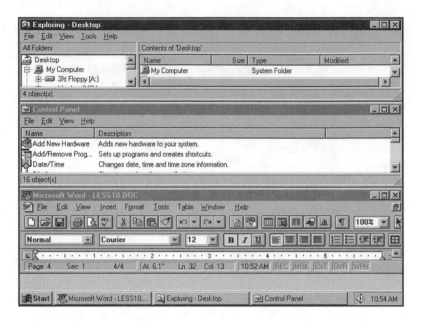

Figure 8.2   Horizontally tiled windows.

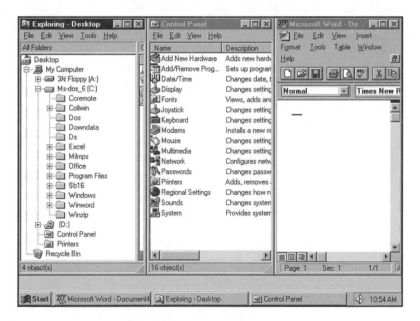

Figure 8.3   Vertically tiled windows.

Moving Between Applications

Windows 95 enables you to have multiple applications open at the same time. This section tells you how to move between applications using the taskbar.

Moving Between Applications   The Task List in Windows 3.1 has been replaced by the taskbar in Windows 95. In Windows 95, when you press **Alt+Tab** to switch to a different application, the icons and application names of all open windows appear in one dialog box. In Windows 3.1, you have to cycle through all the open applications until you get to the one you want.

The taskbar is a button bar that appears at the bottom of your screen by default. Each button on the taskbar represents an open window. The taskbar button of the currently active window looks like it's pressed in.

To quickly switch between applications using the taskbar, simply click on the button for the application to which you want to switch. Windows 95 immediately takes you to the application. Figure 8.4 shows two applications represented on the taskbar.

Bypass the Taskbar   Press and hold the **Alt** key and press the **Tab** key (continue to hold down **Alt**), and a dialog box appears displaying the icons and application names of all open applications. Each time you press **Tab**, a new (open) application is selected, and a border appears around the selected icon. When the application you want is selected, release the **Alt** key, and Windows 95 switches you to that application. If (while the dialog box is still on-screen) you decide you don't want to switch to that application, press **Esc** and release the Alt key.

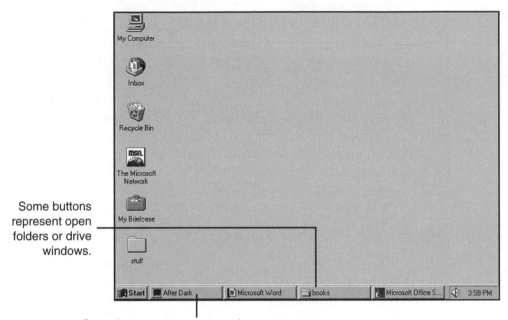

Some buttons represent open folders or drive windows.

Some buttons represent running programs.

Figure 8.4   The taskbar buttons.

Moving Between Windows in the Same Application

As I said earlier, in addition to working in multiple applications in Windows 95, you also can open multiple windows within an application. Moving to a new window means you are changing the window that is active. If you are using a mouse, you can move to a window by clicking on any part of it. When you do, the title bar becomes highlighted, and you can work in the window.

To move to the next document window using the keyboard, press **Ctrl+F6**; to move to the previous document window, press **Ctrl+Shift+F6**. Figure 8.5 shows Microsoft Word with three open documents. One document, Win01.doc, is minimized. Minimized windows within applications appear at the bottom of the application window, rather than in the taskbar.

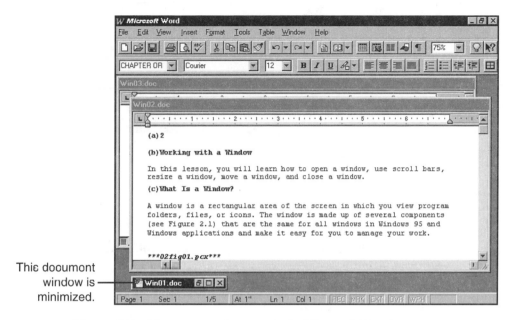

This document
window is —
minimized.

Figure 8.5   Three open documents in Microsoft Word.

Active Window   The window currently in use. You can tell which window is active because its title bar is highlighted a different color than the others.

Moving Between Windows   In Windows 3.1 and Windows 95, you can also use the Window menu to move between windows in the same application.

In this lesson, you learned how to arrange windows, switch between open applications, and switch between windows in the same application. In the next lesson, you'll learn how to copy and move information between windows.

Copying and Moving Information Between Windows

In this lesson, you learn about the Clipboard and how to copy and move information between windows.

What Is the Clipboard?

One of the handiest features of the Windows 95 environment is its capability to copy or move information (both text and graphics) from one window to another. This includes windows (documents) in the same applications, as well as those in different applications. When you copy or cut information, Windows places it in a storage area called the Clipboard.

The Clipboard holds only the information most recently copied or cut. When you copy or cut something else, it replaces anything that was previously on the Clipboard.

Copy and Cut   When you copy information, the application copies it to the Clipboard without disturbing the original. When you cut information, the application removes it from its original location and places it on the Clipboard.

Paste   When you paste data, the application inserts the information that's on the Clipboard in the location you specify, but the copy on the Clipboard remains intact (so you can use it again, if necessary).

You can see the contents of the Clipboard at any time by following these steps:

1. Click on the **Start** button to open the Start menu, and select the **Programs** menu.

2. From the Programs menu, open the **Accessories** folder.

3. Click the **Clipboard Viewer** icon, and the Clipboard Viewer window appears.

4. Click the **Maximize** button in the Clipboard Viewer window's title bar. The contents of the Clipboard appear in the Clipboard Viewer window. Figure 9.1 shows an address in the Clipboard.

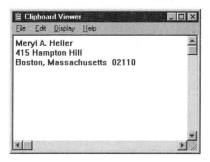

Figure 9.1   The contents of the Clipboard, as seen through the Clipboard Viewer.

Take a look at the contents of your Clipboard. Unless you have recently copied or cut information, the Clipboard is empty.

   **Without a Trace**   When you turn off your computer or exit Windows 95, the contents of the Clipboard are lost.

   Clipboard Viewer   The Clipboard Viewer in Windows 95 works the same as it did in Windows 3.1.

Selecting Text

Before you can copy or cut text, you must identify which text you want copied or cut. This is called selecting text. Selected text appears highlighted so you can quickly distinguish it. Figure 9.2 shows selected text in a WordPad document.

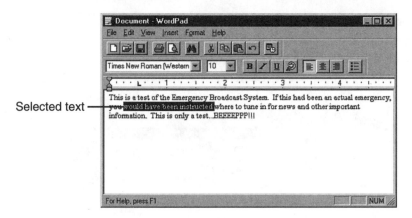

Selected text

Figure 9.2 Selected text in a WordPad document.

To select text with the mouse:

1. Position the mouse pointer just before the first character you want to select.

2. Press and hold the left mouse button, and drag the mouse pointer to the last character you want selected.

3. Release the mouse button. The selected text is highlighted.

To select text with the keyboard:

1. Use the arrow keys to position the insertion point (the blinking vertical line) just before the first character you want to select.

2. Press and hold down the **Shift** key, and use the arrow keys to move the highlight to the last character you want to select.

3. Release all keys, and the selected text appears highlighted.

Text Selection Shortcuts   To select a single word using the mouse, double-click on the word. To select text word-by-word (instead of character-by-character) with the keyboard, hold down both the **Shift** and **Ctrl** keys while using the arrow keys.

To get rid of the highlight on the selection (deselect it), click anywhere in the document or press an arrow key.

 Typing over Selected Text   If you press an alphanumeric key (a letter, number, or other character) while text is highlighted, the text will be deleted and replaced with that character.

Selecting Graphics

The procedure for selecting graphics depends on the Windows application you are using. In some word processing programs, such as WordPad, you select graphics in the same way you select text. In Word (and the other Office applications too), you click on a graphic to select it. In a program like Paint, there are special tools for copying and cutting either rectangular or irregular shapes. Since the procedure varies, it is best to refer to the documentation for each application.

Copying Information Between Windows

Once you have selected the text or graphics, the procedures for copying and pasting are the same in all Windows applications. To copy and paste information between windows of the same application, as well as between windows of different applications, follow these steps:

1. Select the text or graphic to copy (following the instructions earlier in this lesson).

2. Open the **Edit** menu and choose **Copy**. A copy of the selected material is placed on the Clipboard; the original selection remains in place.

3. Position the insertion point where you want to insert the selection. (You may need to open another application or document.)

4. Open the **Edit** menu and choose **Paste**. Windows copies the selection from the Clipboard to your document. (The original selection remains in its original location, and a copy remains on the Clipboard until you copy or cut something else.)

Multiple Copies Because the selected item remains on the Clipboard until you copy or cut again, you can paste information from the Clipboard multiple times. You can also perform other tasks before you paste. (For example, you can leave the selection on the Clipboard while you type new text, and then paste the selection whenever you're ready for it.)

Moving Information Between Windows

After you have selected text or graphics, the procedures for cutting and pasting are the same in all Windows applications. To cut and paste information between windows of the same application or windows of different applications, follow these steps:

1. Select the text or graphic to cut (following the instructions earlier in this lesson).

2. Open the **Edit** menu and choose **Cut**. Windows 95 removes the selection from its original location and places it on the Clipboard.

3. Position the insertion point where you want to insert the selection. (You may need to open another application or document.)

4. Open the **Edit** menu and choose **Paste**. Windows copies the selection from the Clipboard to your document. (A copy remains on the Clipboard until you cut or copy something else.)

Copy, Cut, and Paste Copying, cutting, and pasting in Windows 95 and Windows 3.1 work the same way.

In this lesson, you learned how to copy and move information between windows. In the next lesson, you'll learn how to browse through the files and folders on different drives.

Viewing Drives, Folders, and Files with My Computer

In this lesson, you will learn how to use the My Computer window to examine the contents of your hard, floppy, and CD-ROM drives.

Understanding Drives, Folders, and Files

A drive is the hardware that seeks, reads, and writes information from and to a disk. A hard disk and its drive are considered one inseparable unit, while a floppy disk can easily be removed from its drive and replaced with a different disk.

Drives are given letter names. For most computers, drives A and B are floppy disk drives, used to store and retrieve data on diskettes. Drive C generally designates the hard disk inside the computer. (Since hard disks and their drives are not easily separated, the terms disk and drive are often used interchangeably when referring to hard disks.) If the computer has more than one hard disk, or if the hard disk has been divided into multiple partitions (sections), the additional drives are usually labeled D, E, F, and so on.

Because so much information can be stored on a hard disk, hard disks are usually divided into folders. For example, drive C probably has a separate folder for every program you have. Floppy disks can contain folders too, but they usually don't. (Because of their limited capacity, it is easy to keep track of files on a floppy disk without using folders.)

Disk space is not set aside for individual folders; in fact, folders take up hardly any disk space at all. If you think of a disk as a file drawer full of papers, folders are like tabbed file folders used to organize the papers into manageable groups.

Folders   What Windows 95 refers to as folders, Windows 3.1 refers to as directories.

Folders hold files just as paper file folders hold pieces of paper. Files come in two varieties: program (or executable) files and document files. A program file contains the instructions the computer needs to perform. A document file contains a text document that you can read. Regardless of the type of files you're working with, you can use the Windows Explorer to view and control them.

 File Names   File names in Windows 95 can have up to 255 characters (including spaces) and do not require a file extension; file names in Windows 3.1 can only have up to eight characters and usually have a file extension with a maximum of three characters.

 Displaying Extensions   To display the file extensions for file names, choose **View, Options** from the Explorer, My Computer, or any open folder menu. In the Options dialog box, click the **View** tab, and click the **Hide MS-DOS File Extensions for File Types that are Registered** check box. The check mark disappears from the check box. Choose **OK** to display the file extensions.

Viewing a Disk's Contents with My Computer

My Computer enables you to view all files, folders, disk drives, and printers on your computer as icons. This feature is similar to the Windows Explorer.

Using My Computer, you can browse through your computer right from the desktop to find the files you want to open. Follow these steps:

1. Double-click the My Computer icon on the Windows 95 desktop to open the My Computer window. This window contains icons for

all the disk drives on your computer as well as the Control Panel folder.

2. Double-click the icon for the drive or folder you want to examine. A window opens that displays that drive's or folder's contents.

3. Select the folder you want to browse by highlighting its icon and choosing **File, Open** or by double-clicking its icon. You can select additional folders in the same way.

By default, each folder you select opens in its own window, as shown in Figure 10.1. To straighten up the screen and prevent one window from being hidden by the others, you can arrange the windows on the desktop any way you want by dragging each window by its title bar to a new location. For more on arranging multiple windows, refer to Lesson 8.

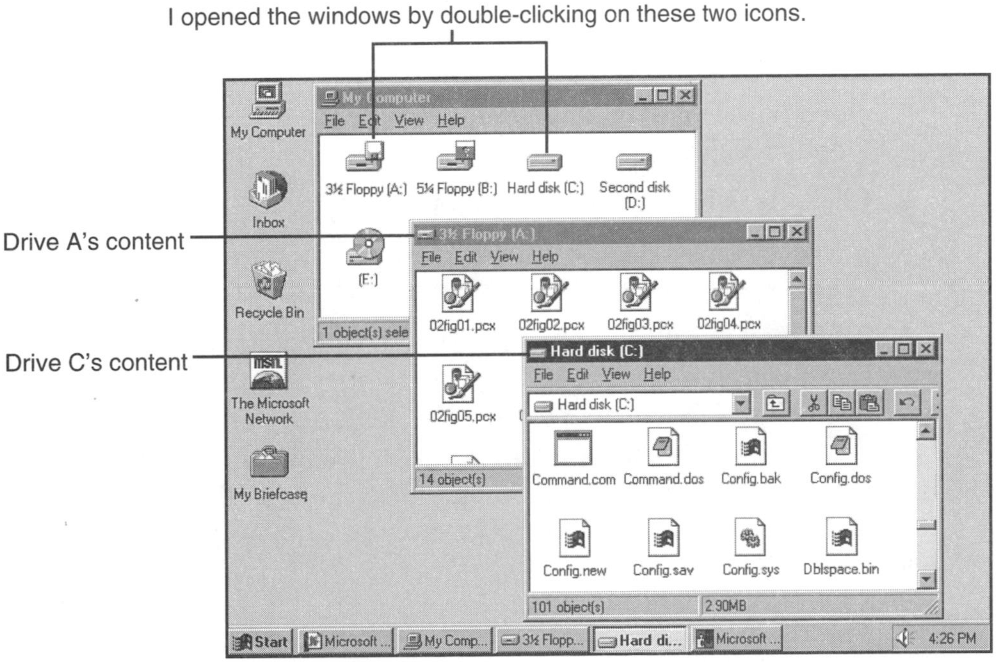

I opened the windows by double-clicking on these two icons.

Drive A's content

Drive C's content

Figure 10.1 Browsing the contents of the A drive and C drive from the My Computer window.

59

Changing the My Computer Display

By default, when you browse through folders in the My Computer window, Windows displays a separate window for each folder. However, you can control how Windows displays information in the My Computer window. For example, you can set up My Computer as a single window, and you can use the commands on My Computer's View menu to change the size of the icons and how they're displayed.

Setting Up a Single Window

If you don't like having all those windows onscreen while you're browsing through your files, you can set Windows 95 to display a single window that changes as you open each folder. Then, no matter how many windows you open, you will only see one window on the desktop at a time.

To set Windows 95 so that you only see a single window as you browse, follow these steps:

1. Open the current window's **View** menu and select **Options**. The Options dialog box appears.

2. Click the **Folder** tab. The Folder options appear (see Figure 10.2).

3. Select the second option (**Browse Folders By Using a Single Window that Changes as You Open Each Folder**).

4. Click the **OK** button. When you open a different folder in My Computer now, the content of the already-open window changes, rather than opening a new window.

If you want to change back to the default view in which Windows displays multiple browsing windows, repeat the preceding steps but choose the first option (**Browse Folders Using a Separate Window for Each Folder**) from the Folder tab.

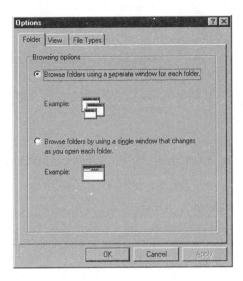

Figure 10.2   Browsing options in the Options dialog box.

Arranging Icons

By default, the items in the My Computer window (and any windows you open from this window) appear in Large Icon view. If you have a lot of icons in a window, you may want to open the View menu and choose Small Icons so you can view more icons at a glance. (You can always change back to the default view later by choosing **Large Icons** from the **View** menu.)

When arranging a window to suit your needs, you may need to move your icons out of the way by dragging them with the mouse. However, suppose that later you want to return your icons to their original positions. No problem! Choose **View, Arrange Icons, Auto Arrange** (a check mark appears next to the option when it's selected), and Windows 95 arranges the icons for you automatically. To turn off Auto Arrange, select the same command sequence again; the option is deselected, and the check mark disappears.

Arranging Icons   The Auto Arrange command works the same way in Windows 95 that it does in Windows 3.1. Also, in Windows 95 you can use the **Arrange Icons** command to sort the items in the window by Drive Letter, Type, Size, or Free Space, depending on the view you select. In Windows 3.1, when you select the **Arrange Icons** command, the icons appear in a window in the order of most usage (for example, programs you use most appear at the top of the window).

To sort the icons in a My Computer window, follow these steps:

1. Open My Computer's **View** menu.

2. Choose **Arrange Icons**, and a submenu appears.

3. Choose the sort type you want (**Drive Letter**, **Type**, **Size**, or **Free Space**). Windows rearranges the icons in the window accordingly.

Another way to clean up the icons in the window is to arrange the icons so that they line up in rows. To do so, choose **View, Line Up Icons**, and Windows 95 arranges the icons neatly in rows.

Closing My Computer

To close the My computer window, click the **Close** button in the upper-right corner of the window. The window shrinks to an icon on the desktop.

In this lesson, you learned how to view the contents of the drives on your computer by using the My Computer window. In the next lesson, you learn how to use the Windows Explorer to view a disk's contents.

Viewing Drives, Folders, and Files with Windows Explorer

In this lesson, you will learn how to use the Windows Explorer to view a disk's contents.

Starting the Windows Explorer

To start the Windows Explorer, follow these steps:

1. Open the **Start** menu and choose **Programs**.

2. From the Programs menu, choose **Windows Explorer**. The Windows Explorer window appears (see Figure 11.1).

Managing Files   The Windows Explorer in Windows 95 replaces Windows 3.1's File Manager.

Using the Windows Explorer Window

Figure 11.1 shows the Windows Explorer window. The All Folders window (the left side of the screen) shows all the folders on the selected drive (in this case, drive C).

The left side of the Windows Explorer window contains the folder list, a graphical representation of the folders and subfolders on your system. (The folder list on your screen will probably contain different folders from those shown in Figure 11.1.) In Figure 11.1, you can see that drive C contains a folder named Windows, and the Windows folder has many subfolders, including one named Command.

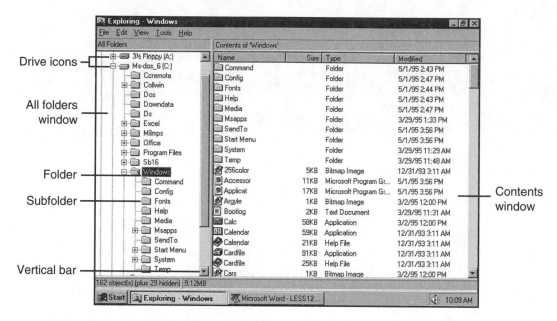

Figure 11.1 The Windows Explorer window, displaying the All Folders window.

Folders and Subfolders The folder that leads to all other folders (much like the trunk of a tree leads to all branches and leaves) is the main folder. In Figure 11.1 the main folder is C:\. Any folder can have a subfolder. Subfolders are like file folders within file folders; they help you organize your files. In Figure 11.1, Command is a subfolder of Windows.

The right side of the window contains a list of the files in the folder that's currently highlighted in the folder list. Notice that the folder icon next to the Windows folder (the highlighted folder) appears as an open folder. In this figure, the files in the Windows folder are listed in the right half of the Windows Explorer window.

Selecting Folders

When you select a folder using the folders list, its contents are displayed on the right side of the Explorer window. To select a folder with the mouse, simply click on the folder you want. Table 11.1 shows the keys you can use to select a folder with the keyboard.

Table 11.1 Keys for Selecting a Folder

Key	Function
↑	Selects the folder above the selected one.
↓	Selects the folder below the selected one.
←	Closes the selected folder.
→	Opens the selected folder.
Home	Selects the first folder in the folder list.
End	Selects the last folder in the folder list.
First letter of	Selects the first folder that begins with that folder name letter. Press the letter again if necessary, until you select the folder you want.

Opening and Closing Folders

In Figure 11.1, the folders list shows the subfolders of the Windows folder. You can close (decrease the detail of) the folders list so that subfolders do not appear, or you can open (increase the detail of) the folders list so it shows all folders. A plus sign (+) next to a folder indicates that there are subfolders to display; a minus sign (−) next to a folder indicates that the folder has been opened and can be closed.

To open or close a folder with the mouse, just double-click on the folder icon. To open or close a folder with the keyboard, use the arrow keys to select the folder and press + (plus) to open it or − (minus) to close it.

 **It's Only for Show**   Closing and opening affects this display only; it doesn't alter your folders in any way.

Changing Drives

You can change drives to see the folders and files contained on a different disk. To change drives with the mouse, click on the drive icon on the All Folders list. Using the keyboard, to change to a floppy drive press the first number for the drive type (for example, press 3 for a 3.5" floppy drive). Press H to change to your hard disk, or arrow keys to move from any other drive in the tree to your hard drive.

Changing the Windows Explorer Display

The commands in Windows Explorer's View menu enable you to change how the folders window and the files list window display information. You can control the size of the windows, whether or not the toolbar and status bar are displayed, and how the files in the files list window are displayed.

When you change the Windows Explorer's display settings to suit your needs, Windows remembers those settings. They remain the same every time you start Windows (until you change them again).

Sizing the Windows

In the Windows Explorer screens you've seen so far, both the folders window and the list of files were shown. You can change the way each is shown by changing the amount of window space allotted to each. For example, you may want to see more files and less white space around the folders list. Follow these steps to change the way the window space is divided between the panes:

1. A vertical gray line appears in the Folders window, representing the divider between the two panes. Point to the gray line, and the mouse pointer changes to a short vertical bar with two arrows.

2. Drag the line to where you want it. The window display changes accordingly (see Figure 11.2).

Changing the Display   You change the size of the window panes in Windows 95's Explorer the same way you changed them in Windows 3.1's File Manager window.

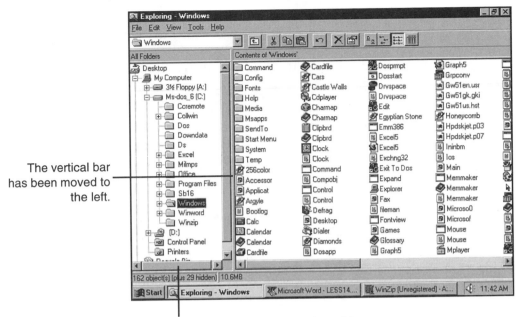

The vertical bar has been moved to the left.

Notice that the All Folders window now has a horizontal scroll bar.

Figure 11.2 The changed window.

Changing the File List Display

By default, the Windows Explorer shows only the file names and icons for each folder. However, you can change the display to include more information about each file if you want. The View menu provides you with four options you can use to customize the file list display: Large Icons, Small Icons, List, and Details.

The **View, List** command tells Windows to display only the icons and file names for each folder (as shown in Figure 11.2). This is the default display. Choose **View, Details** to have Windows display the following information about each file:

- Size in bytes
- File type (to describe the file such as Folder, Application, Help, Settings, and so on)
- Last modification day and date

You can also change the size of the icons that Windows displays in the files list window. Choose **View, Large Icons** to display large icons with the file names beneath the icons. Choose **View, Small Icons** to display small icons with the file names to the right of the icons.

Changing the Files List   The View, Large Icons and View, Small Icons commands in Windows 95 are not available in Windows 3.1. The View, List and View, Details commands in Windows 95 replace the View, Partial Details and View, All Files Details commands in Windows 3.1.

Small Icons versus List   Small Icons and List views both show small icons with the name to the right. The difference is how the files and folders are arranged. In List view, they're arranged in columns. In Small Icons view, they're arranged in rows.

Controlling the Order of the Display

As you can see in Figure 11.2, the files in the folder are listed in alphabetical order by file name. If you prefer, you can have Windows arrange the icons by the following methods:

- Choose **View, Arrange Icons, by Type** to arrange files alphabetically by their file type.

- Choose **View, Arrange Icons, by Size** to arrange files from smallest to largest.

- Choose **View, Arrange Icons, by Date** to arrange files alphabetically by date from newest to oldest.

Controlling the Order of the Display   The View, Arrange Icons command in Windows 95 replaces the View, Sort command in Windows 3.1.

Displaying the Toolbar

You can display the Windows Explorer toolbar at the top of the Windows Explorer window (as shown in Figure 11.2) by choosing **View, Toolbar**. Then you can click on the buttons on the toolbar instead of choosing menu commands. Table 11.2 shows the buttons on the Windows Explorer toolbar.

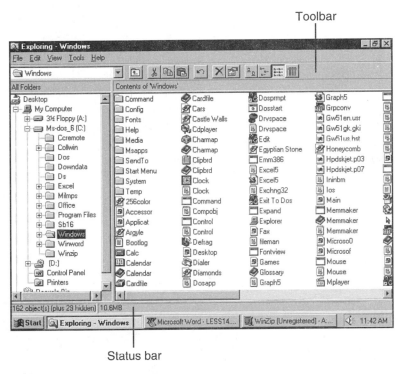

Figure 11.3   The toolbar and status bar are displayed.

Table 11.2   Windows Explorer's Toolbar Buttons

Button	Name	Description
	Up One Level	Displays the folder up one level from the folder currently displayed in the Folder text box.
	Cut	Cuts the selected file or folder and places it on the Clipboard.

continues

Table 11.2 Continued

Button	Name	Description
	Copy	Copies the selected file or folder to the Clipboard.
	Paste	Pastes the contents of the Clipboard to the location selected in the list.
	Undo	Undoes last file or folder operation.
	Delete	Deletes the selected file or folder.
	Properties	Displays the properties of the selected file or folder.
	Large Icons	Displays large icons in the contents window.
	Small Icons	Displays small icons in the contents window.
	List	Displays a list of files and folders with names and icons.
	Details	Displays a detailed list of files and folders.

Displaying the Status Bar

Initially, Windows displays the status bar at the bottom of the Windows Explorer window (as shown in Figure 11.3). If you want to hide the status bar, open the **View** menu and select **Status Bar** (to deactivate it). To redisplay it, repeat the previous command sequence.

Closing the Windows Explorer

If you're not going to use the Windows Explorer again right away, you should close it instead of minimizing it, to conserve system resources. To close the Windows Explorer, click the **Close** button or double-click the Control menu icon.

In this lesson, you learned how to use the Windows Explorer to examine the contents of a disk. In the next lesson, you'll learn how to create and delete files and folders.

Creating and Deleting Files and Folders

In this lesson, you learn how to create and delete files and folders.

Creating a File or Folder

Some files and folders are created automatically when you install a program. For example, when you install Word for Windows, the installation program creates a folder on your hard drive and places the Word for Windows files in that folder. However, you can also create files and folders yourself.

There are several reasons you may want to create a folder. Many application installation programs create a folder when you install the application on your computer. If one of your application installation programs does not, you will want to create a folder for that application.

A more common reason to create a folder is to store document files. For example, you may want to create a folder to store documents you create with WordPad so the document files won't be scattered among the more than one hundred Windows program files in the Windows folder. Having a separate folder for WordPad documents makes it much easier to find and manipulate the documents you create.

My Documents   Microsoft Office creates a folder called My Documents in your Windows directory, where it stores your files from Office programs by default.

Creating a Folder with Windows Explorer

To create a folder using the Windows Explorer, follow these steps:

1. Open the **Start** menu and choose **Programs**, then **Windows Explorer**. The Windows Explorer window appears.

2. Highlight the folder in the folders window under which you want to create the new folder. (The folder you create will be a subfolder of the folder you highlight.) If you don't want the new folder to be a subfolder of another folder, highlight the (C:) folder.

3. Select **File, New, Folder**. A folder icon named New Folder appears at the bottom of the files list.

4. Type the new folder name using up to 255 characters (including spaces) in the text box that appears next to the new folder icon. The name you type replaces the words "New Folder" as you type.

5. Press **Enter**, and Windows renames the new folder.

 Creating and Deleting Folders   The File, New Folder command in Windows 95 replaces the File, Create Directory command in Windows 3.1. You use the same process to delete a folder in Windows 95 (see "Deleting a File or Folder") that you did to delete a directory in Windows 3.1.

Creating a Folder with My Computer

To create a folder with My Computer, follow these steps:

1. In My Computer, open the icon or folder in which you want to create a folder.

2. Select **File, New**. Windows creates a new folder icon.

3. Type a new name for the folder and press **Enter**.

Deleting a File or Folder

There will come a time when you need to delete a file or folder. For example, you may have created a file or folder by mistake, you may want to remove the files or folder for an application you no longer use, or you may need to make more room on your hard drive.

 **Better Safe Than Sorry**   Before you delete anything, it is a good idea to make a backup copy of any files or folders you might need later. See Lesson 13 for directions on how to copy files and folders.

To delete a file or folder, follow these steps:

1. In a My Computer window or the Windows Explorer folders list, select the file or folder to delete. Be aware that when you delete a folder, Windows 95 deletes all files in that folder.

2. Choose **File, Delete** or press the **Delete** key. The Confirm Folder Delete dialog box appears, indicating what will be deleted and asking you to confirm the deletion.

3. Check the Confirm Folder Delete dialog box carefully to make certain you are deleting what you intended to delete.

4. Select **Yes**.

 Deleting a File or Folder   The File, Delete commands in Windows 95 and Windows 3.1 are similar. In Windows 95, however, you see only the Confirm Delete dialog box; in Windows 3.1, you see the Delete dialog box and then the Confirm Delete dialog box. Also, Windows 95 deletes the files from the Windows Explorer or the My Computer window and moves them to the Recycle Bin. Then, from the Recycle Bin you can restore any files you might need.

 **I Didn't Mean to Do That!**   If you delete a folder or file by mistake, immediately choose Edit, **Undo Delete** to restore the deleted folder(s) and file(s).

Working with the Recycle Bin

The files you delete in Windows are stored temporarily in the Recycle Bin. You can retrieve files from the Recycle Bin if you decide you need them again, or you can purge the deleted files when you're sure you no longer need them. By purging deleted files, you make more room on your disk.

To retrieve files you've deleted, follow these steps:

1. Double-click the Recycle Bin icon. The Recycle Bin window appears.

2. Click on the file you want to retrieve. To select multiple files, hold down Ctrl and click on each file.

3. Select **File, Restore**. Windows restores the files to their original locations.

Follow these steps to purge deleted files in the Recycle Bin:

1. Select **File, Empty Recycle Bin**. A confirmation dialog box appears.

2. Choose **Yes** to delete all the files.

3. Click the **Close** button to close the Recycle Bin window.

Purge Files Individually   To delete only one file from the Recycle Bin, select the file, open the File menu, choose Delete, and click on Yes. Windows purges that file only.

Recycle Bin   The Recycle Bin is a new feature in Windows 95; it is not available in Windows 3.1.

In this lesson, you learned how to create and delete files and folders. In the next lesson, you'll learn how to move and copy files and folders.

Moving and Copying Files and Folders

In this lesson, you learn how to select multiple files and folders and how to copy and move them.

Selecting Multiple Files or Folders

To really speed up operations, you will want to select multiple files or folders and then execute commands that affect the entire group. For example, you may want to select several files to copy to a disk. Copying them all at once is much faster than copying each file individually. The following sections explain how you can select multiple files and folders.

Selecting Multiple Contiguous Files or Folders

It is easy to select multiple files or folders that are displayed contiguously in Windows Explorer's files list window or My Computer.

 Contiguous Files   When the files that you want to select are listed next to each other in the Windows Explorer, without any files that you don't want in between them, they are *contiguous*.

To select contiguous files or folders with the mouse:

1. Click the first file or folder that you want to select. When you click it, it becomes highlighted.

2. Hold down the **Shift** key and click the last file or folder that you want to select. All the items between (and including) the first and last selections are highlighted. Figure 13.1 shows a selection of contiguous files.

Selected contiguous files

Figure 13.1 Selected contiguous files are highlighted.

To select contiguous files or folders with the keyboard:

1. Use the arrow keys to move the highlight to the first file or folder that you want to select. (Press **Tab** to move the highlight bar between the folders window and the files list window.)

2. Hold down the **Shift** key and use the arrow keys to extend the highlight to the last file or folder you want to select.

To deselect a contiguous group of files or folders, select a file or folder outside the selected items.

Selecting Noncontiguous Files or Folders

Often, the files or folders you want to select are noncontiguous: they are separated by several files that you do not want. To select such noncontiguous files or folders, you use the **Ctrl** key.

To select items with the mouse, hold down the **Ctrl** key and click on the files or folders you want. Each item you click on becomes highlighted and remains highlighted until you release the **Ctrl** key. Figure 13.2 shows a selection of multiple noncontiguous files. To deselect items with the mouse, click on any file or folder.

77

Figure 13.2 Selecting multiple noncontiguous files.

TIP

Narrowing the Selection   If you want to select or deselect files with related names, choose the **Tools, Find, Files or Folders** command. Enter the characters you want to find in the Named text box and choose **(C:)** from the Look in drop-down list. Then choose **Find Now**. When Windows 95 displays the files you want to select or deselect, choose **Edit, Select, All** in the menu bar of the Find dialog box to select all the files in the Search Results window. Then deselect the files you don't want selected. Lesson 14 explains how to use the Find command.

TIP

Selecting Files or Folders   You select files or folders in Windows 95 the same way you select files and directories in Windows 3.1.

Moving or Copying Files or Folders

To move or copy files or folders through the Windows Explorer or My Computer, you drag and drop—that is, you select the items you want from your source folder, "drag" them to the destination folder, and "drop" them there. You'll learn the details of using this technique later in this section.

Move vs. Copy   When you move the file or folder, it no longer exists in its original location, but only in the new location. When you *copy* a file or folder, the original file or folder remains in its original location, and a copy of the file or folder is placed in a second location.

Before you move or copy, make sure the source file or folder is visible, so you can highlight the file(s) you're going to drag. Also, make sure that the destination drive or folder is visible. In Figure 13.3, My Documents (the source folder), the **memoa** file (the source file), and the empty **WordPadDOC** folder (the destination folder) are all visible.

Figure 13.3   The selected file can be moved or copied.

Copying Files and Folders

With the mouse, use this procedure to copy:

1. Select the files or folders to copy.

2. Press the **Ctrl** key and drag the files or folders to the destination drive or folder.

3. Release the mouse button and the **Ctrl** key.

    With the keyboard, use this procedure to copy:

1. Select the files or folders to copy.

2. Select **Edit**, **Copy**.

3. Select the destination drive or folder.

4. Select **Edit**, **Paste**. Figure 13.4 shows the result of the copy and paste operations. The WordPad document file has been copied into the WordPadDOC folder.

Figure 13.4   The completed copy operation.

TIP **The File Is Already There** If you attempt to copy a file or folder to a location in which a file or folder with the exact same name exists, Windows 95 lets you know with a message that says This folder already contains a file called 'filename'. Would you like to replace the existing file with this one? Choose **Yes** to replace the existing file or **No** to stop the copy operation.

Moving Files and Folders

With the mouse, follow these steps to complete a move:

1. Select the files or folders to move.

2. Drag the files or folders to the destination drive or folder.

3. Release the mouse button.

    With the keyboard, complete a move using these steps:

1. Select the files or folders to move.

2. Select **Edit, Cut**.

3. Select the destination drive or folder.

4. Select **Edit, Paste**.

 Copying and Moving Files and Folders Copying and moving files and folders in Windows 95 and Windows 3.1 is similar. The **Edit, Copy** and **Edit, Cut** commands in Windows 95 replace the File, Copy and File, Move commands in Windows 3.1. Also, the Copy and Move confirmation dialog boxes you saw in Windows 3.1 do not appear in Windows 95, which makes it quicker to copy and move files and folders.

TIP **Wrong Move or Copy?** If you move or copy the wrong files or folders, you can choose **Edit, Undo Copy** in the Windows Explorer menu bar or click the **Undo** button on the Windows Explorer toolbar to undo the operation.

In this lesson, you learned how to select multiple files and folders and how to copy and move files and folders. In the next lesson, you'll learn how to rename and find files and folders.

Renaming and Finding Files and Folders

In this lesson, you learn how to rename and find files and folders.

Renaming Files or Folders

To rename your files, follow these steps:

1. In the Windows Explorer or a My Computer window, select the file or folder you want to rename.

2. Choose **File,Rename**. A box appears around the file or folder name, and the name is highlighted.

3. Type the new name for the file or folder. As you type, the new name replaces the old name. Press **Enter** when you finish typing.

 **It Worked Yesterday** Never rename program files. Many applications will not work if their files have been renamed.

 Renaming Files or Folders The File, Rename commands in Windows 95 and Windows 3.1 are similar. However, you type the new name next to the icon in Windows 95, whereas in Windows 3.1, you type the new name into the Rename dialog box.

Searching for a File

As you create more files, the ability to find a specific file becomes more critical. You can search for either a single file or a group of files with similar names using the **Tools, Find** command. To search for a group of files, use the asterisk wild card (*) with a partial file name to narrow the search. You can also perform a partial name search without wild cards, search by last modification date, save complex searches, and do a full text search. Table 14.1 shows some search examples and their potential results.

Wild Cards   When you're not sure of the file name you want to find, you can use the asterisk wild card (*) to replace multiple characters in the file name or the question mark wild card (?) to replace one character in the file name.

Table 14.1   Search Examples and Their Results

Characters Entered for Search	Sample Search Results
mem?.doc	mem1.doc, mem2.doc, mem5.doc
mem1.doc	mem1.doc
mem*.doc	mem1.doc, mem2.doc, mem11.doc
c*.exe	calc.exe, calendar.exe
*.exe	calc.exe, calendar.exe, notepad.exe
c*.*	calc.exe, calendar.exe, class.doc

To search for a file, follow these steps:

1. Click the **Start** button, select **Find**, and select **Files or Folders**. The Find dialog box appears (see Figure 14.1).

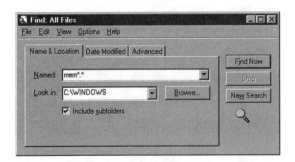

Figure 14.1   The completed Find dialog box.

2. In the Named text box, enter the characters you want to find, using wild cards to identify unknown characters.

3. If you want to search the entire drive, choose **C:** in the Look In text box (if it's not already there) and make sure the **Include subfolders** check box is selected.

If you want to search only the main folder, make sure the **Include Subfolders** check box is not selected.

If you want to search a specific folder, click the **Browse** button and select a folder from the folders list.

4. If you want to search for a file according to its last modification date, select the **Date Modified** tab and select the date options you want.

5. If you want to search for a certain type of file, select the **Advanced** tab and choose a file type in the Of Type drop-down list box.

6. Select the **Find Now** button to begin the search. The search results window appears under the Find dialog box, showing the files that were found (see Figure 14.2).

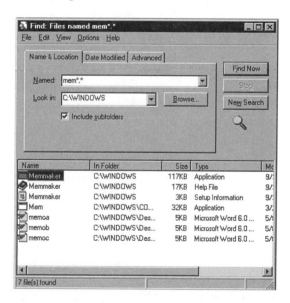

Figure 14.2   The search results appear below the Find settings.

Searching for a File   The Find command in Windows 95 replaces the File, Search command in Windows 3.1.

In this lesson, you learned how to rename a file or folder and search for a file or folder. In the next lesson, you'll learn how to work with fonts in Windows.

Working with Windows Fonts

In this lesson, you learn to find what fonts you have, display font samples, add new fonts, and delete fonts.

Finding Out What Fonts You Have

Many printers can print more than one character style or typeface (called a font). Check your printer manual to see if your printer is capable of printing multiple fonts. If it is, you will want to check the font setup in Windows 95 before you print. Fonts may be stored on floppy disks or on cartridges that slide into the printer.

Windows provides and supports different fonts, including TrueType fonts. Bit-mapped fonts store a unique bit map (or graphic) image for each font in each size. TrueType fonts are easily accessible, built-in, scalable fonts that don't care what kind of printer or display monitor you have.

When you set up Windows 95, the fonts that are stored directly in your printer were identified. Figure 15.1 shows the list of fonts in the Properties sheet for an HP DeskJet 500 printer. Font cartridges are available for this printer, and the Cartridge B: Prestige Elite is selected. You can select a maximum of two cartridges for this printer at any time.

Use the Fonts page in the Properties sheet (shown in Figure 15.1) to see the Font options. From this dialog box, you can determine which font cartridges are installed.

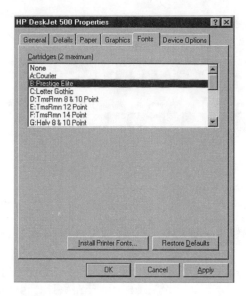

Figure 15.1   Selecting a font cartridge.

To check the font cartridge setup:

1. Choose **Start**, **Settings, Printers**. The Printers window appears.

2. From the Printers window, right-click the printer icon. The short-cut menu appears.

3. Choose **Properties**. The Properties sheet appears.

4. Click the Fonts tab. The font options for the selected printer appear (see Figure 15.1).

5. If your fonts are stored on cartridges, highlight the cartridge(s) you'll use (based on the maximum number identified in the dialog box).

A more common type of font used in Windows 95 is TrueType. These fonts are stored on your hard disk, and can be used with any printer. Use the Fonts folder shown in Figure 15.2 to check the setup of the fonts stored on the hard disk drive. Follow these steps:

1. Choose **Start**, **Settings**, **Control Panel**. The Control Panel window appears.

3. Double-click the **Fonts** icon. The Fonts window appears (see Figure 15.2).

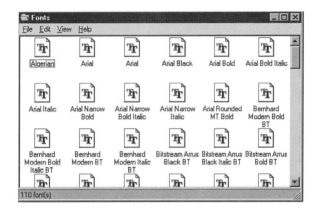

Figure 15.2 The Fonts folder.

Displaying Font Samples

Windows displays detailed information about any font you select in the Fonts window. You can see a sample of a font and all the sizes it comes in on-screen, as well as print a copy of the sample font.

To display a font sample:

1. Open the Fonts window, as described in the previous steps.

2. Double-click a font and Windows displays a sample with all the sizes it comes in (see Figure 15.3).

3. Click the **Print** button in the font's dialog box to print font information and font size samples.

Figure 15.3 A font sample with all its sizes.

Installing Fonts from Disk

You may find that you want to add fonts to the operating environment. These fonts become available for use in all Windows applications. When you add a font to Windows, you use disk space (however, TrueType fonts take up much less space than bit-mapped fonts.)

To install fonts from disk, follow these steps:

1. Display the Fonts window, as described earlier in this lesson.

2. From the Fonts menu bar, choose **File, Install New Font**. The Add Fonts dialog box appears.

3. Insert the disk that contains the fonts you want to add into the correct drive.

4. In the Add Fonts dialog box, select the drive letter for the fonts disk (A:, B:, or D:) and click the **OK** button. The fonts available on the disk or CD appear in the List of Fonts list box.

5. Select the fonts you want to add and click the **OK** button. The fonts are copied to the Fonts folder.

Deleting a Font from Disk

Fonts take up space in active memory as well as on your hard disk.
There may come a time when you want to either delete fonts you don't
use from active memory, or remove them entirely from your disk. To
delete a font, follow these steps:

1. Open the Fonts window, as described earlier in this lesson.

2. Select the fonts you want to delete.

3. From the Fonts menu bar, choose **File, Delete**. Windows asks you
   to confirm deleting the font(s).

4. Click the **OK** button. Windows removes the font(s) from disk.

Quickly Delete the Fonts   You can drag the unwanted fonts
to theRecycle Bin to quickly delete the fonts you no longer use.

In this lesson, you learned how to view, install, and delete fonts. In
the next lesson, you'll learn how to set up Windows for printing.

Getting Ready to Print

In this lesson, you learn to check printer installation and add a printer.

Checking the Printer Installation

When you installed Windows 95, Setup configured any printers connected to your computer and created the links to those printers automatically. Before you attempt to print, however, you need to make sure the settings are correct.

To check the print setup from Windows 95, go to the Printers folder by choosing **Start, Settings, Printers**. The Printers folder appears (see Figure 16.1).

Figure 16.1   The Printers folder. You may have different printers.

Easy Access to the Printers Folder   You can access the Printers folder from three other places in Windows 95: the My Computer window, the bottom of the folders list in the Windows Explorer, and the Control Panel Printers icon.

From the Printers folder, you can select the installed printer you want to check and open the Properties sheet to check the settings. To do so, right-click the printer icon in the Printers window to open the shortcut menu, then choose **Properties** to display the Properties sheet. Figure 16.2 shows the Properties sheet for the HP DeskJet 500 printer.

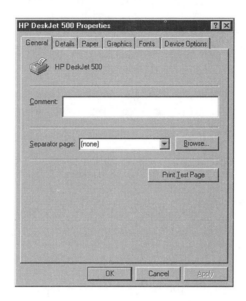

Figure 16.2   The Properties sheet for the HP DeskJet 500 printer.

You can choose from the following tabs in the Properties sheet to check the settings.

- The General options include the printer name, comments, separator page, and print test page.

- The Details tab displays the details about your installed printer. On it, you see the port connection to which your printer is attached (Print to the following port). This port is usually LPT1 (for parallel printers) or COM1 (for serial printers).

Printer Port   The connection on your computer to which your printer's cable is attached. If the port description indicates Not Present, Windows 95 doesn't detect that port on your computer. Check your printer manual to see whether your printer uses the parallel or serial port.

93

- The Paper options enable you to enter information about the paper size and paper source, and to set the orientation to either Portrait (the short side of the paper is at the top) or Landscape (the long side of the paper is at the top).

- The Graphics options enable you to enter information about resolution in dots per inch (the more dots the finer the resolution), dithering (none, coarse, fine, line art, error diffusion), and intensity (from darkest to lightest). If you have a PostScript printer, your options will be different.

- The Fonts options list the installed printer fonts and enable you to install and remove printer fonts (see Lesson 15).

- The Device options enable you to change the print quality and printer memory. Check your printer manual if you are not sure of the amount of memory in your printer.

 Checking the Printer Installation The Printers folder in Windows 95 replaces the Printers feature in the Control Panel of Windows 3.1.

You may have other tabs too, depending on the printer model. For example, PostScript printers will have a PostScript tab.

Once you have all the options set the way you want them, click the **OK** button in the Properties sheet to return to the Printers folder.

Setting a Default Printer

The default printer is the printer that the computer assumes is connected to your computer unless you select another printer. The default printer is the first one that appears in the Printers folder list. Windows automatically sets up a default printer when you install Windows. Almost all Windows 95 applications print using the Printers folder and the default printer defined through it. To set up a default printer:

1. From the Printers folder, double-click the icon that represents the printer you want to set as the default. The print queue window opens.

2. In the print queue, choose the **Printer, Set as Default** command to specify the default printer.

Quick Method   Right-click on a printer icon and choose **Set As Default** from the shortcut menu.

Checking Your Equipment

In addition to making sure Windows 95 is ready for printing, you'll want to check your equipment. Be sure to double-check the following things:

- Is the cable between the computer and the printer securely attached on each end?

- Is the printer turned on?

- Is the printer ready for the computer's transmission with the On Line light on?

- Is paper loaded in the printer?

Adding a Printer

The Add Printer wizard in the Printers folder lets you add new printers to the list of installed printers available in the Printers folder. This wizard simplifies the process of adding a printer.

To add a new printer, follow these steps:

1. In the Printers window, double-click the **Add Printer** icon. The Add Printer Wizard dialog box appears.

2. Click the **Next** button.

3. Choose **Local Printer** or (**Network Printer** if you are using a networked printer) and click the **Next** button.

4. Select a printer from the Manufacturers list box. The wizard displays a list of printer models in the Models list box.

5. Select a printer model.

6. Choose **OK**, then follow the prompts in each wizard dialog box to install the new printer.

What Disk?   When you install new features to your Windows environment, have your installation diskettes close at hand. In the example above, Windows will probably ask you to insert one of the disks containing the printer drivers before it can carry out your instructions.

Adding a Printer   You can add a printer with the Add Printer Wizard in Windows 95 instead of choosing the Add button in the Printer dialog box in Windows 3.1.

In this lesson, you learned how to check your printer's installation and add a printer. In the next lesson, you learn how to manage print jobs in Windows.

Printing with the Printers Folder

In this lesson, you learn to manage jobs you send to any printer.

Printing from a Windows Application

To print from any Windows application, choose **File, Print**. A Print dialog box appears for you to specify a number of options. The options available depend on the application. When you click **OK** in this dialog box, the application hands off the font and file information to the Printers folder. This enables you to continue working in your application while your job is printing. The Printers folder acts as the "middleman" between your printer and the application from which you are printing.

Print Jobs Windows creates a print job (or simply a job) when you choose the Print command from the application you are working in.

Printers Folder Each printer icon in the Printers folder in Windows 95 handles print jobs rather than using a separate Print Manager in Windows 3.1.

Checking the Print Queue

When you print a document, the printer usually begins processing the job immediately. But what happens if the printer is working on another job that you (or someone else if you're working on a network printer) sent? In this case, the Printers folder acts as a print queue and holds the job until the printer is ready for it.

Print Queue   A holding area for jobs waiting to be printed. If you were to list the contents of the queue, the jobs would appear in the order they were sent to the Printer.

Figure 17.1 shows a document in the print queue. As you can see, the print queue window displays the document name, status, owner, progress (pages), and started at (time and date). Notice also that the printer's status shows that it is printing. This indicates the document was just sent to the queue and is beginning to print.

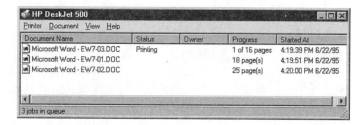

Figure 17.1   The print queue window.

To display the print queue, follow these steps:

1. Click the **Start** button, and choose **Settings**. The Settings menu appears.

2. Choose **Printers** and the Printers folder appears.

3. Double-click the printer icon for the printer to which you are printing. The print queue window appears with a list of queued documents. If no documents are waiting to print, there won't be any jobs listed below the column headings.

Display the Print Queue Quickly   Double-click the printer icon that appears on the taskbar immediately after printing a document.

Controlling the Print Job

You can control print jobs once they're in the queue. This includes changing the order in which the jobs print, pausing and resuming the print job, and deleting a job before it prints.

Reordering Jobs in the Queue

To change the order of a job in the queue, simply drag the job entry to a new position in the list.

First Come, First Served You can't reorder or place a job before the job that is currently printing.

Pausing and Resuming the Print Queue

You may want to pause the queue and then resume printing later. For example, the paper in the printer may be misaligned. Pausing the print queue will give you time to correct the problem.

To pause the print queue, choose **Printer, Pause Printing** or press **Alt+P** and then **A** while in the print queue window. To resume printing, choose **Printer, Pause Printing** again from the print queue menu bar or press **Alt+P** and then **A**.

Printer Stalled Your printer may stall while it's processing your print job. If it does, Windows displays the word stalled in the printer status line. Press **Alt+P** and then **A** to start printing again. This gets the printer going again, but chances are that a problem such as the printer being out of paper or ink caused the printer to stall. If so, the queue will stall again, and you'll have to refer to your printer manual or contact a technical person to help you.

Deleting a Print Job

Sometimes, you'll send a document to be printed and then change your mind. For example, you may think of other text to add to the document or realize you forgot to spell-check your work. In such a case, deleting the print job is easy. Follow these steps:

1. Click the **Start** button, and choose **Settings**. The Settings menu appears.

2. Choose **Printers**. The Printers folder appears.

3. Double-click the printer icon for the printer to which you are printing. The print queue window appears.

4. Select the job to delete.

5. Choose **Document, Cancel Printing**.

 Clear the Queue! To delete all the files in the print queue, choose **Printer, Purge Print Jobs** from the print queue menu bar or click the **Close** button in the top right corner of the window.

In this lesson, you learned how to control print jobs. In the next lesson, you learn how to change the desktop and regional settings.

Controlling the Appearance of Windows 95

In this lesson, you'll learn to control specific aspects of the Control Panel, such as on-screen colors, the appearance of your desktop, and the locale and units settings.

Changing Your Desktop

The Control Panel is a folder available through the Settings menu that enables you to control various aspects of Windows 95 (see Figure 18.1).

The Display Properties sheet lets you control many things about your desktop. To access this dialog box, follow these steps:

Figure 18.1 The Windows 95 Control Panel.

1. Choose **Start, Settings, Control Panel**. The Control Panel appears (see Figure 18.1).

2. Double-click the **Display** icon. The Display Properties dialog box appears.

Display Settings   The Display icon in Windows 95's Control Panel replaces the Color and Desktop icons in Windows 3.1's Control Panel.

The Display Properties sheet contains several tabs that control different sets of options. The following sections explain how to use these tabs.

Changing the Desktop Background

You can changea number of visual and performance elements of your desktop through the Control Panel. To change the desktop background, follow these steps:

1. Open the Display Properties sheet (as described earlier in the lesson).

2. If necessary, click the **Background** tab. The Pattern and Wallpaper options appear in the window (see Figure 18.2).

3. Select the options you want, and choose **OK**.

 Tile or Center?   Tile repeats the graphic to cover the entire desktop; Center places a single copy of the graphic in the center.

From the Background page, you can change any of the following options:

Pattern   Select the pattern to be displayed on the desktop. You can choose from a number of simple, two-color patterns; see the sample screen displayed at the top of the dialog box to see an example.

Wallpaper   More elaborate than the Pattern selection, the Wallpaper option enables you to display .BMP files on your desktop. Windows 95 comes with some very attractive wallpapers. The wallpaper you select is displayed in the sample screen at the top of the dialog box.

Display   Select the type of display you want for the wallpaper. Tiled wallpaper repeats pictures to cover the whole desktop. Centered wallpaper places one picture in the middle of the desktop; extra space around the wallpaper is filled with the desktop color.

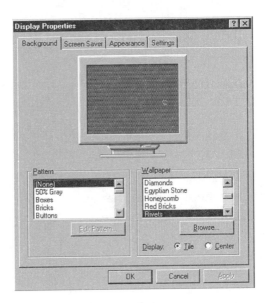

Figure 18.2   Rivets is selected in the wallpaper options.

Setting a Screen Saver

Screen savers were originally designed to protect your screen from "burning in" an image that was displayed there too long. Even though today's monitors are advanced enough to eliminate this problem, screen savers are still fun to use. If you select a screen saver, Windows automatically blanks the screen and runs a pattern across it anytime your computer is inactive for the default length of time. To return to the screen you left and continue working, press a key or move the mouse.

To select a screen saver, follow these steps:

1. Open the Display Properties sheet (as described earlier in this lesson).

2. Click the **Screen Saver** tab.

3. Open the Screen Saver drop-down list box and click on a screen saver. The sample screen at the top of the page shows the current selection.

4. In the Wait text box, enter the number of minutes you want to delay the screen saver, and then choose **OK**.

Changing Appearance Settings

With the Control Panel, you can change the appearance of your desktop by setting the colors of many components in Windows 95. The capability to control the color of certain Windows elements can help you learn to use the program faster: you're able to look for a particular color and shape, instead of just a shape. Or you can adjust the colors displayed on your color monitor just for a change of pace.

Follow these steps to change the Windows screen colors from the Control Panel:

1. Open the Display Properties sheet (as described earlier in the lesson).

2. Click the **Appearance** tab. The color scheme options appear in the window.

3. Select a color scheme from the Scheme drop-down list box by clicking the down arrow or by pressing **Alt+S** and then **Alt+O**. The predefined scheme options appear.

4. Use the arrow keys to scroll through the scheme options. The display above the Scheme text box illustrates the current selection. Select the scheme you want to use.

5. Press **Enter** to make your choice. Figure 18.3 shows the Slate color scheme selected in the Appearance page.

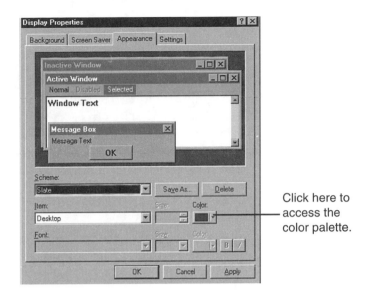

Figure 18.3   The Slate scheme as selected on the Appearance page.

Click here to access the color palette.

After you become more comfortable with Windows 95, go into the Appearance page and create your own color scheme. You can assign different colors to the various Windows elements (title bar, buttons, menus, and so on). To do so, click on the element in the sample area that you want to change, and choose a color from the **Color** drop-down list. To save your creation as a Windows 95 scheme, click the **Save As** button, enter a name for the color scheme, and choose **OK**.

Color Scheme   A color scheme is a set of predefined or customized colors that applies a different color to a different part of the screen. Color schemes make each Windows element easy to identify.

Changing Regional Settings

Most readers will use Windows 95 in the United States. However, if you work in an international setting, you may want to make some changes in the Regional Settings Properties sheet. You can configure Windows to use settings familiar to your region, nationality, and number system. For example, if a United States firm creates letters or documents to be sent abroad to Spain, regional settings would benefit everyone by ensuring that all numeric and other settings are indigenous to Spain. Follow these steps to control the regional settings:

1. Select **Start, Settings, Control Panel**. The Control Panel window opens.

2. Double-click the **Regional Settings** icon. The Regional Settings Properties sheet appears (see Figure 18.4).

3. Make the selections for the changes you desire.

4. Choose **OK** and the changes are made.

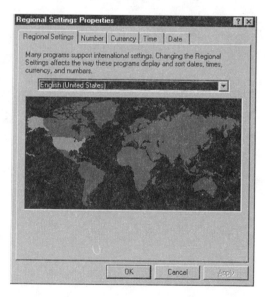

Figure 18.4 The Regional Settings Properties sheet.

In the Regional Settings Properties sheet, you can make changes on any of the following pages:

- **Regional Settings**   Windows has a number of standard locale settings on how units are displayed, page setup defaults, and so on. Use the Locale option on the Regional Settings page to choose the locale setting you want to use.

- **Number**   Use the Number options to change the way Windows displays numbers.

- **Currency**   Use the Currency options to change the way Windows displays positive and negative currency values.

- **Time**   Use the Time options to change the way Windows displays time values.

- **Date**   Use the Date options to change the way Windows displays long and short dates.

 Regional Settings   The Regional Settings icon in Windows 95's Control Panel replaces the International Settings icon in Windows 3.1's Control Panel.

In this lesson, you learned to change the desktop and change regional settings from the Control Panel. In the next lesson, you'll learn how to run DOS applications.

Running DOS Applications

In this lesson, you learn to use Windows features in DOS applications, understand new DOS commands, and configure DOS applications.

Using the MS-DOS Prompt Program

The MS-DOS Prompt program icon lets you install and run DOS applications while running Windows. The MS-DOS Prompt program appears at the bottom of the Programs menu.

Using Windows Features in DOS Applications

You can run your DOS applications under Windows 95, just as you did in Windows 3.1. There are several Windows features you can use in a DOS application, including a toolbar, a window you can size, and a Close button. These features enable you to work in a DOS application just as you would in a Windows application.

More support for Running DOS Applications   Windows 95 provides more support for running DOS applications than Windows 3.1. Applications that wouldn't run under Windows 3.1 now run properly in Windows 95, including applications that require special hardware (such as a joystick for games). When you run a DOS application in a window under Windows 95, you can now use a toolbar and a Close button, and you can size a window.

To open a DOS program in a window, follow these steps:

1. Choose Start, Programs. The Programs menu appears.

2. Choose MS-DOS Prompt. You see the MS-DOS prompt in a window.

3. At the MS-DOS prompt, type the command that starts your MS-DOS program. The DOS program appears in a window, as shown in Figure 19.1.

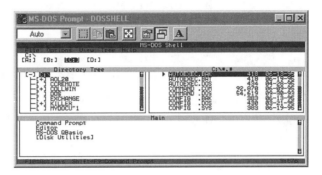

Figure 19.1   A DOS program in a window.

Displaying a Toolbar

When you run a DOS application in a window under Windows 95, a toolbar appears at the top of the window. The buttons on the toolbar provide access to the most common commands, enabling you to work with the DOS application as if it were a Windows application. You can click a button on the toolbar to quickly perform the following functions:

- Cut, copy, and paste text and graphics between DOS and Windows applications

- Switch between a window and full-screen mode

- View properties of the DOS application

- Access font options for displaying text in a DOS application window

Sizing a DOS Window

You can change the size of a DOS application window the same way you resize a Windows 95 window. Simply point to the border of the DOS application window until the mouse pointer becomes a double-headed arrow, then drag the border of the window in the direction you want to shrink or enlarge the window.

The Minimize, Maximize, and Restore buttons appear in the upper-right corner of the DOS application window. These buttons are identical to the Minimize, Maximize, and Restore buttons in a Windows 95 window. Click the **Minimize** button in the DOS application window to change the window to a button on the taskbar. Click the **Maximize** button to enlarge the display to full-screen size in the window. Click the **Restore** button to restore the full-screen window to its previous size.

If you press **Alt+Enter**, the DOS application displays as full size without a window. When you press **Alt+Enter** again, the DOS application displays in a window again.

Using the Close Button

When you open a DOS application in a window, you'll see a Close button (the button with an X on it) in the upper-right corner of the window. This button is the same as the Close button in a Windows 95 window.

To close a DOS application, follow these steps:

1. Exit your DOS application as you normally do. You see the MS-DOS prompt.

2. Click the Close button to close the MS-DOS prompt window.

Understanding the New DOS Commands

There are new DOS commands that make it easy for you to work with DOS applications under Windows 95. For instance, the Start command enables you to access new capabilities supported by Windows 95. Also, there are commands that work with files that have long file names in Windows 95.

New DOS Commands   The Start command and the commands (such as Dir and Copy) that work with long file names in Windows 95 aren't available under Windows 3.1.

The Start Command

The Start command enables you to start a Windows or DOS application from the MS-DOS command prompt. To use this command, follow these steps:

1. Choose **Start, Programs**, **MS-DOS Prompt** program. The MS-DOS window appears.

2. At the MS-DOS prompt, type **start**, press the **Spacebar**, then type the application name. For example, type **start excel**. If you want to start an application and open a document, type the document name and file type. For example, type **start budget.xls**.

It Won't Start   If the program doesn't start, type it in again including the path. For example, to start the Norton Utilities, type **start C:\NU\Norton**. You can also edit the path in the AUTOEXEC.BAT file to include that folder, so you won't have to type the complete path in the future.

Long File Names

You can now use long file names in Windows 95 and in DOS applications that run under Windows 95. There are several commands in DOS that work with files that have long file names. For example, the DIR command shows long file names as well as the corresponding 8.3 file name (a file name with a maximum of 8 characters and a 3 character extension indicating file type).

You can also display additional file details with the DIR command. To do so, type **dir/v**. (The v stands for verbose mode.) The additional file details include the file name, file type, file size, allocated space, last modified date and time, last accessed date, and attributes such as D for directory and A for archived.

The COPY command also supports long file names. You can copy to or from short or long file names. You must precede the long file name with a double quote ("). For example, type **copy budget.xls** "annual budget. This example creates a new file with a long file name.

Configuring DOS Applications

DOS applications have properties just like Windows applications do. You can configure DOS applications by changing the information in a DOS application property sheet. There are several tabs in the Property sheet that allow you to change options related to the following elements: Program, Font, Memory, Screen, and Misc. To view properties for a DOS application, follow these steps:

MS-DOS Properties   MS-DOS properties contain settings that control the objects for your DOS application in a window. You can change these settings at any time by right-clicking on the object you want to change and choosing Properties. You can change the program, font, memory, screen, and miscellaneous properties for a DOS application in a window.

1. Click the **Properties** button on the MS-DOS Prompt toolbar at the top of the MS-DOS prompt window. The Properties sheet appears.

2. Click the appropriate tab to see the options you want to change. For example, click the **Screen** tab to change the screen settings for the MS-DOS prompt window.

3. Make the necessary changes to the properties information. For example, by default, the MS-DOS Prompt toolbar displays at the top of the MS-DOS prompt window. Choose the **Display Toolbar** option to remove the toolbar from the window. Then click **OK**.

In this lesson, you learned to run DOS programs under Windows. In the next lesson, you learn how to use HyperTerminal Connections and Phone Dialer.

Using the Other Accessories

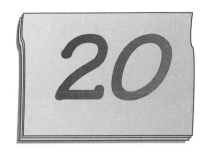

In this lesson, you learn to use HyperTerminal Connections and Phone Dialer.

Using HyperTerminal Connections

The HyperTerminal Connections program lets you connect to a remote computer that isn't running under Windows. You can use Hyper-Terminal and your modem to send and receive files or connect to a mainframe, a computer bulletin board, or another PC.

The first time you make a particular connection, you must go through the setup procedure to enter the information for that connection. In future uses, you can just double-click on the connection icon in the HyperTerminal window.

To set up a new HyperTerminal connection, follow these steps:

1. Choose **Start, Programs, Accessories**.

2. Click on **HyperTerminal**. The HyperTerminal window appears (see Figure 20.1).

Figure 20.1   The Windows 95 HyperTerminal window.

3. Double-click on **Hypertrm**. The Connection Description dialog box appears.

4. In the Connection Description dialog box (Figure 20.2), enter a name for the connection in the Name text box. Then choose an icon for the connection in the Icon list box. Click **OK.**

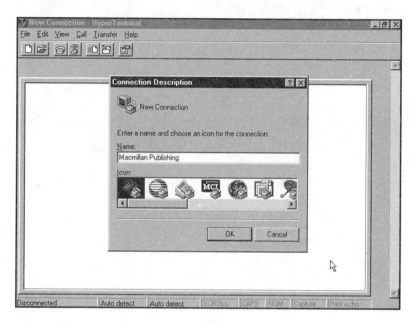

Figure 20.2 Enter the description for the connection you'll make.

5. In the Phone Number dialog box, enter the phone number and other calling information. Click **OK**.

6. The Connect dialog box opens. Click the **Dial** button to dial the number.

7. Communicate with the computer you're calling; then when you're finished, disconnect by selecting **Call**, **Disconnect**.

8. When you exit HyperTerminal, it asks if you want to save your session. Click **Yes**.

HyperTerminal The HyperTerminal program in Windows 95 replaces the Terminal program in Windows 3.1.

When you want to make the same connection again, just double-click on its icon in the HyperTerminal folder, then click the Dial button in the dialog box that appears.

Using the Phone Dialer

The Phone Dialer program enables you to place phone calls from your computer by using your modem or another Windows telephone device. You can dial another computer modem's phone number and make a connection. To use Phone Dialer, follow these steps:

1. Choose **Start, Programs, Accessories**.

2. Click **Phone Dialer**. The Phone Dialer appears (see Figure 20.3).

Figure 20.3   The Windows 95 Phone Dialer.

3. Type a phone number in the Number to Dial text box. Or, if you've entered numbers before, select one from the drop-down list. Then click **Dial**. You can also click on a Speed Dial button to dial the phone number.

To store a frequently used phone number, click an empty Speed Dial button and the Program Speed Dial dialog box appears. Enter the information requested, and click **Save** or **Save And Dial**.

Phone Dialer The Phone Dialer program in Windows 95 replaces the Phone Dial command in the Terminal program in Windows 3.1.

In this lesson, you learned how to use HyperTerminal Connections and Phone Dialer. In the next lesson, you learn how to control multimedia with Windows.

Working with Multimedia

In this lesson, you learn to use CD Player, Media Player, Sound Recorder, and Volume Control to work with multimedia.

Using the CD Player

Windows 95 provides a built-in CD Player so you can play audio CDs while you're working. This CD Player contains features just like a regular advanced CD player, such as random play, programmable playback order, and the capability to save programs. If you save a program, you don't have to recreate the play list each time you insert a CD. That way, you can skip over songs you don't want to play. To use the CD Player, follow these steps:

1. Choose **Start, Programs, Accessories, Multimedia, CD Player**. The CD Player window appears (see Figure 21.1).

Figure 21.1   The Windows 95 CD Player.

   Autoplay   When you insert a compact disc, the CD Player launches and begins playback automatically.

2. Insert a CD in your CD-ROM drive. The CD's artist, title, and track appear in the CD Player window if you've entered this information before.

3. To set up a play list, choose **File, Edit Play List**. The Edit Play List dialog box appears. Specify which tracks you want to play and in which order. Click **Add** to add each track to the play list. Click **Set Name** to save a program.

4. Click the **Play** button in the CD Player window to play the CD. To pause the CD, click the **Pause** button. To resume playing the CD, click the **Play** button. To play the CD in random order, choose **Options, Random Order**.

 Change Tracks Click the **Previous Track** button to play the previous track. Click the **Next Track** button to play the next track.

 Skip Around Click the **Skip Backwards** button to move backward within a track. Click the **Skip Forward** button to move forward within a track.

5. Click the **Stop** button to stop playing your CD.

6. Click the **Eject** button to eject your CD.

Using the Media Player

The Media Player program enables you to play multimedia files such as Windows-compatible multimedia voice, animated video files, and MIDI-based music files. Windows supports the following digital video file formats: .AVI, .BMP, .PCX, .TXT, .WAV, and .WRI.

 MIDI File A MIDI file contains electronic instructions for playing a song and can be compared to sheet music. A device such as a sound card can play the song contained in a MIDI file. Musicians can use MIDI as a development tool to control music equipment and add music to titles and games. Windows 95 supports MIDI and waveform audio .WAV files.

To use the Media Player, follow these steps:

1. Choose **Start, Programs, Accessories, Multimedia, Media Player**. The Media Player window appears (see Figure 21.2).

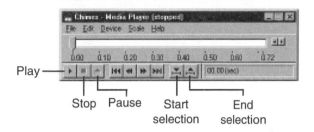

Figure 21.2   The Windows 95 Media Player window.

2. Open the **Device** menu and select the device you want to play. The Open dialog box appears.

3. Double-click the file you want to play. (Change the drive and/or folder if necessary to locate it.)

4. Click the **Play** button in the Media Player window to play the file.

Rewind and Fast Forward   Drag the slider to the left to rewind to the previous selection mark or to the beginning of the file. Drag the slider to the right to fast forward to the next selection mark or to the end of the file.

5. Click the **Stop** button to stop playing your file.

To play a specific selection, move the slider to the location where you want to start playing the selection. Click the **Start Selection** button to mark the beginning of the selection. Move the slider to the location where you want to stop playing the selection. Click the **End Selection** button to mark the end of the selection. Press **Alt+P** and then click the **Play** button to perform the selection you specified.

Media Player The Media Player program in Windows 95 is similar to the Media Player program in Windows 3.1. Windows 95's AutoPlay feature makes it easier for you to install and run audio CD-ROMs. When you put a Windows 95 audio CD disk into a CD-ROM drive, Windows automatically spins the disk, opens it, and follows the setup instructions.

Using the Sound Recorder

The Sound Recorder program lets you record, modify, and mix sounds. To play a sound using the Sound Recorder, follow these steps:

1. Choose **Start, Programs, Accessories, Multimedia, Sound Recorder**. The Sound Recorder window appears (see Figure 21.3).

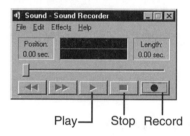

Play—⌐ Stop Record

Figure 21.3 The Windows 95 Sound Recorder window.

2. Choose **File, Open** from the Sound Recorder menu bar. The Open dialog box appears.

3. Double-click the sound file you want to play. (Change the drive and/or folder if needed to find the sound file.)

4. Click the **Play** button in the Sound Recorder window to play the sound. As the sound plays, you see a visual representation of the sound waves in the Wave box.

To be able to record sounds you must have some type of input device such as a microphone or a MIDI instrument. You must also have a sound card, even if you're just recording a CD to a file.

To record a sound, follow these steps:

1. Choose **File, New** from the Sound Recorder menu bar. The New Sound dialog box appears.

2. Enter a name for the sound file and specify the file format and attributes. Choose **OK**.

3. Click the **Record** button to begin recording.

4. Speak into the microphone to record the message.

5. When you're finished recording, click the **Stop** button to stop recording.

6. Choose **File, Save As** from the Sound Recorder menu bar to save the sound file.

You can edit sounds by adding effects and mixing sounds together. Open the **Options** menu and choose commands there to add affects. Choose **Edit, Mix File** to mix sounds.

Using Volume Control

The Volume Control program enables you to control the balance between the left and right speakers, adjust the volume, and turn the sound off for all multimedia devices. To use Volume Control, follow these steps:

1. Choose **Start, Programs, Accessories, Multimedia, Volume Control**. The Volume Control window appears (see Figure 21.4).

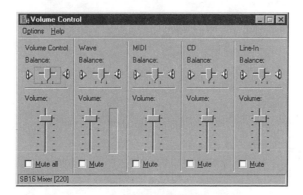

Figure 21.4   The Windows 95 Volume Control window.

2. For Volume Control, Wave, MIDI, CD, or Line-in, drag the Balance slider bar left and right to balance the sound between the left and right speakers.

3. For Volume Control, Wave, MIDI, CD, or Line-in, drag the Volume slider bar up or down to increase or decrease the volume.

4. For Volume Control, Wave, MIDI, CD, or Line-in, click the Mute check box to turn the sound off. An X appears in the Mute check box, indicating that the sound is turned off. To turn the sound on, click the Mute check box to remove the X in the check box.

Adjusting Volume   The Volume Control button appears on the taskbar. If you click on the taskbar's Volume Control, you can turn the sound up or down easily. If you double-click on the taskbar's Volume Control, you see the Volume Control dialog box.

Volume Control The Volume Control program in Windows 95 isn't available in Windows 3.1.

In this lesson, you learned to use CD Player, Media Player, Sound Recorder, and Volume Control.

WORD

Starting Word

In this lesson, you'll start Microsoft Word for Windows 95, learn the parts of the Word screen, and learn how to quit the program. You'll also learn about the toolbar.

Starting Word for Windows

Install First To start Word for Windows, you must first install it on your system.

To start Word for Windows, follow these steps:

1. Click on the **Start** button in Windows 95. The Start menu opens.

2. Point to **Programs**. The Programs menu appears.

3. Click on **Microsoft Word**. Word starts.

Parts of the Screen

When you start Word for Windows, you will see its opening logo for a few seconds and then the main screen appears with a blank document, ready for your input. Take a moment to familiarize yourself with the Word for Windows screen. It contains a number of useful components, as shown in Figure 1.1.

Title bar Displays the program name and the name of the document being edited.

Menu bar Contains the main Word for Windows menu.

Standard toolbar Displays buttons that you can select to perform common editing tasks. You must have a mouse to use the toolbar.

Formatting toolbar Use to select character- and paragraph-formatting commands. You must have a mouse to use this toolbar, too.

TipWizard Displays helpful tips about using Word. This is a new feature in Word for Windows 95.

Ruler Controls margins, indents, and tab stops.

Work area Where your document appears.

Status bar Displays information about your document.

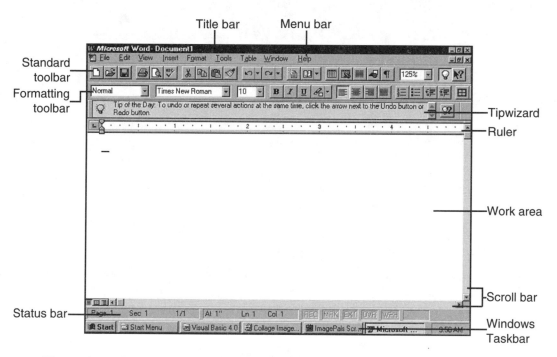

Figure 1.1 Components of the Word for Windows screen.

Depending on how you set up your system, one or more of these screen components may not appear. Don't worry—you'll see how to display them later.

The Toolbar

The toolbar contains buttons that you select with the mouse to perform common tasks. For example, the far left button represents the File New command, and the button next to it represents the File Open command. If you position the mouse pointer on a toolbar button (without clicking) Word displays a *tool tip* next to the mouse pointer, with a brief description of the button's function.

You'll probably find that clicking a toolbar button is quicker and more convenient than entering the entire command sequence. Tables 1.1 and 1.2 show the tools on the Standard and Formatting toolbars.

Table 1.1   The Standard Toolbar

Button	Purpose
	Starts a new document
	Opens a document
	Saves the current document
	Prints the current document
	Enters Print Preview mode
	Checks spelling
	Cuts the selection to the Clipboard
	Copies the selection to the Clipboard
	Pastes the contents of the Clipbord
	Activates Format Painter
	Undoes the previous action
	Redoes an action that you undid

continues

127

Table 1.1   Continued

Button	Purpose
	Applies an AutoFormat
	Inserts an address
	Inserts a new table
	Inserts an Excel worksheet
	Sets text in multiple columns
	Starts Microsoft Draw
	Shows or hides paragraph marks and other hidden characters
85%	Changes the magnification of the document view
	Turns on/off the Tip of the Day feature
	Gets help with an onscreen area or feature

Table 1.2   The Formatting Toolbar

Button	Purpose
Normal	A drop-down list of styles available
Times New Roman	A drop-down list of fonts
10	A drop-down list of font sizes
B	Toggles Bold on/off
I	Toggles Italic on/off

Button	Purpose
U	Toggles Underline on/off
	Applies highlighting
	Aligns text left
	Centers text
	Aligns text right
	Justifies text across the page
	Creates a numbered list
	Creates a bulleted list
	Decreases indent
	Increases indent
	Turns the Borders toolbar on/off

Quitting Word for Windows

When you finish using Word for Windows, quit the program by doing one of the following:

- Press **Alt+F4** on the keyboard.
- With the mouse, position the pointer on the box at the left of the title bar and double-click.
- Click the **Close** button (the button with the **X**) at the right of the title bar.
- Select **File**, **Exit**.

If you have any unsaved documents, Word for Windows prompts you to save them. Then the program terminates, and you return to the Windows desktop.

In this lesson, you learned how to start and quit Word for Windows and about the parts of the screen. In the next lesson, you'll learn how to use the Word for Windows Help system.

The Word Help System

In this lesson, you'll learn how to use Word's online Help system.

The Help Command

The Help command lets you access Word's online Help system, which can display program information and instructions on your screen. One way to access the Help system is via the Help command on the main menu. This menu has five commands on it:

- **Microsoft Word Help Topics** displays the main Help screen, titled Help Topics. This is the main portion of the Help system.

- **Answer Wizard** starts the Word Answer Wizard (which you also access via the Help Topics screen).

- The **Microsoft Network** lets you connect to the Microsoft Network. This command is available only if you've set up your system for the network connection.

- **WordPerfect Help** displays help for users who are familiar with the WordPerfect word processing program.

- **About Microsoft Word** displays information about the Word for Windows program, such as the program version number and the license number.

This lesson explains the most useful parts of the Help system. Please refer to your program documentation if you want additional information on the Microsoft Network or WordPerfect Help.

Quick Help   You can display the Help Topics screen as you edit your document by pressing **F1**.

The Help Topics Screen

The Help Topics screen has four tabs that let you access different parts of the Help system. Three of these, Index, Contents, and Find, are identical in operation to those found in Windows 95's Help system. For information about them, see Lesson 5 in the Windows 95 part of this book. The other tab is the Answer Wizard.

The Answer Wizard lets you find Help information by asking questions in your own words. It's one of Word 7.0's new features. You can access the *Answer Wizard* by selecting **Help, Answer Wizard**, or by selecting the **Answer Wizard** tab in the **Help Topics** screen. The Answer Wizard provides an unusual way for you to obtain Help information, as shown in Figure 2.1.

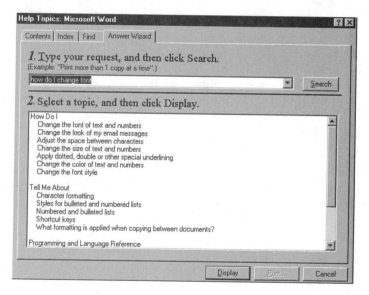

Figure 2.1   The Answer Wizard.

To use the Answer Wizard, type a question or request into the **number 1** text box on the Answer Wizard screen, and then press **Enter** or click the **Search** button. You may be wondering how you check spelling. Word displays a list of topics that it thinks might answer your question. Click the topic you want to view, and then click the **Display** button. For most topics, Word then displays a Help screen with the relevant information. In some cases, Word will "demonstrate" the task to you by issuing the needed menu commands.

The Tip Wizard

When the Tip Wizard is active, it "watches" you work and displays helpful hints about what you are doing. The Tip Wizard appears below the Formatting toolbar, as shown in Figure 2.2. In this figure, the Tip Wizard displays a tip about Word's automatic spell-checking feature (which you'll learn about in Lesson 21).

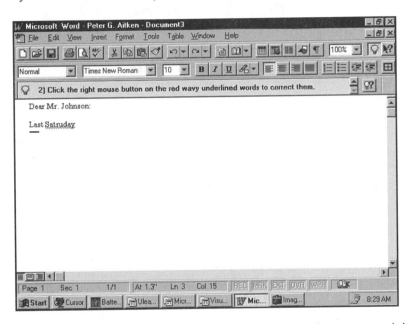

Figure 2.2   The Tip Wizard displays helpful hints about what you are doing.

To turn the Tip Wizard display on or off, select **View Toolbars**, and then click the **Tip Wizard** option. When the Tip Wizard is turned on, it detects you doing certain things and flashes the yellow light bulb in its window; you will see a tip or hint. You can scroll through previously displayed tips using the scroll bar at the right end of the Tip Wizard window.

Normally, the Tip Wizard displays each tip only once. To reset the Tip Wizard so that it will display previous tips again in the future, press **Ctrl** and click the light bulb on the Tip Wizard.

If the Tip Wizard appears but does not display any tips, you may need to activate it:

1. Select **Tools, Options** to display the Options dialog box.

2. Click the **General** tab, if necessary.

3. Click the **TipWizard Active** option to turn it on.

4. Select **OK**.

Context-Sensitive Help

If you are using Word's menus or dialog boxes, you can obtain context-sensitive Help at any time by pressing **F1**. If you highlight a menu command, information about that command appears. If a dialog box is open, pressing **F1** displays information about the dialog box.

After you have read Help, press **Esc** to close it and return to what you were doing.

Context-sensitive Help   Information directly related to what you are doing at the moment.

What's This?

 Word also includes a Help button on the Standard toolbar which can tell you about parts of the screen. Just click on it, and your mouse pointer changes to an arrow with a question mark. Then click on any element you see onscreen to see a pop-up definition.

In this lesson, you learned how to use the Help system. In the next lesson, you'll learn how to enter and delete text, and how to move around a document.

Document Editing: The Basics

In this lesson, you'll learn how to enter text, how to move around the screen, and how to select and delete text.

Entering Text

When starting Word for Windows 95, you see a blank work area that contains only two items:

- **Blinking vertical line**   Marks the insertion point, the location where text you type appears in the document and where certain editing actions occurs.

- **Horizontal line**   The end-of-document marker.

Since your new document is empty, these two markers are at the same location. To enter text, simply type it. As you type, the text appears and the insertion point moves to the right. If the line reaches the right edge of the screen, then Word automatically moves to the start of the next line; this is *word wrapping*. Press **Enter** only when you want to start a new paragraph. As you enter more lines than will fit on the screen, Word automatically scrolls previously entered text upward to keep the insertion point in view.

Leave It to Word Wrap   Press **Enter** only when you want to start a new paragraph.

Moving Around the Screen

As you work on a document, you will often have to move the insertion point so that you can view or work on other regions of text.

Table 3.1   Moving the Insertion Point around the Screen

To Move	*Perform This Action*
With the mouse	
Up or down one line	Click the up or down arrow on the vertical scroll bar.
Up or down one screen	Click the vertical scroll bar between the box and the up or down arrow.
Up or down any amount	Drag the scroll bar box up or down.
To any visible location	Click the location.
With the keyboard	
Left or right one character	Press ← or →.
Up or down one line	Press ↑ or ↓.
Left or right one word	Press Ctrl+← or Ctrl+→.
Up or down one paragraph	Press Ctrl+↑ or Ctrl+↓.
Start or end of a line	Press Home or End.
Up or down one screen	Press PgUp or PgDn.
Top or bottom of current screen	Press Ctrl+PgUp or Ctrl+PgDn.
Start or end of the document	Press Ctrl+Home or Ctrl+End.

Selecting Text

Many Word for Windows 95 operations require that you first *select* the text that you want to modify. For example, to italicize a word, you must select the word first and then specify italics. Selected text appears on the screen in reverse video, as shown in Figure 3.1, which has the phrase **Dear Mr. Johnson** selected.

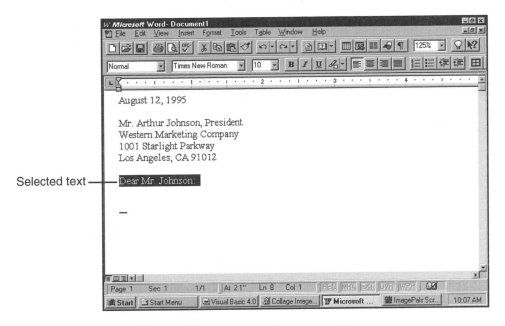

Selected text —

Figure 3.1   Selected text appears in reverse video.

You can select text with either the mouse or the keyboard. With the mouse, you can use the *selection bar*, an unmarked column in the left document margin. When the mouse pointer moves from the document to the selection bar, it changes from an I-beam to an arrow.

Table 3.2   Methods of Selecting Text

To Select Text	*Perform This Action*
With the mouse	
Any amount	Point at the start of the text; drag the highlight over the text.
One word	Double-click anywhere on the word.
One sentence	Press and hold Ctrl and click anywhere in the sentence.
One line	Click the selection bar next to the line.
Multiple lines	Drag in the selection bar next to the lines.

continues

137

Table 3.2 Continued

To select text	Perform this action
With the mouse	
One paragraph	Double-click the selection bar next to the paragraph.
Entire document	Press and hold Ctrl and click anywhere in the selection bar.
With the keyboard	
Any amount	Move the insertion point to the start of the text, press and hold Shift, and move the insertion point to the end of the desired text using the movement keys described earlier.
Entire document	Ctrl+A.

To cancel a selection, click anywhere on the screen or use the keyboard to move the insertion point.

 Fast Select   Double-click a word to select it quickly.

Deleting Text

You can delete single characters or larger blocks of text.

- To delete the character to the right of the insertion point, press **Del**.

- To delete the character to the left of the insertion point, press **Backspace**.

- To delete a block of text, select the text and then press **Del** or **Backspace**.

If you make a mistake, you can recover deleted text with the **Edit, Undo** command. Depending on how you deleted the text, this command appears on the Edit menu as either Undo Typing or Undo Edit Clear. In either case, the effect is the same: the deleted characters are replaced in their original position. You must select this command immediately after deleting and before performing any other action. You can also click on the **Undo** button or press the shortcut key, **Ctrl+Z**. You can select Undo more than once to undo several most recent editing actions.

In this lesson, you learned how to enter, select, and delete text. In the next lesson, you'll learn how to create a new document using Word's templates and Wizards.

Using Templates and Wizards

In this lesson, you'll learn how to use Word's templates and wizards to create a new document.

Documents and Templates

As you learned in the previous lesson, when you start Word, it displays a blank document for you to work with. The new document uses Word's Normal template. The question is, what is a template?

You may not be aware of it, but every Word for Windows document uses a *template*. A template is a model, or pattern, for a document. A template can contain boilerplate text, graphics, and formatting. Any document that uses a template automatically contains all the elements of the template. Then, you add additional text and formatting as needed.

For example, a business-letter template might contain your company's logo and address, the date, and a salutation. When you use the template, you need to type in only the text of the letter; the standard elements are provided by the template. You can create your own templates (as you'll learn in a later lesson); you can also use the predefined templates that come with Word.

Specialized Templates

The Normal template is pretty basic; it contains no boilerplate text or special formatting. It is fine for many documents. However, Word provides a variety of specialized templates that are designed to simplify the task of creating certain types of documents, such as FAXes, memos, invoices, newsletters, and more.

Roll Your Own   You'll learn how to create your own templates in Lesson 16.

Wizards

A wizard goes a step beyond a regular template. In addition to providing predefined formatting and tcxt, a wizard automates part of the process of creating a document. For example, a FAX Wizard would prompt you to enter the recipient's name and telephone number, and then automatically insert them in the proper locations in the document.

Creating a New Document from a Template

Here are the steps for creating a new document based on a template:

1. Select **File, New**. Word displays the New dialog box.

2. Click the tab corresponding to the type of document you are creating. The figure shows the **Letters & Faxes** tab selected.

3. Click the desired template.

4. Select **OK**.

Click Yourself a New Document   To create a new document based on the Normal template, click the **New** button on the Standard toolbar.

Word will load the template. If the template contains any text, it will appear on your screen. You can now edit the document in the usual fashion. If you selected a wizard in step 3, see the next section for details on how to use it.

Using a Wizard

Each Word wizard is different, so it's impossible to provide detailed instructions that will apply to all of them. However, the basic steps involved are similar for all wizards. Once you understand these steps, you can handle any of the Word for Windows wizards.

A Wizard consists of a series of dialog boxes. Each dialog box presents you with options to select or text boxes where you enter information. A typical wizard dialog box is shown.

A simple wizard might have only two or three dialog boxes; a more complex one may have a dozen. After entering the required information in a dialog box, here's what to do:

- Click the **Next** button to go on to the next wizard dialog box. In the last dialog box, the Next button is not available.

- If you want to change information that you entered, click the **Back** button to return to the previous dialog box.

- If you want the Wizard to create the document using the information you have entered so far, click the **Finish** button.

- Click the **Cancel** button to cancel the wizard (your document will not be created).

Once the Wizard finishes, you can edit your new document using the standard techniques.

In this lesson, you learned how to use Word's templates and wizards to simplify the task of creating a new document. In the next lesson, you'll learn how to control the way Word displays documents on your screen.

Controlling the
Screen Display

In this lesson, you'll learn how to control the Word for Windows screen display to suit your working style.

Document Display Views

Word for Windows offers four different views in which you can display your document.

Normal View

You'll probably want to work most often in *Normal* view. This is the Word for Windows default display. Figure 5.1 shows a document in Normal view. As you can see, all special formatting is visible on-screen. Different font sizes, italics, boldface, and other enhancements display on the screen very much as they will appear on the printed page. Certain aspects of the page layout, however, are not displayed in order to speed editing; for example, you do not see headers and footers. Normal view is fine for most editing tasks.

To select or change your view to Normal, select **View, Normal** or click the **Normal View** button at the left end of the horizontal scroll bar. In the View menu, the currently selected view has a dot displayed next to it.

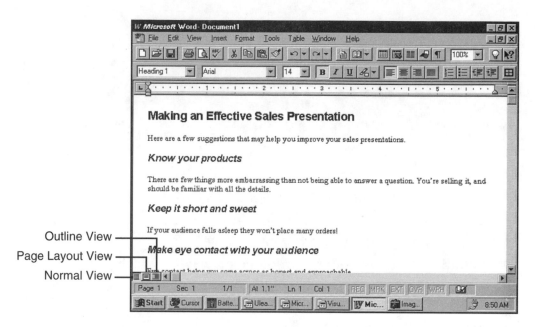

Outline View ——
Page Layout View ——
Normal View ——

Figure 5.1 A document displayed in Normal view.

Outline View

Use *Outline* view to create outlines and to examine the structure of a document. Figure 5.2 shows the sample document in Outline view. Here you can choose to view only your document headings—hiding all subordinate text. You can quickly promote, demote, or move document headings—along with subordinate text—to a new location.

Select **View, Outline** to switch to Outline view, or click the **Outline View** button at the left end of the horizontal scroll bar (refer to Figure 5.1).

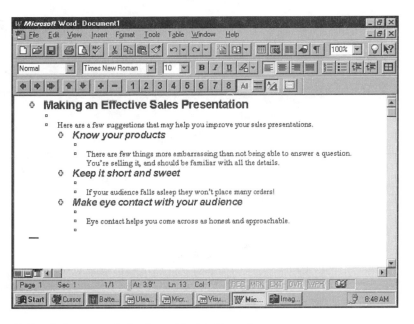

Figure 5.2 A document displayed in Outline view.

Page Layout View

Page Layout view displays your document exactly as it will print. Headers, footers, and all the details of page layout appear on the screen. You can edit in Page Layout view; this view is ideal when you are fine-tuning the details of page composition. Be aware, however, that the additional computer processing required makes display changes relatively slow in Page Layout view, particularly when you have a complex page layout. Figure 5.3 shows the sample document in Page Layout view.

TIP

Sneak Preview Use Page Layout view to see what your printed document will look like before you actually print.

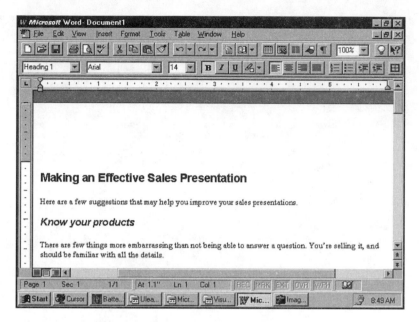

Figure 5.3 A document displayed in Page Layout view.

Select **View, Page Layout**, or click the **Page Layout View** button (refer to Figure 5.1), to switch to Page Layout view.

Draft Font Mode

Draft Font mode is a display option that you can apply in both Normal and Outline views. As Figure 5.4 illustrates, a single generic font appears on-screen and special formatting such as italics and boldface are indicated by underlining. Draft Font mode provides the fastest editing and screen display. This component is ideal when you're concentrating on the contents of your document rather than its appearance.

To turn Draft Font mode on or off:

1. Select **Tools, Options** to display the Options dialog box.

2. If necessary, click the **View** tab to display the View options.

3. Select the **Draft Font** option to turn it on or off.

4. Select **OK**.

Zoom button

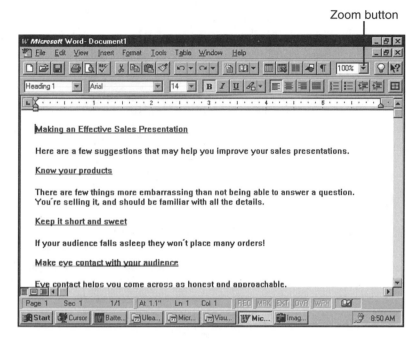

Figure 5.4   A document displayed in Draft Font mode.

Full Screen Display

To see the maximum amount of text on the screen, select **View, Full Screen**. In Full Screen view, the title bar, menu, toolbars, status line, and all other Word elements are hidden, and you can use the full screen for your text. You can enter and edit text in this view and select from the menus using the usual keyboard commands. To turn off Full Screen view, select **View, Full Screen** again, or click the **Full Screen** icon that appears in the lower right corner of the screen.

Ruler and Toolbar Display

The Word for Windows default is to display the Ruler, Standard toolbar, and Formatting toolbar at the top of the editing screen. The TipWizard usually appears, too. At times, you may want to hide one or more of these items to give yourself a larger work area and a less-cluttered screen. Of course, you will not have access to the editing features of the item(s) you have hidden.

Select **View**, **Ruler** to toggle the Ruler display between on and off. To control the toolbars and the TipWizard, select **View**, **Toolbars** to display the Toolbars dialog box. Turn the Standard, Formatting, and TipWizard options on or off as desired, then select **OK**.

Put 'em Away Hide the Ruler and toolbars when you need maximum text displayed but don't want to use Full Screen view.

Zooming the Screen

The **View, Zoom** command lets you control the size of your document as displayed on the screen. You can enlarge it to facilitate reading small fonts or decrease the size to view an entire page at one time. When you select **View, Zoom**, the Zoom dialog box appears (see Figure 5.5).

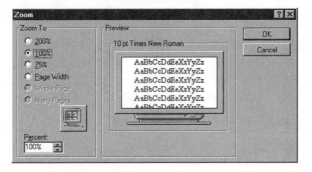

Figure 5.5 The Zoom dialog box.

In the Zoom dialog box, you have the following options. As you make selections, the Preview section of the dialog box shows you what the selected zoom setting will look like.

- Under **Zoom To**, select the desired page magnification. 200 percent is twice normal size, 75 percent is three-quarters normal size, and so on. In the **Percent** box, you can enter a custom magnification in the range 10–200 percent.

- Select **Page Width** to have Word for Windows automatically scale the display to fit the entire page width on the screen.

- Select **Whole Page** to have Word for Windows automatically scale the display to fit the entire page on the screen.

- Select **Many Pages** to display two or more pages at the same time. Click the monitor button under the **Many Pages** option, and then drag to specify how many pages to display.

- You can also change the zoom setting by pulling down the **Zoom** control on the Standard toolbar and selecting the desired zoom setting.

Note that the **Whole Page** and **Many Pages** options are available only if you are viewing the document in Page Layout view.

In this lesson, you learned how to control the Word for Windows screen display. In the next lesson, you'll learn how to save documents.

Saving Documents

In this lesson, you'll learn how to name your document, save it to disk, and enter summary information.

Saving a Document for the First Time

When you create a new document in Word for Windows, it is stored temporarily in your computer's memory under the default name Doc*n*, where *n* is a number that increases by 1 for each new unnamed document. The document is only "remembered" until you quit the program or the computer is turned off. To save a document permanently so you can retrieve it later, you must save it to a disk. This is done with the **File**, **Save** command, or by selecting the **Save** button.

1. When you save a document for the first time, you must assign it another name. When you select **File**, **Save** for an unnamed document (or **File**, **Save As** for any document), Word displays the Save As dialog box.

2. In the **File Name** text box, enter the name you want to assign to the document file. The name can be up to 256 characters long and should be descriptive of the document contents.

3. If you want to save the document in a different folder, pull down the **Save in** list to select a different folder.

4. Click **Save**. Word for Windows automatically adds the DOC extension when it saves the file.

Extension   The extension is the one- to three-letter part of a file name to the right of the period.

Saving a Named Document

 As you work on a document, save it periodically to minimize possible data loss in the event of a power failure or other system problem. Once you have assigned a name to a document, the **File**, **Save** command saves the current document version under its assigned name; no dialog boxes appear. You can also click the **Save** button on the Standard Toolbar.

 **Don't Forget!**   Save your document regularly as you work on it. If the power goes off unexpectedly, your most recent saved version will be all you have left.

Changing a Document Name

You may want to save a named document under a new name, for example, you can keep the old version under the original name and the revised version under a new name. To change a document name, select **File**, **Save As**. The Save As dialog box appears showing the current document name in the **File Name** text box. Then take the following steps:

1. Change the file name to the desired new name.

2. (Optional) Select a different folder in the **Save in** list to save the document in a different folder.

3. Select **OK**. Word saves the document under the new name.

Entering and Changing Summary Information

You can enter or change the summary information associated with a document at any time. Select **File**, **Properties**, and the Properties dialog box will appear. Make the desired changes; then select **OK**. The new information will be registered with the document the next time you save the file.

In this lesson, you learned how to save a document and change a document name. In the next lesson, you'll learn how to retrieve a document from a disk.

Retrieving Documents

In this lesson, you'll learn how to retrieve a document from a disk into Word for Windows, to search for a specific file, and to import documents you created with other programs.

Retrieving a Word for Windows Document

You can retrieve any document created with Word for Windows for further editing, printing, and other functions. To do so, select **File**, **Open** or click the **Open** button on the Standard Toolbar. The Open dialog box will be displayed, as shown in Figure 7.1.

Retrieving a Document   This means to reopen a document from your disk into Word for Windows so you can work on it.

The file list shows all of the Word documents and folders in the current folder. The Look in box shows the name of the current folder. Here are the actions you can take:

- To open a file, click its name in the list or type its name into the File name box. Then, press **Enter** or click the **Open** button.

- To preview the contents of a file, click the file name, then click the **Preview** button.

- To move up one folder, click the **Up One Level** button.

- To move down one level to a different folder, double-click the folder name in the file list.

- To move to another folder, open the **Look in** list and select the desired folder.

Look in box   Up One Level button   Preview button

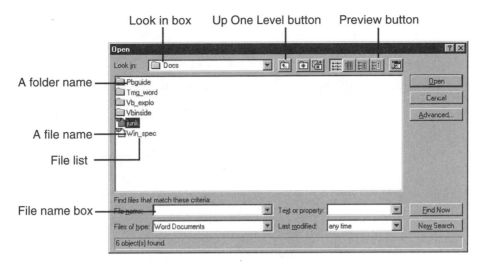

A folder name

A file name

File list

File name box

Figure 7.1   The File Open dialog box.

Folder   A *folder* is a method of organizing files on a disk. Before Windows 95, folders used to be called *subdirectories*.

To quickly open a file you worked on recently, you can use Word's Recently Used File List. To view this list, select **File** to display the File menu—the list is displayed at the bottom of the menu just above the Exit command. To open a file on the list, press the number corresponding to the file or click the file name with the mouse.

Controlling how many files appear   You can control how many files are displayed on the Recently Used File List, and whether or not the list is displayed at all. Select **Tools**, **Options**, and click the **General** tab. Turn the **Recently Used File List** option on or off to control display of the list. To change the number of files displayed in the list, enter a number in the **Entries** box, or click the up and down arrows.

153

Finding a File

If you cannot remember the full name or location of the file that you want to retrieve, use the **Find** command in the Open dialog box to find it by name, contents, and/or summary information. When you select the **Find Now** button, Word for Windows searches for files that meet the criteria you specify in the boxes at the bottom of the Open dialog box:

1. Enter a partial file name in the **File name** box if you remember part of the file's name. For example, to find all Word documents whose names start with the word SALES, enter the template **SALES***. To search, regardless of file name, leave this box blank.

2. To search for files of a particular type, such as WordPerfect documents, pull down the Files of type list and select the desired file type. Select **All Files** from this list to search regardless of file type.

3. To find files that contain specified text in the document or summary information, enter the text in the **Text or property** box. For example, Figure 7.2 shows that the Open dialog box is set up to find files containing the text, *ruler*, before the search began.

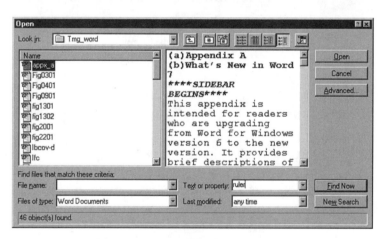

Figure 7.2   Using the Open dialog box to find files.

4. To find files based on when they were last modified, pull down the **Last modified** list and select the desired criterion.

5. Click the **Find Now** button to start the search. The names of matching files, if any, will be displayed in the file list. Figure 7.3 shows the Open dialog box after performing the search for files containing the text "ruler." You can see that only five documents in the current folder were found.

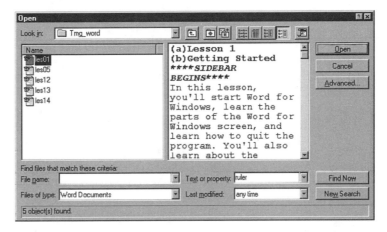

Figure 7.3   The Open dialog box displaying the results of a search.

   Opening from Windows   You can open any file directly from My Computer or Windows Explorer. Just double-click the file. (See Part I of this book for info on Windows.)

Importing Documents

It is possible to import documents that were created with other applications, converting them to Word for Windows format. For example, you can import a document that was created with WordPerfect, therefore, retaining all of its special formatting and fonts. Word for Windows imports from a wide variety of programs. To import a file, follow these steps:

   1. Select **File**, **Open** or click the **Open** button on the Standard Toolbar. The Open dialog box appears.

155

2. Pull down the **Files of type** list and select the type of file you want to import.

3. The File List shows all files of the type shown in the Files of Type box that are located in the current folder. Select the file to import, or type its name directly into the **File name** box.

4. Select **Open**.

In this lesson, you learned how to retrieve a document from a disk into Word for Windows, how to search for a specific file, and how to import documents that were created with other programs. In the next lesson, you'll learn how to print your document.

Printing Your Document

In this lesson, you'll learn how to print your document.

Quick Printing

To print a Word for Windows document, you must have installed and selected the printer you are going to use. The printer must be turned on and online. To print the entire document using the current settings:

1. Select **File**, **Print**, or press **Ctrl+P**. The Print dialog box appears (see Figure 8.1).

2. Select **OK**. The document will print.

Quick Printing   To print one copy of the entire document without going to the Print dialog box, click the **Print** button.

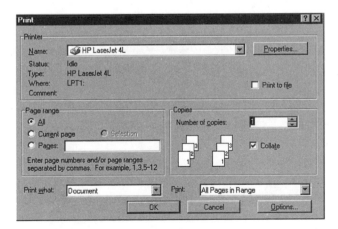

Figure 8.1   The Print dialog box.

Printing Part of a Document

You can print a single page of a document or a range of pages. This can be useful for checking the results of your editing changes when you've only modified part of the document. Here's how:

1. If you're printing a single page, position the insertion point anywhere on the page that you want to print.

2. Select **File**, **Print** or press **Ctrl+P**. The Print dialog box appears.

3. Under Page range, select **Current page** to print the page where you have placed the insertion point. Select **Pages** to print a range of pages. Then, enter the beginning and ending page numbers in the box separated by a dash (for example, **2–6**).

4. Select **OK**. The selected page or pages will print. To print noncontiguous pages, enter the page numbers separated by commas (for example: 1, 6, 10).

There are some other options in the Print dialog box that you may find useful:

- To print information from the document other than its text, such as its Summary Information, pull down the **Print what** list and select.

- To print just the odd- or even-numbered pages, pull down the **Print** list and select.

- To print more than one copy, enter the desired number of copies, or click the up and down arrow, in the **Number of copies** box.

- To print pages in reverse order (last to first), which will produce collated output on printers with face-up output, click the **Options to display** button and, in the dialog box that is displayed, turn on the **Reverse Print Order** option.

Two-sided printing? For do-it-yourself, two-sided printing, print the odd-numbered pages of your document, place the printed pages in your printer's paper tray, then print the even-numbered pages. You'll have to experiment with the paper orientation in the paper tray to get it right.

Using Print Options

There are several printing options available that you may find useful. To use these options:

1. Select **File**, **Print** or press **Ctrl+P**. The Print dialog box appears.

2. Select **Options**. The Options dialog box, as shown in Figure 8.2, appears.

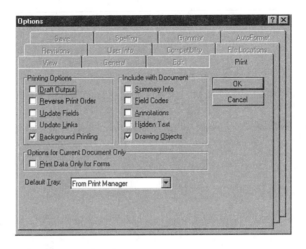

Figure 8.2 The Options dialog box.

3. Under Printing Options, select one or more of the following:

   - **Draft Output**   Produces draft output that prints faster but may lack some graphics and formatting (depending on your specific printer).

   - **Reverse Print Order**   Prints pages in last-to-first order. This setting produces collated output on printers that have face-up output.

   - **Update Fields**   Automatically updates all document fields (except locked ones) before printing.

4. Select **OK**. You are returned to the Print dialog box.

5. Select **OK** to begin printing.

Setting Up the Page

By default, Word for Windows formats printer output for 8 1/2-by-11-inch paper in *portrait orientation*. You can modify these settings if needed (if you want to print on 8 1/2-by-14-inch legal paper, for example).

 Portrait Orientation   This is the default and prints lines parallel to the short edge of the paper. *Landscape orientation*, by contrast, prints lines parallel to the long edge of the paper.

To change the print orientation and the paper size:

1. Select **File**, **Page Setup**. The Page Setup dialog box appears.

2. Click the **Paper Size** tab.

3. Open the **Paper Size** drop-down box, which lists several common paper sizes.

4. Select the desired paper size.

5. If you select **Custom Size** from the list, use the **Height** and **Width** boxes to specify the actual paper size.

6. Under **Orientation**, select **Portrait** or **Landscape**.

7. Select **OK**. The new settings will be in effect for your document the next time you print.

Previewing the Print Job

You can view a screen display that previews exactly what your document will look like when printed. To do this:

 1. Select **File**, **Print Preview** or click the Print Preview button . The current page appears in preview mode (see Figure 8.3).

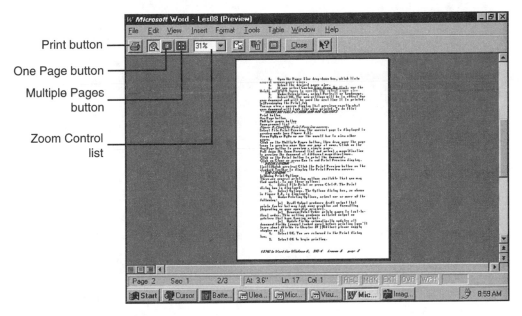

Print button

One Page button

Multiple Pages button

Zoom Control list

Figure 8.3   The Print Preview screen.

2. Press **PgUp** or **PgDn**, or use the scroll bar to view other pages.

3. Click the **Multiple Pages** button; then drag over the page icons to preview more than one page at once. Click the **One Page** button to preview a single page.

4. Pull down the **Zoom Control** list and select a magnification to preview the document at different magnifications.

5. Click the **Print** button to print the document.

6. Click **Close** or press **Esc** to end Print Preview display.

In this lesson, you learned how to print your documents. In the next lesson, you'll learn how to move and copy text.

Moving and Copying Text

In this lesson, you'll learn how to move and copy text in your document.

Copying Text

Before you can move or copy text, you must select it. In Lesson 3, you learned how to select a block of text in order to delete it. You use the same procedures to select text you want to move or copy. Remember, selected text appears on the screen in reverse video.

When you copy text, you place a duplicate of the selected text in a new location. After you copy, the text exists in both the original and new locations. There are several methods available for copying text.

Save Your Fingers   Copying text can save you from having to type. For example, copy a paragraph to a new location when you need to modify it only slightly.

Using the Clipboard to Copy

The Clipboard is a temporary storage location offered in Windows programs. You can copy text from one location in your document to the Clipboard and then paste it from the Clipboard to the new location in your document.

1. Select the text you want to copy. The selected text appears highlighted, as shown in Figure 9.1.

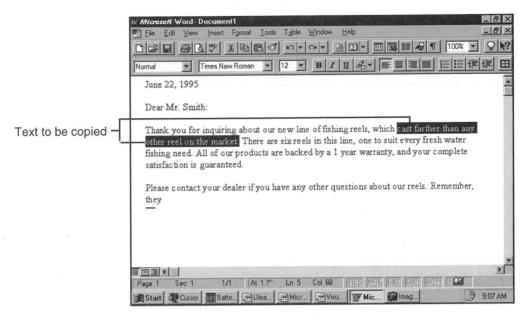

Text to be copied ⌐

Figure 9.1   Highlighted text to be copied.

 2. Select **Edit, Copy**. You can also click on the **Copy** button, or press **Ctrl+C**.

3. Move the insertion point to the new location for the text.

 4. Select **Edit, Paste**. You can also select the **Paste** button or press **Ctrl+V**. The text appears at the new location, as shown in Figure 9.2.

 Again and Again   You can paste the same text from the Clipboard more than once. The text remains on the Clipboard, throughout your work session, until you replace it with new text.

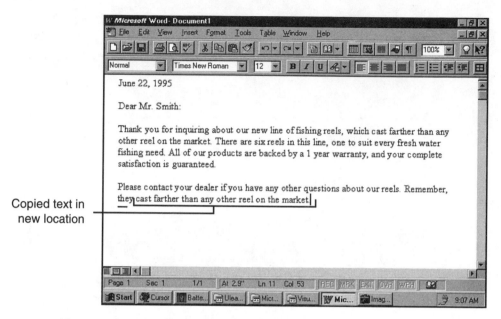

Copied text in
new location

Figure 9.2 The copied text in the new location.

Using the Mouse to Copy

A shortcut for copying is available if you're using the mouse:

1. Select the text to copy.

2. Using the mouse, point at the location where you want the text copied. If necessary, you can first scroll the document to bring the location into view.

3. Press and hold **Ctrl+Shift** and click the right mouse button. Word copies the selected text to the location you pointed to.

Copying Text That You Just Typed

You can quickly insert a copy of text that you just typed at a different document location:

1. At one document location, type the text that you want to copy.

2. Move the insertion point to the second location for the text.

3. Select **Edit Repeat Typing**, or press **F4**.

Moving Text

You can move text from one document location to another. When you move text, Word *deletes* it from the original location and inserts it at the new location.

Moving Text Using the Clipboard

You can move text with the Clipboard. These are the steps to follow:

1. Select the text to move.

2. Select **Edit**, **Cut**, click the **Cut** button, or press **Ctrl+X**. Word deletes the selected text from the document and places it on the Clipboard.

3. Move the insertion point to the new location.

4. Select **Edit**, **Paste**, click the **Paste** button, or press **Ctrl+V**. Word inserts the text into the document.

Moving Text with the Mouse

You can drag selected text to a new location using the mouse. This technique is particularly convenient for small blocks of text.

1. Select the text to be moved. (Figure 9.3 shows an example.)

2. Point at the selected text with the mouse; press and hold the left mouse button.

3. Drag to the new location. As you drag, a dotted vertical line indicates where Word will insert the text.

 Copy with the Mouse   To copy the text instead of moving it, press and hold **Ctrl** while dragging.

4. Position the dotted line at the desired insertion point, and release the mouse button. Word moves (or copies, if you were holding **Ctrl**) the text. (Figure 9.4 shows the new position of the selected text in Figure 9.3.)

In this lesson, you learned how to move and copy text. In the next lesson, you'll learn how to format paragraphs.

Text to be moved

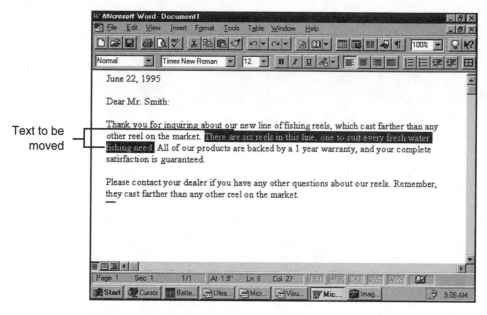

Figure 9.3 To move text, first highlight it.

Moved text in new location

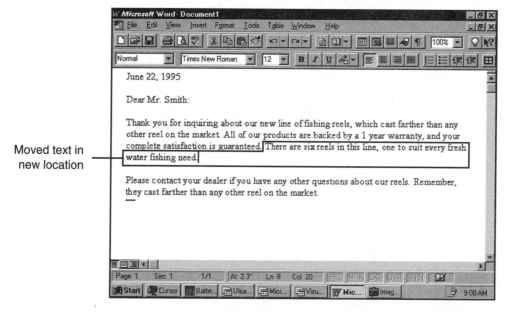

Figure 9.4 Cut the text and paste it in the new location or drag it to the new location with the mouse.

Formatting Your Document

This lesson introduces you to the concept of formatting (or changing the appearance of) your document and also tells you where to turn for information on specific kinds of formatting.

What Is Formatting?

The term *formatting* refers to changes you make in your document's appearance. Whenever you underline a word, set a paragraph off with italics, display a list as a table, or change the page margins you are working with formatting.

Formatting is an important part of many documents. An attractive and well-formatted document has a definite edge on clarity and impact over another document that may have the same content but is poorly formatted. Most of the remaining lessons in this book deal with formatting; this brief lesson serves as a general introduction.

How Is Formatting Applied?

There are two different methods for applying most of Word's formatting commands. The difference depends on whether you want to format text that already exists in the document, or text that you are about to type:

- To format existing text, you first select the text (as you learned in Lesson 3) and then issue the formatting command. The format change affects only the selected text.

- To format new text, move the insertion point to the location where you want the text to appear; then issue the formatting command. The format change will affect new text that you type in.

Where Do I Turn Next?

If it's possible, I recommend that you continue working through the book's lessons in order. If you need to find information on a particular formatting topic right away, you can refer to this list.

For information on...	*Please turn to...*
Using fonts, underlining, boldface, and italics	Lesson 11
Changing the page margins and line spacing	Lesson 12
Using and setting tabs	Lesson 13
Modifying text alignment	Lesson 14
Adding page numbers, headers, and footers	Lesson 17
Creating numbered and bulleted lists	Lesson 22
Arranging text in columns	Lesson 23
Using Word's automatic formatting	Lesson 24
Putting data in tables	Lesson 25

Formatting Characters

In this lesson, you'll learn how to apply special formatting to characters.

What Is Character Formatting?

The term character formatting refers to attributes that apply to individual characters in a document. Font, type size, underlining, italic, and boldface are examples of character formatting. A character format can apply to anything from a single letter to the entire document.

Using Fonts

What Is a Font?   The appearance of text is determined—in large—by its font. A font specifies both the style of text—that is, the appearance of individual characters—and its size. For example, the text you are reading now is printed using the Palatino font in 11 point size.

The style of a font is denoted by a name, such as Times New Roman or Courier. The size of a font is specified in terms of points, with one point equal to 1/72 of an inch. As you enter text in a document, the formatting toolbar displays the font name and point size currently in use. For example, in Figure 11.1, Courier 12 point is the current font.

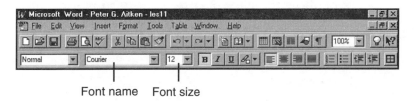

Font name   Font size

Figure 11.1   The formatting toolbar displays the name and size of the current font.

Changing the Font of Existing Text

Although the exact fonts and sizes will vary, depending on your Windows installation and the printer you are using, you can change the font style and/or size of any portion of your document. To change font and/or size, follow these steps:

1. Select the text to change. If the selected text currently contains only a single font and size, it displays on the formatting toolbar. If it contains more than one font or size, then none display.

 Fast Select!   Remember that you can quickly select an entire document by pressing **Ctrl+A**.

2. To change the font, open the **Font Name** drop-down box and select a different font.

3. To change point size with the mouse, open the **Font Size** drop-down box on the formatting toolbar and select the desired point size.

    If you are in Page Layout view or in Normal view with Draft mode off, the screen display will immediately update to show the new font. In Draft mode, different fonts are not displayed on the screen, but the formatting toolbar will display the name and size of the current font. See Lesson 5 to learn about the views and modes you can use.

Changing the Font of New Text

You change the font that will be used for new text that you type as follows:

1. Move the insertion point to the location where you will type in the new text.

2. Follow the steps the preceding section for changing the font of existing text, but do not select any text first.

3. Type the new text. It will appear in the newly specified font. Other text in your document will not be affected.

Bold, Underline, and Italic

The attributes boldface, italic, and/or underlining can be applied alone or in combination to any text in your document. These attributes are controlled by the toggle buttons on the Formatting toolbar:

B   Bold

I   Italic

U   Underline

Toggle Buttons   These are buttons that, when selected, turn the corresponding attribute on if it is off, and off if it is on.

To apply attributes to new text that you type:

1. Move the insertion point to the location of the new text.
2. Click the toolbar button(s) for the desired formatting, or press **Ctrl+B** (bold), **Ctrl+I** (italic) or Ctrl+U (underlining).
3. Type the text.
4. To turn off the attribute, click the button again or press the corresponding key combination.

To change existing text:

1. Select the text.
2. Click the toolbar button(s) for the desired formatting, or press **Ctrl+B** (bold), **Ctrl+I** (italic) or **Ctrl+U** (underlining).

In Draft mode, the presence of any character formatting is indicated by underlining. In all other modes, the text appears on-screen with all formatting displayed.

In this lesson, you learned how to format characters. In the next lesson, you'll learn how to set page margins and line spacing.

Setting Margins and Line Spacing

In this lesson, you'll learn how to set page margins and line spacing.

Setting Left and Right Margins with the Ruler

Word provides default margins for every template, but you can easily adjust them to suit your purposes.

The Ruler displayed across the top of the Word for Windows work area makes setting margins easy. You can work visually rather than thinking in terms of inches or centimeters. The Ruler is designed to be used with a mouse. To use the Ruler to change margins, you must be working in Page Layout mode (select View Page Layout).

Displaying the Ruler   If your Ruler is not displayed, select **View, Ruler** to display it.

Margin settings made with the Ruler affect the entire document. The white bar on the Ruler shows the current margin settings, as shown in Figure 12.1. To change the left or right margin, point at the margin symbol on the Ruler, at the left or right end of the white bar (the mouse pointer will change to a two-headed arrow). Then, drag the margin to the new position.

Margins   The left and right margins are the distances, respectively, between the text and the left and right edges of the page.

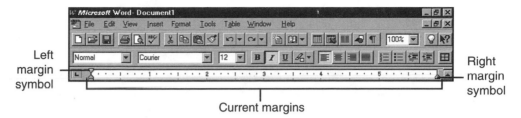

Left margin symbol

Right margin symbol

Current margins

Figure 12.1   The Ruler displays a white bar showing the current left and right margin settings.

Note that the margin symbols on the Ruler are the vertical edges of the white margin bar, *not* the small triangular buttons. These buttons are the indent symbols, which you'll learn about in Lesson 14. If your mouse pointer has changed to a 2-headed arrow, then you know you have found the margin symbol.

Changing Margins   To change the margins for only a portion of a document, change the left and/or right indent (covered in Lesson 14).

Setting Left and Right Margins with a Dialog Box

If you prefer not to use the Ruler, or want to enter specific values, you can set the left and right margins using a dialog box. This technique also allows you to set the margins for only a part of the document:

1. If you want the new margins to affect only a portion of the document, move the insertion point to the location where the new margin settings should begin.

2. Select **File**, **Page Setup**, then click the **Margins** tab to display the Margin options.

3. In the **Left** box, click the up or down arrows to increase or decrease the left margin. The numerical value is the distance in inches between the left edge of the page and the left edge of text. The sample page in the dialog box shows what the settings will look like when printed.

4. In the **Right** box, click the up or down arrows to increase or decrease the right margin. The value is the distance between the right edge of the page and the right edge of text.

5. Open the **Apply To** box and select where the new margins should be used: **Whole Document** or **This Point Forward.**

6. Select **OK.**

Setting Top and Bottom Margins

You also use the Page Setup dialog box to change the top and bottom margins. These margins specify the distance between text and the top and bottom of the page. As with the left and right margins, the top and bottom margin settings affect the entire document.

1. Select **Format, Page Setup** to display the Page Setup dialog box.

2. If necessary, click the **Margins** tab to display the margins options.

3. In the **Top** box, click the up or down arrows to increase or decrease the top margin. In the **Bottom** box, click the up or down arrows to increase or decrease the bottom margin. The sample page in the dialog box shows what the settings will look like when printed.

4. Select **OK.**

Header and Footer Margins   Top and bottom margins do not affect the position of headers and footers.

Changing Line Spacing

Line spacing controls the amount of space between lines of text. Different spacing is appropriate for different kinds of documents. If you want to print your document on as few pages as possible, use single line spacing to position lines close together. In contrast, a document that will later be edited by hand should be printed with wide line spacing to provide space for the editor to write comments.

Word offers a variety of line-spacing options. If you change line spacing, it affects the selected text; if there is no text selected, it affects the current paragraph and text you type at the insertion point. To change line spacing:

1. Select **Format, Paragraph** to display the Paragraph dialog box. If necessary, click the **Indents and Spacing** tab.

2. Pull down the **Line Spacing** list and select the desired spacing. The Single, 1.5 Lines, and Double settings are self-explanatory. The other settings are:

   - **Exactly:**   Space between lines will be exactly the value, in points, that you enter in the **At** box.

   - **At Least:**   Space between lines will be at least the value you enter in the **At** box; Word will increase the spacing as needed if the line contains large characters.

   - **Multiple:**   Changes spacing by the factor you enter in the At box. For example, enter 1.5 to increase spacing by one and a half times, and enter 2 to double the line spacing.

In this lesson, you learned how to set page margins and line spacing. The next lesson shows you how to use and set tabs.

Setting Tabs

In this lesson, you'll learn how to use and set tabs.

What Are Tabs?

Tabs provide a way for you to control the indentation and vertical alignment of text in your document. When you press the Tab key, Word inserts a tab in the document, which moves the cursor (and any text to the right of it) to the next tab stop. By default, Word has tab stops at 0.5-inch intervals across the width of the page. You can modify the location of tab stops and control the way that text aligns at a tab stop.

Types of Tab Stops

There are four types of tab stops; each aligns text differently:

- **Left-aligned**   Left edge of text aligns at tab stop. Word's default tab stops are all left-aligned.

- **Right-aligned**   Right edge of text aligns at tab stop.

- **Center-aligned**   Text is centered at the tab stop.

- **Decimal-aligned**   Decimal point (period) is aligned at tab stop (used for aligning columns of numbers).

Figure 13.1 illustrates the effects of the four tab alignment options. This figure also shows the four different symbols that are displayed on the Ruler to indicate the position of tab stops.

Click here until it
shows the symbol
for the type of tab
you want.

Left-aligned
tab stop

Decimal-
aligned
tab stop

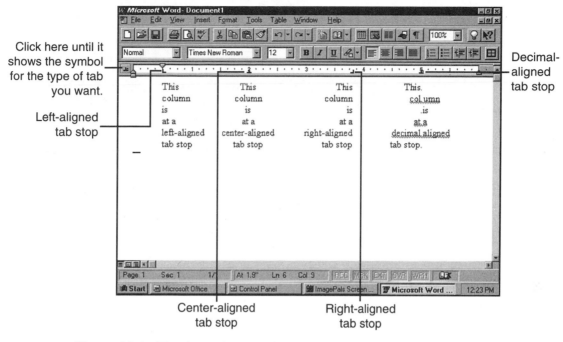

Center-aligned
tab stop

Right-aligned
tab stop

Figure 13.1   The four tab stop alignment options.

Changing the Default Tab Stops

You cannot delete the default tab stops, but you can change the spacing between them. Here are the steps to follow:

1. Select **Format**, **Tabs** to display the Tabs dialog box.

2. In the **Default Tab Stops** box, click the up or down arrow to increase or decrease the spacing between default tab stops.

3. Select **OK**.

The default tab stop spacing affects the entire document.

Good-bye Tab   To effectively "delete" the default tab stops, set the spacing between them to a value larger than the page width.

Creating Custom Tab Stops

If the default tab stops are not suited to your needs, you can add custom tab stops.

1. Select the paragraphs that will have custom tabs. If no text is selected, the new tabs will affect text that you type at the insertion point.

2. Click the tab symbol at the left end of the Ruler until it displays the symbol for the type of tab you want to insert (see Figure 13.1).

3. Point at the approximate tab stop location on the Ruler, and press and hold the left mouse button. A dashed vertical line will extend down through the document showing the tab stop position relative to your text.

4. Move the mouse left or right until the tab stop is at the desired location.

5. Release the mouse button.

 If your Ruler is not displayed, select **View, Ruler**.

When you add a custom tab stop, all of the default tab stops to the left are temporarily inactivated. This ensures that the custom tab stop will take precedence. Custom tab stop symbols are displayed on the Ruler for the paragraph containing the insertion point.

Moving and Deleting Custom Tab Stops

Follow these steps to move a custom tab stop to a new position:

1. Point at the tab stop symbol on the Ruler.

2. Press and hold the left mouse button.

3. Drag the tab stop to the new position.

4. Release the mouse button.

To delete a custom tab stop, follow the same steps, but, in step 3, drag the tab stop symbol off the **Ruler**, then release the mouse button.

Using Tab Leader Characters

A tab leader character is a character displayed in the blank space to the left of text that has been positioned using a tab. Typically, periods or hyphens are used for leader characters to create effects such as that shown in Figure 13.2. This menu was created by setting a decimal align tab stop with a dot leader character at the 5.25" position.

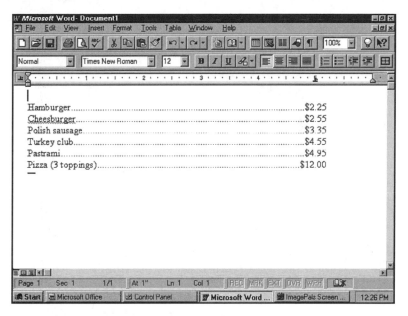

Figure 13.2. Using tabs with a leader character.

To change the leader character for a custom tab stop:

1. Point at the tab stop symbol on the **Ruler** and double-click. Word displays the Tabs dialog box.

2. Under **Leader**, select the desired leader character.

3. Select **OK**.

In this lesson you learned how to set and use tabs. The next lesson shows you how to indent and justify text.

Indenting and Justifying

In this lesson, you'll learn how to use indents and justification in your documents. These features help further customize the overall flow and appearance of your text.

Indenting Paragraphs

Indentation lets you control the amount of space between your text and the left and right edges of the page. Unlike margins, which you learned about in Lesson 12, indentation works for single lines and small sections of text. You can set different indentations for left and right edges, and for the first line of a paragraph.

What Is Indentation?   Indentation is the space between the edges of a paragraph and the page margins.

Setting Indents with the Ruler

The easiest way to set indents is with the Ruler and the mouse (If your Ruler is not displayed, select **View, Ruler**). The Ruler is calibrated in inches from the left margin. The Ruler elements that you use to set indents are illustrated in Figure 14.1.

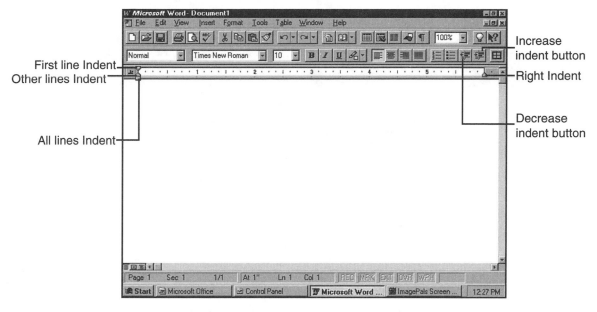

Figure 14.1   The Ruler can be used to set indentation.

To change indent positions, drag the indent symbols to the desired positions. As you drag, a dotted vertical line is displayed in the document showing the new position.

- To change the indent of the first line of a paragraph, drag the **First Line Indent** symbol to the desired position.

- To change the indent of all lines of a paragraph, except the first one, drag the **Other Lines Indent** symbol to the desired position (this is called a hanging indent).

- To change the indent of all lines of a paragraph, drag the **All Lines Indent** symbol to the desired position.

- To change the indent of the right edge of the paragraph, drag the **Right Indent** symbol to the desired position.

If you select one or more paragraphs first, the new indents will apply only to the selected paragraphs. Otherwise, the new indents will apply only to new paragraphs that you type from the insertion point forward.

Quick Indents   To quickly increase or decrease the left indent for the current paragraph or selected paragraphs, click the **Increase Indent** or **Decrease Indent** button on the Formatting Toolbar.

Displaying the Formatting Toolbar   If the Formatting Toolbar is not displayed, select **View, Toolbars**, then select the **Formatting** option.

Setting Indents with a Dialog Box

If you prefer, you can set indents using a dialog box:

1. Select **Format**, **Paragraph** to display the Paragraph dialog box, then click the **Indents and Spacing** tab if necessary to display the indents and spacing options (Figure 14.2).

2. Under **Indentation**, click the up and down arrows in the **Left or Right** boxes to increase or decrease the indentation settings. For a first line or a hanging indent, select the indent type in the **Special** pull-down list, then enter the indent amount in the **By** box. The sample page in the dialog box illustrates how the current settings will appear.

3. Select **OK**. The new settings are applied to any selected paragraphs or to new text.

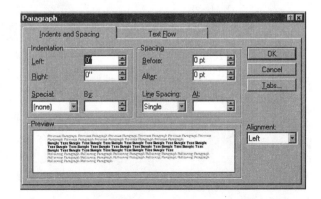

Figure 14.2. Setting Indents in the Paragraph dialog box.

Justifying Text

Word for Windows offers four justification options:

- **Left justification** aligns the left ends of lines. (This book is printed with left justification.)

- **Right justification** aligns the right ends of lines.

- **Full justification** aligns both the left and right ends of lines.

- **Center justification** centers lines between the left and right margins.

To change the justification for one or more paragraphs, first select the paragraphs to change; then, click one of the justification buttons on the formatting toolbar, as shown in Figure 14.3.

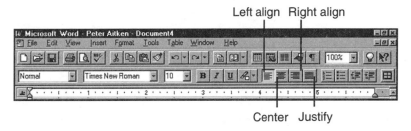

Figure 14.3. Click these buttons to set text justification.

What Is Justification?   Justification refers to the way in which lines on the page are aligned with the lines above and below them.

If you prefer to use a dialog box to change justification, select the paragraphs and then:

1. Select **Format**, **Paragraph** to display the Paragraph dialog box.

2. Open the **Alignment** drop-down box.

3. Select the desired alignment.

4. Select **OK**.

Changing Justification If you change justification without selecting any paragraphs, then the new justification will apply *only* to any new paragraphs that you type.

In this lesson, you learned how to set indentation and justification in your documents. In the next lesson, you'll learn how to search for and replace text.

Searching and Replacing

In this lesson, you'll learn how to search for specific text in your document, and how to automatically replace each occurrence of it with new text.

Searching for Text

You can have Word for Windows search through your document to find occurrences of specific text. For example, you are writing a 40 page report and want to edit the section on the New York Sales Office. You'll quickly find it by searching for "New York." Word's default is to search the entire document. If there is text selected, the search will be limited to the selection.

To search for text, follow these steps:

1. Select **Edit**, **Find**. The Find dialog box will display, as shown in Figure 15.1.

2. In the **Find What** text box, enter the text to find. This is the search template.

Search Template   The *search template* is a model for the text you want to find.

3. *(Optional)* Select **Find Whole Words Only** to match whole words only. With this option off, a search template of *light* would match *light*, *lightning*, *lighter*, and so on. With this option on, it would match only *light*.

Figure 15.1   The Find dialog box.

4. *(Optional)* Select **Match Case** to require an exact match for upper- and lowercase letters. If this option is not selected, Word will find matching text of either case.

5. In the Search box, select **All** to have Word search the entire document. You can also select **Down** to have Word for Windows search from the insertion point to the end of the document, or from the beginning of the selected text to the end. Select **Up** to search in the opposite direction.

6. Select **Find Next**. Word for Windows looks through the document for text that matches the search template. If Word finds matching text, it highlights the text in the document and stops, with the Find dialog box still displayed.

   Now, you can do one of two things:

   - Select **Find Next** to continue the search for another instance of the template.

   - Press **Esc** to close the dialog box and return to the document. The found text remains selected.

If, after searching only part of the document, Word for Windows reaches the start of the document (for an upward search) or the end of the document (for a downward search), you are given the option of continuing the search from the other end of the document. Once the entire document has been searched, a message to that effect is displayed.

Finding and Replacing Text

Use the Replace command to search for instances of text, and to replace them with new text. Imagine that you're almost finished with your 400-page novel, and decide to change the main character's name from Brad to Lance. This command will save you a lot of work!

To replace text, follow these steps:

1. Select **Edit, Replace**. The Replace dialog box appears, shown in Figure 15.2.

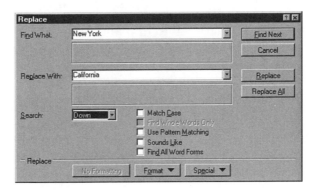

Figure 15.2 The Replace dialog box.

2. In the **Find What** text box, enter the target text that is to be replaced.

3. In the **Replace With** text box, enter the replacement text.

4. If desired, select the **Match Case**, **Find Whole Words Only**, and **Search** options, as explained earlier in this lesson.

5. Select **Replace All** to have Word for Windows go through the entire document, replacing all instances of the target text with the replacement text. You can also select **Find Next** to highlight the first instance of the target text.

Deleting Text   To delete the target text, leave the **Replace With** box blank.

If you select Find Next, Word will highlight the first occurrence of the template in the document. You now have three options:

- Select **Replace** to substitute the highlighted text with the replacement text and then find the next instance of the target text.

- Select **Find Next** to leave the highlighted text unchanged and then find the next instance of the target text.

- Select **Replace All** to find and replace all remaining instances of the target text. Use caution, as the Replace All command can be dangerous!

Saving Time   To save typing, use abbreviations for long words and phrases. Later, use **Replace** to change them to final form.

Recovery!   If you make a mistake replacing text, you can recover with the **Edit Undo Replace** command.

In this lesson, you learned how to search for and optionally replace text. In the next lesson, you'll learn how to use Word for Windows templates.

Using Templates

In this lesson, you'll learn how to create and modify templates.

What Is a Template?

You learned in Lesson 4 that every Word for Windows document is based on a template, and you also learned how to create a new document based on one of Word's predefined templates. You can also create your own template, or modify existing ones.

Creating a New Template

You can create new templates to suit your specific word-processing needs. To create a new template from scratch:

1. Select **File, New**. The New dialog box is displayed.

2. In the dialog box, select the **Template** option.

3. In the box displaying template icons, be sure that **Blank Document** is selected.

4. Select **OK**. A blank document-editing screen appears with a default name, such as **TEMPLATE1**.

5. Enter the boilerplate text and other items that you want to be part of the template. Apply formatting to the text as desired; create any styles that you want in the template.

6. Select **File, Save**. The Save As dialog box is displayed.

7. In the File name text box, enter a descriptive name up to 256 characters long for the template.

8. Select **OK**. The template is saved under the specified name and is now available for use each time you start a new document.

Boilerplate   This is text that appears the same in all documents of a certain type.

Modifying an Existing Template

You can retrieve any existing template from disk and modify it. Then, you can save it under a new name. To modify a template:

1. Select **File, New** to display the New dialog box, shown in Figure 16.1.

2. Select the template that you want to modify. If necessary, select a different folder in the **Look In** list.

3. Be sure the **Template** option is selected.

4. Click **OK**.

5. Make the desired modifications and additions to the template's text and styles.

6. To save the modified template under its original name, select **File, Save**. This is not advised, however. It's better to save the modified template under a new name (see step 7) so the original template will still be available.

7. To save the modified template under a new name (leaving the original template unchanged), select **File, Save As** and enter a new template name.

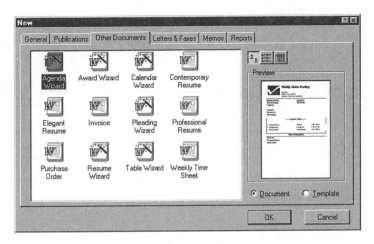

Figure 16.1   Opening a template for modification.

Note that changes you make to a template are not reflected in documents that were created based on the template before it was changed.

Creating a Template from a Document

To create a template based on an existing Word document you created, follow these steps:

1. Open the document; delete any text and formatting that you do not want to appear in the template.

2. Select **File, Save As** to display the Save As dialog box.

3. Open the **Save as Type** list and select **Document Template**.

4. Open the **Save in** list and select the **Template** folder.

5. Type the name for the template in the **File name** box.

6. Select **Save**.

In step 4, it's important to select the proper template folder. If you don't, the new template will not be available in Word's New dialog box.

In this lesson, you learned how to create and modify document templates. In the next lesson, you'll learn how to add page numbers, headers, and footers to your documents.

Page Numbers, Headers, and Footers

In this lesson, you'll learn how to add page numbers, headers, and footers to your documents.

Adding Page Numbers

Many documents, particularly long ones, benefit from having numbered pages. Word for Windows offers complete flexibility in the placement and format of page numbers. To add page numbers to your document:

1. Select **Insert, Page Numbers**. The Page Numbers dialog box displays.

2. Pull down the **Position** list and select the desired position on the page: Top of Page or Bottom of Page.

3. Pull down the **Alignment** list and select **Left, Center,** or **Right.** You can also select **Inside** or **Outside** if you're printing two-sided pages and want the page numbers positioned near to (Inside) or away from (Outside) the binding.

4. The default number format consists of Arabic numerals (1, 2, 3, etc.). To select a different format (for example, i, ii, iii), select **Format** and select the desired format.

5. Select **OK**.

When you add a page number using the above procedure, Word for Windows makes the page number part of the document's header or footer. The next section describes headers and footers.

What Are Headers and Footers?

A header or footer is text that prints at the top (a header) or bottom (a footer) of every page of a document. A header or footer can show the page number, or it can contain chapter titles, authors' names, or any other information you desire. Word for Windows offers several header/footer options:

- The same header/footer on every page of the document.

- One header/footer on the first page of the document and a different header/footer on all other pages.

- One header/footer on odd-numbered pages and a different header/footer on even-numbered pages.

Headers and Footers   The header is at the top of the page, and the footer is at the bottom.

Adding or Editing a Header or Footer

To add a header or footer to your document, or to edit an existing header or footer, follow these steps:

1. Select **View, Header and Footer**. Word displays the current page's header enclosed by a nonprinting dashed line (Figure 17.1). Regular document text is dimmed, and the Header and Footer toolbar is displayed. On the toolbar, click the **Switch** button to switch between the current page's header and footer.

2. Enter the header or footer text and formatting using the regular Word editing techniques.

3. If you want the date, time, or page number inserted, click the appropriate button on the toolbar.

4. Click the **Show Next** and **Show Previous** buttons on the Header and Footer toolbar to switch between the various sections. As you edit, each header or footer will be labeled (for example, "First Page Header", "Odd Page Footer").

5. When finished, click the **Close** button on the toolbar to return to the document.

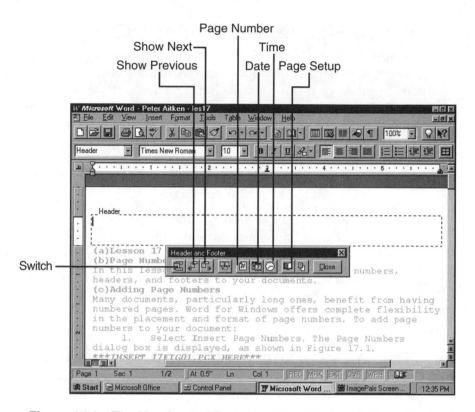

Figure 17.1 The Header and Footer Toolbar displayed after selecting View Header and Footer.

Goodbye, header! To delete a header or footer, follow the steps above for editing the header or footer. Select all of the text in the header or footer; press **Del**.

Creating Different Headers and Footers for Different Pages

Normally, Word displays the same header and footer on all the document's pages. In addition, you have the following options:

- One header/footer on the first page with a different header/footer on all other pages.

- One header/footer on odd-numbered pages with another header/footer on even-numbered pages.

To activate one or both of these options:

1. Select **View, Header and Footer**.

2. Click the **Page Setup** button on the Header and Footer toolbar. Word displays the Page Setup dialog box. If necessary, click the **Layout** tab to display the page layout options (Figure 17.2).

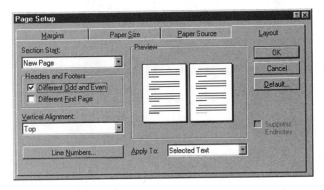

Figure 17.2   The Page Setup dialog box.

3. In the Headers and Footers section of the dialog box, turn on the **Different Odd and Even** option and/or the **Different First Page** option.

4. Select **OK** to close the Page Setup dialog box.

In this lesson, you learned to add page numbers, headers, and footers to a document. The next lesson shows you how to save time with Word's AutoCorrect feature.

Footnotes and Endnotes

In this lesson, you will learn how to use footnotes and endnotes in your documents.

Footnotes versus Endnotes

You use footnotes and endnotes to explain, comment on, or provide references for text in your document. A reference mark is placed in the text at the location of the text the note refers to, and the same reference mark is used at the beginning of the corresponding footnote or endnote to identify it. A footnote is positioned at the bottom of the page where its reference mark appears, whereas endnotes are grouped together at the end of the document.

The reference marks for footnotes can be either a symbol, such as *, or sequential numbers. Endnotes are almost always referenced by sequential numbers. Word manages your footnotes and endnotes for you, automatically renumbering them when you delete or insert a note in the document.

Inserting a Footnote or Endnote

These are the steps required to insert a footnote or endnote in your document:

1. Position the insertion point where you want the reference mark located in the text.

2. Select **Insert, Footnote** to display the Footnote and Endnote dialog box (Figure 18.1). Be sure the desired type of note, Footnote or Endnote, is selected.

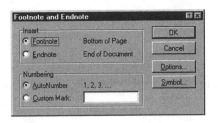

Figure 18.1   The Footnote and Endnote dialog box.

3. For sequentially numbered notes, click the **AutoNumber** option. For a symbol, click the **Custom Mark** option, then enter the desired symbol in the box. You can also click the **Symbol** button and select the desired symbol from the dialog box that is displayed.

4. Click the **OK** button. Depending on which view you are in, one of the following happens:

   • If you are in Normal view, Word opens a pane in which you enter the footnote text; when you are finished, click the **Close** button.

   • In Page Layout view, you edit the footnote in its actual position on the page. Click the regular document text when you are done.

Quick note keys   To insert a footnote, press **Alt+Ctrl+F**. For an endnote, press **Alt+Ctrl+E**.

Viewing and Editing Notes

Editing and viewing footnotes and endnotes is done in the actual note position if you are in Page Layout view, or in a special pane if you are in Normal view. Select **Normal** or **Page Layout** from the **View** menu to change views.

If you are in Page Layout View, you can edit and view footnotes and endnotes in the actual note position. Select **View, Page Layout** to change to Page Layout view. (In Normal view you edit footnotes and endnotes in a special pane.)

To view a note, select **View, Footnotes** or double-click the note's reference mark in the text. Then, edit the note text using Word's usual editing and formatting commands, including defining and assigning styles and using the Ruler. Click the **Close** button (if in Normal view) or the regular document text (if in Page Layout view) when you are done editing the note.

Moving and Deleting Notes

To move a note's reference mark to a new location in the text, select either the reference mark alone or with its surrounding text. Then drag it to the new location, or

1. Select **Edit, Cut**, press **Ctrl+X**, or click the **Cut** button on the standard toolbar.

2. Move the insertion point to the new location.

3. Select **Edit, Paste**, press **Ctrl+V**, or click the **Paste** button on the standard toolbar.

To delete a note, select its reference mark and press **Del**. When you move or delete a numbered note, Word automatically renumbers the remaining notes.

Customizing Footnotes and Endnotes

Word's default settings are to number footnotes with arabic numerals (1, 2, 3...) and endnotes with lowercase Roman numerals (i, ii, iii...). You can change the numbering style of your document's notes as follows:

1. Select **Insert, Footnote** to display the Footnote and Endnote dialog box (shown earlier in Figure 18.1).

2. Click the **Options** button to display the Note Options dialog box, shown in Figure 18.2.

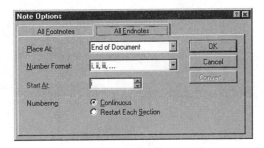

Figure 18.2   The Note Options dialog box with the All Endnotes tab displayed.

3. Click the **All Footnotes** or **All Endnotes** tab depending on which type of note you are changing the numbering for.

4. Pull down the Number Format list and select the desired numbering style.

5. Click **OK** to return to the Footnote and Endnote dialog box, then click **OK** again to return to your document.

In this lesson you learned how to include footnotes and endnotes in your Word documents. The next lesson covers Word's AutoCorrect feature.

Using AutoCorrect Entries

In this lesson, you'll learn how to use Word's AutoCorrect feature.

What Is AutoCorrect?

The AutoCorrect feature lets you define a collection of commonly used words, phrases, or sentences that can be inserted into a document without typing them each time. You insert an AutoCorrect entry in the document by typing a short abbreviation or name that you assigned to it. Each time you type the abbreviation into the document, the corresponding word or phrase automatically replaces it. Typical uses for AutoCorrect entries are your company name, the closing sentence for a business letter, and your name and title. AutoCorrect can also catch common typographical errors, for example replacing "teh" with "the". An AutoCorrect entry can contain just text or text along with special formatting.

Creating an AutoCorrect Entry

One way to create an AutoCorrect entry requires that you first type the replacement text into your document and add any special formatting that you want included. Then:

1. Select the text for the AutoCorrect entry.

2. Select **Tools, AutoCorrect**. The AutoCorrect dialog box displays (Figure 19.1) with the selected text displayed in the With box.

3. In the **Replace** box, enter the name or abbreviation that you want to use for the AutoCorrect entry. This should be a short name that describes the entry. You will later use this name when inserting the AutoCorrect entry into documents.

4. Select the **Plain Text** option to have the AutoCorrect entry inserted as plain text, adopting the formatting of the surrounding text. Select the **Formatted Text** option to have the AutoCorrect entry's original formatting retained when it is inserted.

5. Select **Add**.

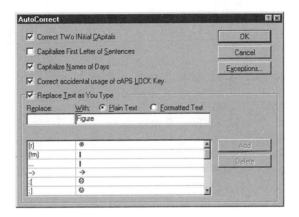

Figure 19.1   The AutoCorrect dialog box.

 Return Address   Save time by creating an AutoCorrect entry that contains your name and address.

Inserting an AutoCorrect Entry

Word will automatically insert AutoCorrect entries as you type:

1. Move the insertion point to the location where you want the AutoCorrect entry inserted.

2. Type the name you assigned to the AutoCorrect entry, preceded by a space, and followed by a space or punctuation mark.

3. The corresponding AutoCorrect entry is inserted in place of its name.

You can control whether Word will automatically replace AutoCorrect entries by selecting **Tools, AutoCorrect**. Then, turn the **Replace Text as You Type** option on or off.

Modifying an AutoCorrect Entry

You can modify an existing AutoCorrect entry. Such modifications will not affect previous instances of the AutoCorrect entry in your documents.

1. Insert the existing AutoCorrect entry into a document as described earlier in this lesson.

2. Change the text that you just inserted and/or its formatting as desired.

3. Select the newly edited text.

4. Select **Tools, AutoCorrect**. The text you selected will be displayed in the With box. Type the abbreviation to be associated with the modified AutoCorrect entry into the Replace box.

5. Select **Replace**.

6. When asked whether to redefine the AutoCorrect entry, select **Yes**.

Deleting an AutoCorrect Entry

You can delete an unneeded AutoCorrect entry from the AutoCorrect list. Deleting an AutoCorrect entry does not affect instances of the entry that were inserted previously.

1. Select **Tools, AutoCorrect**.

2. Type the AutoCorrect entry's abbreviation in the Replace box, or select it from the list.

3. Select **Delete**. The entry is deleted.

In this lesson you learned how to use AutoCorrect entries. The next lesson shows you how to use symbols and special characters.

Symbols and
Special
Characters

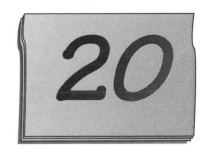

In this lesson, you'll learn how to use symbols and special characters in your Word documents.

What Are Symbols and Special Characters?

Symbols and special characters are not part of the standard character set. The Greek letter mu (µ) and the copyright symbol (©) are examples. If it's not on your keyboard, Word can probably still display and insert it in your documents.

Inserting a Symbol

To insert a symbol at the insertion point, follow these steps:

1. Select **Insert, Symbol** to display the Symbol dialog box. If necessary, click the **Symbols** tab to display the symbols section, as shown in Figure 20.1.

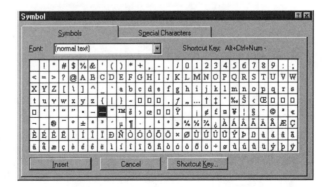

Figure 20.1 The Symbols dialog box.

2. Look through the grid of symbols for the one you want. To see an enlarged view of a symbol, click it.

3. To view other symbol sets, open the Font list and select the desired font.

4. To insert the highlighted symbol, select **Insert**. To insert any symbol, double-click it.

5. Click the **Cancel** button to close the dialog box without inserting a symbol. Click **Close** to close the dialog box after you insert a symbol.

What Are Special Characters?

Some of the special characters that Word offers may seem unfamiliar to you, but they can be quite useful in certain documents. The following lists brief descriptions of the less well-known ones.

En dash   A dash that looks slightly longer than the standard dash made with minus sign on the keyboard. The en dash is properly used in combinations of figures and/or capital letters, as in "Please refer to part 1–A."

Em dash   Slightly longer than an en dash, the em dash has a variety of purposes, the most common of which is to mark a sudden change of thought. For example, "She said—and no one dared disagree—that the meeting was over."

En space   A space slightly longer than the standard space. This space is an en space.

Em space   A space slightly longer than the en space. This space   is an em space.

Non-breaking space   A space that will not be broken at the end of the line. The words separated by a non-breaking space always stay on the same line.

Non-breaking hyphen   Similar to a non-breaking space. That is to say, two words separated by a non-breaking hyphen will always stay on the same line.

Optional hyphen   A hyphen that will not display unless the word it is in needs to be broken at the end of a line.

Inserting a Special Character

To insert a special character in your document at the location of the insertion point:

1. Select **Insert, Symbol** to display the Symbol dialog box. If necessary, click the **Special Characters** tab to display the special characters list, as shown in Figure 20.2.

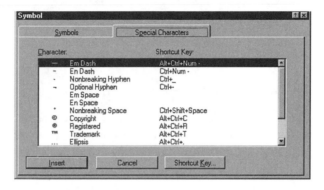

Figure 20.2 The Special Characters list.

2. Look through the list of special characters for the one you want.

3. To insert the highlighted character, select **Insert**. To insert any character in the list, double-click it.

4. Click the **Cancel** button to close the dialog box without inserting a symbol. Click **Close** to close the dialog box after you insert a symbol.

In this lesson you learned how to use symbols and special characters in your Word documents. The next lesson covers proofing your document.

Checking Your Spelling

In this lesson, you'll learn how to use the Word for Windows Speller to help proof your document.

Using the Spelling Checker

The spelling checker lets you verify and correct the spelling of words in your document. Word for Windows checks words against a standard dictionary and lets you know when it encounters an unknown word. You then can ignore it, change it, or add it to the dictionary.

To check spelling in a portion of a document, select the text to check. To check the entire document, first move the insertion point to the start of the document by pressing **Ctrl+Home**. Then:

1. Select **Tools**, **Spelling**, press F7, or click the **Spelling** button. Word for Windows starts checking words beginning at the insertion point.

2. If a word found in the document is not in the dictionary, it becomes highlighted in the text and the Spelling dialog box displays (see Figure 21.1).

Figure 21.1 The Spelling dialog box.

3. In the Spelling dialog box, the Not in Dictionary box displays the word that was not found in the dictionary. If the spelling checker has found any likely replacements, they are listed in the Suggestions list box. In the dialog box, you have the following options:

- To ignore the highlighted word and continue, select **Ignore**.

- To ignore the highlighted word and any other instances of it in the document, select **Ignore All**.

- To change the highlighted word, type the new spelling in the **Change To**-box or highlight the desired replacement word in the **Suggestions list** box. Then select **Change** (to change the current instance of the word) or **Change All** (to change all instances of the word in the document).

- To add the word to the dictionary, select **Add**.

4. The spelling checker proceeds to check the rest of the document. When it finishes checking, it displays a message to that effect. To cancel spell checking at any time, select **Cancel** in the Spelling dialog box.

Fast Check!   To check the spelling of a single word, double-click the word to select it, then press **F7**.

Checking Spelling as You Type

In addition to checking your document's spelling as described above, you can instruct Word to check each word as you type it in. Any word not found in the dictionary will be underlined with a wavy red line, and you can deal with it whenever you choose. To turn automatic spell checking on or off:

1. Select **Tools**, **Options** to display the Options dialog box.

2. If necessary, click the **Spelling** tab.

3. Turn the **Automatic Spell Checking** option on or off.

4. Click **OK**.

To deal with a word that has been underlined by Automatic Spell Checking, click the word with the right mouse button. Word displays a pop-up menu containing suggested replacements for the word (if any are found) as well as several commands. Your choices are

- To replace the word with one of the suggestions, click the replacement word.

- To ignore all occurrences of the word in the document, click **Ignore All**.

- To add the word to the dictionary, click **Add**.

- To start a regular spelling check, click **Spelling**.

Hide Misspelling Marks If your document contains words underlined by the automatic spelling checker and you want to hide the underlines, select **Tools**, **Options**, click the **Spelling** tab, and turn on the **Hide Spelling Errors** in Current Document option. Turn this option off to redisplay the underlines.

In this lesson you learned how to use the Speller to proof your document. The next lesson shows you how to create numbered and bulleted lists.

Creating Numbered and Bulleted Lists

In this lesson you'll learn how to create numbered and bulleted lists in your document.

Why Use Numbered and Bulleted Lists?

Numbered and bulleted lists are useful formatting tools for setting off lists of information in a document; you've seen plenty of both in this book! Word for Windows automatically creates these elements. Use bulleted lists for items that consist of related information, but are in no particular order. Use numbered lists for items with a specific order. Figure 22.1 shows examples of numbered and bulleted lists.

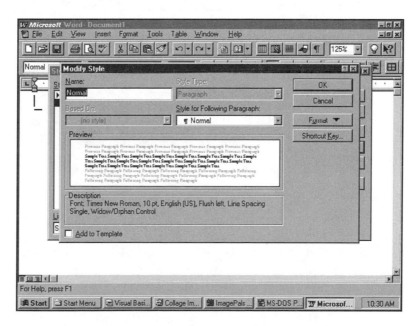

Figure 22.1 Word automatically creates numbered and bulleted lists such as these.

When creating a list, each paragraph is considered a separate list item and receives its own number or bullet.

Creating a Numbered or Bulleted List

To create a numbered or bulleted list from existing text, follow these steps:

1. Select the paragraphs that you want in the list.

2. Select **Format, Bullets and Numbering** to display the Bullets and Numbering dialog box.

3. Depending on the type of list you want, click the **Bulleted** tab or the **Numbered** tab. Figure 22.2 shows the Numbered style options, and Figure 22.3 shows the Bulleted style options.

4. Click the bulleting or numbering option that you want.

5. Select **OK**.

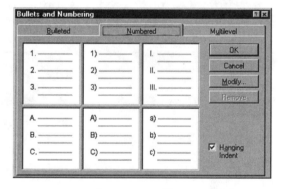

Figure 22.2 List numbering style options displayed in the Bullets and Numbering dialog box.

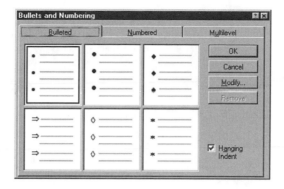

Figure 22.3   List bulleting style options displayed in the Bullets and Numbering dialog box.

To create a numbered or bulleted list as you type:

1. Move the insertion point to the location for the list. Press **Enter**, if necessary, to start a new paragraph.

2. Select **Format, Bullets and Numbering** to display the Bullets and Numbering dialog box.

3. Depending on the type of list you want, click the **Bulleted** tab or the **Numbered** tab.

4. Click the bulleting or numbering style that you want.

5. Select **OK**.

6. Type in the list elements, pressing **Enter** at the end of each paragraph. Each paragraph will be automatically numbered or bulleted as it is added.

7. At the end of the last paragraph, press **Enter**. Word will insert an extra, empty list item that will be removed in the next step.

8. Select **Format, Bullets and Numbering** to display the Bullets and Numbering dialog box, then select **Remove**.

Quick Lists   Create a numbered or bulleted list quickly—in the default style—by clicking the Numbered List or Bulleted List button before typing, or after selecting the list text.

Undoing a Numbered or Bulleted List

Follow these steps to remove bullets or numbers from a list:

1. Select the paragraphs that you want the bullets or numbering removed. This can be the entire list or just part of it.

2. Select **Format, Bullets and Numbering** to display the Bullets and Numbering dialog box.

3. Select **Remove**.

Adding Items to Numbered and Bulleted Lists

You can add new items to a numbered or bulleted list as follows:

1. Move the insertion point to the location in the list where you wan the new item.

2. Press **Enter** to start a new paragraph. Word automatically inserts new bullet or number, and renumbers the list items as needed.

3. Type in the new text.

4. Repeat as many times as needed.

This lesson showed you how to create numbered and bulleted li: In the next lesson you'll learn how to arrange text in columns.

Arranging Text in Columns

In this lesson you'll learn how to use columns in your documents.

Why Use Columns?

Columns are commonly used in newsletters, brochures, and similar documents. The shorter lines of text provided by columns are easier to read and also provide greater flexibility in formatting a document with graphics, tables, and so on. Word for Windows makes it easy to use columns in your documents. Figure 23.1 shows a document formatted with three columns.

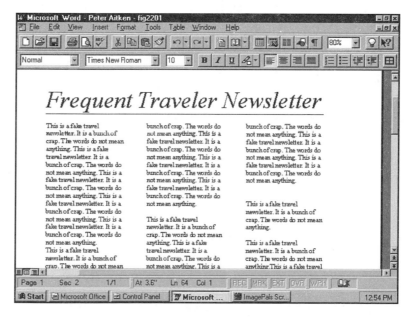

Figure 23.1 A document formatted with three columns.

Note that the Word for Windows columns feature creates *newspaper* style columns, in which the text flows to the bottom of one column and then continues at the top of the next column on the page. For side-by-side paragraphs, such as you would need in a resume or a script, use Word's table feature, covered in Lesson 25.

Creating Columns

Word for Windows has four predefined column layouts:

- Two equal width columns
- Three equal width columns
- Two unequal width columns with the wider column on the left
- Two unequal width columns with the wider column on the right

You can apply any of these column formats to all or part of a document, to selected text, or from the insertion point onward. Follow these steps:

1. If you want only a part of the document in columns, select the text that you want in columns, or move the insertion point to the location where you want columns to begin.

2. Select **Format, Columns** to display the Columns dialog box (Figure 23.2).

3. Under Presets, click the column format that you want.

4. Pull down the **Apply To** list and specify the extent to which the columns should apply.

5. Turn on the **Line Between** option to display a vertical line between columns.

6. Select **OK**.

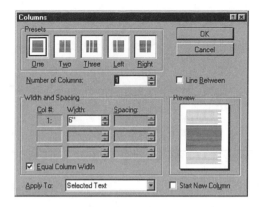

Figure 23.2   The Columns dialog box.

Quick Columns   To display selected text or the entire document in 1 to 4 equal width columns, click the Columns button, and then drag over the desired number of columns.

Screen Display of Columns

To view columns on-screen while you are editing, you must be working in Page Layout mode. In Normal mode, Word displays only a single column at a time (although your columns will be printed). To switch to Page Layout mode, select **View, Page Layout**.

Modifying Columns

Here are the steps to follow to modify existing columns:

1. Select the text in columns that you want to modify.

2. Select **Format, Columns** to display the Columns dialog box. The options in the dialog box will reflect the current settings for the selected columns.

3. Make changes to the column settings as desired.

4. Select **OK**.

Turning Columns Off

To convert multiple column text back to normal one column text, follow these steps:

1. Select the text that you want to change from multiple to a single column.

2. Select **Format, Columns** to display the Columns dialog box.

3. Under Presets, select the **One style** option.

4. Select **OK**.

This lesson showed you how to arrange text in columns. The next lesson shows you how to use AutoFormat.

Using AutoFormat

In this lesson you'll learn how to have Word automatically format your document.

What Is Automatic Formatting?

Automatic Formatting refers to Word's ability to analyze the structure of a document and recognize certain common elements, such as body text, headings, bulleted lists, and quotations. Word will then apply appropriate styles to the various text elements to create an attractively formatted document. You can accept or reject all or part of the automatically applied format and can later make any desired modifications to the document. In addition to applying styles, Automatic Formatting can remove extra "returns" between paragraphs, create bulleted lists, and more.

Is automatic formatting right for you? You'll have to try it out to find out. Take a document that characterizes one you usually work on, save it under a new name (so the original is not changed) and experiment. You'll soon find out whether you like automatic formatting, or whether you prefer manual application.

Applying Automatic Formatting

You can apply automatic formatting to all or part of a document:

1. To format part of a document, select the text. To format the entire document, the insertion point can be anywhere in the document.

2. Select **Format, AutoFormat**, then select **OK**. Word analyzes and reformats the document, and displays the AutoFormat dialog box, shown in Figure 24.1.

Figure 24.1   Use the AutoFormat dialog box to accept or reject the formatting applied by the AutoFormat command.

3. Use the vertical scroll bar to scroll through the document and examine the new formatting. The dialog box will remain displayed; grab its title bar and drag it to another location if it is blocking your view of the document.

4. Select **Reject All** to undo all formatting changes and return the document to its original state. Select **Accept** to accept all the changes. Select **Review Changes** if you want to review the changes and accept or reject them individually (see below).

Reviewing the Formatting Changes

If you select **Review Changes** in step 4 above, you can scroll through the document and examine each individual formatting change, then either accept it or reject it. The Review AutoFormat Changes dialog box will be displayed during this procedure, as shown in Figure 24.2. Scroll through the document using the vertical scroll bar; Word indicates the changes that were made using the following marks, as listed in Table 24.1. These marks also appear in the document in Figure 24.2.

Table 24.1   Word Indicates Formatting Changes Made

Change made	Mark displayed
New style applied to the paragraph	Blue paragraph mark
Paragraph mark deleted	Red paragraph mark
Text or spaces deleted	Strikethrough
Characters added	Underline
Text or formatting changed	Vertical bar in left margin

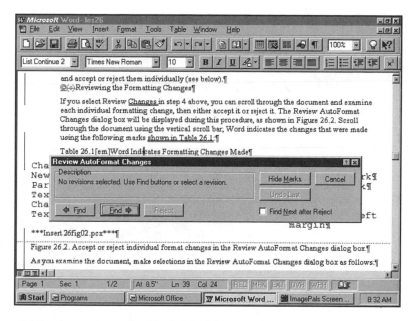

Figure 24.2 Accept or reject individual format changes in the Review AutoFormat Changes dialog box.

As you examine the document, make selections in the Review AutoFormat Changes dialog box as follows:

- Select ←**Find** or **Find**→ to highlight the next or previous change.
- Select **Reject** to undo the highlighted change.
- Select **Undo Last** to reverse the last Reject command (restoring the rejected change).

- Select **Hide Marks** to display the document as it would appear if all remaining changes are accepted. Select **Show Marks** to return to revisions display.

- Turn on the **Find Next After Reject** option to have Word automatically find the next revision after you reject the current one.

- Select **Close** to accept the remaining revisions and return to the AutoFormat dialog box.

Setting the AutoFormat Options

The AutoFormat feature has a number of settings that control which document elements it will modify. You can change these options to suit your preferences:

1. Select **Tools, Options** to display the Options dialog box.

2. Click the **AutoFormat** tab to display the AutoFormat options (Figure 24.3).

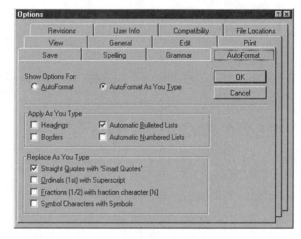

Figure 24.3   Use the Options dialog box to set Word's AutoFormat options.

3. Under Show Options For, select **Autoformat**.

4. Turn options on or off to control which document elements the AutoFormat command will affect.

5. Select **OK**.

Autoformatting as You Type

The first part of this chapter showed you how Word automatically formats an existing document. Word can also format certain elements of your text as you type them. For example, if you start a line with a dash and a space, Word interprets it as being the start of a bulleted list and formats it accordingly. To control which aspects of "format as you type" are active, follow these steps:

1. Select **Tools, Options** to display the Options dialog box. If necessary, click the **AutoFormat** tab in the dialog box.

2. Under Show Options For, select **Autoformat as You Type**.

3. Turn options on or off to control the formatting that will be applied as you type.

4. Select **OK**.

This lesson showed you how to use Word's automatic formatting capability. In the next lesson you'll learn how to use tables.

Tables

In this lesson, you'll learn how to add tables to your documents.

Uses for Tables

A *table* lets you organize information in a row and column format. Each entry in a table, called a *cell*, is independent of all other entries. You can have almost any number of rows and columns in a table. You also have a great deal of control over the size and formatting of each cell. A table cell can contain anything that a Word document can contain except another table–text, graphics, and so on.

Why Tables?   Use tables for columns of numbers, lists, and anything else that requires a row and column arrangement.

Inserting a Table

You can insert a new, empty table at any location within your document. Just follow these steps:

1. Move the insertion point to where you want the table.

2. Select **Table, Insert Table**. The Insert Table dialog box, as shown in Figure 25.1, is displayed.

3. If you want to use the Table Wizard to create your table, click the Wizard button. Lesson 4 showed you how to use Wizards. Otherwise, continue with the next step.

4. In the **Number of Columns and Number of Rows** boxes, click the arrows or enter the number of rows and columns the table should have. (You can adjust these numbers later if you wish.)

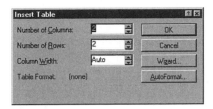

Figure 25.1 The Insert Table dialog box.

5. In the Column Width box, select the desired width for each column, in inches. Select **Auto** in this box to have the page width evenly divided among the specified number of columns.

6. Select **OK**. A blank table is created with the insertion point in the first cell. Figure 25.2, for example, shows a blank table with 4 rows and 3 columns.

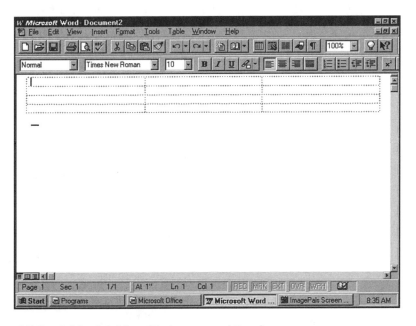

Figure 25.2 A blank table with 4 rows and 3 columns.

Quick Tables To quickly insert a table, click the Table button on the Standard Toolbar, then drag over the desired number of rows and columns.

Working in a Table

When the insertion point is in a table cell, you can enter and edit text as you would in the rest of the document. Text entered in a cell automatically wraps to the next line within the column width. Navigate in a table using the special key combinations listed below:

Press this	To
Tab	Move to the next cell in a row.
Shift+Tab	Move to the previous cell in a row.
Alt+Home	Move to the first cell in the current row.
Alt+PgUp	Move to the top cell in the current column.
Alt+End	Move to the last cell in the current row.
Alt+PgDn	Move to the last cell in the current column.

If the insertion point is at the edge of a cell, you can also use the arrow keys to move between cells.

Editing and Formatting a Table

Once you've created a table and entered some information, you can edit its contents and format its appearance to suit your needs.

Deleting and Inserting Cells, Rows, and Columns

You can delete individual cells, erasing their contents and leaving a blank cell. You can also delete entire rows and columns. When you do so, columns to the right or rows below move to fill in for the deleted row or column.

 Fast Select!   To select an entire cell, click in the left margin of the cell, between the text and the cell border. The mouse pointer changes to an arrow when it's in this area.

To delete the contents of a cell:

1. Select the cell.

2. Press **Del**.

To delete an entire row or column:

1. Move the insertion point to any cell in the row or column to be deleted.

2. Select **Table, Delete Cells**. A dialog box is displayed (see Figure 25.3).

Figure 25.3   The Delete Cells dialog box.

3. In the dialog box, select **Delete Entire Row** or **Delete Entire Column**.

4. Select **OK**. The row or column is deleted.

To insert a single row or column:

1. Move the insertion point to a cell to the right of where you want the new column or below where you want the new row.

2. Select **Table, Insert Columns** to insert a new, blank column to the left of the selected column. Select **Table, Insert Rows** to insert a new, blank row above the selected row.

It Varies!   The commands on the Table menu change according to circumstances. For example, if you have selected a column in a table, the Insert Columns command is displayed but the Insert Rows command is not.

To insert more than one row or column:

1. Select cells that span the number of rows or columns you want to insert. For example, to insert three new rows between rows 2 and 3, select cells in rows 3, 4, and 5 (in any column).

2. Select **Table, Select Row** if inserting rows or **Table, Select Column** if inserting columns.

3. Select **Table, Insert Rows** or **Table, Insert Columns**, as appropriate.

To insert a new row at the bottom of the table:

1. Move the insertion point to the last cell in the last row of the table.

2. Press **Tab**. A new row is added at the bottom of the table.

To insert a new column at the right edge of the table:

1. Click just outside the table's right border.

2. Select **Table, Select Column**.

3. Select **Table, Insert Columns**.

Moving or Copying Columns and Rows

Here's how to copy or move and entire column or row from one location in a table to another.

1. Select the column or row.

  2. To copy, press **Ctrl+C** or click the **Copy** button on the Standard Toolbar. To move, press **Ctrl+X** or click the **Cut** button.

3. Move in insertion point to the new location for the column or row. It will be inserted above or to the left of the location of the insertion point.

 4. Press **Ctrl+C** or click the **Paste** button on the Standard Toolbar.

Changing Column Width

You can quickly change the width of a column with the mouse:

1. Point at the right border of the column whose width you want to change. The mouse pointer changes to a pair of thin vertical lines with arrowheads pointing left and right.

2. Drag the column border to the desired width.

You can also use a dialog box to change column widths:

1. Move the insertion point to any cell in the column you want to change.

2. Select **Table, Cell Height and Width**. The Cell Height and Width dialog box is displayed (see Figure 25.4). If necessary, click the **Column tab** to display the column options.

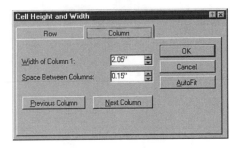

Figure 25.4 The Cell Height and Width dialog box, with the Column tab showing.

3. In the Width of Column box, type in the desired column width, or click the up and down arrows to change the setting. To automatically adjust the column width to fit the widest cell entry, click the **Autofit** button.

4. Change the value in the Space Between Columns box to modify spacing between columns.

5. Click **Next Column** or **Previous Column** to change the settings for other columns in the table.

6. Select **OK**. The table changes to reflect the new column settings.

Automatic Table Formatting

The AutoFormat command makes it a snap to apply attractive formatting to any table:

1. Place the insertion point anywhere in the table.

2. Select **Table, Table AutoFormat**. The Table AutoFormat dialog box is displayed (Figure 25.5).

3. The Formats box lists the available table formats. As you scroll through the list, the Preview box shows the appearance of the highlighted format.

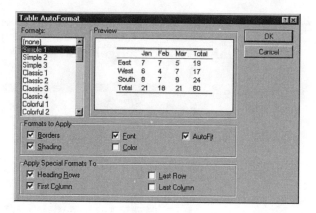

Figure 25.5   Use the Table AutoFormat dialog box to apply table formatting.

4. In the lower section of the dialog box are a number of formatting options. Select and deselect options as needed until the preview shows the table appearance you want.

5. Select **OK**. The selected formatting is applied to the table.

In this lesson, you learned how to add tables to your documents.

EXCEL

Starting and Exiting Excel

In this lesson, you'll learn how to start and end a typical Excel work session and how to get online help.

Starting Excel

To start Excel, follow these steps:

1. Click the **Start** button. The Start menu appears.

2. Choose **Programs**. The Programs menu appears, as shown in Figure 1.1.

3. Choose the **Microsoft Excel** program item to start the program.

Choose Programs on the Start menu.

Choose Microsoft Excel to start Excel.

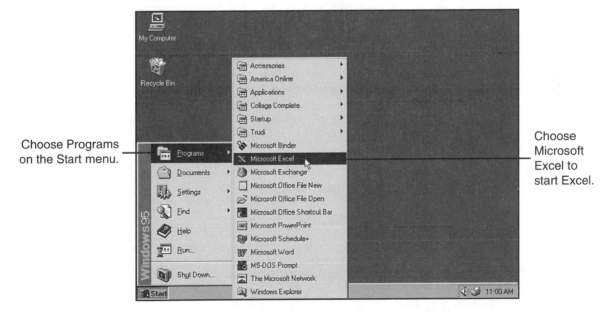

Figure 1.1 Select the Microsoft Excel program item to start the program.

The Excel opening screen appears (see Figure 1.2) with a blank workbook labeled Book1. Excel is now ready for you to begin creating your workbook.

Workbook   An Excel file is called a *workbook*. Each workbook consists of 16 worksheets. Each worksheet consists of columns and rows that intersect to form boxes called *cells* into which you enter text. The tabs at the bottom of the workbook (which are labeled Sheet1, Sheet2, and so on) let you flip through the worksheets when you click on them with the mouse.

You will perform most operations in Excel using the menu bar, at the top of the screen, and the Standard toolbar, just below it. In the next two lessons, you'll learn about the various operations available from the menu bar and the Standard toolbar.

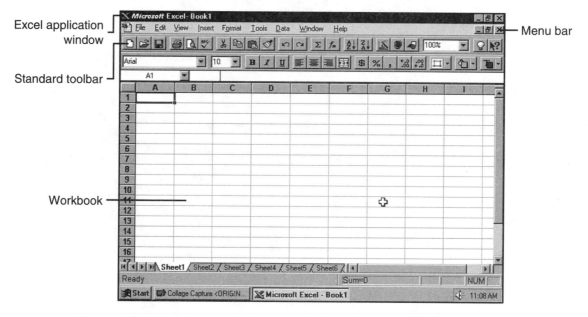

Figure 1.2   Excel's opening screen displays a blank workbook named Book1.

Getting Help

There are several ways to get Help in Excel, as explained in the following sections.

Help Déjà vu The Excel Help system is just like the one in Windows and the ones in the other MS Office programs. For complete information, see the Windows section of this book.

Pull Down the Help Menu

Pull down the **Help** menu for various help options. You can then select **Microsoft Excel Help Topics** (for groups of help topics), **Answer Wizard** (to search for a specific topic), **The Microsoft Network** (for specific details on how to work with Excel and the Microsoft Network), **Lotus 1-2-3 Help** (for specific details on how to make the transition from this program), or **About Microsoft Excel** (for licensing and system information and technical support for Excel from Microsoft).

Click on the Help Button

The Help button is in the Standard toolbar; it's the button that has the arrow and the question mark on it. When you click on the Help button, the mouse pointer turns into an arrow with a question mark. Click on any item or part of the screen with which you need help, and Excel displays help for that item or screen area. Double-click on the **Help** button to search for a Help topic.

Click on the What's This? Button in a Dialog Box

The What's This? button appears in the upper right corner of a dialog box. It's the button that has a question mark on it. When you click on this button, the mouse pointer turns into an arrow with a question mark. Click on any item in the dialog box with which you need help, and Excel displays a pop-up box that contains information about that item. To close the Help box, click anywhere on the screen or press the **Esc** key.

Quick Description   You also can right-click an option in a dialog box to see a description of the selected option, or press Tab to select the option (so that a dotted line appears around it) and then press F1.

Discovering More with the TipWizard

Excel's TipWizard shows you a few of the many shortcuts in Excel. The TipWizard gives you pointers or shortcuts on how to perform a command. For example, if you are summing a group of numbers, an alternate way to sum numbers displays in the TipWizard box.

To use the TipWizard, follow these steps:

1. Click the **TipWizard** button on the Standard toolbar, as shown in Figure 1.3. This button turns the TipWizard on or off.

2. After you perform any commands, you can click the **down arrow** button at the end of the TipWizard box, located beneath the Formatting toolbar. The down arrow button displays the next tip.

3. Click the **up arrow** button at the end of the TipWizard box. The up arrow button displays the previous tip.

4. If a tip suggests clicking a button on a toolbar, the button displays at the end of the TipWizard box. You can click the button at the end of the TipWizard box to try out the TipWizard's suggestion.

Standard toolbar —

Here's where the TipWizard appears.

— TipWizard button

Button suggested by the TipWizard

Use these buttons to move to the next or previous tip.

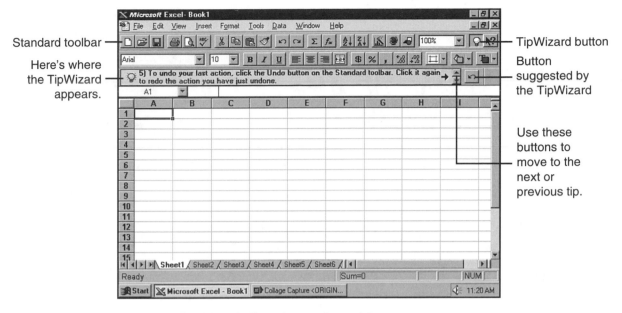

Figure 1.3   The TipWizard offers timesaving advice.

Exiting Excel

To exit Excel and return to the Windows 95 desktop, follow these steps:

1. Press **Alt+F** or click on **File** on the menu bar.

2. Press **X**, or click on **Exit**.

If you changed the workbook in any way without saving the file, Excel will display a prompt asking if you want to save the file before exiting. Select the desired option.

Quick Exit   For a quick exit, press **Alt+F4**, or double-click on the **Control-menu** in the upper left corner of the Excel window. You can also click the **Close** (X) button in the upper right corner of the Excel window.

In this lesson, you learned how to enter and exit Excel and get online help. In the next lesson, you'll learn about the Excel workbook window.

Examining the
Excel Window

2

In this lesson, you'll learn the basics of moving around in the Excel window and in the workbook window.

Navigating the Excel Window

As you can see in Figure 2.1, the Excel window contains several elements that allow you to enter commands and data:

Menu bar   Displays the names of the available pull-down menus (just like in Windows 95 itself).

Toolbars   Contain several icons, buttons, and drop-down lists that give you quick access to often-used commands and features.

Formula bar   Shows the contents of the selected cell. You can edit it by clicking in the formula bar and typing.

Workbook window   Contains the workbook where you will enter your data and formulas.

Status bar   Displays information about the current activity, including help information and keyboard and program modes.

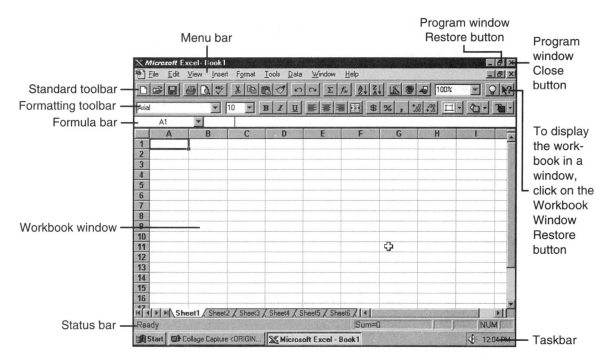

Figure 2.1 Elements of the Excel window.

Navigating the Workbook Window

Inside the Excel program window is a workbook window with the current worksheet in front. In this window, you will enter the labels (text), values (numbers), and formulas (calculations) that make up each worksheet. Figure 2.2 illustrates the various parts of the workbook. Table 2.1 describes these parts.

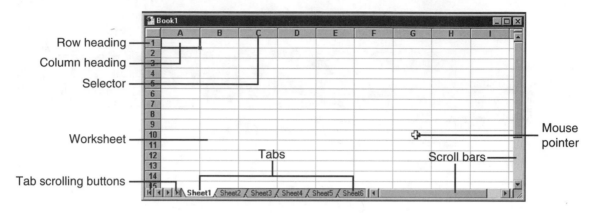

Figure 2.2   Elements of the workbook window.

Table 2.1   Workbook Window Items

Item	Function
Tabs	A workbook starts with 16 worksheets, and you can add or delete sheets as needed. You can use the tabs to flip worksheets.
Tab scrolling buttons	Allow you to scroll through the worksheets in the workbook.
Scroll bars	Allow you to view a section of the current worksheet that is not displayed.
Column heading	Identifies the column by letters.
Row heading	Identifies the row by numbers.
Selector	Outline that indicates the active cell (the one in which you are working).
Split bars	Let you split the workbook window into more than one pane to view different portions of the same worksheet.

Each page in a workbook is a separate worksheet. Each worksheet contains a grid consisting of alphabetized columns and numbered rows. When a row and column intersect, they form a box called a *cell*. Each cell has an *address* that consists of the column letter and row number

(A1, B3, C4, and so on). You will enter data and formulas in the cells to form your worksheets. You will learn more about cells in Lessons 4 and 5.

Moving Between Worksheets

Because each workbook consists of several worksheets, you need a way to move from worksheet to worksheet. Pressing **Ctrl+PgDn** and **Ctrl+PgUp**, or click on the tab for the worksheet you want to view (see Figure 2.3). If the tab is not shown, use the scroll buttons to bring the tab into view, and then click on the tab.

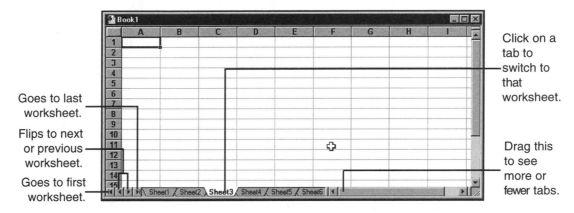

Goes to last worksheet.

Flips to next or previous worksheet.

Goes to first worksheet.

Click on a tab to switch to that worksheet.

Drag this to see more or fewer tabs.

Figure 2.3 You can move from worksheet to worksheet with tabs.

Moving Around on a Worksheet

Once the worksheet you want to work on is displayed, you need some way of moving to the various cells on the worksheet. Keep in mind that the part of the worksheet displayed on-screen is only a small part of the worksheet, as illustrated in Figure 2.4.

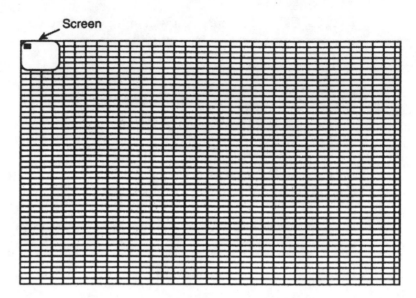

Figure 2.4 The worksheet area displayed on-screen is a small portion of the worksheet.

To move around the worksheet with your keyboard, use the keys as described in Table 2.2.

Table 2.2 Moving Around a Worksheet with the Keyboard

Press	To Move
↑ ↓	One cell in the direction of the arrow.
← →	
Ctrl+↑ or Ctrl+↓	To the top or bottom of a data region (an area of the worksheet that contains data).
Ctrl+← or Ctrl→	To the leftmost or rightmost cell in a data region.
PgUp	Up one screen.
PgDn	Down one screen.
Home	Leftmost cell in a row.
Ctrl+Home	Upper left corner of a worksheet.
Ctrl+End	Lower left corner of a worksheet.

Press	*To Move*
End+↑, End+↓, End+←, End+→	If the active cell is blank, moves to the next blank cell in the direction of the arrow. If the active cell contains an entry, moves in the direction of the arrow to the next cell that has an entry.
End+Enter	Last column in row.

If you have a mouse, moving on a worksheet is easier. Use the scroll bars to scroll to the area of the screen that contains the cell you want to work with. Then, click on the cell. To use the scroll bars:

- Click once on a scroll arrow at the end of the scroll bar to scroll incrementally in the direction of the arrow. Hold down the mouse button to scroll continuously.

- Drag the scroll box inside the scroll bar to the area of the worksheet you want to view. For example, to move to the middle of the worksheet, drag the scroll box to the middle of the scroll bar.

- Click once inside the scroll bar, on either side of the scroll box, to move the view one screenful at a time.

F5 (Goto) for Quick Movement! To move to a specific cell on a worksheet, select **Edit, Go To**, or press **F5**. Type the cell's address in the Reference text box; the address consists of the column letter and row number that define the location of the cell, for example **m25**. To go to a cell on a specific page, type the page name, an exclamation point, and the cell address (for example, **sheet3!m25**). Click on the **OK** button.

In this lesson, you learned how to move around in the Excel window and move around in workbooks. In the next lesson, you will learn how to use Excel's toolbars.

241

Using Excel's Toolbars

In this lesson, you will learn how to use Excel's toolbars to save time when you work.

Using the Toolbars

Unless you tell it otherwise, Excel displays the Standard and Formatting toolbars as shown in figure 3.1. To select a tool from a toolbar, click on that tool.

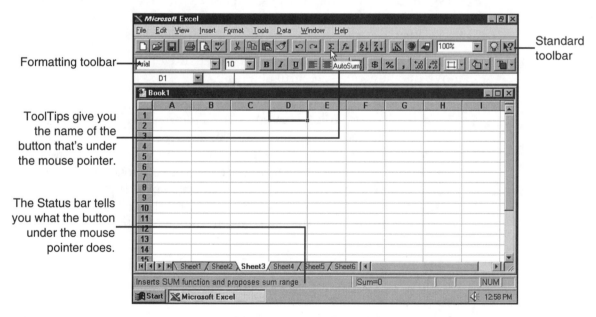

Figure 3.1 The Standard and Formatting toolbars contain buttons for Excel's most commonly used features.

What Is a Toolbar?   An Excel toolbar is a collection of tools or shortcut icons displayed in a long bar. It can be moved and reshaped to make it more convenient for you to use, as you'll learn later in this lesson.

Learning More About Toolbar Buttons

The following tables show you all the tools in the Standard and Formatting toolbars.

Table 3.1   Excel Standard Toolbar Buttons

Button	Name	Description
	New Workbook	Creates a new workbook.
	Open	Opens an existing workbook.
	Save	Saves the workbook.
	Print	Prints the workbook.
	Print Preview	Changes to print preview.
	Spelling	Starts the Spelling checker.
	Cut	Cuts selected ranges to the Clipboard.
	Copy	Copies selected range to the Clipboard.
	Paste	Pastes data from the Clipboard.
	Format Painter	Copies formatting.
	Undo	Undoes last command.
	Repeat	Repeats last command.

continues

243

Table 3.1 Continued

Button	Name	Description
Σ	AutoSum	Creates a sum function.
f*	Function Wizard	Starts the FunctionWizard.
A↓Z	Sort Ascending	Sorts selection in ascending order.
Z↓A	Sort Descending	Sorts selection in descending order.
📊	ChartWizard	Starts the ChartWizard.
🌐	Map	Starts Data Map.
🖊	Drawing	Displays the Drawing toolbar.
▾	Zoom Control	Enables you to zoom the worksheet to percent you specify.
💡	TipWizard	Starts the TipWizard.
⮐?	Help	Enables you to get context-sensitive help.

Table 3.2 Excel Formatting Toolbar Buttons

Button	Name	Description
▾	Font	Enables you to select font from drop-down list.
▾	Font Size	Enables you to select font size from drop-down list.
B	Bold	Applies bold to selected range.
I	Italic	Applies italic to selected range.

Button	Name	Description
U	Underline	Underlines selected range.
≡	Align Left	Aligns selected range to the left.
≡	Center	Centers selected range.
≡	Align Right	Aligns selected range to the right.
⊞	Center Across Columns	Centers text across selected range.
$	Currency Style	Applies currency style to the selected range.
%	Percent Style	Applies percent style to the selected range.
,	Comma Style	Applies comma style to the selected range.
.0/.00	Increase Decimal	Increases the number of decimal points displayed in the selected range.
.00/.0	Decrease Decimal	Decreases the number of decimal points displayed in the selected range.
⊡	Borders	Enables you to select and apply borders to selected range.
◨	Color	Enables you to select and apply color to selected range.
◨	Font Color	Enables you to select and apply color to text in selected range.

In addition to the tools on the Standard and Formatting toolbars, there are other toolbars that contain tools in Excel. Here are some easy ways to learn about the buttons for yourself:

- To see the name of a button, move the mouse pointer over the button. Excel displays a *ToolTip* that provides the name of the button, as shown in Figure 3.1.

- To learn what a button does, move the mouse pointer over the button and look at the status bar at the bottom of the screen (see Figure 3.1). If the button is available for the task you are currently performing, Excel displays a description of what the button does.

- To learn more about a button, click on the **Help** button in the Standard toolbar (the button with the arrow and question mark), and then click on the button for which you want more information.

Turning Toolbars On or Off

Excel initially displays the Standard and Formatting toolbars. If you never use one of these toolbars, you can turn one or both of them off to free up some screen space. In addition, you can turn on other toolbars. You can turn a toolbar on or off by using the View Toolbars command or the shortcut menu.

To use the View Toolbars option:

1. Select **View, Toolbars**. The Toolbars dialog box appears, as shown in Figure 3.3.

2. Select the toolbar(s) you would like to hide or display. A check mark in the toolbar's check box means the toolbar will be displayed. A blank box means the toolbar will be hidden.

3. Click **OK** to accept the toolbar changes.

To use the shortcut menu to hide or display a toolbar, follow these steps:

1. Move the mouse pointer anywhere inside any toolbar.

2. Click the right mouse button. The Toolbars shortcut menu appears.

3. Click on a toolbar name to turn it off. To display a toolbar, click on a toolbar name that doesn't have a check mark next to it. Excel places a check mark next to the name of a displayed toolbar. You'll see the check mark when you display the shortcut menu again.

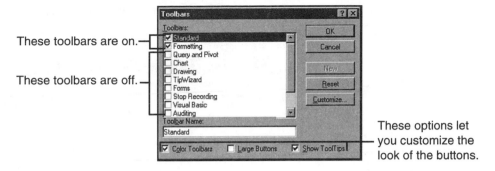

These toolbars are on.

These toolbars are off.

These options let you customize the look of the buttons.

Figure 3.2   Use the Toolbars dialog box to display or hide the toolbars.

Is It Getting Crowded in Here?   Display only the toolbars you need. Toolbars take up screen space and memory.

Moving Toolbars

After you have displayed the toolbars you need, you may position them in your work area where they are most convenient. Figure 3.3 shows an Excel screen with three toolbars in various positions on the screen.

Here's what you do to move a toolbar:

1. Move the mouse pointer over a buttonless part of the toolbar.

2. Hold down the mouse button and drag the toolbar where you want it. You can drag it to a dock or let it "float" anywhere in the window.

If you decide to drag the toolbar to a dock, you can position it in one of four toolbar docks: between the formula bar and menu bar, on the left and right sides of the Excel window, and at the bottom of the Excel window. You'll know that you've found a dock when the toolbar outline changes from square to rectangular. Then you can release the mouse button.

Formatting toolbar
was left at the top.

Floating toolbar.

Standard toolbar moved
to the bottom.

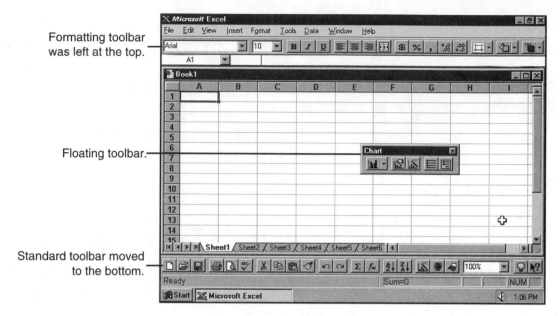

Figure 3.3 Three toolbars in various positions.

If a toolbar contains a drop-down list (such as the Zoom Control tool in the Standard toolbar and the Font tool in the Formatting toolbar), you cannot drag it to a left or right toolbar dock. The list boxes make these toolbars longer and therefore won't display the entire toolbar when moved to the side.

Floating Toolbar   A floating toolbar acts just like a window. You can drag its title bar to move it or drag a border to size it. If you drag a floating toolbar to the top or bottom of the screen, it turns back into a horizontal toolbar.

Quickly Docking a Floating Toolbar   To quickly move a floating toolbar to the top of the screen, double-click on its title bar.

In this lesson, you learned how to use Excel's toolbars. In the next lesson, you will learn how to enter different types of data.

Entering Different Types of Data

In this lesson, you will learn how to enter different types of data in an Excel worksheet.

Types of Data

To create a worksheet that does something, you must enter data into the cells that make up the worksheet. There are many types of data that you can enter, including text, numbers, dates, times, formulas, and functions.

Entering Text

You can enter any combination of letters and numbers as text. Text is automatically left-aligned in a cell.

To enter text into a cell:

1. Select the cell into which you want to enter text by clicking the cell.

2. Type the text. As you type, your text appears in the cell and in the formula bar, as shown in Figure 4.1.

3. Click on the **Enter** button on the formula bar (the button with the check mark on it), or press the **Enter** key, **Tab** key, or an arrow key on your keyboard.

Cancel button ——

Enter button ——

Function Wizard
button ——

Text appears in
cell and on the ——
formula bar

Insertion point ——

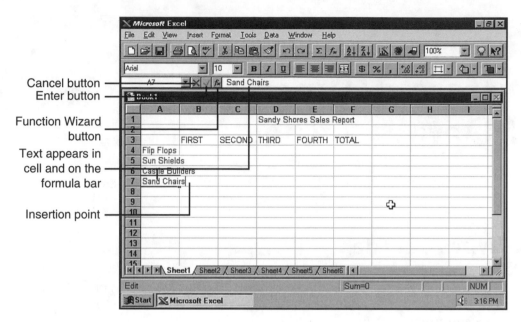

Figure 4.1   Data that you enter also appears on the formula bar as you type it.

Bail out!   To cancel an entry before you are done, click on the **Cancel** button (the button with the X on it), or press **Esc**.

Column and row headings are a type of text you can enter. The column headings are usually entered in one of the top rows on the worksheet, describing the data you're going to enter into each column. For instance, in Figure 4.1, we entered a worksheet title in row 1, so we could enter column headings in row 2 or 3. The row headings are usually entered into column A.

Sometimes your column and row headings may spill over into the adjacent cells. This means the column is too narrow for the text to fit. Don't worry. You'll learn how to correct this later. For now, Just double-click on the column letter (for example, A) to widen the column to accommodate the longest entry.

Numbers as Text   You may want to enter a number as text (for example, a ZIP code). Precede your entry with a single quotation mark ('), as in '46220. The single quotation mark is an alignment prefix that tells Excel to treat the following characters as text and left-align them in the cell.

Entering Numbers

Valid numbers can include the numeric characters 09 and any of these special characters: + ( ) , $ % . . Numbers are automatically right-aligned. You can include commas, decimal points, dollar signs, percentage signs, and parentheses in the values that you enter.

To enter a number:

1. Select the cell into which you want to enter a number by clicking the cell.

2. Type the number. To enter a negative number, precede it with a minus sign, or surround it with parentheses.

3. Click on the **Enter** button on the formula bar, or press **Enter**.

#######   If you enter a number, and it appears in the cell as all number signs (#######) or scientific notation (for example, 7.78E+06), don't worry—the number is okay. The cell is not wide enough to display the number. For a quick fix, select the cell, double-click on the column letter, or choose **Format, Column, AutoFit Selection**. For more information, see Lesson 19.

Entering Dates and Times

You can enter dates and times in a variety of formats. When you enter a date using a format shown in Table 4.1, Excel converts the date into a number which represents the number of days since January 1, 1900. Although you won't see this number (Excel displays it as a normal date), the number is used whenever a calculation involves a date. This feature is called AutoFormat.

251

Table 4.1 Valid Formats for Dates and Times

Format	Example
MM/DD/YY	4/8/58 or 04/08/58
MMMYY	Jan92
DDMMMYY	28Oct91
DDMMM	6Sep
HH:MM	16:50
HH:MM:SS	8:22:59
HH:MM AM/PM	7:45 PM
HH:MM:SS AM/PM	11:45:16 AM
MM/DD/YY HH:MM	11/8/80 4:20
HH:MM MM/DD/YY	4:20 11/18/80

To enter a date or time:

1. Select the cell into which you want to enter a date or time.

2. Type the date or time in the format in which you want it displayed.

3. Click on the **Enter** button on the formula bar, or press **Enter**.

To Hyphen or to Slash   You can use hyphens (-) or slashes (/) when typing dates. Capitalization is not important. For example, 21 FEB becomes 21Feb and FEB 21 also becomes 21Feb.

Day or Night?   Unless you type AM or PM, Excel assumes that you are using a 24-hour military clock. Therefore, 8:20 is assumed to be AM, not PM. If you type 8:20 PM, Excel displays the military time equivalent: 20:20 in the formula bar.

Entering Data Quickly

Excel offers several features for helping you copy entries into several cells at the same time. For example, you might want to avoid typing the same data over and over.

- To copy an existing entry into several surrounding cells, you can use the Fill feature.

- To have Excel insert a sequence of entries in neighboring cells (for example Monday, Tuesday, Wednesday), you can use AutoFill.

- To have Excel calculate and insert a series of entries according to your specifications (for example 5, 10, 15, 20), you can fill with a series.

These features are explained in greater detail in the following sections.

Copying Entries with Fill

You can copy an existing entry into any surrounding cells, by performing the following steps:

1. Select the cell whose contents you want to copy.

2. Position the mouse pointer over the selected cell, and click and drag it over all the cells into which you want to copy the cell entry.

3. Select **Edit**, **Fill**. The Fill submenu appears.

4. Select the direction in which you want to copy the entry. For example, if you choose Right, Excel inserts the entry into the selected cells to the right.

An easier way to fill is to drag the fill handle in the lower right corner of the selected cell to highlight the cells into which you want to copy the entry (see Figure 4.2). When you release the mouse button, the contents of the original cell are copied to the selected cells.

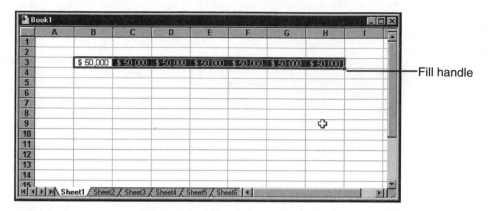

Fill handle

Figure 4.2 Drag the fill handle to copy the contents and formatting into neighboring cells.

 TIP **Copying Across Worksheets** You can copy the contents of cells from one worksheet to one or more worksheets in the workbook. First select the worksheet you want to copy from and to: click the sheet tabs while holding down the **Shift** key. Then, select the cells you want to copy. Select **Edit, Fill, Across Worksheets**. Select **All** (to copy the cells' contents and formatting), **Contents**, or **Formats**, and select **OK**.

Smart Copying with AutoFill

Unlike Fill, which merely copies an entry to one or more cells, AutoFill copies intelligently. For example, if you want to enter the days of the week (Monday through Sunday), you type the first entry (Monday), and AutoFill inserts the other entries for you. Try it:

1. Type **Monday** into a cell.

2. Drag the fill handle up, down, left, or right to select six more cells.

3. Release the mouse button. Excel inserts the remaining days of the week, in order, into the selected cells.

Excel has the days of the week stored as an AutoFill entry. You can store your own series as AutoFill entries. Here's how you do it.

1. Select **Tools, Options**. The Options dialog box appears.

2. Click on the **Custom Lists** tab. The selected tab moves up front, as shown in Figure 4.4.

3. Click on the **Add** button. An insertion point appears in the List Entries text box.

4. Type the entries you want to use for your AutoFill entries (for example, **Q1, Q2, Q3, Q4**). Press **Enter** at the end of each entry.

5. Click on the **OK** button.

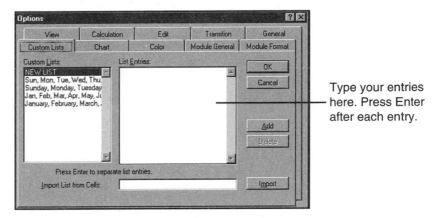

Type your entries here. Press Enter after each entry.

Figure 4.3   Excel lets you create your own AutoFill series.

Now that you have your own AutoFill entry, you can type any item in the list and use AutoFill to insert the remaining entries.

TIP

Transforming Existing Entries to AutoFill   If you have already typed the entries you want to use for your AutoFill entries, select the entries before you choose **Tools, Options**. Click on the Custom Lists tab, and select the **Import** button. Excel lifts the selected entries from your worksheet and sticks them in the **List Entries** text box.

Entering a Series

Although AutoFill is good for a brief series of entries, you may encounter situations in which you need more control or need to fill lots of cells with incremental entries. In such situations, you should use the series feature. Excel recognizes four types of series, shown in Table 4.2.

Table 4.2   Data Series

Series	Initial Entry	Resulting Series
Linear	1,2	3,4,5
	100,99	98,97,96
	1,3	5,7,9
Growth	10, 20	40, 80, 160
	10, 50	250, 1250, 6250
Date	Mon	Tue, Wed, Thur
	Feb	Mar, Apr, May
	Qtr1	Qtr2, Qtr3, Qtr4
	1992	1993, 1994, 1995
Autofill	Team 1	Team 2, Team 3, Team 4
	Qtr 4	Qtr 1, Qtr 2, Qtr 3
	1st Quarter	2nd Quarter, 3rd Quarter, 4th Quarter

Here's what you do to create a series:

1. Enter a value in one cell and press **Enter**. This value will be the starting or ending value in the series.

2. Select the cells with the value and the cells into which you want to extend the series.

3. Select **Edit, Fill, Series**. The Series dialog box, shown in Figure 4.4, appears.

4. Under Series in, select **Rows** or **Columns**. This tells Excel whether to fill down a column or across a row.

5. Under Type, choose a series type (refer to Table 4.2.).

6. Adjust the **Step** value (the amount between each series value), and **Stop** value (the last value you want Excel to enter), if necessary.

7. Click on **OK**, or press **Enter**, and the series is created.

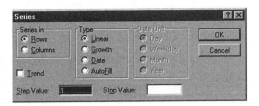

Figure 4.4 The Series dialog box.

In this lesson, you learned how to enter different types of data and how to automate data entry. In the next lesson, you will learn how to edit entries.

Editing Entries

In this lesson, you will learn how to make changes to entries in an Excel worksheet and undo those changes. You'll also learn to check your spelling, and find and replace entries.

Editing Data

After you have entered data into a cell, you may change it by editing it. In Excel, you can edit cell text in either the formula bar or in the cell itself.

To edit an entry, do this:

1. Select the cell in which you want to edit data.

2. Click in the formula bar, or press **F2**, or double-click on the cell.

3. Press ← or → to move the insertion point. Use the **Backspace** key to delete characters to the left, or the **Delete** key to delete characters to the right. Then type any characters you want to add.

4. Click on the **Enter** button on the formula bar, or press **Enter** to accept your changes.

Checking Your Spelling

Excel offers a spell checking feature that rapidly finds and highlights for correction the misspellings in a worksheet. Sometimes Excel won't even attempt to decipher your word, and doesn't give you any suggestions for the word not found in its dictionary.

To run the spell checker:

1. Select **Tools**, **Spelling**, or click the Spelling button on the Standard toolbar. Excel finds the first misspelled word and displays the word at the top of the Spelling dialog box. Excel's estimate of the

correct word appears in the Change To box and in the suggestions list. See Figure 5.1.

2. If a suggestion is correct, click on the word in the Suggestions list, (if necessary), and then click **Change** to change the misspelled word. Or click **Change All** to change all occurrences of the misspelled word. If desired, you can click **Add** to add the word to the custom dictionary.

3. If a suggestion is wrong, you can do any of the following:

    - Click **Suggest** to display words in the Suggestions list.
    - Click **Ignore** to leave the word unchanged.
    - Click **Ignore All** to leave all occurrences of the word unchanged.
    - Or type your own word in the Change To box if Spelling cannot come up with the right one.

4. When the spell checker doesn't find any more misspelled words, it displays a message to that effect. Click **OK**.

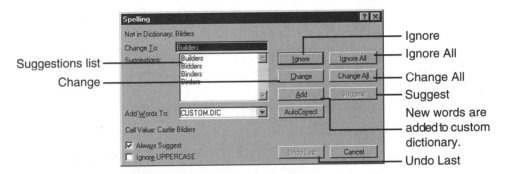

Figure 5.1   Correct spelling mistakes with the Spell options in the Spelling dialog box.

Choose the Wrong Spell Option?   If you mistakenly select the wrong Spell option, you can click the **Undo Last** button in the Spelling dialog box to undo the last option you chose. You can exit Spelling at any time by clicking **Cancel** in the Spelling dialog box.

Using AutoCorrect

Excel's new AutoCorrect feature automatically corrects common typing mistakes as you type. When you press Enter, Excel enters the corrected text in the cell.

With AutoCorrect, you can correct two initial capitals. For example, if you type **MAine** and press Enter, Excel will enter Maine in the cell. AutoCorrect capitalizes the names of days. For example, if you type **monday** and press Enter, Excel will enter Monday in the cell. You can also replace text as you type. For example, if you always type **breif** instead of the correct spelling brief, you can add these entries to the AutoCorrect list and AutoCorrect will fix it for you.

To add entries to the AutoCorrect list, do this:

1. Select **Tools**, **AutoCorrect**. The AutoCorrect dialog box appears, as shown in Figure 5.2.

2. Type the text you want to replace in the Replace text box.

3. Press **Tab** to move the insertion point to the With text box. Type the replacement text in the With text box.

4. Click the **Add** button. This will add the entry to the AutoCorrect list.

To delete an entry from the AutoCorrect list, click on the entry you want to delete. Then click the **Delete** button.

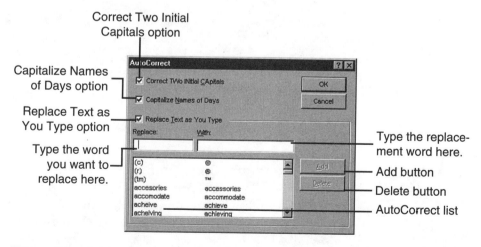

Figure 5.2 Add entries to the AutoCorrect list to correct common typographical errors as you work.

Shorthand Shortcut   You can use AutoCorrect like short-hand. For example, you can type "Div1" and have Excel replace it with "Division 1" as you type.

Undoing an Action

You can undo almost anything you do in a worksheet, including any change you enter into a cell. To undo a change, do one of the following:

- Select **Edit**, **Undo**.

- Press **Ctrl+Z**.

- Click on the **Undo** button in the Standard toolbar.

  To undo an Undo (reverse a change), take one of these actions:

- Open the **Edit** menu, and select **Redo**.

- Click on the **Repeat** button in the Standard toolbar.

Undo/Repeat One Act   The Undo and Repeat features only undo or repeat the most recent action you took.

Replacing Data

With Excel's Replace feature, you can locate data and then replace the original data with new data. When you have a label, a value, or formula that is entered incorrectly throughout the worksheet, you can use the Edit, Replace command to search and replace all occurrences of the incorrect information with the correct data.

To find and replace data, follow these steps:

1. Select the cells that contain the data you want to search. (See Lesson 10 for more information on selecting cells.)

2. Select **Edit**, **Replace**. The Replace dialog box appears, as shown in Figure 5.3.

3. Type the text you want to find and replace in the Find What text box.

4. Click in the Replace With text box or press the **Tab** key. Type the text you want to use as the replacement in the Replace With text box.

5. Click the **Replace All** button to begin the search and replace all occurrences of the data you specified. When Excel finishes replacing all occurrences, click outside the selected cells to deselect them.

You can also search for and replace once occurrence at a time. To do this, click the **Find Next** button to find the next occurrence of the data. Then click the **Replace** button if you want to replace the data or click the **Find Next** button again to skip the occurrence and find the next occurrence.

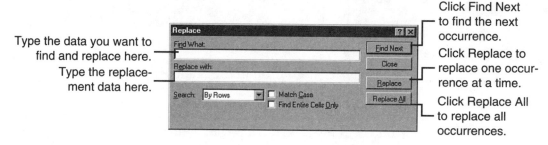

Figure 5.3   Finding and replacing data with the Replace dialog box.

   **Replace One At a Time**   Be sure that you want to replace all occurrences before you select the Replace All button.

In this lesson, you learned how to edit cell data, undo changes, spell check, and replace. In the next lesson, you will learn how to work with workbook files.

Working with Workbook Files

In this lesson you will learn how to save, close, and open workbook files, and how to create new workbooks. You'll also learn how to switch between multiple open workbooks.

Saving and Naming a Workbook

Whatever you type into a workbook is stored only in your computer's temporary memory. If you exit Excel, that data will be lost, so it is important to save your workbook files to disk regularly.

The first time you save a workbook to disk, you have to name it. Here's how you do it:

1. Select **File**, **Save**, or click on the **Save** button. The Save As dialog box appears as shown in Figure 6.1.

2. Type the name you want to give the workbook in the File Name text box, up to 218 characters.

3. To save the file on a different drive, open the Save In drop-down list and click on the desired drive.

4. To save the file to a different folder, double-click on that folder in the files and folders list. (You can move up a folder level by clicking on the **Up One Level** button.)

5. Click the **Save** button, or press **Enter**.

Default Folder   You can set up a default folder where Excel will save all your workbook files. Select **Tools, Options**. Click on the **General** tab. Click inside the **Default File Location** text box, and type a complete path to the drive and folder you want to use (the folder must be an existing one). Select **OK**.

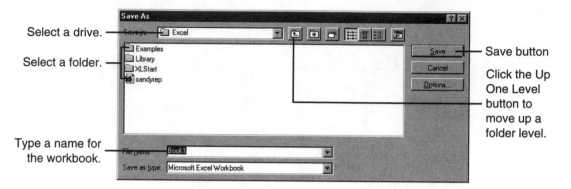

Select a drive.

Select a folder.

Type a name for the workbook.

Save button

Click the Up One Level button to move up a folder level.

Figure 6.1 The Save As dialog box.

To save a file you have already saved (and named), simply click on the **Save** button, or press **Ctrl+S**, or select **File, Save**. Excel automatically saves the workbook (including any changes you entered) without displaying the Save As dialog box.

Saving a Workbook Under a New Name

Sometimes, you may want to change a workbook but keep a copy of the original workbook, or you may want to create a new workbook by modifying an existing one. You can do this by saving the workbook under another name or in another folder. Here's how you do it:

1. Select **File, Save As**. You get the Save As dialog box, just as if you were saving the workbook for the first time.

2. To save the workbook under a new name, type the new file name over the existing name in the File Name text box.

3. To save the file on a different drive or in a different folder, select the drive letter from the Save In box and the folder from the files and folders list.

4. To save the file in a different format (for example, Lotus 1-2-3 or Quattro Pro), open the Save as Type drop-down list, and select the desired format.

5. Click the **Save** button, or press **Enter**.

Backup Files   You can have Excel create a backup copy of each workbook file you save. Click on the **Options** button in the Save As dialog box, select **Always Create Backup**, and click on **OK**. To use the backup file, choose **File, Open** to display the Open dialog box, and select **Backup Files** from the Files of Type list.

Creating a New Workbook

You can create a new workbook by modifying an existing one or by opening a blank workbook and starting from scratch. Here's how you open a blank workbook:

1. Select **File, New** or press **Ctrl+N**. The New dialog box appears, as shown in Figure 6.2.

2. Click on the **Workbook** icon if it's not already selected.

3. Click on **OK**, or press **Enter**. A new workbook opens on-screen.

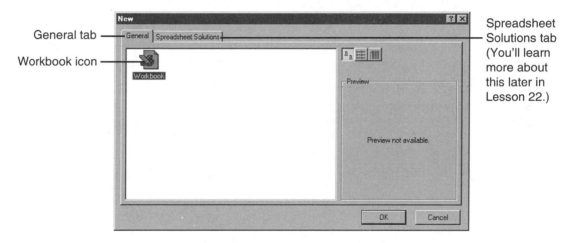

Figure 6.2   The General tab in the New dialog box.

Instant Workbook   You can bypass the New dialog box by simply clicking on the **New Workbook** button in the Standard toolbar. Excel opens a new workbook window without displaying the New dialog box.

265

Closing Workbooks

Closing a workbook removes its workbook window from the screen. To close a workbook, do this:

1. If the window you want to close isn't currently active, make it so by selecting its name from the Window menu.

2. Select **File, Close**. If you have not yet saved the workbook, you will be prompted to do so.

In a Hurry? To quickly close a workbook, press **Ctrl+F4**. You can also click the **Close** (X) button located in the upper right corner of the workbook. If you have more than one workbook open, you can close all of them by holding down the **Shift** key while selecting **File, Close All**.

Opening an Existing Workbook

If you have closed a workbook and then later you want to use it again, you must open it. Here's how you do it:

1. Select **File, Open**, or click on the **Open** button in the Standard toolbar. The Open dialog box appears, as shown in Figure 6.3.

2. If the file is not on the current drive, click on the arrow to the right of the Look In box, and select the correct drive.

3. If the file is not in the current folder, select the correct folder from the files and folders list.

4. Do one of the following:

   • Choose the file you want to open from the files and folders list.

   • Type the name of the file in the File Name box. As you type, Excel highlights the first file name in the list that matches your entry (this is a quick way to move through the list).

5. Click on **Open**, or press **Enter**.

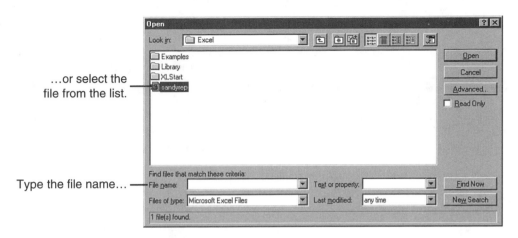

...or select the file from the list.

Type the file name...

Figure 6.3   The Open dialog box.

Recently Used Workbooks   Near the bottom of the File menu is a list of the most recently opened workbooks. You can quickly open the workbook by selecting it from the File menu.

Moving Among Open Workbooks

Sometimes, you may have more than one workbook open at a time. There are several ways to move among open workbooks:

- If part of the desired workbook window is visible, click on it.

- Open the **Window** menu, and select the name of the workbook you want to go to.

- Press **Ctrl+F6** to move from one workbook window to another.

In this lesson, you learned how to save, close, and open workbooks, as well as find misplaced workbook files. The next lesson teaches you how to work with the worksheets in a workbook.

Working with Worksheets

This lesson teaches you how to add worksheets to and delete worksheets from workbooks. You will also learn how to copy, move, and rename worksheets.

Using Worksheets

Each workbook consists of 16 worksheet pages whose names appear on tabs near the bottom of the screen. (You can add more sheets if you need them.) Having multiple pages (sheets) in a single workbook means you can use a separate sheet for each table or chart, enabling you to keep your data organized.

Selecting Worksheets

Before we get into the details of inserting, deleting, and copying worksheets, you should know how to select one or more worksheets.

- To select a single worksheet, click on its tab.

- To select several neighboring worksheets, click on the tab of the first worksheet in the group, and then hold down the Shift key while clicking on the tab of the last worksheet in the group.

- To select several non-neighboring worksheets, hold down the Ctrl key while clicking on each worksheet's tab.

Inserting Worksheets

To insert a new worksheet in a workbook, perform the following steps:

1. Select the worksheet *before which* you want the new worksheet inserted. For example, if you select Sheet4, the new worksheet (which will be called Sheet17 because the workbook already contains 16 worksheets) will be inserted before Sheet4.

2. Select **Insert**, **Worksheet**. Excel inserts the new worksheet, as shown in Figure 7.1.

Worksheet inserted
before Sheet 4.

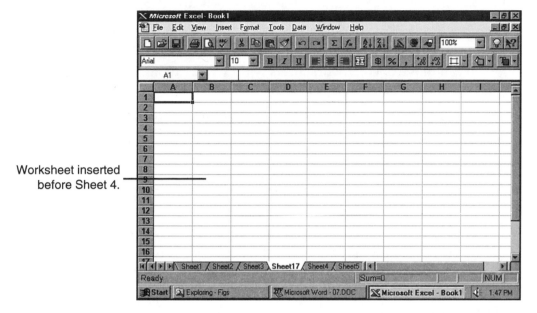

Figure 7.1   Excel inserts the new worksheet before the worksheet you selected.

Shortcut Menu   A faster way to work with worksheets is to right-click on a worksheet tab. This brings up a shortcut menu that lets you insert, delete, rename, move, copy, or select all worksheets. When you choose Insert from the shortcut menu, Excel displays the Insert dialog box. Click the **Worksheet** icon and click **OK** to insert a new worksheet.

Deleting Worksheets

If you plan on using only one worksheet, you can remove the 15 other worksheets to free up memory. Here's how you remove a worksheet:

1. Select the worksheet(s) you want to delete.

2. Select **Edit, Delete Sheet**. A dialog box appears, asking you to confirm the deletion.

3. Click on the **OK** button. The worksheets are deleted.

Moving and Copying Worksheets

You can move or copy worksheets within a workbook or from one workbook to another. Here's how:

1. Select the worksheet(s) you want to move or copy. If you want to move or copy worksheets from one workbook to another, be sure to open the target workbook.

2. Select **Edit, Move or Copy Sheet**. The Move or Copy dialog box appears, as shown in Figure 7.2.

3. To move the worksheet(s) to a different workbook, select the workbook's name from the **To Book** drop-down list. If you want to move or copy the worksheet(s) to a new workbook, select **[new book]** in the To Book drop-down list. Excel will create a new workbook and then copy or move the worksheet(s) to it.

4. In the **Before Sheet** list box, choose the worksheet before which you want the selected worksheet(s) to be moved.

5. To copy the selected worksheet(s) (rather than move), select **Create a Copy** to put a check mark in the check box.

6. Select **OK**. The selected worksheet(s) are copied or moved, as specified.

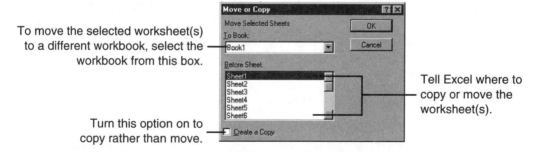

To move the selected worksheet(s) to a different workbook, select the workbook from this box.

Tell Excel where to copy or move the worksheet(s).

Turn this option on to copy rather than move.

Figure 7.2 The Move or Copy dialog box asks you where you want to copy or move a worksheet.

Moving within a Single Workbook

An easier way to copy or move worksheets within a workbook is to use the Drag & Drop feature. First, select the tab of the worksheet(s) you want to copy or move. Move the mouse pointer over one of the selected tabs, click and hold the mouse button, and drag the tab where you want it moved. To copy the worksheet, hold down the **Ctrl** key while dragging. When you release the mouse button, the worksheet is copied or moved.

Moving Between Workbooks

You can also use the Drag & Drop feature to quickly copy or move worksheets between workbooks. First, open the workbooks you want to use for the copy or move. Choose **Window**, **Arrange**, **Tiled**. Click on **OK** to arrange the windows so that a small portion of each one appears on-screen. Select the tab of the worksheet(s) you want to copy or move. Move the mouse pointer over one of the selected tabs, click and hold the mouse button, and drag the tab where you want it moved. To copy the worksheet, hold down the **Ctrl** key while dragging. When you release the mouse button, the worksheet is copied or moved.

Changing the Worksheet Tab Names

By default, all worksheets are named Sheet and are numbered starting with the number 1. So that you'll have a better idea of the information each sheet contains, you can change the names that appear on the tabs. Here's how you do it:

1. Select the worksheet whose name you want to change.

2. Double-click on the worksheet's tab, or right-click on the tab and select **Rename** from the shortcut menu. Excel shows you the Rename Sheet dialog box, as shown in Figure 7.3.

3. Type a new name for the worksheet, and click on the **OK** button.

Type a new name for the worksheet here. ———

Rename Sheet

Name

Sheet1

OK

Cancel

Figure 7.3 Excel lets you give your worksheets more meaningful names.

In this lesson, you learned how to insert, delete, move, copy, and rename worksheets. In the next lesson, you will learn how to print your workbook.

Printing Your Workbook

In this lesson, you will learn how to print an entire workbook or only a portion of it.

Changing the Page Setup

A workbook is a collection of many worksheets, like pages in a note-book. You can print the whole notebook at once, or just one or more pages at a time.

Before you print a worksheet, you should make sure that the page is set up correctly for printing. To do this, select File, Page Setup. You'll see the Page Setup dialog box, as shown in Figure 8.1.

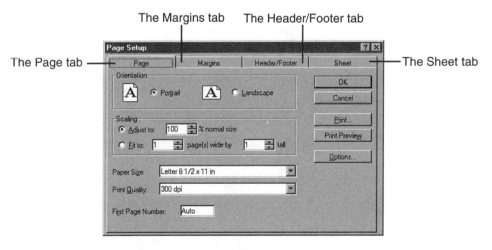

Figure 8.1 The Page Setup dialog box.

Enter your page setup settings as follows:

Page tab

Orientation   Select Portrait to print across the narrow side of the paper or Landscape to print across the wide side.

Scaling   You can reduce and enlarge your workbook or force it to fit within a specific page size (see Lesson 9).

Paper Size   This is 8 1/2 by 11 inches, by default. You can choose a different size from the list.

Print Quality   Print quality is measured in dpi (dots per inch)—the higher the number, the better the printout looks, but the slower it prints.

First Page Number   You can set the starting page number to something other than 1.

Margins tab

Top, Bottom, Left, Right   You can adjust the size of the top, bottom, left, and right margins.

From Edge   You can specify how far you want a Header or Footer printed from the edge of the page.

Center on Page   You can center the printing between the left and right margins (Horizontally) and between the top and bottom margins (Vertically).

Header/Footer tab

Header/Footer   You can add a header or a footer (repeated text on each page at the top or bottom). See Lesson 9 for more information.

Custom Header/Custom Footer   You can choose the Custom Header or Custom Footer button to create headers and footers that insert the time, date, worksheet tab name, and workbook file name.

Sheet tab

Print Area   You can print a portion of a workbook or worksheet by entering the range of cells you want to print. If you do not select a print area, Excel will print either the sheet or the workbook, depending on the options set in the Page tab.

Print Titles   You can repeat a row or column of entries on every page.

Print   You can have the gridlines (the lines that define the cells) printed. You can also have a color spreadsheet printed in black-and-white.

Page Order   If your worksheet is both too tall and too wide to fit on a single page, you can specify which direction Excel should "read"—from left to right, or from top to bottom.

When you are done entering your settings, click on the OK button.

Previewing a Print Job

After you've determined your page setup and print area, you can preview what the printed page will look like before you print.
To preview a print job, select File, Print Preview, or click on the Print Preview button in the Standard toolbar. Your workbook appears as it will when printed, as shown in Figure 8.2.

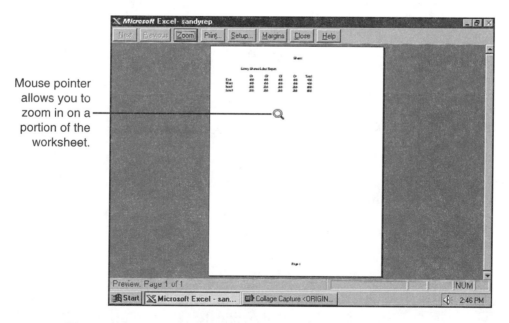

Mouse pointer allows you to zoom in on a portion of the worksheet.

Figure 8.2   You can preview your workbook before printing it.

A Close-Up View Zoom in on any area of the preview by clicking on it with the mouse pointer (which looks like a magnifying glass). You can also use the Zoom button at the top of the Print Preview screen.

Printing Your Workbook

After setting the page setup and previewing your data, it is time to print. You can print selected data, selected sheets, or the entire workbook.

To print your workbook:

1. If you want to print a portion of the worksheet, select the range you want to print (see Lesson 10). If you want to print one or more sheets within the workbook, select the sheet tabs. To print the entire workbook, you don't select anything.

2. Select **File**, **Print** (or press Ctrl+P). The Print dialog box appears, as shown in Figure 8.3.

3. Select the options you would like to use:

   Print What allows you to print the currently selected cells, the selected worksheets, or the entire workbook.

   Copies allows you to print more than one copy of the selection, worksheet, or workbook.

   Collate allows you to print a complete copy of the selection, worksheet, or workbook before the first page of the next copy is printed. This option is available when you print multiple copies.

   Page Range lets you print one or more pages. For example, if you want to print only pages 5–10, select Page(s), and then type 5 in the From box and 10 in the To box.

4. Click on **OK**, or press Enter.

Printing Gridlines By default Excel does not print the gridlines (the lines that define the cells). To print gridlines, click in the Gridlines check box under the Print options in the Sheet tab. When you print your worksheet, you will see your worksheet data in grids on white paper.

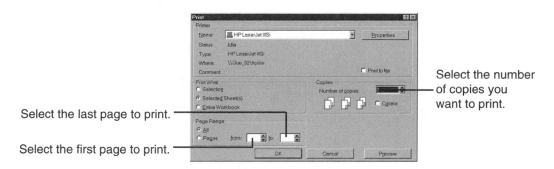

Select the last page to print.

Select the first page to print.

Select the number of copies you want to print.

Figure 8.3 The Print dialog box.

Quick Print To print one copy of all the data in a workbook using the default page setup settings, click on the Print button in the Standard toolbar. Excel bypasses the Print dialog box and immediately starts printing the workbook.

In this lesson, you learned how to print all or part of your workbook. In the next lesson, you will learn how to print large worksheets.

Printing Large Worksheets

In this lesson you learn how to print ranges in a worksheet, and to make the printouts of your large worksheets easier to read and understand.

Selecting a Print Area

By default, Excel prints the entire worksheet. However, you can specify a range of cells to print, and Excel will print only that range.

To select a print area:

1. Select **File**, **Page Setup**. The Page Setup dialog box appears.

2. Click the **Sheet** tab to display the Sheet options.

3. Click in the **Print Area** text box to display the insertion point.

4. Drag the Page Setup dialog box out of the way, and drag the mouse pointer over the desired cells (see Lesson 10), as shown in Figure 9.1. You'll see a dashed line border surrounding the selected area.

5. Click **Print** in the Page Setup dialog box to display the Print dialog box. Then click **OK** to print your worksheet.

To remove the print area, delete the cell coordinates in the Print Area text box.

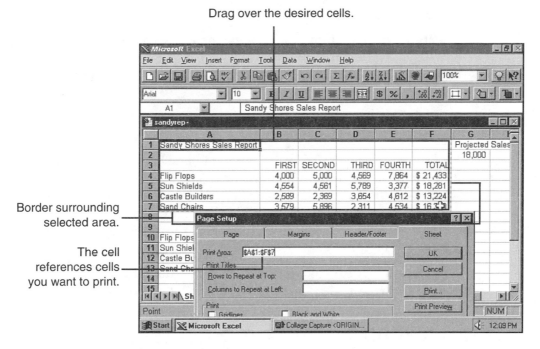

Figure 9.1   Selecting a print area.

Adjusting Page Breaks

When you print a workbook, Excel determines the page breaks based on the paper size and margins and the selected print area. To make the pages look better and break things in logical places, you may want to override the automatic page breaks with your own breaks. However, before you add page breaks, try these options:

- Adjust the widths of individual columns to make the best use of space (see Lesson 19).

- Consider printing the workbook sideways (using Landscape orientation).

- Change the left, right, top, and bottom margins to smaller values.

If after trying these options you still want to insert page breaks, first determine whether you need to limit the number of columns on a page or the number of rows.

279

To insert a page break:

1. Select the row or column that will be the first to appear on the new page. For instance, if you want page 1 to contain columns A through G, select column H. Or if you want page 1 to contain rows 1–20, select row 21.

2. Select **Insert, Page Break**. A dashed line appears at the point where the page break will occur.

You can set both vertical and horizontal page breaks; set one, then repeat the above procedure to set the other. You can also set both at once. Just select the cell that is below and to the right of the last cell for the page, and then select **Insert, Page Break**. For example, if you wanted cell G12 to be the last cell on that page, move to cell H13, and set the page break.

To remove a page break, select the row, column, or cell that you used to set the page break, select **Insert, Remove Page Break**.

Printing Column and Row Headings

Excel provides a way for you to select labels and titles that are located on the top edge and left side of your large worksheet, and print them on every page of the printout. This option is useful when a worksheet is too wide to print on a single page. The extra columns will be printed on subsequent pages without any descriptive information unless you use the Repeat Rows at Top and Repeat Columns at Left options in the Page Setup dialog box.

When you specify the column and row headings, Excel divides the worksheet into sections, showing dashed borders around the column and row headings you want to repeat.

To print column and row headings on every page:

1. Select **File, Page Setup**. The Page Setup dialog box appears.

2. Click the **Sheet** tab to display the Sheet options.

3. Click in the **Rows to Repeat at Top** text box. Then drag the Page Setup dialog box out of the way and drag the mouse pointer over the desired cells (see Lesson 10), as shown in Figure 9.2.

4. Click in the **Columns to Repeat at Left** text box. Then drag the dialog box title bar out of the way and drag the mouse pointer over the desired cells.

5. Click **OK**.

After you finish, you may want to check the headings in Print Preview to make sure they're set correctly.

To remove the rows and columns you want to repeat, delete the cell coordinates in the Rows to Repeat at Top and Columns to Repeat at Left text boxes.

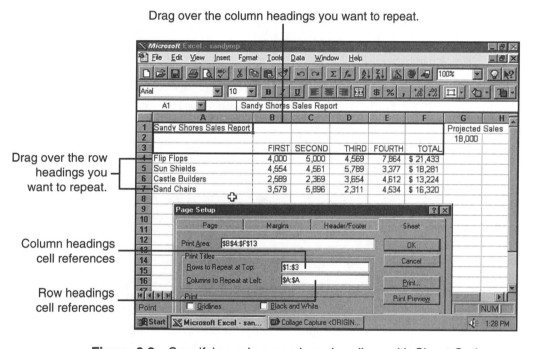

Figure 9.2 Specifying column and row headings with Sheet Options.

Adding Headers and Footers

Excel lets you add headers and footers to print information at the top and bottom of every page of the printout. The information can include any text, page numbers, the current date and time, the workbook file name, and the worksheet tab name.

You can choose the headers and footers suggested by Excel, or you can include any text plus special commands to control the appearance of the header or footer. For example, you can apply bold, italic, or underline to the header or footer text (see Lesson 17). You can also left-align, center, or right-align your text in a header or footer (see Lesson 16).

To add headers and footers:

1. Select **File**, **Page Setup**. The Page Setup dialog box appears.

2. Click the **Header/Footer** tab to display the Header and Footer options, as shown in Figure 9.3.

3. To select a different header, open the Header drop-down list. Click on a header you want. The sample header appears at the top of the Header/Footer tab.

4. To select a different footer, open the Footer drop-down arrow next to the Footer text box and click on a footer you want.

5. Click **OK** to close the Page Setup dialog box and return to your worksheet or click the **Print** button to display the Print dialog box. Then click **OK** to print your worksheet.

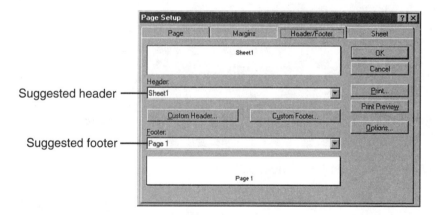

Figure 9.3 Adding headers and footers with Header/Footer options.

Don't Want Any Headers or Footers?   To remove the
header and footer, choose None in the Header and Footer
suggestions lists.

Scaling a Worksheet to Fit on a Page

If your worksheet is still too large to print on one page after you change
the orientation and margins, you might consider using the Fit To option. This option shrinks the worksheet to fit on the specified number of
pages. You can specify the document's width and height.

To scale a worksheet to fit on a page:

1. Select **File**, **Page Setup**. The Page Setup dialog box appears.

2. Click the **Page** tab to display the Page options, as shown in
   Figure 9.4.

3. Enter the number of pages in the **Page(s) Wide By** and the **Tall** text
   boxes.

4. Click **OK**.

Reduce or enlarge
your printout with the
Adjust To option.

Scale your worksheet to
fit on the specified
number of pages with
the Fit To option.

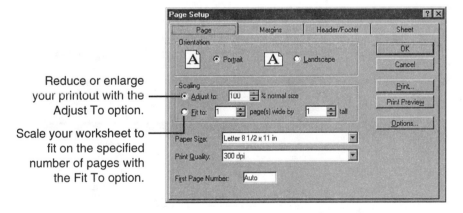

Figure 9.4   Scaling a worksheet to fit on the specified number of pages with
Page options.

In this lesson, you learned how to print a large worksheet. In the
next lesson, you will learn how to work with ranges.

Working with Ranges

In this lesson, you will learn how to select and name cell ranges.

What Is a Range?

A *range* is a rectangular group of connected cells. The cells in a range may all be in a column, or a row, or any combination of columns and rows, as long as the range forms a rectangle, as shown in Figure 10.1. A range can also be a single cell.

Learning how to use ranges can save you time. You can format a range of cells all at once, for instance. You can also use a range to print only a selected group of cells, or refer to a range in a formula.

Ranges are referred to by their anchor points (the top left corner and the lower right corner). For example, the ranges shown in Figure 10.1 are B4:F7, A9:F9, and G2.

Figure 10.1 A range is any combination of cells that forms a rectangle.

Selecting a Range

To select a range, use the mouse:

1. Move the mouse pointer to the upper left corner of a range.

2. Click and hold the left mouse button.

3. Drag the mouse to the lower right corner of the range and release the mouse button.

4. Release the mouse button. The selected range will be highlighted.

There are various selecting techniques that you can use to select a range on a worksheet. They're shown in Table 10.1.

Table 10.1   Selecting Techniques

Selection	Technique
Cell	Click the cell you want to select.
Range	Click the first cell in the range. Hold down the left mouse button and drag across the cells you want to include.
Noncontiguous ranges	Select the first range. Hold down the **Ctrl** key and select the next range. Do this for each range you want to select.
Row	Click on the row heading number at the left edge of the worksheet.
Column	Click on the column heading letter at the top edge of the worksheet.
Entire worksheet	Click the **Select All** button (the blank rectangle in the upper left corner of the worksheet above row 1 and left of column A).
Range that is out of view	Press **F5** (Goto) and type the range address in the **Reference** text box. For example, to move to cell Z50, type **Z50** and press **Enter**. To select the range R100 to T250, type R100:T250 and press Enter.

Deselecting the Selection To remove the selection, click on any cell in the worksheet.

Naming Cells and Cell Ranges

Up to this point, you have used cell addresses to refer to cells. Although that works, it is often more convenient to name cells with more recognizable names. For example, say you want to determine your net income by subtracting expenses from income (see Lesson 13). You can name the cell that contains your total income INCOME, and name the cell that contains your total expenses EXPENSES. You can then determine your net income by using the formula:

=INCOMEEXPENSES

to make the formula more logical and easier to manage. Naming cells and ranges also makes it easier to cut, copy, and move blocks of cells, as explained in Lesson 11.

To name a cell range:

1. Select the range of cells you want to name.

2. Click inside the name box (on the left side of the formula bar). See Figure 10.2.

3. Type a range name (up to 255 characters). Valid names can include letters, numbers, periods, and underlines, but no spaces. A range name cannot begin with a number.

4. Press **Enter**.

To see the list of range names, click the down arrow next to the Name box on the formula bar.

Another way to name a range is to select it and then select **Insert**, **Name**, **Define**. This displays the Define Name dialog box, shown in Figure 10.3. Type a name in the **Names in Workbook** text box, and click on **OK**.

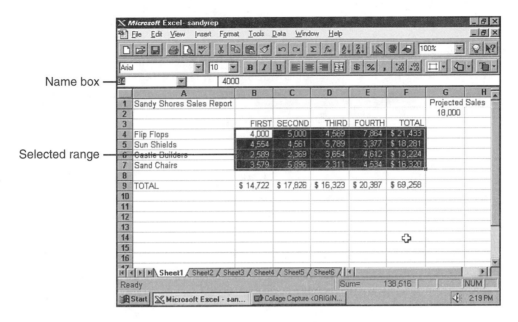

Figure 10.2   Type a name in the name box.

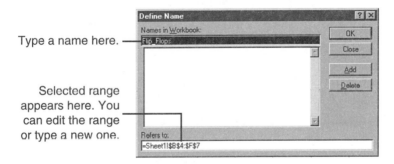

Figure 10.3   The Define Name dialog box.

The Define Name dialog box allows you to see what range a range name contains. Click on a range name in the **Names in Workbook** list. You'll see the cell address(es) assigned to the range name in the Refers To text box.

The dollar signs in the cell addresses indicate absolute cell references, which always refer to the same cell. An absolute cell reference will not be adjusted if changes are made to those cells in the worksheet. You don't have to type the dollar signs in the cell address. When you select cells with the mouse, Excel inserts the dollar signs automatically.

This dialog box also lets you delete names. To delete a range name, click on a name in the Names in Workbook list, click on the **Delete** button.

In this lesson, you learned how to select and name ranges. In the next lesson, you will learn how to copy, move, and erase data.

Copying, Moving, and Erasing Data

In this lesson, you will learn to copy, move, and erase data.

Easy Editing with the Clipboard

When you copy or move data, a copy of that data is placed in a temporary storage area called the *Clipboard*.

What Is the Clipboard?   The Clipboard is an area of memory that holds data you are copying or moving. You can use it to copy or move within the same program, or between programs.

Copying Data

You make copies of data to use in other sections of your worksheet or in other worksheets or workbooks. The original data remains in place, and a copy of it is placed where you indicate.

To copy data:

1. Select the range or cell that you want to copy.

2. Select **Edit**, **Copy**, or press **Ctrl+C**. The contents of the selected cell(s) are copied to the Clipboard.

3. Select the first cell in the area where you would like to place the copy. (To copy the data to another worksheet or workbook, change to that worksheet or workbook.)

4. Select **Edit**, **Paste**, or press **Ctrl+V**.

Watch Out! When copying or moving data, be careful when you indicate the range where the data should be pasted. Excel will paste the data over any existing data in the indicated range.

You can copy the same data to several places in the worksheet by repeating the **Edit, Paste** command. Data copied to the Clipboard remains there until you copy or cut something else.

Quick Copying with Drag & Drop The fastest way to copy is to use the Drag & Drop feature. Select the cells you want to copy, and then hold down **Ctrl** while dragging the cell selector border where you want the cells copied (see Figure 11.1). Without the Ctrl key, Excel moves the data.

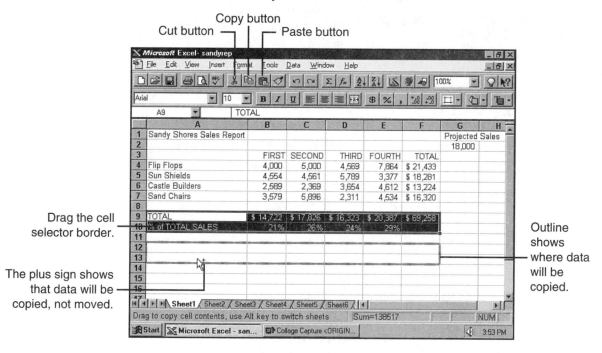

Figure 11.1 To copy data, hold down the Ctrl key while dragging the cell selector border.

Drag & Drop Between Worksheets You can drag cells between worksheets. First select the range. Then hold down the **Ctrl** key and the **Alt** key to copy, or just the **Alt** key to move, while dragging the range to the tab for the other worksheet. Continue to drag the range from the sheet tab up to the new location in the worksheet until the range appears where you want it.

Moving Data

Moving data is similar to copying, except that the data is removed from its original place and moved to the new location.

To move data:

1. Select the range or cell that you want to move.

2. Select **Edit, Cut**, or press **Ctrl+X**.

3. Select the first cell in the area where you would like to place the data. To move the data to another worksheet, change to that worksheet.

4. Select **Edit, Paste**, or press **Ctrl+V**.

To move data quickly, use the Drag & Drop feature. Select the data to be moved, and then drag the cell selector border without holding down the Ctrl key.

Shortcut Menu When cutting, copying, and pasting data, don't forget the shortcut menu. Simply select the cells you want to cut or copy, right-click on the selected cells, and choose the appropriate command from the shortcut menu that appears.

Erasing Data

Although erasing data is fairly easy, you must decide exactly what you want to erase first. Here are your choices:

- Use the **Edit, Clear** command to erase the contents or formatting of the cells. The Edit Clear command is covered next.

- Use the **Edit, Delete** command to remove the cells and everything in them. This is covered in Lesson 12.

With the Clear command, you can remove the data from a cell, or just its formula, formatting, or attached notes. Here's what you do:

1. Select the range of cells you wish to clear.

2. Select **Edit, Clear**. The Clear submenu appears, as shown in Figure 11.2.

3. Select the desired clear option: **All** (clears formats, contents, and notes), **Formats**, **Contents**, or **Notes**.

A Clean Slate To quickly clear the contents of cells, select the cells and press the **Delete** key.

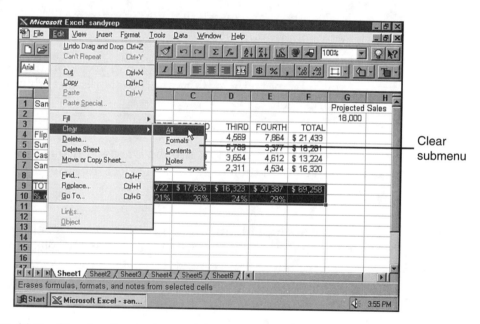

Figure 11.2 Clearing the contents of the selected cells.

In this lesson, you learned how to copy and move data. You also learned how to clear data from cells. In the next lesson, you will learn how to insert and delete cells, rows, and columns.

Inserting and Deleting Cells, Rows, and Columns

In this lesson, you will learn how to rearrange your worksheet by adding and deleting cells, rows, and columns.

Inserting Cells

Sometimes, you will need to insert information into a worksheet, right in the middle of existing data. With the Insert command, you can insert one or more cells, or entire rows or columns.

Shifting Cells Inserting cells in the middle of existing data will cause those other cells to shift down or to the left. If you insert individual cells, your formulas may be thrown off. If you insert entire rows or columns, however, the formulas adjust themselves automatically.

To insert a single cell or a group of cells:

1. Select the cell(s) where you want the new cell(s) inserted. Excel will insert the same number of cells as you select.

2. Select **Insert, Cells**. The Insert dialog box shown in Figure 12.1 appears.

3. Select **Shift Cells Right** or **Shift Cells Down**.

4. Click on **OK**, or press **Enter**. Excel inserts the cell(s) and shifts the data in the other cells in the specified direction.

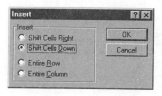

Figure 12.1   The Insert dialog box.

 TIP   **Drag Insert**   A quick way to insert cells is to hold down the Shift key while dragging the fill handle (the little box in the lower right corner of the selected cell(s)). Drag the fill handle up, down, left, or right to set the position of the new cells.

Removing Cells

In Lesson 11, you learned how to clear the contents and formatting of selected cells. This merely removed what was inside the cells. If you want to remove the cells completely, perform the following steps:

1. Select the range of cells you want to delete.

2. Select **Edit**, **Delete**. The Delete dialog box appears, as shown in Figure 12.2.

3. Select the desired Delete option: **Shift Cells Left** or **Shift Cells Up**.

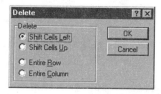

Figure 12.2   The Delete dialog box asks where you want surrounding cells shifted.

Inserting Rows and Columns

Inserting entire rows and columns in your worksheet is similar to inserting a cell(s). Here's what you do:

1. Do one of the following:

   - To insert a single row or column, select it, or a single cell within it. Columns are inserted to the left of the current cell. Rows are inserted above the current cell.

   - To insert multiple rows or columns, select the number of columns or rows you want to insert. To select columns, drag over the column letters at the top of the worksheet. To select rows, drag over the row numbers. For example, select three column letters or row numbers to insert three rows or columns.

2. Select **Insert**, **Rows** or **Insert**, **Columns**. Excel inserts the row(s) or column(s) and shifts the adjacent rows down or adjacent columns right.

 Shortcut Insert   To quickly insert rows or columns, select one or more rows or columns, and then right-click on one of them. Choose **Insert** from the shortcut menu.

Deleting Rows and Columns

Deleting rows and columns is similar to deleting cells. When you delete a row, the rows below the deleted row move up to fill the space. When you delete a column, the columns to the right shift left.

To delete a row or column:

1. Click on the row number or column letter of the row or column you want to delete. You can select more than one row or column by dragging over the row numbers or column letters.

2. Select **Edit**, **Delete**. Excel deletes the row(s) or column(s) and renumbers the remaining rows and columns sequentially. All cell references in formulas and names in formulas are updated appropriately, unless they are absolute ($) values (see Lesson 14).

In this lesson, you learned how to insert and delete cells, rows, and columns. In the next lesson, you will learn how to use formulas.

Performing Calculations with Formulas

In this lesson, you will learn how to use formulas to calculate results in your worksheets.

What Is a Formula?

Worksheets use formulas to perform calculations on the data you enter. With formulas, you can perform addition, subtraction, multiplication, and division using the values contained in various cells.

Formulas typically consist of one or more cell addresses and/or values and a mathematical operator, such as + (addition), – (subtraction), * (multiplication), or / (division). For example, if you wanted to determine the average of the three values contained in cells A1, B1, and C1, you would type the following formula in the cell where you want the result to appear:

=(A1+B1+C1)/3

Every formula must begin with an equal sign (=).

Figure 13.1 shows several formulas in action. Table 13.1 lists the mathematical operators you can use to create formulas.

Table 13.1 Excel's mathematical operators

Operator	Performs	Sample Formula	Result
^	Exponentiation	=A1^3	Enters the result of raising the value in cell A1 to the third power.
+	Addition	=A1+A2	Enters the total of the values in cells A1 and A2.

Operator	Performs	Sample Formula	Result
–	Subtraction	=A1A2	Subtracts the value in cell A2 from the value in cell A1.
*	Multiplication	=A2*3	Multiplies the value in cell A2 by 3.
/	Division	=A1/50	Divides the value in cell A1 by 50.
	Combination	=(A1+A2+A3)/3	Determines the average of the values in cells A1 through A3.

=E4+E5+E6 gives total income for the 4th Quarter.

=E10+E11+E12+E13 gives total expenses for the 4th Quarter.

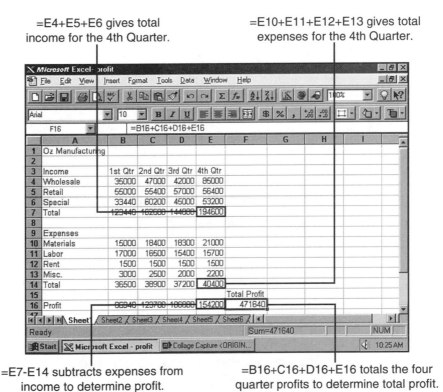

=E7-E14 subtracts expenses from income to determine profit.

=B16+C16+D16+E16 totals the four quarter profits to determine total profit.

Figure 13.1 Type a formula in the cell where you want the resulting value to appear.

Order of Operations

Excel performs a series of operations from left to right in the following order, giving some operators precedence over others:

1st   Exponential and equations within parentheses

2nd   Multiplication and division

3rd   Addition and subtraction

This is important to keep in mind when you are creating equations, because the order of operations determines the result.

For example, if you want to determine the average of the values in cells A1, B1, and C1, and you enter =A1+B1+C1/3, you'll probably get the wrong answer. The value in C1 will be divided by 3, and that result will be added to A1+B1. To determine the total of A1 through C1 first, you must enclose that group of values in parentheses: =(A1+B1+C1)/3.

Entering Formulas

You can enter formulas in either of two ways: by typing the formula or by selecting cell references. To type a formula, perform the following steps:

1. Select the cell in which you want the formula's calculation to appear.

2. Type the equal sign (=).

3. Type the formula. The formula appears in the formula bar.

4. Press **Enter**, and the result is calculated.

To enter a formula by selecting cell references, take the following steps:

1. Select the cell in which you want the formula's result to appear.

2. Type the equal sign (=).

3. Click on the cell whose address you want to appear first in the formula. The cell address appears in the formula bar.

4. Type a mathematical operator after the value to indicate the next operation you want to perform. The operator appears in the formula bar.

5. Continue clicking on cells and typing operators until the formula is complete.

6. Press **Enter** to accept the formula or **Esc** to cancel the operation.

Displaying Formulas

Excel does not display the actual formula in a cell. Instead, Excel displays the result of the calculation. You can view the formula by selecting the cell and looking in the formula bar. If you want to see the formulas in the cells, do this:

1. Select **Tools**, **Options**.

2. Click on the **View** tab.

3. Click on the **Formulas** check box in the Window Options area. A check mark appears, indicating that the option has been turned on (see Figure 13.2).

4. Click on **OK**, or press **Enter**.

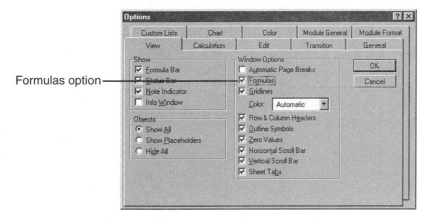

Figure 13.2   Using the Options dialog box to display formulas in the cells.

Display Formulas Quickly   Press **Ctrl+`** to toggle between viewing formulas or viewing values. Hold down the Ctrl key, and press ` (the accent key—it's the key with the tilde (~) on it).

Editing Formulas

Editing formulas is the same as editing any entry in Excel. Here's how you do it:

1. Select the cell that contains the formula you want to edit.

2. Position the insertion point in the formula bar with the mouse, or press **F2** to enter Edit mode.

Quick In-Cell Editing   To quickly edit the contents of a cell, simply double-click on the cell. The insertion point appears inside the cell.

3. Make changes to the formula.

4. Click on the **Enter** button on the formula bar, or press **Enter** to accept your changes.

In this lesson, you learned how to enter and edit formulas. In the next lesson, you will learn how to copy formulas, when to use relative and absolute cell addresses, and how to change Excel's settings for calculating formulas in the worksheet.

Copying Formulas

In this lesson, you will learn how to copy formulas, and use relative and absolute cell references.

Copying Formulas

Copying formulas is similar to copying other data in a worksheet. (For more details, refer to Lesson 11.) To copy formulas:

1. Select the cell that contains the formula you want to copy.

2. Select **Edit**, **Copy**, or press **Ctrl+C**.

3. Select the cell(s) into which you want to copy the formula. To copy the formula to another worksheet or workbook, change to the new worksheet or workbook.

4. Select **Edit**, **Paste**, or press **Ctrl+V**.

Drag and Drop Formulas   To quickly copy a formula, use the Drag & Drop feature. Select the cell that contains the formula you want to copy, and then hold down the **Ctrl** key while dragging the cell selector border where you want the formula copied. When you release the mouse button, the formula is copied to the new location.

Using Relative and Absolute Cell Addresses

When you copy a formula from one place in the worksheet to another, Excel adjusts the cell references in the formulas relative to their new positions in the worksheet. For example, in Figure 14.1, cell B9 contains the formula =B4+B5+B6+B7, which determines the total sales revenue for the first quarter (FIRST). If you copy that formula to cell C9 (to determine the total sales revenue for the second quarter (SECOND), Excel would automatically change the formula to =C4+C5+C6+C7. This is how relative cell addresses work.

Cell references are adjusted for column C.

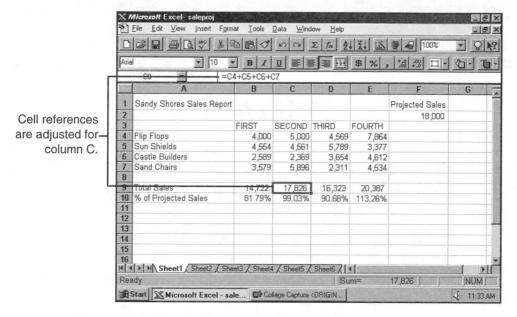

Figure 14.1 Excel adjusts cell references when you copy formulas to different cells.

Sometimes, you may not want the cell references to be adjusted when formulas are copied. That's when absolute references become important.

Absolute vs. Relative An *absolute reference* is a cell reference in a formula that does not change when copied to a new location. A *relative reference* is a cell reference in a formula that is adjusted when the formula is copied.

The formula in cells B10, C10, D10, and E10 uses an absolute reference to cell F2, which holds the projected sales for this year. (B10, C10, D10, and E10 divide the sums from row 9 of each column by the contents of cell F2.) If you didn't use an absolute reference, when you copied the formula from B10 to C10, the cell reference would be incorrect, and you would get an error message.

To make a cell reference in a formula absolute, you must add a $ (dollar sign) before the letter and number that make up the cell address. For example, the formula in B10 would read as follows:

=B9/F2

You can type the dollar signs yourself or press F4 after typing the cell address. Some formulas use mixed references. For example, the column letter may be an absolute reference and the row number may be a relative reference, as in the formula $A2/2. If you had this formula in cell C2, and you copied it to cell D10, the result would be the formula $A10/2. The row reference (row number) would be adjusted, but not the column.

Mixed Reference   A reference that is only partially absolute, such as A$2 or $A2, is called a *mixed reference*. When a formula that uses a mixed reference is copied to another cell, only part of the cell reference is adjusted.

In this lesson, you learned how to copy formulas. You also learned when to use relative and absolute cell addresses and how to change calculation settings. In the next lesson, you will learn how to use Excel's Function Wizard to insert another type of formula, called a function.

Performing Calculations with Functions

15

In this lesson, you will learn how to perform calculations with functions and how to use Excel's new Function Wizard to quickly insert functions in cells.

What Are Functions?

Functions are ready-made formulas that perform a series of operations on a specified range of values. For example, to determine the sum of a series of numbers in cells A1 through H1, you can enter the function =SUM(A1:H1), instead of entering =A1+B1+C1+ and so on. Functions can use range references (such as B1:B3), range names (such as SALES), and/or numerical values (such as 585.86).

Every function consists of the following three elements:

- The = sign indicates that what follows is a function (formula).

- The **function name** (for example, SUM) indicates the operation that will be performed.

- The **argument**, for example (A1:H1), indicates the cell addresses of the values that the function will act on. The argument is often a range of cells, but it can be much more complex.

You can enter functions either by typing them in cells or by using the Function Wizard, as you'll see later in this lesson. Table 15.1 shows Excel's most common functions that you'll use most in your worksheets.

Table 15.1   Excel's most common functions

Function	Example	Description
AVERAGE	=AVERAGE(B4:B9)	Calculates the mean or average of a group of numbers.
COUNT	=COUNT(A3:A7)	Counts the numeric values in a range. For example, if a range contains cells with text and other cells with numbers, you can count how many numbers are in that range.
COUNTA	=COUNTA(B4:B10)	Counts all cells that are not blank in a range. For example, if a range contains cells with text and other cells with numbers, you can count how many cells contain text in that range.
IF	=IF(A3>=100, "Must be less than 100",A3*2)	Uses conditions or tests regarding the value of a cell. The condition answer is either true or false. In the example, if the condition proves true, the first part of the function is calculated (A3<100) and the text Must be less than 100 is the answer. If the condition proves false, the second part of the function is calculated (A3>100) and A3 is multiplied by 2.
MAX	=MAX(B4:B10)	Returns the maximum value in a range of cells.
MIN	=MIN(B4:B10)	Returns the minimum value in a range of cells.

continues

Table 15.1   Continued

Function	Example	Description
PMT	=PMT(A3,A4,A5)	Calculates the periodic payment when you enter the interest rate, periods, and principal as arguments.
SUM	=SUM(A1:A10)	Adds the values and calculates the total in a range of cells.

Using the AutoSum Tool

Because SUM is one of the most commonly used functions, Excel created a fast way to enter it—you simply click on the AutoSum button in the Standard toolbar. AutoSum guesses what cells you want summed, based on the currently selected cell. If AutoSum selects an incorrect range of cells, you can edit the selection.

To use AutoSum:

1. Select the cell in which you want the sum inserted. Try to choose a cell at the end of a row or column of data.

 2. Click on the **AutoSum** tool in the Standard toolbar. AutoSum inserts =SUM and the range of the cells to the left of or above the selected cell (see Figure 15.1).

3. You can adjust the range of cells by doing one of the following:

   • Click inside the selected cell or the formula bar, and edit the range.

   • Click on the first correct cell in the range to deselect the incorrect range, then drag the mouse pointer over the rest of the correct range of cells.

4. Click on the **Enter** box in the formula bar, or press **Enter**. The total for the selected range is calculated.

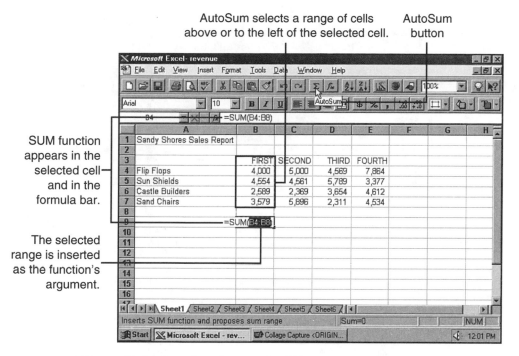

AutoSum selects a range of cells above or to the left of the selected cell.

AutoSum button

SUM function appears in the selected cell and in the formula bar.

The selected range is inserted as the function's argument.

Figure 15.1 AutoSum inserts the SUM function and selects the cells it plans to total.

Using Function Wizard

Although you can type a function directly into a cell, just as you can type formulas, you may find it easier to use the Function Wizard. The Function Wizard leads you through the process of inserting a function. Here's how you do it:

1. Select the cell in which you want to insert the function. (You can insert a function by itself or as part of a formula.)

2. Select **Insert, Function,** or click on the **Function Wizard** button (the fx button) on the Standard toolbar or formula bar. The Function Wizard Step 1 of 2 dialog box appears, as shown in Figure 15.2.

FunctionWizard
button on Standard
toolbar

FunctionWizard
button in
formula bar

Select the
desired
function.

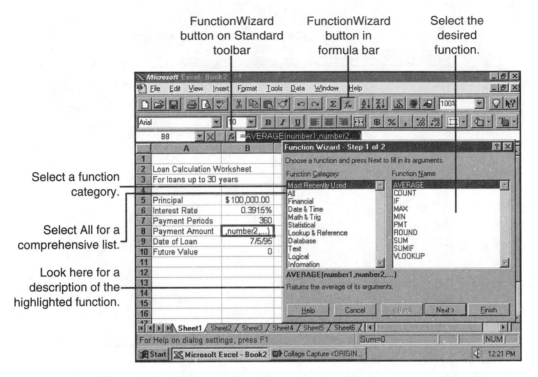

Select a function
category.

Select All for a
comprehensive list.

Look here for a
description of the
highlighted function.

Figure 15.2   The first step is to select the function you want to use.

3. In the **Function Category** list, select the type of function you want to insert. Excel displays the names of the available functions in the Function Name list.

4. Select the function you want to insert from the **Function Name** list, and then click on the **Next** button. Excel displays the Step 2 of 2 dialog box. This box will differ depending on the selected function. Figure 15.3 shows the dialog box you'll see if you chose the PMT function.

5. Enter the values or cell ranges for the argument. You can type a value or argument, or drag the dialog box title bar out of the way and click on the desired cells with the mouse pointer.

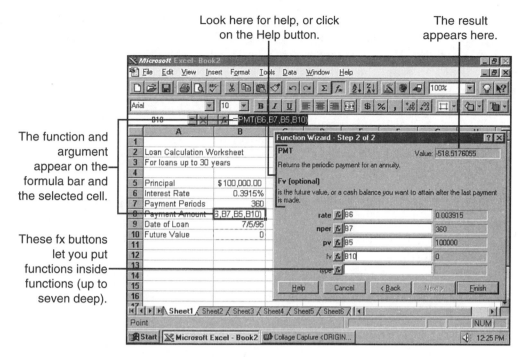

Look here for help, or click
on the Help button.

The result
appears here.

The function and
argument
appear on the
formula bar and
the selected cell.

These fx buttons
let you put
functions inside
functions (up to
seven deep).

Figure 15.3 The second step is to enter the values and cell references that
make up the argument.

6. Click on the **Finish** button. Excel inserts the function and argument in the selected cell and displays the result.

If you are using the PMT function, the result appears in red which
indicates a negative number. This negative number represents the
amount you must pay for the loan.

TIP

Low Interest Rates If the interest rate shown in Figure 15.3
looks too good to be true, it's because Excel works with
monthly percentage rates rather than annual percentage rates.
Whenever you enter a percent on a loan or investment, enter
the annual percentage rate divided by 12. For example, if your
mortgage is at 7% (.07), you would enter =.07/12.

To edit a function, you can type your corrections just as you can with a formula (see lesson 13). You can also use the Function Wizard. To use the Wizard, select the cell that contains the function you want to edit. (You want the cell selected, but you don't want to be in Edit mode; that is, the insertion point should not be displayed in the cell.) Select **Insert**, **Function**, or click on the **Function Wizard** button. The Editing Function 1 of 1 dialog box appears, allowing you to edit the function's argument.

In this lesson, you learned the basics of dealing with functions, and you learned how to use Excel's Function Wizard to quickly enter functions. You also learned how to quickly total a series of numbers with the AutoSum tool. In the next lesson, you will learn how to improve the look of your text by adding character and number formatting and alignment.

Adjusting Number Formats and Text Alignment

In this lesson, you will learn how to customize the appearance of numbers in your worksheet and control the alignment of text inside cells.

Formatting Values

Numeric values are usually more than just numbers. They represent a dollar value, a date, a percent, or some other value. Excel offers a wide range of number formats as listed in Table 16.1. In addition, you can fine-tune each number format with special options, such as making negative numbers appear in red or changing the number of decimal places used.

Table 16.1   Excel's number format categories

Category	Example	Description
General	3400.50	Default number format; the number appears exactly as you type it.
Number	3,400.50	Can be used for general-purpose numbers. Includes a comma for thousand separator and two decimal places.
Currency	$3,400.50	Use for general monetary values. Like a Number format, except with a dollar sign.
Accounting	$3,400.00	Like Currency, except the decimal places or dollar signs are aligned.

continues

Table 16.1 Continued

Category	Example	Description
Date	8/7/94	Displays a number as a date. (The date is calculated as the number of days since 1/1/00).
Time	10:00	Displays a number as the time. (The time is calculated as the number of minutes since 12:00 a.m.).
Percentage	99.50%	Like Number format, except multiplied by 100 and with a percent sign.
Fraction	1/2	Displays decimal numbers as fractions.
Scientific	3.40E+03	Displays numbers in scientfic notation.
Text	135RV90	Displays both text and numbers in a cell as text, exactly as entered.
Special	02110	Use to display ZIP code, phone number, and Social Security numbers in a list or database.
Custom	00.0%	Use to create your own number format.

After deciding on a suitable numeric format, follow these steps:

1. Select the cell or range that you want to format.

2. Select **Format, Cells**, or press **Ctrl+1**. The Format Cells dialog box appears.

3. Click the **Number** tab. (See Figure 16.1.)

4. In the **Category** list, select the category you want to use.

5. In the **Type** list, select the format type you want to use.

6. Click **OK**, or press **Enter**.

When you select a category...   ...a list of format types for that category appears.

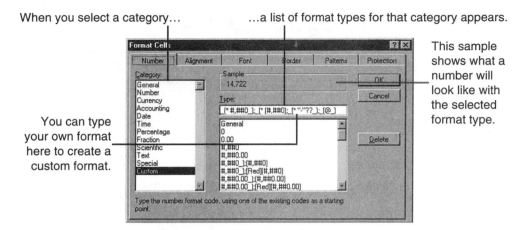

This sample shows what a number will look like with the selected format type.

You can type your own format here to create a custom format.

Figure 16.1 The Format Cells dialog box with the Number tab up front.

The Formatting toolbar (just below the Standard toolbar) contains several buttons for selecting a number format, including the following:

Button	Style
$	Currency Style
%	Percent Style
,	Comma Style
+.0 .00	Increase Decimal
.00 +.0	Decrease Decimal

Select the cell and then click on a formatting tool. You can also change the Number format of a cell by using the shortcut menu; select the cell, click the right mouse button on the cell to display the shortcut menu, and then choose Format, Cells.

Formatting Dates and Times

Dates and time are actually numeric values that have been formatted to appear as dates and times. You can change the way Excel displays the date and time if you like. Excel offers several date and time formats as listed in Table 16.2.

Table 16.2 Excel's date and time formats

Date/Time Format	Example
m/d	4/8
m/d/yy	4/8/95
mm/dd/yy	04/08/95
d-mmm	8-Apr
d-mmm-y	8-Apr-95
dd-mmm-y	08-Apr-95
mmm-yy	Apr-95
mmmm-yy	April-95
mmmm-d, yyyy	April 8, 1995
m/d/yy h:mm	4/8/95 5:30
m/d/yy hh:mm	4/8/95 17:30
hh:mm	17:15
h:mm	5:15
h:mm:ss	5:15:20
mm:ss	20:45
h:mm AM/PM	5:15 PM
h:mm:ss AM/PM	5:15:20 AM

That's Not the Date I Entered!   If you enter a date in a cell that is formatted with the Number format, the date will appear as a number. With the Number format, Excel converts the date to a value that represents the number of days since January 1, 1900. For example, 01/01/1900 equals 1; 12/31/1900 equals 366 (1900 was a leap year). To fix it, change the Number format to the Date format and select a date type from the Type list.

After deciding on a suitable date and time format, follow these steps:

1. Select the cell or range that contains the dates or times you want to format.

2. Select **Format**, **Cells**, or press **Ctrl+1**. The Format Cells dialog box appears.

3. If the Number tab is not up front, click on it.

4. In the **Category** list, select the Date or Time category. (See Figure 16.2.)

5. In the **Type** list, select the format type you want to use.

6. Click **OK**, or press **Enter**.

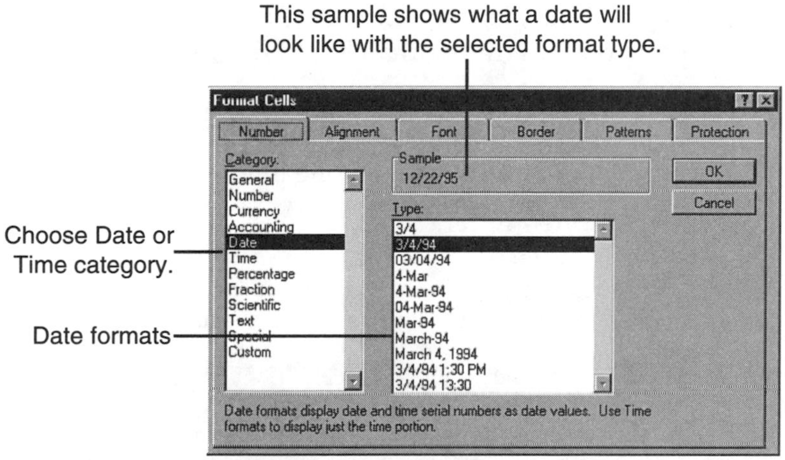

Figure 16.2 The date formats.

Aligning Text in Cells

When you enter data into an Excel worksheet, that data is aligned automatically. Text is aligned on the left, and numbers are aligned on the right. Text and numbers are initially set at the bottom of the cells.

To change the alignment:

1. Select the cell or range you want to align.

   If you want to center a title or other text over a range of cells, select the entire range of blank cells in which you want the text centered, including the cell that contains the text you want to center.

2. Select **Format**, **Cells**, or press **Ctrl+1**. The Format Cells dialog box appears.

3. Click the **Alignment** tab. (See Figure 16.3).

4. Choose from the following options and option groups to set the alignment:

> **Horizontal**   lets you specify a left/right alignment in the cell(s). (The Center across selection option lets you center a title or other text inside a range of cells.)

> **Vertical**   lets you specify how you want the text aligned in relation to the top and bottom of the cell(s).

> **Orientation**   lets you flip the text sideways or print it from top to bottom (rather than left to right).

> **Wrap Text**   tells Excel to wrap long lines of text within a cell without changing the width of the cell. (Normally, Excel displays all text in a cell on one line.)

5. Click **OK**, or press **Enter**.

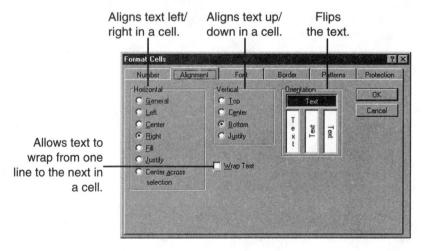

Figure 16.3   The Alignment options.

A quick way to align text and numbers is to use the alignment buttons in the Formatting toolbar. The following buttons allow you to align the text:

 Left

 Right

 Center

 Center Across Columns

Changing the Default Format and Alignment

When you enter the same type of data into a large worksheet, it is sometimes convenient to change the default format for that workbook. You then can change the format for only those cells that are exceptions. Note that when you change the default, it affects all the cells in the worksheet and every sheet in the workbook, but it does not affect other workbooks.

You can change the default settings for number format, alignment, and others. To change the defaults:

1. Select **Format, Style**. The Style dialog box appears, as shown in Figure 16.4.

2. In the **Style Name** list box, select Normal.

3. Click the **Modify** button. Excel displays the Format Cells dialog box, as shown in Figure 16.1.

4. Click the tab for the group of format settings you want to change. For example, you can click Number to change the default numeric formatting.

5. Select the desired format settings such as Currency with 0 decimal places, and then click the **OK** button. Excel returns you to the Style dialog box.

6. Click **OK**, or press **Enter**.

Select the Normal style.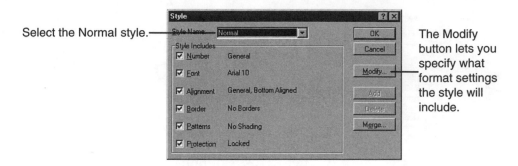

The Modify button lets you specify what format settings the style will include.

Figure 16.4 The Style dialog box.

In this lesson, you learned how to format numbers and align data in cells. In the next lesson, you will learn how to format text.

Improving the Look of Your Text

In this lesson, you will learn how to change the appearance of the text in the cells.

How Can You Make Text Look Different?

When you type text or numbers, Excel inserts it in the Arial font, which doesn't look very fancy. You can change the following text attributes to improve the appearance of your text or set it apart from other text:

Font   For example, Algerian, Desdemona, and Wide Latin.

Font Style   For example, Bold, Italic, Underline, and Strikethrough.

Size   For example, 10-point, 12-point, and 20-point. (The higher the point size, the bigger the text is. There are approximately 72 points in an inch.)

Color   For example, Red, Magenta, and Cyan.

What's a Font?   In Excel, a font is a set of characters that have the same typeface (for example, Helvetica).

Figure 17.1 shows a worksheet after different attributes have been changed for selected text.

Text centered across columns,
set in 16-point, bold, italic type.

Underline
applied to cells.

Row headings
set in italics.

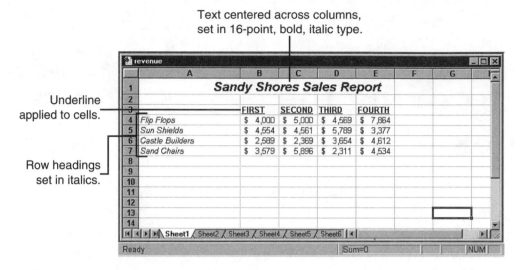

Figure 17.1   A sampling of several text attributes.

Using the Format Cells Dialog Box

You can change the look of your text by using the Format Cells dialog
box or by using the Font buttons in the Formatting toolbar. To use the
Format Cells dialog box, follow these steps:

1. Select the cell or range that contains the text you want to format.

2. Select **Format**, **Cells**, or press **Ctrl+1**.

3. Click the **Font** tab. (See Figure 17.2).

4. Enter your font preferences by selecting them from the lists.

5. Click **OK**, or press **Enter**.

Excel uses a default font to style your text as you type it. To change
the default font, enter your font preferences in the Font tab, and then
click on the Normal Font option. When you click the OK button, Excel
makes your preferences the default font.

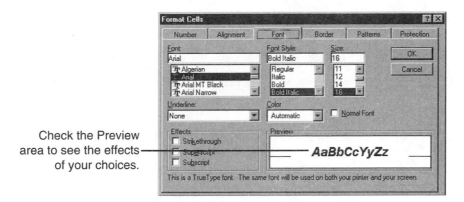

Check the Preview area to see the effects of your choices.

Figure 17.2 The Format Cells dialog box with the Font tab up front.

Font Shortcuts A faster way to change text attributes is to use the keyboard shortcuts. First select the cell(s), then press **Ctrl+B** for bold; **Ctrl+I** for Italic; **Ctrl+U** for Underline; and **Ctrl+5** for Strikethrough.

Changing Text Attributes with Toolbar Buttons

A faster way to enter font changes is to use the buttons and drop-down lists in the Formatting toolbar, as shown in Figure 17.3.

Select a font size here. Italic

Bold Underline Text color

Select a font here.

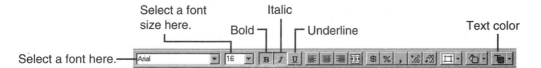

Figure 17.3 Use the Formatting toolbar to quickly make font changes.

To use a tool to change text attributes:

1. Select the cell or range that contains the text whose look you want to change.

321

2. To change the font or font size, pull down the appropriate drop-down list, and click on the font or size you want. You can also type the point size in the Font Size box.

3. To add an attribute (such as bold or underlining), click on the desired button.

Change Before You Type   You can activate the attributes you want before you type text. For example, if you want a title in Bold, 12-point MS Sans Serif, click in the document to position the insertion point where you want to change the attributes, then set these attributes before you start typing.

In this lesson, you learned how to customize your text to achieve the look you want. In the next lesson, you will learn how to add borders and shading to your worksheet.

Adding Cell Borders and Shading

In this lesson, you will learn how to add pizzazz to your worksheets by adding borders and shading.

Adding Borders to Cells

As you work with your worksheet on-screen, each cell is identified by a gridline that surrounds the cell. In print, these gridlines may appear washed out. To have better defined lines appear on the printout, you can add borders to selected cells or cell ranges. Figure 18.1 shows the options for adding lines around cells and cell ranges.

All	All		Outline	Outline		Dotted line	Dotted line
All	All		Outline	Outline		Dotted line	Dotted line
All	All		Outline	Outline		Dotted line	Dotted line

Single	Single		Double	Double		Thick	Thick
Single	Single		Double	Double		Thick	Thick
Single	Single		Double	Double		Thick	Thick

Top	Top		Bottom	Bottom		Left	Right
Top	Top		Bottom	Bottom		Left	Right
Top	Top		Bottom	Bottom		Left	Right

Figure 18.1 A sampling of borders.

To add borders to a cell or range, perform the following steps:

1. Select the cell(s) around which you want a border to appear.
2. Select **Format, Cells**. The Format Cells dialog box appears.
3. Click the **Border** tab. (See Figure 18.2).
4. Select the desired border position, style (thickness), and color for the border.
5. Click **OK**, or press **Enter**.

Select a border position.

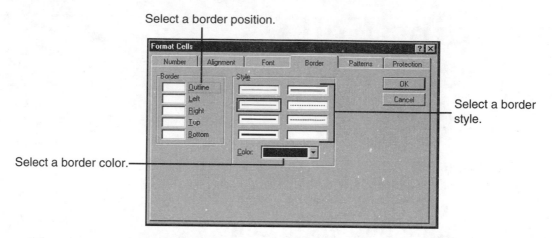

Select a border style.

Select a border color.

Figure 18.2 The Format Cells dialog box with the Border tab up front.

Hiding Gridlines When adding borders to a worksheet, hide the gridlines to get a better idea of how the borders will print. Select **Tools**, **Options**, click on the **View** tab, and select **Gridlines** to remove the check mark from the check box. By default, Excel for Windows 95 does not print the gridlines.

Borders Button To add borders quickly, select the cells around which you want the border to appear, and click on the arrow to the right of the Borders button in the Formatting toolbar. Click on the desired border. If you click on the Borders button itself (rather than on the arrow), Excel automatically adds a bottom borderline or the borderline you last chose to the selected cells.

Adding Shading to Cells

For a simple but dramatic effect, add shading to your worksheets. Figure 18.3 illustrates the effects that you can create with shading.

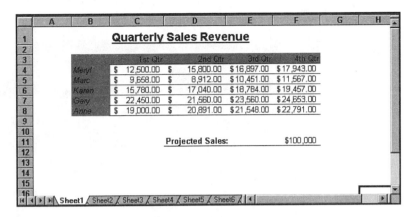

Figure 18.3   A worksheet with added shading.

To add shading to a cell or range:

1. Select the cell(s) you want to shade.

2. Select **Format, Cells**.

3. Click on the **Patterns** tab. The shading options appear, as shown in Figure 18.4.

4. Open the Pattern drop-down list, and you will see a grid that contains all the colors from the color palette, as well as patterns. Select the shading color and pattern you want to use. The Color options let you choose a color for the overall shading. The Pattern options let you select a black-and-white or colored pattern that lies on top of the overall shading. A preview of the result is displayed in the Sample box.

5. Click **OK**, or press **Enter**.

Color Button   A quick way to add cell shading (without a pattern) is to select the cells you want to shade and then click on the arrow to the right of the Color button. Click on the color you want to use. If the shading is dark, consider using the Font Color button to select a light color for the text.

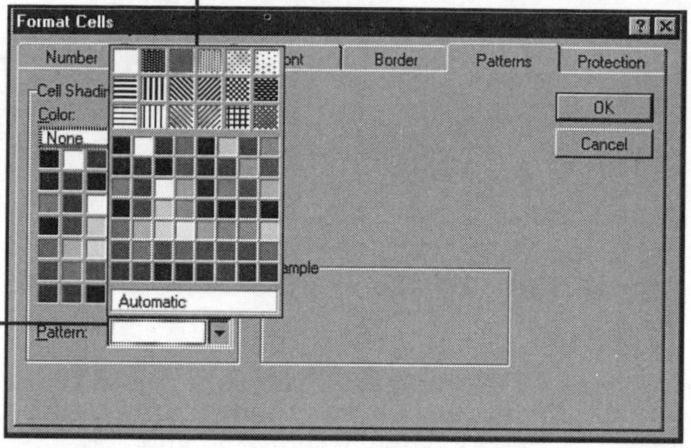

Select an overall color for the selected cell.

Select a pattern to lay
on top of the color.

Figure 18.4 Selecting a shading and a pattern.

Using AutoFormat

Excel offers the AutoFormat feature that takes some of the pain out of
formatting. AutoFormat provides you with 16 predesigned table formats that you can apply to a worksheet.

To use predesigned formats, perform the following steps:

1. Select the worksheet(s) and cell(s) that contain the data you want
   to format.

2. Select **Format, AutoFormat**. The AutoFormat dialog box appears,
   as shown in Figure 18.5.

3. In the **Table Format** list, choose the predesigned format you want
   to use. When you select a format, Excel shows you what it will
   look like in the Sample area.

4. To exclude certain elements from the AutoFormat, click on the
   Options button, and choose the formats you want to turn off.

5. Click the **OK** button. Excel formats your table to make it look like
   the one in the preview area.

> **TIP**
>
> **Deformatting an AutoFormat**   If you don't like what
> AutoFormat did to your worksheet, select the table, then
> choose **Format, AutoFormat**. From the Table Format list,
> choose **None** to remove the AutoFormat.

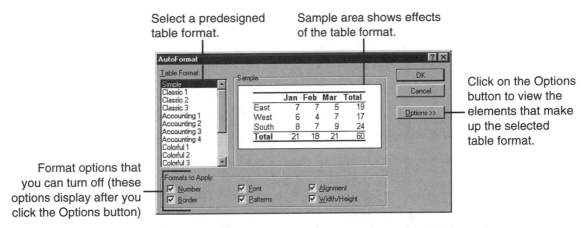

Figure 18.5   Use the AutoFormat dialog box to select a prefab format.

Copying Formats with Format Painter

Excel gives you two ways to copy and paste formatting:

- You can use the Edit Copy command and then the Edit Paste Special command and select Formats from the Paste options in the Paste Special dialog box.

- You can use the Format Painter button in the Standard toolbar.

The Format Painter lets you quickly copy and paste formats that you have already used in a workbook. Because the Format Painter button is faster, I'll give you the steps you need to paint formats:

1. Select the cell(s) that contain the formatting you want to copy and paste.

2. Click on the **Format Painter** button (the one with the paintbrush on it) in the Standard toolbar. Excel copies the formatting. The mouse pointer changes into a paintbrush with a plus sign next to it.

3. Click and drag over the cells to which you want to apply the copied formatting.

4. Release the mouse button. The copied formatting is applied to the selected cells.

In this lesson, you learned some additional ways to enhance the appearance of your worksheets. In the next lesson, you will learn how to change the sizes of rows and columns.

Changing Column Width and Row Height

In this lesson, you will learn how to adjust the column width and row height to make the best use of the worksheet space.

Adjusting Column Width and Row Height with a Mouse

You can adjust the width of a column or the height of a row by using a dialog box or by dragging with the mouse. Here's how you adjust the row height or column width with the mouse:

1. If you want to change two or more rows or columns at once, select them.

2. Position the mouse pointer between the row or column headings, as shown in Figure 19.1.

3. Hold down the mouse button and drag the border. When you release the mouse button, and the row height or column width is adjusted.

Dragging the right border of column C changes its width.

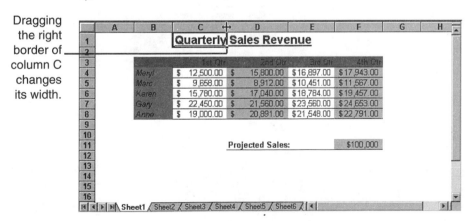

Figure 19.1 The mouse pointer changes to a double-headed arrow when you move it over a border in the row or column heading.

Dragging the border of a row or column does not give as precise sizing as when you provide specific sizes with the Format Row Height and Format Column Width commands.

Custom-Fit Cells   To quickly make a column as wide as its widest entry, double-click on the right border of the column heading. To make a row as tall as its tallest entry, double-click on the bottom border of the row heading.

Changing Height and Width using the Format Menu

The Format menu contains the commands you need to change the column width and row height of selected rows and columns. Here's how to change the column width:

1. Select the column(s) whose width you want to change. To change the width of a single column, select any cell in that column.

2. Select **Format, Column, Width**. The Column Width dialog box appears, as shown in Figure 19.2.

3. Type the number of characters you would like as the width. The default width is 8.43.

4. Click **OK**, or press **Enter**.

Figure 19.2   Changing the column width.

AutoFit Column Width   To make selected columns as wide as their widest entries, select the columns, select **Format, Column**, and select **AutoFit Selection**.

By default, Excel makes a row a bit taller than the tallest text in the row. For example, if the tallest text is 10 points tall, Excel makes the row 12.75 points tall. To use the Format menu to change the row height:

1. Select the row(s) whose height you want to change. To change the height of a single row, select any cell in that row.

2. Select **Format**, **Row**, **Height**. The Row Height dialog box appears, as shown in Figure 19.3.

3. Type the desired height in points.

4. Click **OK**, or press **Enter**.

Figure 19.3   Changing the row height.

In this lesson, you learned how to change the row height and column width. In the next lesson, you will learn how to change the view of your worksheet.

Changing the View of Your Worksheet

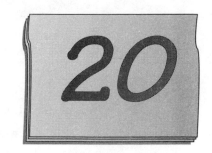

In this lesson, you will learn how to view your worksheet in various ways.

Magnifying and Reducing the View of Your Worksheet

Excel's Zoom feature lets you increase and decrease the percentage of magnification at which you view your worksheet. You can zoom in and get a closer look at data in your worksheet or zoom out so the whole worksheet shows on the screen at one glance.

Here's how you can magnify and reduce the view of your worksheet:

1. Select **View**, **Zoom**. The Zoom dialog box appears, as shown in Figure 20.1.

2. Select a percentage of magnification option. To magnify your data, choose a higher percentage. To reduce your data, choose a lower percentage.

3. Click **OK**, or press **Enter**. Excel enlarges or reduces the worksheet accordingly.

Zoom Control   To quickly change the percentage of magnification in your worksheet, click on the arrow to the right of the Zoom Control box (100% in a box next to the TipWizard tool) on the far right side of the Standard toolbar. Select a percentage of magnification on the Zoom Control list.

How Do I Unzoom?   To restore the percentage of magnification to 100% (default), click **100%** in the Zoom Control box on the Standard toolbar.

Select a higher percentage
to magnify your data.

Select a lower percentage
to reduce your data.

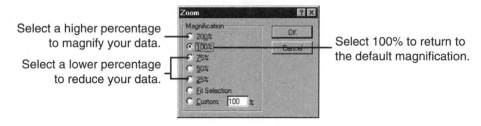

Select 100% to return to
the default magnification.

Figure 20.1   Magnifying and reducing your data in the Zoom dialog box.

Freezing Column and Row Titles

Often, you will enter data in a large worksheet that exceeds one screen. When you scroll to other areas, you cannot see which row or column you are in. No problem. With Excel's Window Freeze Panes command, you can freeze column and row titles so that they remain stationary when you scroll to other parts of the worksheet. Follow these steps:

1. Click on the cell that is located below your column headings and to the right of the row headings. You want to freeze the titles where the column and row headings intersect.

2. Select **Window, Freeze Panes**. Excel splits the window into panes and freezes the titles above and to the left of the cell selector, as shown in Figure 20.2.

Scroll to the far right side of the worksheet. Notice that the row titles remain in view. Scroll to the bottom of the worksheet. The column titles remain on the screen.

To restore the worksheet to the original display, open the **Window** menu and select **Unfreeze Panes**.

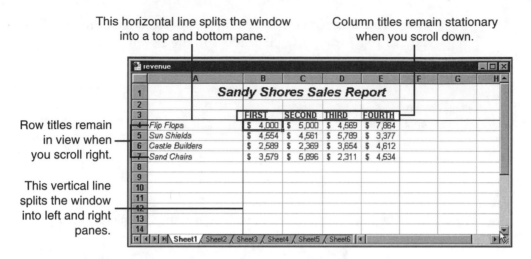

This horizontal line splits the window into a top and bottom pane.

Column titles remain stationary when you scroll down.

Row titles remain in view when you scroll right.

This vertical line splits the window into left and right panes.

Figure 20.2   Freezing column and row titles.

Splitting a Worksheet

Because a worksheet can be so large, you may want to view different parts of the worksheet at the same time. To do this, you need to split the workbook window into panes. Here's how you work with panes:

- To split a workbook window, drag one of the split bars, as shown in Figure 20.3. The horizontal split bar starts above the arrow at the top of the vertical scroll bar. The vertical split bar starts to the right of the arrow at the right end of the horizontal scroll bar.

- To switch from one pane to the other, click in the pane you want to work with.

- To close a pane, drag the split bar to the right side or bottom of the window (depending on which split bar you are using), and release the mouse button.

- To keep the top or left pane from scrolling, select **Window, Freeze Panes**. With the panes frozen, as you scroll in the bottom or right pane, the view in the other pane stays put.

- To free the panes, select **Window, Unfreeze Panes**.

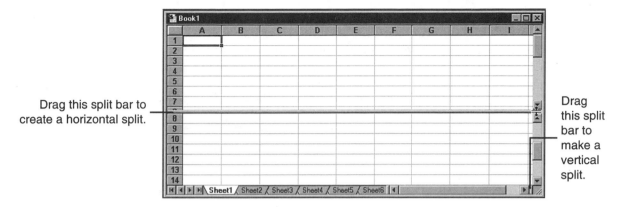

Drag this split bar to create a horizontal split.

Drag this split bar to make a vertical split.

Figure 20.3   Drag one of the split bars to divide the window into two panes.

Hiding and Displaying Columns and Rows

If you work with sensitive data and you do not want other people to see information in your worksheet or printout, you can hide columns and rows. Hidden columns and rows don't print when you print the worksheet. When you hide columns or rows, the formulas that use data in the hidden columns or rows will continue to work properly. To hide and display columns and rows using the mouse, you can do the following:

- To hide one or more columns, drag the right column border past the left column border for each column you want to hide, as shown in Figure 20.4.

- To redisplay one or more columns, place the mouse pointer between the two column headings next to the hidden column. If column C is hidden, for example, place the mouse pointer between column headings B and D. Move the mouse pointer around until it turns from a single, thick border to a double-lined border. Then drag the column border to the right to redisplay each hidden column.

- To hide one or more rows, drag the bottom row border past the top row border for each row you want to hide.

- To redisplay one or more rows, place the mouse pointer between the two row headings next to the hidden row. Then drag the row border down to redisplay each hidden row. See Figure 20.5.

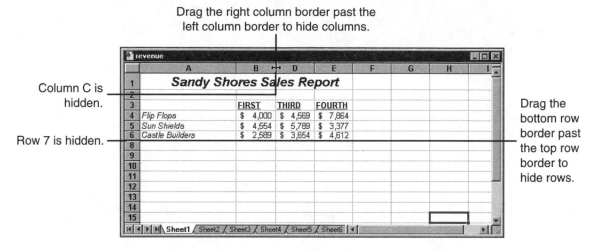

Drag the right column border past the left column border to hide columns.

Column C is hidden.

Row 7 is hidden.

Drag the bottom row border past the top row border to hide rows.

Figure 20.4 Drag a column or row border to hide columns or rows.

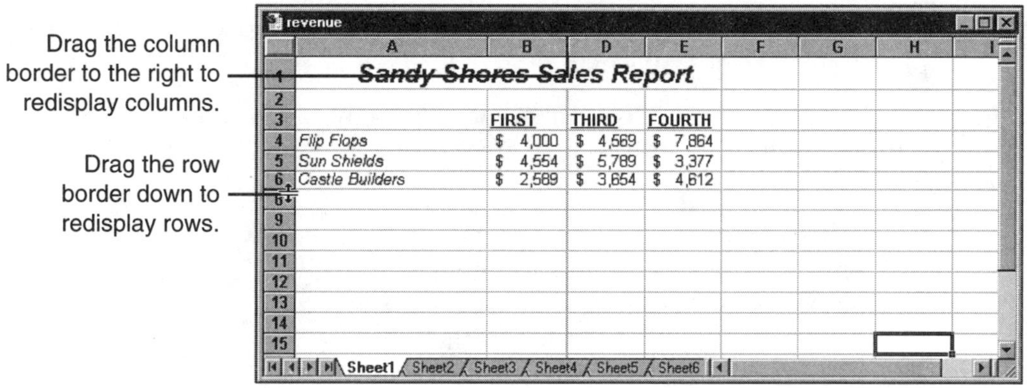

Drag the column border to the right to redisplay columns.

Drag the row border down to redisplay rows.

Figure 20.5 Drag a column or row border to redisplay columns or rows.

In this lesson, you learned how to change the view of your worksheet. In the next lesson, you will learn how to use templates.

Working with Templates

In this lesson, you'll learn how to create a workbook with an Excel template and customize templates.

What Is a Template?

Every workbook is based on a template. The default template is NORMAL.XLT. A template can help you create workbooks that are consistent and customize your workbooks to suit a particular need. For example, if you create a weekly budget report and don't want to recreate the entire report each week, you can just save one of your reports (or use one of Excel's built-in templates) as a template, and then insert new numbers in the basic format each week.

When you save the workbook as a template or use an Excel built-in template, you can create additional workbooks based on the template. These workbooks will include the same text, formatting, and other elements you included when you created the template.

What's a Template?   A template is a collection of patterns and tools for creating a category of workbooks. You can format the template, insert text and graphics, and change the page layout so that the template includes all the key information.

Creating a Workbook with an Excel Template

To create a workbook with an Excel template, perform the following steps:

1. Select **File**, **New**. The New dialog box appears.

2. Click on the **Spreadsheet Solutions** tab, and click on the template icon you want to use. You see a sample of the template in the Preview area, as shown in Figure 21.1.

3. Click **OK** or press **Enter**. Excel copies the template into a new workbook, ready for you to add your own information to it.

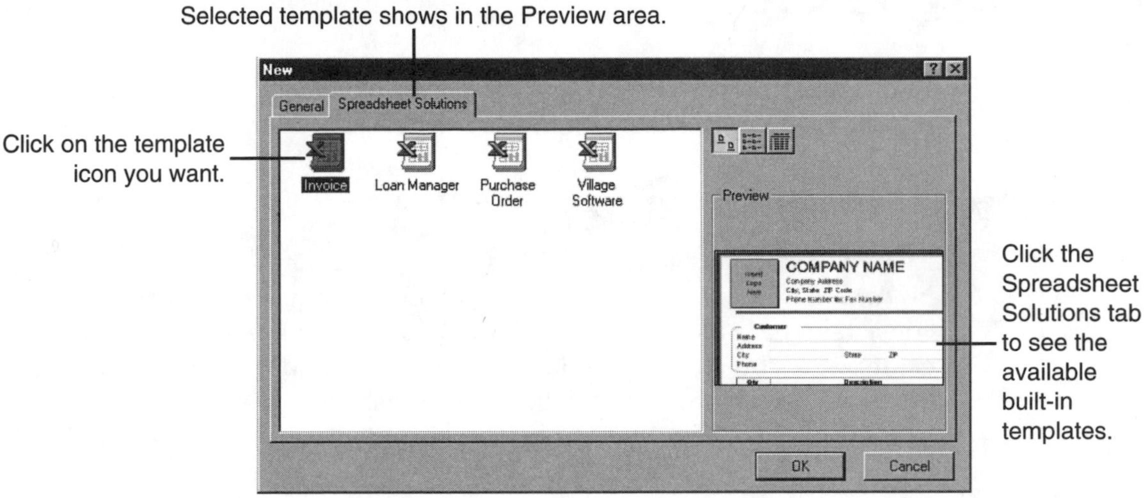

Selected template shows in the Preview area.

Click on the template icon you want.

Click the Spreadsheet Solutions tab to see the available built-in templates.

Figure 21.1   Use the New dialog box to create a new workbook based on a built-in template.

Creating a Template

To save time, save your favorite workbook as a template. You can create your template based on an existing workbook.

To create a template, perform the following steps:

1. Create the workbook or open the workbook you want to save as a template. You can include text, formatting, macros, and so on.

2. Select **File, Save As**. The Save As dialog box appears.

3. Type a name for the template in the **File Name** text box.

4. Select **Template** from the Save as Type drop-down list box. You'll see the Templates folder appear in the Save In box. All templates must be stored in the Templates folder. (See Figure 21.2.)

5. Click **Save**, or press **Enter**. The template is created and saved. When you use this template, you will find it on the General tab in the New dialog box.

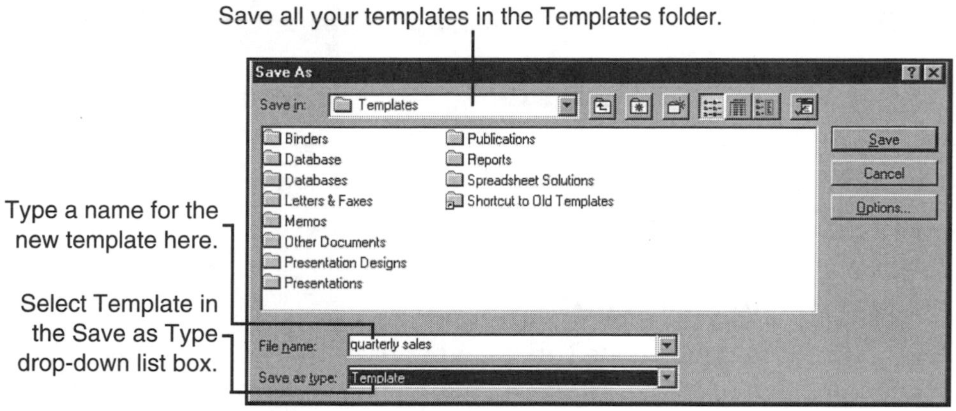

Save all your templates in the Templates folder.

Type a name for the new template here.

Select Template in the Save as Type drop-down list box.

Figure 21.2   Creating a new template.

In this lesson, you learned how to create and use templates. In the next lesson, you will learn how to create charts.

339

Creating Charts

In this lesson, you will learn to create charts to represent your workbook data as a picture.

Charting with Excel

With Excel, you can create various types of charts. Some common chart types are shown in Figure 22.1. The chart type you choose depends on your data and on how you want to present that data. These are the major chart types and their purposes:

Pie   Use this chart to show the relationship among parts of a whole.

Bar   Use this chart to compare values at a given point in time.

Column   Similar to the Bar chart; use this chart to emphasize the difference between items.

Line   Use this chart to emphasize trends and the change of values over time.

Area   Similar to the Line chart; use this chart to emphasize the amount of change in values.

Most of these basic chart types also come in 3-dimensional varieties. In addition to looking more professional than the standard flat charts, 3-D charts can often help your audience distinguish between different sets of data.

Embedded Charts   A chart that is placed on the same worksheet that contains the data used to create the chart. A chart can also be placed on a chart sheet in the workbook so that the worksheet and chart are separate. Embedded charts are useful for showing the actual data and its graphic representation side-by-side.

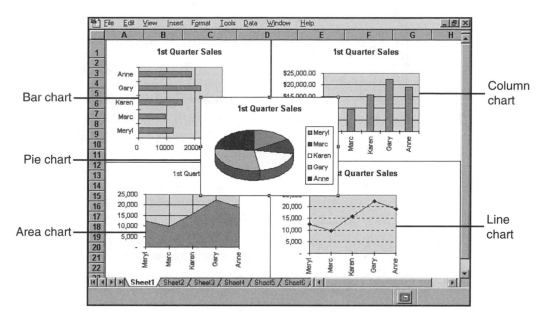

Figure 22.1 Commonly used Excel chart types.

Charting Terminology

Before you start creating charts, familiarize yourself with the following terminology:

Data Series The bar, pie wedges, lines, or other elements that represent plotted values in a chart. For example, a chart might show a set of blue bars that show the value of an item over time. You might also have red bars on the chart which show the value of a different item. Each is considered a separate data series.

Categories Categories reflect the number of elements in a series. For instance, you might have four categories: Spring, Summer, Fall, and Winter, to show your sale in each of the four seasons. Categories normally correspond to the columns that you have in your chart data.

Axis One side of a chart. In a two-dimensional chart, there is an X-axis (horizontal) and a Y-axis (vertical). The X-axis contains the category and/or data series labels. The Y-axis lists the possible values. Your data points meet in the middle to show the value of a category or data series.

341

Legend   Defines the separate elements of a chart. For example, the legend for a pie chart will show what each piece of the pie represents.

Gridlines   Emphasizes the Y-axis or X-axis scale of the data series. For example, major gridlines for the Y-axis will help you follow a point from the X or Y-axis to identify a data point's exact value.

Creating a Chart

You can create charts as part of a worksheet (an embedded chart) or as a separate chart worksheet. If you create an embedded chart, it will print side-by-side with your worksheet data. If you create a chart on a chart worksheet, you can print it separately. Both types of charts are linked to the worksheet data that they represent, so when you change the data, the chart is automatically updated.

Creating an Embedded Chart

The ChartWizard button in the Standard toolbar allows you to create a graph frame on a worksheet. To use the ChartWizard, take the following steps:

1. Select the data you want to chart. If you typed names or other labels (for example, Qtr 1, Qtr 2, and so on) and you want them included in the chart, make sure you select them.

2. Click on the **ChartWizard** button in the Standard toolbar (see Figure 22.2).

3. Move the mouse pointer where you want the upper left corner of the chart to appear. Hold down the mouse button, and drag to define the size and dimensions of the chart.

Precision Dragging   To create a square chart, hold down the **Shift** key as you drag. If you want your chart to exactly fit the borders of the cells it occupies, hold down the **Alt** key as you drag.

4. Release the mouse button. The ChartWizard Step 1 of 5 dialog box asks if the selected range is correct. You can correct the range by typing a new range or by dragging the dialog box title bar out of the way, and dragging over the cells you want to chart.

5. Click on the **Next** button. The ChartWizard Step 2 of 5 dialog box appears, as shown in Figure 22.2, asking you to select a chart type.

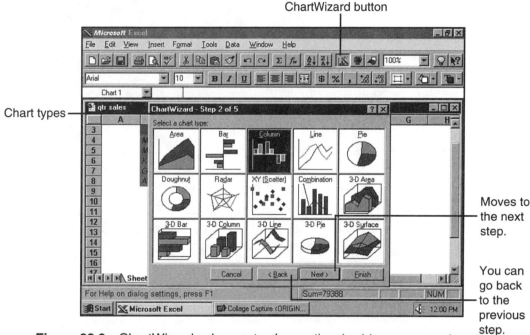

Figure 22.2 ChartWizard asks you to choose the chart type you want.

6. Select a chart type, and click on the **Next** button. The ChartWizard Step 3 of 5 dialog box appears, asking you to select a chart format.

7. Select a format for the chosen chart type, and click on the **Next** button. The ChartWizard Step 4 of 5 dialog box appears, as shown in Figure 22.3. (The Column chart type and column chart format 6 were chosen to get to the dialog box in Figure 22.3. Your dialog box may look different, depending on the chart type you chose.)

8. Choose whether the data series is based on rows or columns, and choose the starting row and column. Click on the **Next** button. The ChartWizard Step 5 of 5 dialog box appears.

343

Select whether you want data
graphed by rows or columns.

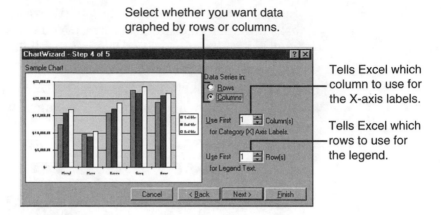

Tells Excel which
column to use for
the X-axis labels.

Tells Excel which
rows to use for
the legend.

Figure 22.3 The ChartWizard prompts you to specify exactly how you want
the data charted.

9. If desired, add a legend, title, or axis labels. Click on the **Finish**
   button. Your completed chart appears on the current worksheet.

Moving and Resizing a Chart To move an embedded chart,
click anywhere in the chart area and drag it to the new location. To change the size of a chart, select the chart, and then
drag one of its handles (the black squares that border the
chart). Drag a corner handle to change the height and width,
or drag a side handle to change only the width.

Creating a Chart on a Separate Worksheet

If you don't want your chart to appear on the same page as your
worksheet data, you can create the chart on a separate worksheet.
To create a chart in this way, select the data you want to chart, and
then select **Insert**, **Chart**, **As New Sheet**. Excel inserts a separate chart
worksheet (named Chart 1) to the left of the current worksheet and
starts the ChartWizard. Perform the same steps given in the previous
section for creating a chart with the ChartWizard.

Using the Chart Toolbar

You can use the Chart toolbar to create a chart, or to change an existing chart, as shown in Figure 22.4. If the Chart toolbar is not displayed, you can turn it on by choosing **View, Toolbars**, placing a check mark in the **Chart** check box, and clicking on **OK**.

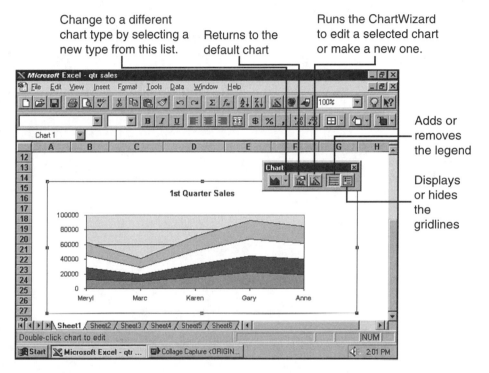

Change to a different chart type by selecting a new type from this list.

Returns to the default chart

Runs the ChartWizard to edit a selected chart or make a new one.

Adds or removes the legend

Displays or hides the gridlines

Figure 22.4   The Chart toolbar.

Still Not Satisfied?   If you need to make changes to your chart, select the chart, and then click on the **ChartWizard** tool to redefine the data area and make other changes.

Saving Charts

The charts you create are part of the current workbook. To save a chart, simply save the workbook that contains the chart. For more details, refer to Lesson 6, "Working with Workbook Files."

Printing a Chart

If a chart is an embedded chart, it will print when you print the worksheet that contains the chart. If you created a chart on a separate worksheet, you can print the chart separately by printing only the chart worksheet. For more information about printing, refer to Lesson 8, "Printing Your Workbook."

In this lesson, you learned about the different chart types and how to create them. You also learned how to save and print charts. In the next lesson, you will learn how to enhance your charts.

Giving Charts a
New Look

In this lesson, you will learn how to enhance your charts to display data more clearly and more attractively.

Opening a Chart Window

Before you can add enhancements to a chart, you must open the chart in its own window. This means the chart must be in a special edit mode. For instance, you must double-click an embedded chart—that is, a chart on the same sheet as its data—to edit it (see the chart on the Sheet 2 tab in Figure 23.1). On the other hand, a chart on its own sheet (see the chart on the Chart 1 tab in Figure 23.1) is ready to edit when you select its worksheet tab.

Chart on a worksheet

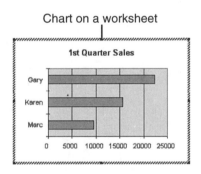

Chart on its own chart sheet

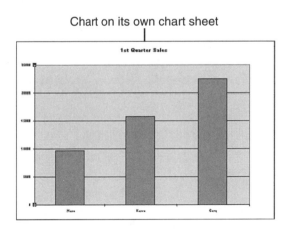

Figure 23.1 Before you add enhancements, you must display the chart in a worksheet or chart sheet.

Before you start adding enhancements to a chart, you should understand that a chart is made up of several objects. By clicking on an object, you make it active, and handles appear around it, as shown in Figure 23.2. You can then move or resize the object or change its appearance, by doing any of the following:

- Double-click on an object to display a dialog box that lets you change the object's appearance. For example, if you double-click on a column in a column chart, you can change its color.

- Right-click on the object and then select the desired formatting option from the shortcut menu.

- Select the object, and then select an option from the Insert or Format menu. The Insert menu lets you add objects to a chart, including a legend, data labels, and a chart title.

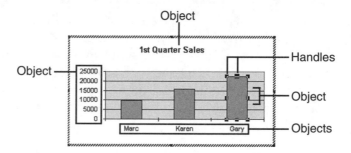

Figure 23.2   Each chart consists of several individual objects.

The following sections tell you how to add some more commonly used enhancements to a chart.

Adding Titles

You can add various titles to a chart to help indicate what the chart is all about. You can add a chart title that appears at the top of the chart, and you can add axis titles that appear along the X and Y axes. Here's how you do it:

1. Make sure the chart is in edit mode (double-click on an embedded chart on the same worksheet as its data or click on the chart tab to select the chart on its own sheet).

2. Right-click on the chart, and choose **Insert Titles**, or select **Insert, Titles**.

3. Click on each title type you want to add, to put a check mark in their check boxes.

4. Click on the **OK** button. Excel returns you to the chart window and inserts a text box for the title you want to add, as shown in Figure 23.3.

5. Click on a text box to select it, click inside the text box, and then edit the text as desired.

6. To enter the text for the axis titles, click on the **X** or **Y** next to its axis to display a text box. Click inside the text box, and then edit the text as desired.

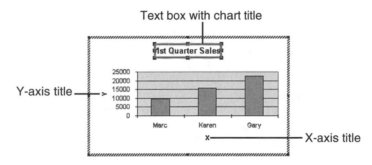

Figure 23.3   Excel inserts text boxes for each specified title.

Formatting Text on a Chart

Any text you add to a chart is added inside a text box. (You'll learn how to format text that was lifted from the worksheet data later in this section.) To format text you added, do this:

1. Right-click on the text that you want to format. A text box appears around the text, and a shortcut menu appears.

2. Select the **Format** option. The Format option differs depending on the object. If you right-click on the chart title, for example, the option reads Format Chart Title.

3. Enter your preferences in the Format dialog box. This dialog box typically contains tabs for changing the font, adding borders and shading to the text box, and changing the alignment of text in the box.

4. Click **OK** when you are done.

Formatting Text You Did Not Add   Charts may contain some text that was obtained from the worksheet data. A quick way to format this text is to right-click on the chart (not on any specific object), and choose **Format Chart Area**. Click on the **Font** tab, enter your preferences, and click on **OK**.

Formatting the Axes

You can enhance the X, Y, and Z axes in a number of ways, including changing the font of the text, scaling the axes, and changing the number format. The Z axis is the vertical plane that only occurs in 3D charts. Here's how you do it:

1. Right-click on the axis you want to format, and choose **Format Axis** from the shortcut menu, or click on the axis and select **Format**, **Selected Axis**. The Format Axis dialog box appears, as shown in Figure 23.4.

2. Enter your preferences in the dialog box.

3. Click **OK** or press **Enter**.

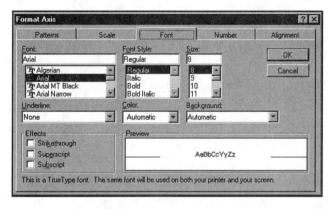

Figure 23.4   The Format Axis dialog box lets you change the look of the axis and its text.

In this lesson, you learned how to improve the appearance of your chart. In the next lesson, you will learn about keeping a database in Excel.

POWERPOINT

Starting and Exiting PowerPoint

In this lesson, you will learn how to start and exit PowerPoint.

Starting PowerPoint

Before you start PowerPoint, you must have PowerPoint installed on your computer, and you should have a basic understanding of Windows 95. If you need a refresher course in Windows 95, read Part I of this book.

To start PowerPoint, follow these steps:

1. Click the **Start** button.

2. Move your mouse pointer to **Programs**. A menu of programs appears.

3. Move your mouse pointer to **Microsoft PowerPoint** and click on it (see Figure 1.1). PowerPoint starts and displays the introductory screen.

The first thing you see when you start PowerPoint is the Tip of the Day box. Click **OK** to bypass it, and you'll see a dialog box in which you choose whether you want to start a new presentation or open an existing one. You'll learn about this dialog box in Lesson 2. For now, click **Cancel** to exit this dialog box.

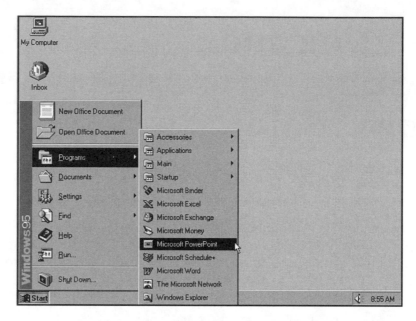

Figure 1.1 To start PowerPoint, move through the Start button's menu system to Microsoft PowerPoint.

Exiting PowerPoint

When you finish using PowerPoint, you should exit. Don't just turn off your computer! If you've made any changes to a presentation and haven't saved them yet, PowerPoint asks if you want to save them when you exit. For now, answer No if asked about this. You'll learn about saving in Lesson 6.

To exit PowerPoint:

1. If the PowerPoint dialog box is still on-screen, click on the **Cancel** button to close it.

2. If this dialog box is not on-screen, do one of the following (see Figure 1.2):

   - Open the **File** menu and select **Exit**.

   - Press **Alt+F4**.

   - Click the PowerPoint window's **Close** button.

You can click this Close
button to close the
PowerPoint window.

You can select Exit
from the File menu.

Figure 1.2 There are several ways to exit PowerPoint.

3. If you're asked if you want to save your changes, select **Yes** if you want to save your changes. (If you choose Yes, see Lesson 6 to learn how to complete the Save As dialog box that appears.) Select **No** if you haven't created anything you want to save yet.

In this lesson, you learned to start and exit PowerPoint. In the next lesson, you'll learn how to create a new presentation.

Creating a New Presentation

In this lesson, you will learn how to create a presentation in several different ways.

Three Choices for Starting a New Presentation

PowerPoint offers you several ways to create a new presentation. Before you begin, decide on the method that's right for you:

- AutoContent Wizard offers the highest degree of help. It walks you through each step of creating the new presentation.

- A template offers a standardized group of slides, all with a similar look and feel, for a particular situation. Each template slide includes dummy text which you can replace with your own text.

- You can choose to start from scratch and create a totally blank presentation, building the presentation from the ground up. This is not recommended for beginners.

 Wizards Wizards are a special feature in most Microsoft products. A wizard displays a series of dialog boxes that ask you design and content questions. You select options and type text. When you are done, the Wizard creates something (in this case, a presentation) according to your instructions.

 Template A template is a predesigned slide that comes with PowerPoint. When you select a template, PowerPoint applies the color scheme and general layout of the slide to each slide in the presentation.

Actually, there is a fourth way to start a presentation too; you can select **New Office Document** from the **Start** menu in Windows. You don't have to have started PowerPoint first. You'll learn more about this in the Working Together section near the end of this book.

A Word About the PowerPoint Dialog Box

If you just started PowerPoint and the PowerPoint dialog box is displayed, you are ready to start a new presentation (see Figure 2.1). From here, you can choose to create a new presentation using the AutoContent Wizard, a Template, or a Blank Presentation. Just click on your choice, and then click OK, and follow along with the steps in the remainder of this lesson to complete the presentation.

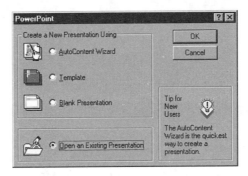

Figure 2.1   When you first start PowerPoint, this dialog box greets you. It's one method you can use to create a new presentation.

Unfortunately, this dialog box is available only when you first start the program. Once you close the dialog box, you won't see it again until the next time you start the program. That's why the steps in the remainder of this lesson don't rely on it; instead they show alternative methods for starting a presentation if this dialog box is not available.

Creating a New Presentation with the AutoContent Wizard

With the AutoContent Wizard, you select the type of presentation you want to create (strategy, sales, training, reporting, conveying bad news, or general) and PowerPoint creates an outline for the presentation. Here's how you use the AutoContent Wizard:

1. Open the **File** menu and click **New**. The New Presentation dialog box appears (see Figure 2.2).

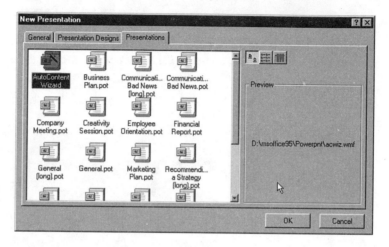

Figure 2.2   You can start a new presentation from here.

2. Click the **Presentations** tab if it's not already on top.

3. Double-click the **AutoContent Wizard** icon. The AutoContent Wizard starts.

4. Click the **Next** button to begin.

5. When prompted (see Figure 2.3), fill in your name, the subject of your presentation, and any other information you want to include on the title slide, such as your company name. Then click **Next**.

6. Select the type of presentation you want to give (for example, I'm choosing Reporting Progress), then click **Next**.

7. Choose a visual style for the presentation (I'm choosing Default).

8. Choose whether you want the presentation to be under 30 minutes or over 30 minutes. (Or, you can indicate that you haven't decided yet.) Then click **Next**.

9. Choose the type of output you need (I'm choosing On-screen Presentation), and whether or not you need handouts (Yes or No). Then click **Next**.

10. Click **Finish**. The beginnings of your presentation, with dummy text in place, appears on-screen.

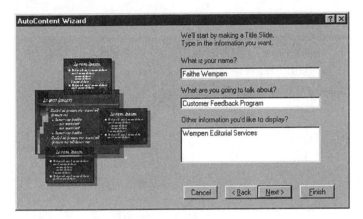

Figure 2.3   Just answer the AutoContent Wizard's questions and click Next.

Replacing Dummy Text   You can start personalizing your presentation right away by replacing the dummy text with your own text. Just select the existing text and type right over it. See Lesson 11 for more information about editing text.

Creating a New Presentation with a Template

A template is the middle ground between maximum hand-holding (the AutoContent Wizard) and no help at all (Blank Presentation). There are two kinds of templates: Presentation Templates and Presentation Design Templates:

- **Presentation Templates**   These templates offer much of the same help as the AutoContent Wizard—in fact, the AutoContent Wizard bases its presentation types on these. The templates provide a color scheme for slides and a basic outline for slide text. Their names reflect the purpose of the presentation, for example, "Communicating Bad News."

- **Presentation Design Templates**   These templates offer only a color scheme and a "look" for slides—you're on your own to provide the content for each slide.

To start a new presentation using a template, follow these steps:

1. Open the **File** menu and select **New**. The New Presentation dialog box opens (as shown in Figure 2.2).

2. If you want to use a Presentation Template, click the **Presentations** tab. If you want to use a Presentation Design, click the **Presentation Designs** tab.

3. Click on the template you want to use. You can identify the templates easily because they end with the file extension .POT. A preview of the template appears in the Preview area.

4. After you select the template you want to use, click **OK**. PowerPoint creates the new presentation based on that template.

5. If you selected a Presentation Template, you are ready to start editing the slides, just like with the AutoContent Wizard. If you selected a Presentation Design Template, you see the New Slide dialog box (see Figure 2.4). Click on the AutoLayout you want to use, and click **OK**.

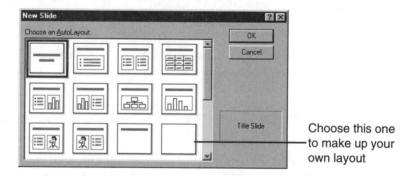

Choose this one to make up your own layout

Figure 2.4   In the New Slide dialog box, you can choose a predesigned slide layout, or you can choose to design your own.

 TIP

The Next Step?   To start customizing a Presentation Template, just click on the dummy text and type new text to replace it. You can work through the whole presentation that way—the upcoming lessons, especially Lesson 11, can help. To customize a Presentation Design Template, just add more slides by clicking on the Add Slide button at the bottom of the screen and create your presentation one slide at a time. See Lesson 9 for help.

Creating a Blank Presentation

Are you sure you want to attempt a blank presentation on your first time out? A blank presentation has no preset color scheme or design, and no dummy text to help you know what to write. To create a blank presentation, follow these steps:

1. Open the **File** menu and select **New**.

2. Click the **General** tab.

3. Double-click the **Blank Presentation** icon. The New Slide dialog box appears. (See Figure 2.4.)

4. Select the **AutoLayout** you want to use, click on it, and click **OK**.

What Next?

Now you have the basic shell of your presentation, but you need to modify and customize it. If you're not in a hurry, I suggest reading the lessons in this book in order so you can learn PowerPoint fully. However, if you're in a hurry, refer to the following lessons:

- To change the view of the presentation so you can work with it more easily, see Lesson 5, "Working with Slides in Different Views."

- To apply a different design template or slide layout, see Lesson 8, "Changing a Presentation's Look."

- To add new slides, see Lesson 9, "Inserting, Deleting, and Copying Slides."

- To rearrange slides, see Lesson 10, "Rearranging Slides in a Presentation."

- To add and edit text, see Lesson 11, "Adding Text to a Slide."

In this lesson, you learned how to create a new presentation. In the next lesson, you'll learn how to control the PowerPoint program with menus and toolbars.

Getting Around in PowerPoint

In this lesson, you learn how to get around in PowerPoint and enter commands.

A Look at PowerPoint's Application Window

If you created a new presentation using the AutoContent Wizard or a template, your screen looks something like the screen shown in Figure 3.1. This screen contains many of the same elements you find in any Windows 95 program: a title bar, window control buttons (Minimize, Maximize, and Close), and a menu bar. For an explanation of these elements, refer to Part I of this book.

In addition, you see three toolbars and a presentation window that are unique to PowerPoint. The following sections explain how to work with these unique items.

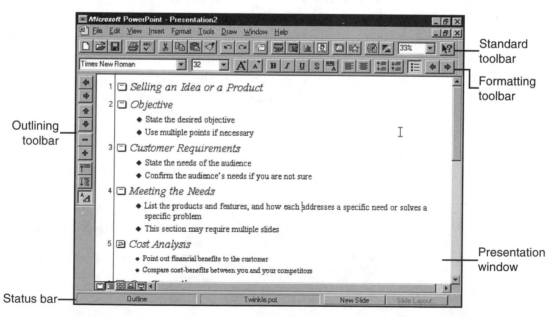

Figure 3.1   PowerPoint provides many tools for quickly entering commands.

The Presentation Window

In the center of the PowerPoint window is a presentation window. (It's probably maximized, so it flows seamlessly into the larger PowerPoint window.) You use this window to create your slides and arrange them into a presentation. At the bottom of the presentation window are several buttons that enable you to change views. Figure 3.1 shows a presentation in Outline view, whereas Figure 3.2 shows the same presentation in Slide view. For details about changing views, see Lesson 5.

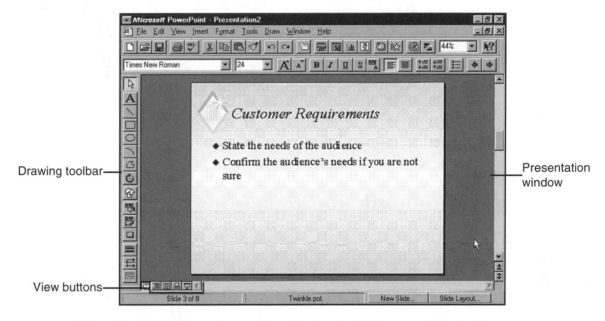

Figure 3.2   You can change views by simply clicking on a View button.

Using Shortcut Menus

Although you can enter all commands in PowerPoint using menus, PowerPoint offers a quicker way: context-sensitive *shortcut menus* like the ones in Windows 95. To use a shortcut menu, move the mouse pointer over the object you want the command to act on, and then click the right mouse button. A shortcut menu pops up (as shown in Figure 3.3), offering commands that pertain to the selected object. Click on the desired command.

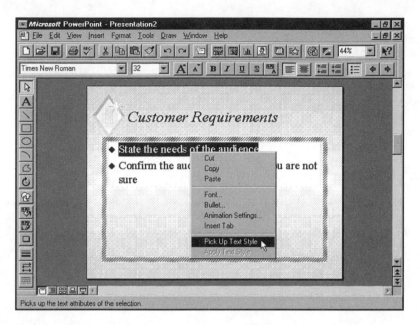

Figure 3.3 Display a shortcut menu by right-clicking on the object.

Working with Toolbars

PowerPoint displays three toolbars by default: the Standard and Formatting toolbars below the menu bar (see Figure 3.1) and the Outlining or Drawing toolbar to the left of the presentation window. (The toolbar on the left varies, depending on which view you're using.) To select a button from the toolbar, just click on the button.

Learning More About Toolbar Buttons

Although I could list and explain all the tools in the Standard toolbar and in all the other toolbars, here are some better ways to learn about the buttons for yourself:

- **To see the name of a button**, move the mouse pointer over the button. PowerPoint displays a ToolTip that provides the name of the button.

- **To learn what a button does**, move the mouse pointer over the button and look at the status bar (shown in Figure 3.1). If the button is available for the task you are currently performing, PowerPoint displays a description of what the button does.

* **To learn more about a button**, click on the **Help** button in the Standard toolbar (the button with the arrow and question mark), and then click on the button for which you want more information.

Turning Toolbars On or Off

If you never use a particular toolbar, you can turn it off to free up some screen space. In addition, you can turn on other toolbars that come with PowerPoint but don't appear automatically. To turn a toolbar on or off:

1. Right-click on any toolbar, in any area where there isn't a button. A shortcut menu appears (see Figure 3.4). A check mark appears beside each toolbar that is turned on.

2. Click on the displayed toolbar you want to hide, or click on a hidden toolbar that you want to display.

Figure 3.4   The shortcut menu for toolbars displays the names of all the toolbars.

When you click on a toolbar name on the menu, the menu disappears and that toolbar appears (if it was hidden) or the toolbar disappears (if it was displayed).

Moving Toolbars

After you have displayed the toolbars you need, you can position them in your work area wherever they are most convenient. Here's how to move a toolbar:

1. Position the mouse pointer over an area of the toolbar where there isn't a button.

2. Hold down the left mouse button, and drag the toolbar where you want it according to these guidelines:

   • Drag the toolbar to a toolbar dock. There are four docks: just below the menu bar, on the left and right sides of the application window, and just above the status bar.

   • Drag the toolbar anywhere else inside the application window to create a floating toolbar (see Figure 3.5).

3. Release the mouse button.

What About Drop-Down Lists? If a toolbar contains a drop-down list, you cannot drag it to the left or right toolbar dock.

Figure 3.5 A floating toolbar.

A floating toolbar acts just like a window. You can drag its title bar to move it or drag a border to size it. If you drag a floating toolbar to a toolbar dock, the toolbar turns back into a normal (nonfloating) toolbar.

Customizing a Toolbar To customize a toolbar, right-click on it and choose **Customize**. You can then drag a toolbar button from one toolbar to another or drag a button off a toolbar (to remove it). To add a button, select a feature category from the Categories list in the dialog box, and then drag the desired button to any of the toolbars.

In this lesson, you learned about the PowerPoint application and presentation windows, and you learned how to enter commands with shortcut menus and toolbars. In the next lesson, you learn how to use the PowerPoint Help system.

Getting Help

In this lesson, you'll learn about the various types of help available to you in PowerPoint.

Help: What's Available?

Because every person is different, PowerPoint offers many different ways to get help with the program. You can use any of these methods to get help:

- Click the **Help** button on the Standard toolbar, and then click on the object you need help with.

- Choose what you're interested in learning about from a series of Help Topics from the Help menu.

- Use the Answer Wizard to enter your question in plain English and see a demonstration on how to use a feature.

- Press **F1** to get context-sensitive help (i.e. help that changes depending on what you're doing).

- Learn tricks and tips along the way with the Tip Wizard.

 Just Like Windows   PowerPoint's Help system is based on the Windows 95 Help system. Review Lesson 5 in the Windows section of this book for a quick refresher.

Getting Help with Screen Elements

If you wonder what a particular button or tool on the screen is used for, wonder no more. Just follow these steps:

1. Click the **Help** button on the Standard toolbar.

2. Click on the screen element for which you want help. A box appears explaining the element (see Figure 4.1).

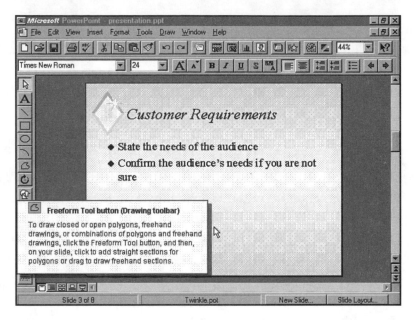

Figure 4.1 To get help on a screen element, click the Help button, and then click the element.

Using the PowerPoint Help Topics

A more conventional way to get help is through the Help menu. When you open the PowerPoint Help system, you move through the topics listed to find the topic you're interested in.

There are several tabs in the Help system, so you can use Help the way you want. To access the Help system:

1. Select **Help, Microsoft PowerPoint Help Topics**.

2. Click on the tab for the type of help you want.

3. Click on the topic you're interested in, if there's a list, or type in your topic and press **Enter**.

Three of the four tabs you will see in the Help window will be familiar to you: Context, Index, and Find. These are present in Windows 95 itself. Refer to Lesson 5 in the Windows section of this book for a full explanation of each of these three tabs. The fourth tab, which doesn't appear in Windows itself, is the Answer Wizard. It is explained in the following section.

The Answer Wizard

The Answer Wizard is a tab in the Help Topics dialog box, but you can also access it in other ways: you can select it directly from the Help menu, or you can press F1 (as explained in the next section). The Answer Wizard provides help based on plain-English questions you type in. You enter a question and the Answer Wizard actually shows you how to perform the task.

Follow these steps to use the Answer Wizard:

1. Select **Help**, **Microsoft PowerPoint Help Topics**.

2. Click on the **Answer Wizard** tab.

3. Type what you want to do in the top box, and then click the **Search** button.

4. In the bottom box, double-click on the topic that appears that matches your interest (see Figure 4.2).

5. Depending on the topic, normal Help text may appear, or a dialog box may appear telling you that the Answer Wizard will show you how to perform the procedure. If you get a dialog box, click **Next**.

6. Watch as the Answer Wizard shows you how to perform the task.

When the Answer Wizard is showing you something (step 6), it'll be like someone else is controlling your mouse and keyboard; menus open and commands execute automatically, for example. Just watch and learn.

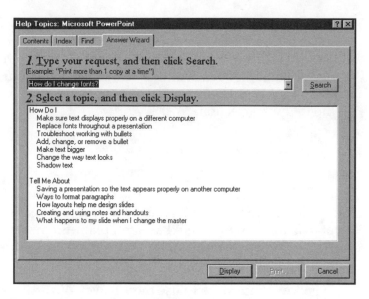

Figure 4.2   The Answer Wizard lets you ask questions in your own words.

F1 for Help

Pressing F1 for help is an old standby in Windows programs, and it still works. When you press F1, the Answer Wizard appears with what it thinks you're doing already typed in as a question. You can modify the question if it's not exactly what you want to ask, or just click Search to accept it. See the previous section about the Answer Wizard for more information.

Extra Help with the Tip of the Day

Some people cram for exams, while others prefer to learn more casually, soaking up little facts here and there as they work. For the casual learner, the Tip of the Day feature provides a great way to learn little extras about PowerPoint.

When you start PowerPoint, the Tip of the Day box appears automatically. You just click OK to remove it. If you want to see another tip later, you can make the box reappear by following these steps:

1. Select **Help, Tip of the Day**.

2. Read the tip.

3. To read another tip, click **Next Tip**.

4. To review tips you've read before, click **Previous Tip**.

5. (Optional) To prevent the Tip of the Day box from appearing at startup, deselect the **Show Tips at Startup** check box.

6. When you finish viewing tips, click **OK**.

In this lesson, you learned about the many ways that PowerPoint offers help. In the next lesson, you'll learn about the different views PowerPoint offers for working with your presentation.

Working with Slides in Different Views

In this lesson, you will learn how to display a presentation in different views, and to edit slides in Outline and Slide views.

Changing Views

PowerPoint can display your presentation in different views. Having the option of selecting a view makes it easier to perform certain tasks. For example, Outline view shows the overall organization of the presentation, whereas Slide Sorter view enables you to quickly rearrange the slides. Figure 5.1 shows the available views.

To change views, open the **View** menu and choose the desired view: **Slides**, **Outline**, **Slide Sorter**, or **Notes Pages**. A quicker way to switch views is to click the button for the desired view at the bottom of the presentation window, as shown in Figure 5.2.

Outline to Slide View   If you're using Outline view, you can quickly display a slide in Slide view by double-clicking on the desired slide icon in the outline.

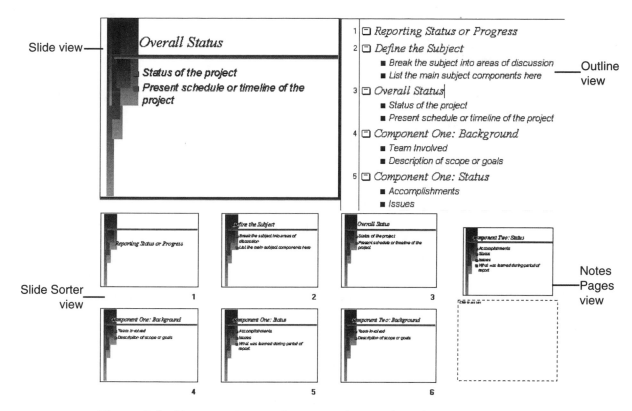

Figure 5.1   You can change views to make a task easier.

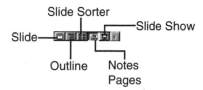

Figure 5.2   Use these buttons to change views.

What About the Slide Show Button? The Slide Show button enables you to view your presentation as a timed slide show. For details, see Lesson 18.

Moving from Slide to Slide

When you have more than one slide in your presentation, you will need to move from one slide to the next in order to work with a specific slide. The procedure for selecting a slide depends on which view you are currently using:

- In Outline view, use the scroll bar to display the slide you want to work with. Click on the **Slide** icon (the icon to the left of the slide's title) to select the slide, or click anywhere inside the text to edit it.

- In Slide view, click on the **Previous Slide** or **Next Slide** button just below the vertical scroll bar (as shown in Figure 5.3), or drag the box inside the scroll bar until the desired slide number is displayed.

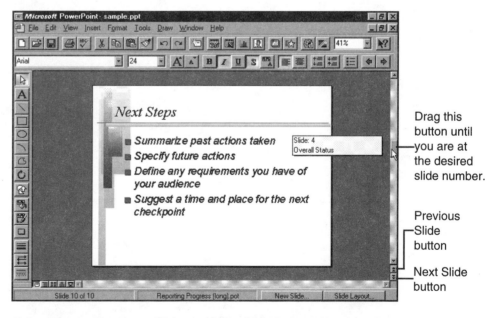

Figure 5.3 Use the Previous Slide and Next Slide buttons to move between slides in Slide or Notes Pages view.

- In Slide Sorter view, click on the desired slide. A thick border appears around the selected slide.

- In Notes Pages view, click on the **Previous Slide** or **Next Slide** button, or drag the box inside the scroll bar until the desired slide number is displayed.

Editing Slides

If you created a presentation in Lesson 2 using the AutoContent Wizard or a template, you already have several slides, but they may not contain the text you want to use. If you created a blank presentation, you have one slide on the screen that you can edit.

In the following sections, you will learn the basics of how to edit text in Outline and Slide views. In later lessons, you will learn how to add and edit text objects, pictures, graphs, organizational charts, and other items.

Object   An object is any item on a slide, including text, graphics, and charts.

Editing in Outline View

Outline view (see Figure 5.4) provides the easiest way to edit text. You simply click to move the insertion point where you want it, and then type in your text. Press the **Del** key to delete characters to the right of the insertion point or the **Backspace** key to delete characters to the left.

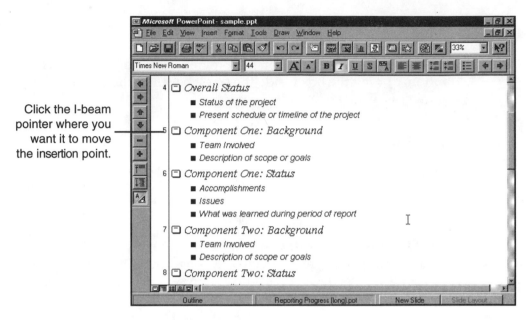

Click the I-beam pointer where you want it to move the insertion point.

Figure 5.4   Switch to Outline view to edit text.

To select text, hold down the left mouse button and drag the mouse pointer over the desired text. You can then press the Del or Backspace key to delete the text, or you can drag the text where you want to move it.

Auto Word Select   When you select text, PowerPoint selects whole words. If you want to select individual characters, open the **Tools** menu, select **Options**, click the **Edit** tab, and select **Automatic Word Selection** to turn it off. Click the **OK** button.

Editing in Slide View

Slide view provides an easy way to edit all objects on a slide, including text and graphic objects. As shown in Figure 5.5, you can edit an object by clicking or double-clicking it. For a text object, click on the object to select it, and then click where you want the insertion point moved. For a graphic object, double-click it to bring up a set of tools that will help you edit it.

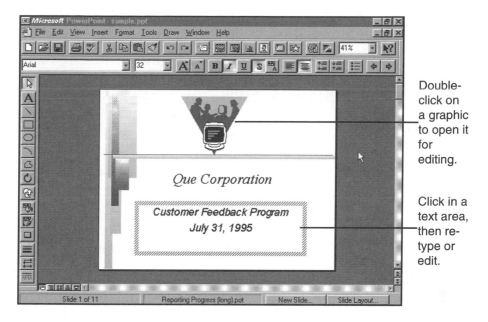

Double-click on a graphic to open it for editing.

Click in a text area, then re-type or edit.

Figure 5.5 Slide view enables you to edit both text and graphic objects.

Working with a Bulleted List

The bulleted list is a powerful tool that helps you organize and present ideas and supporting data for your presentation. As you type entries, keep in mind that you can change an entry's level and position in the list. To change the position or level of an entry (in Outline view), use the arrow keys or mouse to place the insertion point anywhere inside the entry, and then perform one of the following actions:

Click on this button to move the entry up in the list.

Click on this button to move the entry down in the list.

Click on this button to indent the entry to the next lower level in the list. (When you do, the item is indented, the bullet style changes, and the text usually appears smaller.)

Click on this button to remove the indent and move the entry to the next higher level in the list. (When you do, the item is moved to the left, the bullet style changes, and the text appears larger.)

Dragging Paragraphs You can quickly change the position or level of a paragraph by dragging it up, down, left, or right. To drag a paragraph, move the mouse pointer to the left side of the paragraph until it turns into a four-headed arrow. Then hold down the left mouse button and drag the paragraph to the desired position.

In Lesson 12, you will learn how to change the appearance of the bullet, and the size and formatting of text for each entry, as well as how much the text is indented for each level.

In this lesson, you learned how to change views for a presentation, move from slide to slide, and edit text. In the next lesson, you'll learn how to save, close, and open a presentation.

Saving, Closing, and Opening a Presentation

In this lesson, you will learn how to save a presentation to disk, close a presentation, and open an existing presentation.

Saving a Presentation

Soon after creating a presentation, you should save it in a file on disk to protect the work you have already done. To save a presentation for the first time, follow these steps:

1. Select **File**, **Save**, or press **Ctrl+S**, or click the **Save** button on the Standard toolbar. The File Save dialog box appears (see Figure 6.1).

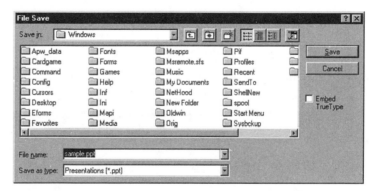

Figure 6.1 The File Save dialog box.

2. In the File name text box, type the name you want to assign to the presentation. Do not type a file extension; PowerPoint automatically adds the extension .PPT.

New Name Possibilities Because Powerpoint 7.0 is a Windows 95 application, you are not limited to the old 8-character file names. Your file names can be as long as you like (within reason—the limit is 255 characters) and can include spaces.

3. The Save In box shows which folder the file will be saved in. If you want to save to a different drive or folder, see the next section in this lesson. Otherwise, continue to step 4.

4. Click **Save**.

Now that you have named the file and saved it to a disk, you can save any changes you make simply by pressing **Ctrl+S** or clicking the **Save** button on the Standard toolbar. Your data is saved under the file name you assigned.

To create a copy of a presentation under a different name, select **File, Save As**. Use the Save As dialog box in the same way you use the File Save dialog box shown in Figure 6.1.

Changing the Drive or Folder

The dialog boxes for opening and saving files in Windows 95 are different from the ones in Windows 3.1. The File Save and File Open dialog boxes take a bit of getting used to. Figures 6.1 and 6.2 show the dialog boxes; Table 6.1 explains the buttons and other controls you see in them.

Table 6.1 Buttons for Changing Drives and Folders in Windows 95 Dialog Boxes

Control	Purpose
Powerpnt	Shows every drive your computer has access to, plus your Network Neighborhood and Briefcase. Use this button to choose a different drive.
	Moves to the folder "above" the one shown in the Save In box (that is, the folder in which the current one resides).
	Shows the C:\WINDOWS\FAVORITES folder, no matter which folder was displayed before.

	Creates a new folder.
	Shows the folders and files in the currently displayed folder list.
	Shows details about each file and folder.
	Shows the properties of each file and folder.
	Opens a dialog box of settings you can change that affect the dialog box.
	(Appears in File Open dialog box only.) Switches to Preview view, in which you can see the first slide of a presentation before you open it.

Closing a Presentation

You can close a presentation at any time. Note that although this closes the presentation window, it does not exit PowerPoint. To close a presentation, follow these steps:

1. If more than one presentation is open, open the Window menu and select the one you want to close.

2. Select **File, Close**, or press **Ctrl+F4**. If you have not saved the presentation, or if you haven't saved since you made changes, a dialog box appears asking if you want to save.

3. To save your changes, click **Yes**. If this is a new presentation, refer to the steps earlier in this lesson for saving a presentation. If you have saved the file previously, the presentation window closes.

Opening a Presentation

Once you save a presentation to a disk, you can open the presentation and continue working on it at any time. Follow these steps:

 1. Select **File, Open**, or press **Ctrl+O**, or click the **Open** button on the Standard toolbar. The File Open dialog box appears.

2. If the file isn't in the currently displayed folder, change drives and/or folders. Refer to "Changing the Drive or Folder" earlier in this lesson.

3. Double-click on the file to open it.

Finding a Presentation File

If you're having trouble locating your file, PowerPoint can help you look. Follow these steps to find a file.

1. Select **File, Open** if the File Open dialog box is not already open.

2. In the File name box at the bottom of the dialog box, type the name of the file you're looking for.

Wild Cards You can use wild cards if you don't know the entire name of a file. The asterisk wild-card character stands in for any character or set of characters, and the question mark wild-card character stands in for any single character. For instance, if you know the file begins with P, you could type P*.ppt to find all PowerPoint files that begin with P.

3. (Optional) If desired, enter other search criteria:

   - If you're looking for a different file type, choose it from the Files of type drop-down list.

   - If you're looking for a file containing certain text, type it in the Text or property box.

   - If you know when you last modified the file, choose the time interval from the Last modified drop-down list.

4. Click the **Advanced** button. The Advanced Find dialog box appears (see Figure 6.2).

5. In the Look in section at the bottom of the Advanced Find dialog box, narrow down the search area as much as possible using these techniques:

   - If you are sure the file is in a certain folder, type that folder's path (such as C:\WINDOWS) in the Look in box.

- If you are sure the file is on a certain drive, select it from the Look in drop-down list.

- If you don't know which drive contains the file, select **My Computer** from the Look in drop-down list.

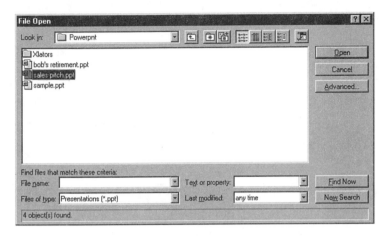

Figure 6.2   Use the Advanced Find dialog box to select the folders and drives you want to search.

6. Make sure the **Search Subfolders** check box is marked. If it isn't, click on it.

7. Click the **Find Now** button. The File Open dialog box reappears and displays the files that match your search criteria.

8. Double-click on the desired file to open it.

More Search Options   As you may have noticed in Figure 6.2, there are a lot more complex search options available—too many to cover here. See your PowerPoint documentation for more details.

In this lesson, you learned how to save, close, open, and find presentations. In the next lesson, you will learn how to print a presentation.

Printing Presentations, Notes, and Handouts

In this lesson, you learn how to select a size and orientation for the slides in your presentation and how to print the slides, notes, and handouts you create.

Quick Printing—No Options

The quickest way to print is to use all the default settings. You don't get to make any decisions about your output, but you do get your printout without delay.

To print a quick copy, follow either of these steps:

- Click the **Print** button on the Standard toolbar.

- Select **File**, **Print**, and click the **OK** button.

When you use either of these methods for printing, you get a printout of your entire presentation in whatever view is on-screen. The following list describes what type of printout you can expect from each view.

- Slide view: The entire presentation prints in Landscape orientation with one slide per page. Each slide fills an entire page.

- Outline view: The entire outline prints in Portrait orientation.

- Slide Sorter view: The entire presentation prints in Portrait orientation with six slides per page.

- Notes Pages view: The entire presentation prints in Portrait orientation with one slide per page. Each slide prints with its notes beneath it.

Orientation   The orientation setting tells the printer which edge of the paper should be at the "top" of the printout. If the top is across the wide edge, it's Landscape; if the top is across the narrow edge, it's Portrait.

Changing the Slide Setup

If you didn't get the printouts you expected from the previous procedures, you can change the selected presentation output, size, and orientation of the presentation in the Slide Setup dialog box. To customize your printouts, follow these steps:

1. Select **File, Slide Setup**. The Slide Setup dialog box appears on-screen, as shown in Figure 7.1.

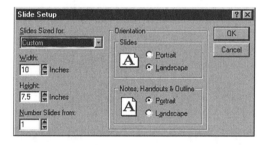

Figure 7.1   The Slide Setup dialog box enables you to set the position and size of the slides.

2. Perform one of the following procedures to set the slide size:

   - To use a standard size, select a size from the **Slides Sized for** drop-down list. For example, you can have slides sized for regular 8.5 × 11 paper, 35mm slides, or an on-screen slide show.

   - To create a custom size, enter the dimensions in the **Width** and **Height** text boxes.

Spin Boxes   The arrows to the right of the Width and Height text boxes enable you to adjust the settings in those boxes. Click on the up arrow to increase the setting by .1 inch, or on the down arrow to decrease it by .1 inch.

385

3. In the Number Slides from text box, type the number with which you want to start numbering slides. (This is usually 1, but you may want to start with a different number if the presentation is a continuation of another.)

4. Under the Slides heading, choose **Portrait** or **Landscape** orientation for your slides.

5. In the Notes, Handouts & Outline section, choose **Portrait** or **Landscape** for those items.

Can I Print Notes and Handouts Differently? If you want your notes printed in portrait orientation and your handouts printed in landscape orientation, just choose **Portrait** from the Notes, Handouts & Outline section of the Slide Setup dialog box and print the notes. Then, before you print the handouts, go back to this dialog box and choose **Landscape** from the Notes, Handouts & Outline section.

6. Click **OK**. If you changed the orientation of your slides, you may have to wait a moment while PowerPoint repositions the slides.

Choosing What and How to Print

If the default print options don't suit you, you can change them. Do you have more than one printer? If so, you can choose which printer to use. For example, you may want to use a color printer for overhead transparencies and a black-and-white printer for your handouts. You can also select options for printing multiple copies and for printing specific slides only.

To set your print options, follow these steps, and then print.

1. Select **File**, **Print**. The Print dialog box appears, with the name of the currently selected printer in the Name box (Figure 7.2).

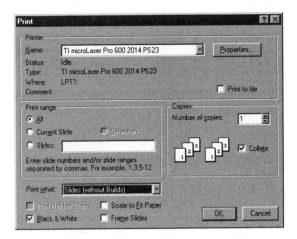

Figure 7.2   Choose your printing options in the Print dialog box.

2. If you want to use a printer different from the one that appears, open the Name drop-down list and select a different printer.

Printer Properties   To make adjustments to your printer's settings, click on the **Properties** button in the Print dialog box. The adjustments you can make vary from printer to printer, but you should be able to adjust graphics quality, select paper size, and choose which paper tray to use, among other things.

3. Choose what to print in the Print Range section:

   • Choose **All** to print all the slides in the presentation.

   • Choose **Current Slide** to print only the currently displayed slide.

   • Enter a range of slide numbers in the Slides text box—for example, **2-4** to print slides 2, 3, and 4.

4. Open the **Print what** drop-down list and choose what you want to print. You can print slides, handouts, notes, or outlines.

5. If you want more than one copy, enter the number of copies you want in the **Number of copies** box.

6. Select or deselect any of these check boxes in the dialog box as desired:

Print Hidden Slides   If you have any hidden slides, you can choose whether to print them or not. If you don't have any hidden slides, this check box will be unavailable. You'll learn about hidden slides in Lesson 10.

Black & White   If you have a black-and-white printer, select this check box to make the color slides print more crisply. You can also select this check box to force a color printer to produce black and white output.

Scale to Fit Paper   If the slide (or whatever you're printing) is too large to fit on the page, select this check box to decrease the size of the slide to make it fit on the page. Now you won't have to paste two pieces of paper together to see the whole slide.

Frame Slides   Select this check box if you want to print a border around each slide.

Collate   If you are printing more than one copy, select this check box to collate (1, 2, 3, 1, 2, 3) each printed copy instead of printing all the copies of each page at once (1, 1, 2, 2, 3, 3).

Print to File   Select this option to send the output to a file rather than to your printer.

Why Would I Print to File?   If you don't have the printer that you want to use hooked up to your computer, you can print to a file, and then take that file to the computer where the printer is. The other computer does not need to have PowerPoint installed on it in order to print PowerPoint documents.

7. Click **OK** to print.

In this lesson, you learned how to print slides, outlines, and notes, and how to set options for your printouts. In the next lesson, you will learn how to change the overall appearance of the slides in a presentation.

Changing a Presentation's Look

In this lesson, you will learn various ways to give your presentation a professional and consistent look.

Giving Your Slides a Professional Look

PowerPoint comes with 150 professionally designed slides you can use as *templates* for your own presentations. That is, you can apply one of these predesigned slides to an already existing presentation to give the slides in your presentation a professional look.

Template   A template is a predesigned slide that comes with PowerPoint. When you select a template, PowerPoint applies the color scheme and general layout of the slide to each slide in the presentation.

There's another way to make global changes to the entire presentation: you can alter the Slide Master. The Slide Master is not really a slide, but it looks like one. It's a design grid that you make changes on; these changes affect every slide in the presentation. For instance, if you want a graphic to appear on every slide, you can place it on the Slide Master instead of pasting it onto each slide individually. When you apply a template, you are actually applying that template to the Slide Master, which in turn applies the template's formatting to each slide.

Changing the Colors on a Single Slide   If you want to make some slides in the presentation look different from the others, you're in the wrong lesson.

Applying a Presentation Design Template

You can apply a different template to your presentation at any time, no matter how you originally create your presentation. To change the template, follow these steps:

1. Choose **Format, Apply Design Template**. The Apply Design Template dialog box appears (Figure 8.1).

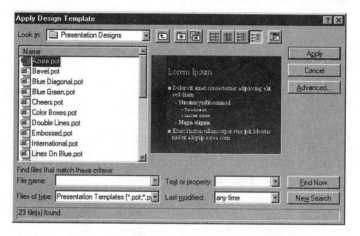

Figure 8.1 Choose a different template from the Apply Design Template dialog box.

 TIP **Faster Templates**   To bypass the Format menu, click on the **Apply Design Template** button on the Standard toolbar.

2. Click on a template name in the Name list. A sample of it appears to the right of the list.

3. When you find a template you want to use, click **Apply**.

Using AutoLayouts

While templates enable you to change the color and design of a presentation, AutoLayouts enable you to set the structure of a single slide in a presentation. For example, if you want a graph and a picture on a slide, you can choose an AutoLayout that positions the two items for you.

Individual Slides?   PowerPoint applies AutoLayouts to individual slides, but the template you choose and the Master Layout modifications you make affect the AutoLayouts. This will become more evident later in this lesson.

To use an AutoLayout, do the following:

1. In Slide view, display the slide you want to change.

2. Select **Format, Slide Layout**. The Slide Layout dialog box appears (see Figure 8.2).

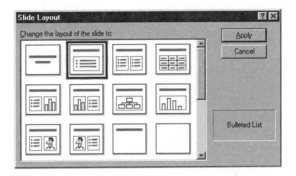

Figure 8.2   You can change an individual slide's layout with this dialog box.

Right-Click   A quick way to display the Slide Layout dialog box is to right-click on the slide in Slide view and select **Slide Layout**.

3. Click on the desired layout, or use the arrow keys to move the selection border to it.

4. Click on the **Apply** button. PowerPoint applies the selected layout to the current slide.

Editing the Slide Master

Every presentation has a Slide Master that controls the overall appearance and layout of each slide. The Slide Master contains all the formatting information that the template brings to the presentation, such as colors and background patterns, and it also marks where the elements you use from the AutoLayout feature will appear on the slide.

To make changes to the Slide Master for your presentation, follow these steps:

1. Select **View**, **Master**, **Slide Master**. Your Slide Master appears, as in Figure 8.3.

Click any of these buttons to exit the Slide Master.

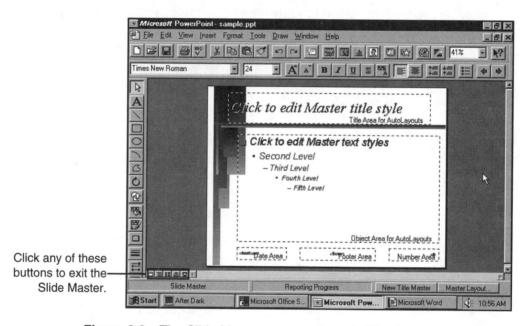

Figure 8.3 The Slide Master ensures that all slides in a presentation have a consistent look.

2. Make any changes to the Slide Master, as you'll learn in upcoming lessons in this book. (Anything you can do to a regular slide, you can do to a Slide Master.)

3. When you're done working with the Slide Master, click any of the view buttons at the bottom left corner of the screen to switch to any other view.

The two most important elements on the Slide Master are the Title Area and Object Area for the AutoLayout objects. The Title Area contains the formatting specifications for each slide's title; that is, it tells PowerPoint the type size, style, and color to use for the text in the title of each slide. The Object Area contains the formatting specifications for all remaining text on the slide.

For most of PowerPoint's templates the Object Area sets up specifications for a bulleted list, including the type of bullet, as well as the type styles, sizes, and indents for each item in the list.

In addition to the Title and Object Areas, the Slide Master can contain information about background colors, borders, page numbers, company logos, clip art objects, and any other elements you want to appear on *every* slide in the presentation.

The Slide Master is like any slide. In the following lessons, when you learn how to add text, graphics, borders, and other objects to a slide, keep in mind that you can add these objects on individual slides or on the Slide Master. When you add the objects to the Slide Master, the objects will appear on *every* slide in the presentation.

In this lesson, you learned how to give your presentation a consistent look with templates and AutoLayouts. You also learned how to use the Slide Master to make global changes to your slides. In the next lesson, you will learn how to insert, delete, and copy slides.

Inserting, Deleting, and Copying Slides

In this lesson, you will learn how to insert new slides, delete slides, and copy slides in a presentation.

Inserting a Slide

You can insert a slide into a presentation at any time and at any position in the presentation. To insert a slide, follow these steps:

1. Select the slide that appears just before the place where you want to insert the new slide. (You can select the slide in any view: Outline, Slides, Slide Sorter, or Notes Pages.)

2. Select **Insert**, **New Slide**, or press **Ctrl+M**. In Outline view, PowerPoint inserts a blank slide, allowing you to type in a title and bulleted list. In all other views, the New Slide dialog box appears (see Figure 9.1).

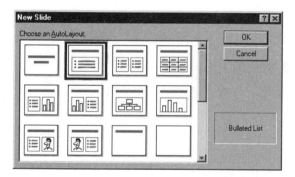

Figure 9.1 In the New Slide dialog box, you can choose a layout for the slide you're inserting.

New Slide Button   Instead of selecting the Insert, New Slide command, you can click on the **New Slide** button on the status bar or the **Insert New Slide** button on the Standard toolbar to insert a new slide.

3. In the **Choose an AutoLayout** list, click on a slide layout, or use the arrow keys to highlight it.

4. Click on the **OK** button. PowerPoint inserts a slide that has the specified layout. See Figure 9.2.

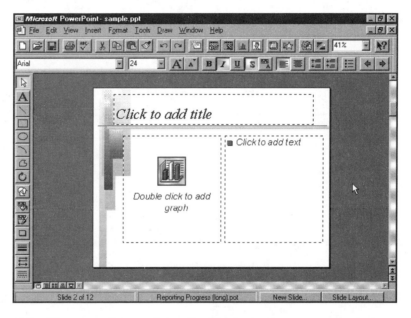

Figure 9.2   The new slide contains the blank structure you selected; you supply the content.

5. Follow the directions indicated on the slide layout to add text or other objects. In most cases, you click on an object to select it and then you type in your text.

Cloning a Slide To create an exact replica of a slide (in Outline or Slide Sorter view), select the slide you want to duplicate. Then select **Edit**, **Duplicate**, or press **Ctrl+D**. The new slide is inserted after the original slide. You can move the slide anywhere you want, as you'll learn in Lesson 10.

Adding Slides from Another Presentation

If you want to insert all the slides from another presentation into the current presentation, perform these steps:

1. Open the presentation into which you want to insert the slides.

2. Select the slide located before the position where you want to insert the slides.

3. Select **Insert**, **Slides from File**. The Insert File dialog box appears.

4. Change the drive and/or folder if needed. (Refer to the section "Changing the Drive or Folder" in Lesson 6.)

5. Double-click on the name of the presentation that contains the slides you want to insert into the open presentation. PowerPoint inserts the slides after the currently selected slide. The new slides take on the color and style of the current presentation.

I Just Wanted One Slide! Unfortunately, you cannot insert just one slide from one presentation into another. However, you can open a presentation and copy a slide using **Edit**, **Copy**, then paste the slide into another presentation using **Edit**, **Paste**. You learn how to select slides for copying later in this lesson.

Creating Slides from a Document Outline

If you have a word-processing document with outline-style headings in it, PowerPoint can pull the headings from the document and use the headings to create slides with bulleted lists. To create slides from a document outline:

1. Select **Insert, Slides from Outline**.

2. Use the Insert Outline dialog box to locate the document file you want to use.

3. Double-click on the name of the document file.

Selecting Slides

In the following sections, you learn to delete, copy, and move slides. However, before you can do anything with a slide, you have to select the slide. To select slides, follow these directions:

- To select a single slide, click on it. (In Slide or Notes Pages view, the currently displayed slide is selected; you don't have to click on it.)

- To select two or more neighboring slides (in Outline view only), click on the first slide, and then hold down the Ctrl and Shift keys while clicking on the last slide in the group.

- To select two or more non-neighboring slides (in Outline or Slide Sorter view), hold down the Shift key while clicking on each slide.

Can I Select Neighboring Slides in Slide Sorter View? Yes, you can. Just use the same procedure for selecting non-neighboring slides.

Deleting Slides

You can delete a slide from any view. To delete a slide, perform the following steps:

1. Display the slide you want to delete (in Slide or Notes Pages view), or select the slide (in Outline or Slide Sorter view). You can delete multiple slides by displaying or selecting more than one slide.

2. Select **Edit, Delete Slide**. The slide disappears.

Quicker Deleting   In Outline or Slide Sorter view, you can just select the slides you want to delete and press the **Delete** key on the keyboard.

Oops! If you deleted a slide by mistake, you can get it back by selecting **Edit, Undo,** or by clicking on the **Undo** button on the Standard toolbar.

Cutting, Copying, and Pasting Slides

In Lesson 10, you will learn how to rearrange slides in Slide Sorter and Outline views. However, you can also use the cut, copy, and paste features to copy and move slides into other presentations. To cut (or copy) a slide and paste it in a presentation, perform the following steps:

1. Change to Slide Sorter or Outline view.

2. Select the slide(s) you want to copy or cut.

3. Open the **Edit** menu, and select **Cut** or **Copy** to either move or copy the slide(s) to the Windows Clipboard.

Windows Clipboard The Windows Clipboard is a temporary holding area for cut or copied items. You can cut or copy items to the Clipboard and then paste them on a slide.

Quick Cut or Copy To bypass the Edit menu, press **Ctrl+C** to copy or **Ctrl+X** to cut, or click on the **Cut** or **Copy** button on the Standard toolbar.

4. If you want to paste the slide(s) into a different presentation, open that presentation.

5. In Slide Sorter view, select the slide after which you want to place the cut or copied slide(s). In Outline view, move the insertion point to the end of the text in the slide after which you want to insert the cut or copied slide(s).

6. Select **Edit, Paste** or press **Ctrl+V**. (You can also click on the **Paste** button on the Standard toolbar.) PowerPoint inserts the cut or copied slides.

Dragging and Dropping Slides

A quick way to move or copy a slide is to use the Drag and Drop feature. Follow these steps to drag and drop slides:

1. Change to Slide Sorter or Outline view.

2. Click on the slide you want to move or copy, and leave the mouse pointer pointing to the slide.

3. To move the slide, hold down the mouse button and drag the slide to the desired position, as shown in Figure 9.3. To copy the slide, hold down the mouse button and the Ctrl key, and drag the slide to the desired position. (If you don't hold down the Ctrl key, PowerPoint moves the slide rather than copying it.)

Drag the slide to the desired location before or after another slide.

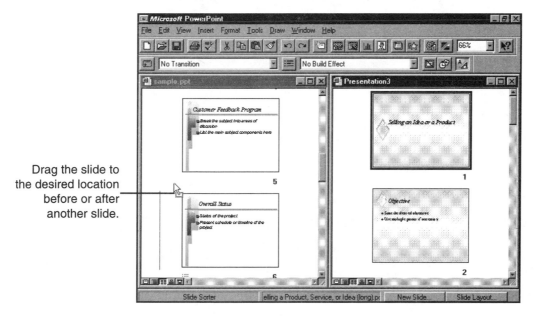

Figure 9.3   You can drag and drop a slide within a presentation or from one presentation to another.

4. Release the mouse button (and the Ctrl key, if you were holding it down) to drop the slide.

Dragging and Dropping Between Presentations   You can drag and drop slides from one presentation to another. Open both presentations (see Lesson 6 for instructions on how to open presentations). Then select **Window, Arrange All**. The two windows appear side-by-side. Change to Slide Sorter view in each window. You can now drag and drop slides from one window to the other.

In this lesson, you learned how to insert, delete, cut, copy, and paste slides. In the next lesson, you will learn how to rearrange the slides in your presentation.

Rearranging Slides in a Presentation

In this lesson, you will learn how to rearrange your slides.

There will be times when you need to change the sequence of slides in a presentation. PowerPoint gives you the ability to reorder slides in either Slide Sorter view or Outline view.

Rearranging Slides in Slide Sorter View

Slide Sorter view shows miniature versions of the slides in your presentation. This enables you to view many of your slides at one time. To rearrange slides in Slide Sorter view, perform the following steps:

1. Switch to Slide Sorter view by selecting **View**, **Slide Sorter**, or clicking the **Slide Sorter** button on the status bar.

2. Move the mouse pointer over the slide you want to move.

3. Hold down the left mouse button, and drag the mouse pointer over the slide before or after which you want to insert the slide. As you drag the mouse pointer, a line appears (see Figure 10.1), showing where you are moving the slide.

4. Release the mouse button. PowerPoint places the slide in its new position and shifts the surrounding slides to make room for the new slide.

Copying a Slide   You can copy a slide in Slide Sorter view as easily as you can move a slide. Simply hold down the Ctrl key while you drag the slide.

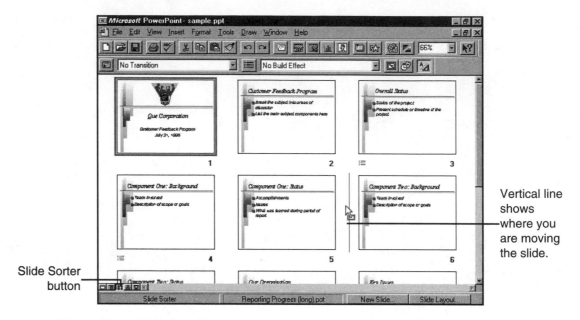

Slide Sorter button

Vertical line shows where you are moving the slide.

Figure 10.1 Switch to Slide Sorter view.

Rearranging Slides in Outline View

In Outline view, you see the titles and text on each slide. This view gives you a clearer picture of the content and organization of your presentation than in Slide Sorter view, so you may prefer to rearrange your slides in Outline view. Here's how you do it:

1. Switch to Outline view by selecting **View**, **Outline** or clicking on the **Outline** button.

2. Click on the slide number or slide icon to the left of the slide you want to move. This action highlights the contents of the entire slide.

Moving the Contents of a Slide If you just want to insert some of the information from a slide into your presentation, you don't have to move the entire slide. You can move only the slide's data—text and graphics—from one slide to another by selecting only what you want to move and dragging it to its new location.

3. Move the mouse pointer over the selected slide icon, hold down the mouse button, and drag the slide up or down in the outline, or click on the **Move Up** or **Move Down** buttons on the Outlining toolbar, as shown in Figure 10.2.

4. Release the mouse button when the slide is at the desired new position. Be careful not to drop the slide in the middle of another slide! If you do, just select **Edit**, **Undo** and try again.

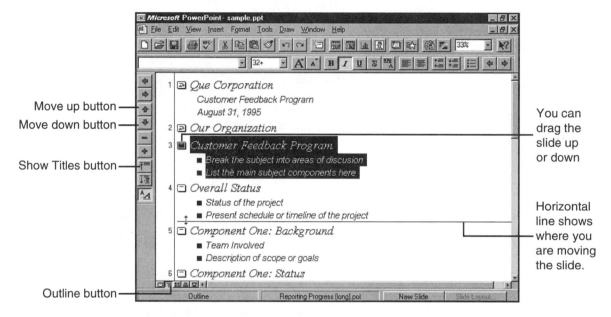

Figure 10.2   Drag the selected icon, or click on the Move Up or Move Down button.

Collapsing the Outline   You can *collapse* the outline to show only the slide titles. This allows you to view more slides at one time and rearrange the slides more easily. To collapse the outline, click on the **Show Titles** button on the Outlining toolbar (refer to Figure 10.2). To restore the outline, click on the **Show All** button.

Hiding Slides

Before you give a presentation, you should try to anticipate any questions that your audience may have and be prepared to answer those questions. You may even want to create slides to support your answers to these questions and then keep the slides hidden until you need them. To hide one or more slides, perform the following steps:

1. Display or select the slide(s) you want to hide. (You can hide slides in Slide, Outline, or Slide Sorter view.)

2. Select **Tools, Hide Slide**. If you are in Slide Sorter view, the hidden slide's number appears in a box with a line through it.

3. To unhide the slide(s), display or select the hidden slide(s), select **Tools, Hide Slide** again.

Printing Hidden Slides?   In Lesson 7, you learned about the Print Hidden Slides check box in the Print dialog box. Select this check box when printing to print the hidden slides.

In this lesson, you learned how to rearrange the slides in a presentation in either the Slide Sorter or Outline view, and how to hide slides. In the next lesson, you will learn how add text to a slide.

Adding Text
to a Slide

In this lesson, you will learn how to add text to a slide, change the text alignment and line spacing, and transform text into a bulleted list.

Creating a Text Box

If the only text you need in your presentation is the title and a bulleted list, you can add text simply by typing it in Outline or Slide view. However, if you want to type additional text on the slide, you must first create a text box.

Text Box   A text box in PowerPoint acts as a receptacle for the text. Text boxes often contain bulleted lists, notes, and labels (used to point to important parts of illustrations).

To create a text box, perform the following steps:

1. Switch to Slide view or Slide Sorter view. (Refer to Lesson 5 for help with views.)

2. Click on the **Text** button on the Drawing toolbar.

3. Move the mouse pointer to where you want the upper left corner of the box to appear.

4. Hold down the left mouse button and drag the mouse pointer to the right until the box is the desired width.

5. Release the mouse button. A one-line text box appears. (See Figure 11.1.)

Figure 11.1   The text box appears with a blinking insertion point inside.

6. Type the text that you want to appear in the text box. When you reach the right side of the box, PowerPoint wraps the text to the next line and makes the box one line deeper. To start a new paragraph, press **Enter**.

7. Click anywhere outside the text box.

Framing a Text Box   The border that appears around a text box when you create or select it will not appear on the printed slide. To add a border that *does* print, see Lesson 17.

Selecting, Deleting, and Moving a Text Box

If you go back and click anywhere inside the text box, a *selection box* appears around it. If you click on the selection box border, handles appear around the text box, as shown in Figure 11.2. You can drag the box's border to move the box, or drag a handle (as shown) to resize it. PowerPoint wraps the text automatically as needed to fit inside the box. To delete a text box, select it (so handles appear around it), and then press the **Delete** key.

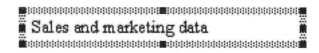

Figure 11.2   Click on the selection box border to display handles.

Editing Text in a Text Box

To edit text in a text box, first click anywhere inside the text box to select it; then, perform any of the following steps:

- To select text, drag the I-beam pointer over the text you want to select. (To select a single word, double-click on it. To select an entire sentence, triple-click.)

TIP   **Auto Word Select**   When you drag over text, PowerPoint selects whole words. If you want to select individual characters, select **Tools**, **Options**, and deselect the **Automatic Word Selection** check box.

- To delete text, select the text and press the **Delete** key. You can also use the Delete or Backspace keys to delete single characters to the right or left of the insertion point, respectively.

- To insert text, click the I-beam pointer where you want to insert the text and type the text.

- To replace text, select the text you want to replace and type the new text. When you start typing, PowerPoint deletes the selected text.

- To copy and paste text, select the text you want to copy and choose **Edit**, **Copy** or press **Ctrl+C**. Move the insertion point to where you want the text pasted (it can be in a different text box) and choose **Edit**, **Paste** or press **Ctrl+V**.

- To cut and paste (move) text, select the text you want to cut and choose **Edit**, **Cut** or press **Ctrl+X**. Move the insertion point to where you want the text pasted (it can be in a different text box), and choose **Edit**, **Paste** or press **Ctrl+V**.

Changing the Text Alignment and Line Spacing

When you first type text, PowerPoint automatically sets it against the left edge of the text box. To change the paragraph alignment, perform the following steps:

1. Click anywhere inside the paragraph you want to realign.

2. Select **Format**, **Alignment**. The Alignment submenu appears.

3. Select **Left**, **Center**, **Right**, or **Justify**, to align the paragraph as desired. (See Figure 11.3 for examples.)

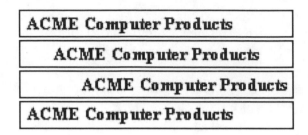

Figure 11.3 You can align each paragraph in a text box.

Some Alignment Shortcuts   To quickly set left alignment, press **Ctrl+L** or click the **Left Alignment** button on the Formatting toolbar. To quickly apply right alignment, press **Ctrl+R.** To quickly apply centered alignment, click the **Center Alignment** button on the Formatting toolbar.

The default setting for line spacing is single-space. To change the line spacing in a paragraph, perform these steps:

1. Click inside the paragraph you want to change, or select all the paragraphs you want to change.

2. Select **Format, Line Spacing**. The Line Spacing dialog box appears, as shown in Figure 11.4.

Figure 11.4   The Line Spacing dialog box.

3. Click on the arrow buttons to the right of any of the following text boxes to change the line spacing:

Line Spacing   This setting controls the space between the lines in a paragraph.

Before Paragraph   This setting controls the space between this paragraph and the paragraph that comes before it.

After Paragraph   This setting controls the space between this paragraph and the paragraph that comes after it.

Lines or Points?   The drop-down list box that appears to the right of each setting allows you to set the line spacing in *lines* or *points*. A line is the current line height (based on text size). A point is a unit commonly used to measure text. A point is approximately 1/72 of an inch.

4. Click on the **OK** button.

Adding a WordArt Object

PowerPoint comes with an auxiliary program called WordArt that can help you create graphic text effects. To insert a WordArt object into a slide, perform the following steps:

1. Display the slide on which you want to place the WordArt object.

2. Select **Insert**, **Object**. The Insert Object dialog box appears.

3. In the Object Type list, click on **Microsoft WordArt 2.0**, and click on the **OK** button. The Microsoft WordArt toolbar and text entry box appear, as shown in Figure 11.5.

4. Type the text you want to use. Whatever you type replaces the **Your Text Here** message. (As you type, press **Enter** when you need to start a new line.)

5. Select a WordArt font from the Font list (see Figure 11.5).

6. Select a text size from the Size list. If you do not specify a size, Word adjusts the text automatically to fit the size of the WordArt box (i.e. Best Fit).

7. Select a shape from the Shape list. Shapes act as cookie cutters to form the text.

8. Use the formatting buttons, as shown in Table 11.1, to create additional effects. (For more formatting options, open the Format menu.)

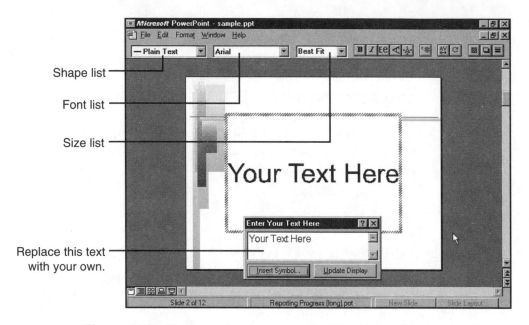

Shape list

Font list

Size list

Replace this text with your own.

Figure 11.5 Type your text and use the WordArt toolbar to style it.

Table 11.1 Buttons on the WordArt Toolbar

Button	Purpose
B	Boldfaces text.
I	Italicizes text.
Ee	Reverses upper and lower cases.
A	Turns text sideways.
A	Stretches text to the edges of the frame.

Button	Purpose
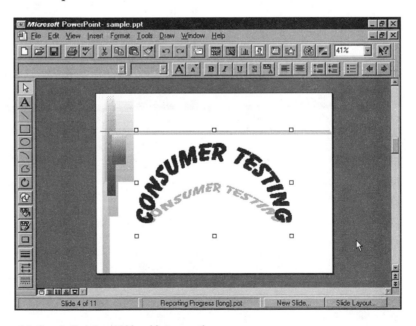	Opens a drop-down list of alignment options.
	Opens the Spacing Between Characters dialog box.
	Opens the Special Effects dialog box.
	Opens the Shading dialog box.
	Opens a drop-down list of shadow options.
	Opens the Border dialog box.

9. Click anywhere inside the presentation window to return to your slide. The WordArt appears on your slide. Figure 11.6 shows the finished product.

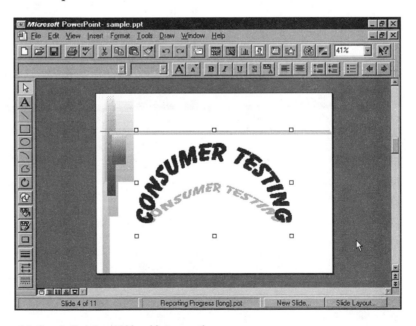

Figure 11.6   A finished WordArt creation.

To edit the WordArt object, double-click on it to display the WordArt toolbar and text entry box. Enter your changes; then, click outside the WordArt object. You can move the object by dragging its border, or resize it by dragging a handle.

In this lesson, you learned how to add text to a slide, change the text alignment and spacing, transform text into a bulleted list, and add WordArt objects. In the next lesson, you will learn how to use tables, tabs, and indents to create columns and lists.

Creating Columns and Lists

In this lesson, you will learn how to use tabs to create columns of text and use indents to create bulleted lists, numbered lists, and other types of lists.

Using Tabs to Create Columns

A presentation often uses tabbed columns to display information. For example, you may use tabs to create a three-column list like the one shown in Figure 12.1.

In addition to hardware products, we carry a varied line of software:

Business	Home	Education
WordPerfect	Quicken	Reader Rabbit 2
Microsoft Word	The New Print Shop	Oregon Trail
PowerPoint	Microsoft Works	BodyWorks
Excel	TurboTax	Where in the World is Carmen Sandiego?

Figure 12.1   You can use tabs to create a multi-column list.

In PowerPoint, you create multiple columns using tab stops. To set the tabs for a multi-column list, perform the following steps:

1. Open the presentation and view the slide you want to work with in Slide View.

2. Create a text box for the text. (For instructions on how to create a text box, see Lesson 11.)

3. Click anywhere inside the text box for which you want to set the tabs.

4. If you already typed text inside the text box, select the text.

5. Select **View**, **Ruler** to display the ruler, if it does not already appear.

6. Click on the tab icon in the upper left corner of the presentation window until it represents the type of tab you want to set:

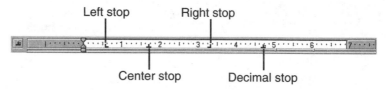

Left stop   Right stop

Center stop   Decimal stop

Figure 12.2 The ruler lets you enter and change tab stop settings.

- **Left stop**   Aligns the left end of the line against the tab stop.
- **Center stop**   Centers the text on the tab stop.
- **Right stop**   Aligns the right end of the line against the tab stop.
- **Decimal stop**   Aligns the tab stop on a period. This is called a decimal tab, and is useful for aligning a column of numbers that use decimal points.

7. Click on each place in the ruler where you want to set the selected type of tab stop, as shown in Figure 12.2.

8. Repeat steps 4 and 5 if you want to set different types of tab stops at different positions.

9. To change the position of an existing tab stop setting, drag it on the ruler to the desired position. To delete an existing tab stop setting, drag it off the ruler.

10. **(Optional)** To turn off the ruler, select **View**, **Ruler**.

Don't Forget the Slide Master   Throughout this lesson, keep in mind that you can enter your changes on the slide master or on individual slides. If you change the slide master, the change affects all slides in the presentation. For details on displaying the slide master, see Lesson 8.

Creating a Bulleted List

PowerPoint offers an easy way to create a bulleted list with standard indents. Follow these steps:

1. Click inside the paragraph you want to transform into a bulleted list, or select one or more paragraphs.

2. Select **Format, Bullet**. The Bullet dialog box appears.

3. Select the **Use a Bullet** check box to enable bullet use.

4. Click **OK**. PowerPoint transforms the selected text into a bulleted list. (If you press Enter at the end of a bulleted paragraph, the next paragraph starts with a bullet.)

Quick Bullets   To bypass the Format menu and Bullet dialog box, simply click on the **Bullet** button on the Formatting toolbar to insert a bullet. You can click on the **Bullet** button again to remove the bullet.

Changing the Bullet Character

By default, whenever you click on the Bullet button on the Formatting toolbar to insert a bullet, PowerPoint inserts a large dot for the bullet. However, you can change the appearance of the bullet at any time by following these steps:

1. Select the paragraph(s) in which you want to change the bullet character.

2. Select **Format, Bullet**. The Bullet dialog box appears. (See Figure 12.3.)

3. Pull down the **Bullets From** list, and select the character set from which you want to choose a bullet. The dialog box displays the characters in the selected set.

Character Set   Each character set is nothing more than a font that's installed on your computer. Some fonts are better suited for bullets than others—open several and examine the characters each one contains.

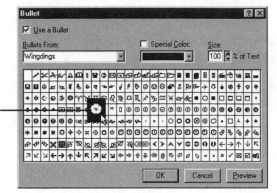

When you click on a character, PowerPoint shows it enlarged.

Figure 12.3 The Bullet dialog box lets you choose an alternative bullet character.

4. Click on the character you want to use for the bullet. When you click on a character, PowerPoint shows it enlarged so you can see it clearly, as shown in Figure 12.3.

5. To set the size of the bullet, use the up and down arrows to the right of the Size text box. Notice that the size of the bullet is not a fixed value—it is relative to the text around it.

6. To select a color for the bullet, pull down the **Special Color** drop-down list and select the desired color.

7. Select the **OK** button. PowerPoint changes the bullet character for all selected paragraphs.

Moving a Bulleted Item You can move an item in a bulleted list by clicking on the item's bullet and then dragging the bullet up or down in the list.

Creating Custom Indents for Lists

Indents allow you to move one or more lines of a paragraph in from the left margin. You can use indents in any text object to create a similar list or your own custom list. To indent text, perform the following steps:

1. Select the text box that contains the text you want to indent.

2. If you already typed text, select the text you want to indent.

3. If the ruler is not visible, select **View, Ruler**.

4. Drag one of the following indent markers to set the indents for the paragraph. (These indent markers appear on the ruler, as shown in Figure 12.4.)

Indent markers

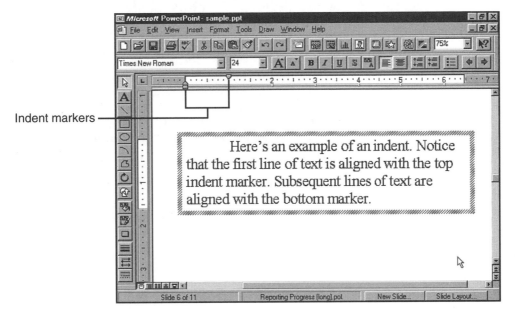

Figure 12.4   Drag the indent markers to indent your text.

- **Drag the top marker** to indent the first line.
- **Drag the bottom marker** to indent all subsequent lines.
- **Drag the box below the bottom marker** to indent all the text.

5. (Optional) To turn the ruler off, select **View, Ruler**.

You can create up to five levels of indents within a single text box. To add an indent level, click on the Demote button on the Formatting toolbar, or press the Tab key when the insertion point is at the beginning of the paragraph. A new set of indent markers appears on the ruler, showing the next level of indents. You can change these new indent settings as explained above.

Once you have set your indents, you can create a numbered or bulleted list by performing the following steps:

1. Type a number and a period, or type the character you want to use for the bullet.

2. Press the Tab key to move to the second indent mark.

3. Type the text you want to use for this item. As you type, PowerPoint wraps the text to the second indent mark.

4. Repeat steps 1 through 3 for each additional item you add to the list.

In this lesson, you learned how to create columns with tabs, create lists with indents, and change the bullet character for bulleted lists. In the next lesson, you will learn how to change the style, size, and color of text.

Changing the Look of Your Text

In this lesson, you will learn how to change the appearance of text by changing its font, style, size, and color.

Enhancing Your Text with the Font Dialog Box

You can enhance your text by using the Font dialog box or by using various tools on the Formatting toolbar. Use the Font dialog box if you want to add several enhancements to your text at one time. Use the Formatting toolbar to add one enhancement at a time.

Fonts, Styles, and Effects   In PowerPoint, a *font* is a family of text that has the same design or *typeface* (for example, Arial or Courier). A *style* is a standard enhancement, such as bold or italic. An *effect* is a special enhancement, such as shadow or underline.

You can change the fonts for existing text or for text you are about to type by performing the following steps:

1. To change the look of existing text, select text by dragging the I-beam pointer over the text.

2. Select **Format**, **Font**. The Font dialog box appears, as shown in Figure 13.1.

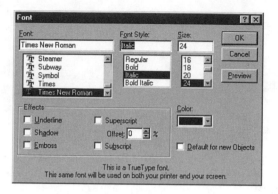

Figure 13.1   The Font dialog box enables you to select a font.

3. From the Font list, select the font you want to use.

4. From the Font Style list, select any style you want to apply to the type. (To remove styles from text, select Regular.)

5. From the Size list, select any size in the list, or type a size directly into the box. (With TrueType fonts, you can type any point size, even sizes that do not appear on the list.)

6. In the Effects group, select any special effects you want to add to the text, such as Underline, Shadow, or Emboss. You can also pick Superscript or Subscript, though these are less common.

7. To change the color of your text, click on the arrow button to the right of the Color list, and click on the desired color. (For more colors, click on the **Other Color** option at the bottom of the list and use the dialog box that appears to select a color.)

8. Click on the **OK** button to apply the new look to your text. (If you selected text before styling it, the text appears in the new style. If you did not select text, any text you type appears in the new style.)

Title and Object Area Text   If you change a font on an individual slide, the font change applies only to that slide. To change the font for all the slides in the presentation, you need to change the font on the Slide Master. To change the Slide Master, select **View**, **Master**, **Slide Master**. Select a text area and perform the steps above to change the look of the text on all slides.

Styling Text with the Formatting Toolbar

As shown in Figure 13.2, the Formatting toolbar contains many tools for changing the font, size, style, and color of text.

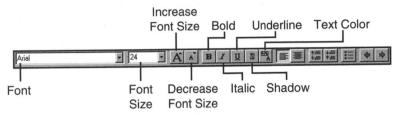

Figure 13.2   The Formatting toolbar contains several tools for styling text.

To use the tools, follow these steps:

1. To change the look of existing text, select the text.

2. To change fonts, open the **Font** drop-down list (see Figure 13.2) and click on the desired font.

3. To change font size, open the **Font Size** drop-down list (shown in Figure 13.2) and click on the desired size, or type a size directly into the box.

Incrementing the Type Size   To increase or decrease the text size to the next size up or down, click on the **Increase Font Size** or **Decrease Font Size** buttons on the Formatting toolbar.

4. To add a style or effect to the text (bold, italic, underline, and/or shadow), click on the appropriate button:

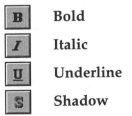

   Bold

   Italic

   Underline

   Shadow

5. To change the color of the text, click on the **Text Color** button and then click on the desired color. (For more colors, click on the **Other Color** option at the bottom of the list and use the dialog box that appears to select a color.)

Changing the Background Color Each presentation has its own color scheme, which includes background and text colors.

Copying Text Formats

If your presentation contains text with a format you want to use, you can pick up the format from the existing text and apply it to other text. To copy text formats, perform the following steps:

1. Highlight the text with the format you want to use.

2. Select **Format, Pick Up Text Style**. PowerPoint copies the format.

3. Select the text to which you want to apply the format.

4. Select **Format, Apply Text Style**. The selected text takes on the look of the source text.

The text format you pick up remains in a temporary holding area until you pick up another format, so you can continue to apply the format to other text until you pick up another format.

Painting Formats You can bypass the Format menu by using the Format Painter button on the Standard toolbar. Drag over the text with the format you want to copy, and click on the **Format Painter** button. Drag over the text to which you want to copy the format. When you release the mouse button, PowerPoint applies the format to the selected text.

In this lesson, you learned how to change the appearance of text by changing its font, size, style, and color. You also learned how to copy text formats. In the next lesson, you will learn how to draw objects on a slide.

Adding Pictures, Sounds, and Video

In this lesson, you will learn how to add PowerPoint clip art, drawings from other graphic programs, sounds, and video clips to a slide.

Adding PowerPoint Clip Art

PowerPoint comes with hundreds of clip art images that you can use in your presentations.

 Clip Art   Clip art is a collection of previously created images or pictures that you can place on a slide.

 Where's the Clip Art?   If you start this procedure and find that it doesn't work correctly, you may not have ClipArt Gallery installed. Re-run the Microsoft Office setup program, and choose ClipArt when asked what component you want to install.

To insert a clip art image onto a slide, perform the following steps:

1. In Slide view, display the slide on which you want to insert the clip art image.

 2. Select **Insert**, **Clip Art**, or click on the **Insert Clip Art** button on the Standard toolbar. The Microsoft ClipArt Gallery appears, as shown in Figure 14.1.

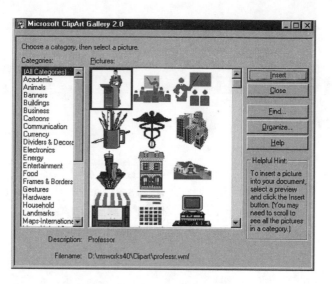

Figure 14.1 Select a category and a clip art image.

First Time? If this is the first time you are inserting a clip art image, PowerPoint displays a dialog box asking for your confirmation and warning that it will take some time. PowerPoint uses this time to organize the clip art library and prepare the images for your use.

3. In the **Categories** list, select the desired group of clip art images. PowerPoint displays the clip art images that are in the selected category.

4. Click on the desired image. A selection border appears around it.

5. Click on the **Insert** button. PowerPoint places the selected image on your slide.

6. Move the mouse pointer over the clip art object, hold down the mouse button, and drag the object to the desired position.

Picture Too Big? If the picture is too big or too small, you can drag the selection handles (the small squares) around the edge of the image to resize it. (Hold down Shift to proportionally resize.) Refer to Lesson 16 for more details about resizing and cropping.

Inserting Pictures from Other Applications

In addition to inserting clip art images, PowerPoint enables you to insert pictures created in other graphics programs. To insert a picture, perform the following steps:

1. Select **Insert, Picture**. The Insert Picture dialog box appears, as shown in Figure 14.2.

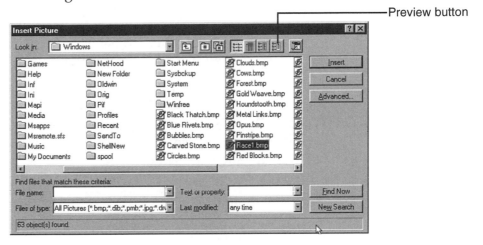

Preview button

Figure 14.2   Use the Insert Picture dialog box to insert a picture from another program.

2. Locate the drive and folder that contain the desired picture file. (See Lesson 6 if you don't remember how to navigate dialog boxes like this.)

3. Click on a file name in the list.

4. If you want to preview the graphic before you import it, click the **Preview** button in the Insert Picture dialog box (see Figure 14.2).

5. Click on the **OK** button. PowerPoint inserts the picture on the slide.

6. Move the mouse pointer over the picture, hold down the mouse button, and drag the picture to the desired position.

Adding Sounds

You can add sound files (.WAV files) to your presentations, so that the sound plays when you click on an icon in the presentation. Or, you can make a sound play automatically when a certain slide appears.

Special Equipment Needed? To add a sound file to a presentation, you don't need any special equipment; however, on the computer you're using to give the presentation, you should have a sound board (such as SoundBlaster) and speakers, so your audience can hear a high-quality sound.

Creating a Sound Object on a Slide

The first way to include a sound on a slide is to insert the sound as an "object" onto the slide, the same as you would insert a piece of clip art. With this method, you can control precisely when the sound plays.

To insert a sound file (.WAV) on a slide, do the following:

1. Display the slide to which you want to apply the sound.

2. Select **Insert, Sound**. The Insert Sound dialog box appears. (It looks almost exactly like the Insert Picture dialog box.)

3. Change the drive and folder if needed to locate the sound, and then click on the sound's title to select it.

Sample Sounds? There are a few sounds in your Windows\Sounds folder, if you just want to practice with one.

4. Click on the **OK** button. A small icon of a speaker appears on the slide to represent the sound. You can drag this icon to any location on the slide you like. It will appear on the slide like any other object.

5. Select **Tools, Animation Settings,** or right-click on the sound icon and then choose **Animation Settings** from the shortcut menu. The Animation Settings dialog box appears, as shown in Figure 14.3.

Figure 14.3 Use the Animation Settings dialog box to tell PowerPoint when to play the sound.

6. Open the **Play Options** drop-down list and select **Play**.

7. Click the **More** button at the bottom of the dialog box to open the More Animation Settings dialog box.

- To have the sound play when the slide first appears, click **Automatically**, and set the **Seconds** to 0. (You can set the Seconds to another number if you prefer a delay.)

- To have the sound play only when you click on its icon, click **In Sequence**.

- To hide the icon, click **Hide while not playing**. (Don't do this if you selected In Sequence, or there will be no icon visible with which to activate the sound!)

8. Click **OK** to close that dialog box, and **OK** again to return to the slide.

Assigning a Sound to an Object

The other way to play sounds in a presentation is to assign a sound to an object that's already on the slide. The sound plays whenever the object appears during the presentation.

The drawback to this method is that you have to set up the slide to "build"—that is, not to display its entire contents at once—in order to assign the sound. This means you have to advance the presentation an extra time for that slide (by pressing Page Down or whatever method you prefer) as you're giving the presentation.

Follow these steps to assign a sound to an object:

1. Right-click on any object on a slide. (To have the sound play when the slide first appears, right-click on the slide's title.)

2. Select **Tools**, **Animation Settings**. The Animation Settings dialog box appears.

3. Open the **Build Options** drop-down list, and select **All at Once**.

4. Open the **Sound** drop-down list (it's the bottom one in the Effects area), and select one of the sounds there, or select **Other Sound** to choose one from another folder.

Sound Locations   The sounds that appear on the list in step 4 are in the Sounds folder of your Microsoft Office folder. (Mine is **C:\msoffice95\Sounds**.) You can move or copy sound files into that folder to make them appear on the list.

5. Click **OK** when you select a sound. The sound plays whenever you display the object with which you associate the sound.

Adding Video Clips

A new feature in PowerPoint for Windows 95 is the capability to insert and control video clips (also called media clips or movies). You can acquire movie clips by downloading them from online services or by buying disks of them at your local computer store.

Inserting a video clip is much like inserting a sound. To insert a video clip, follow these steps.

1. Select **Insert**, **Movie**. The Insert Movie dialog box appears.

2. Select a movie file, and click **OK**. (There's one in the **C:\WINDOWS\MEDIA** folder you can practice with.)

3. Select **Tools**, **Animation Settings**. The same dialog box as that shown in Figure 14.3 appears.

4. Open the **Play Options** drop-down list and select **Play**.

5. If you have more than one thing to play on this slide (for instance, a video clip and a sound), choose the priority of your movie from the **Build/Play object** drop-down list (for example, First to have the video clip play before the sound.)

6. Click the **More** button at the bottom of the dialog box to open the More Animation Settings dialog box, and choose any additional settings. Choose **Automatically** to have the clip play when the slide appears, or **In Sequence** to set it to play only when you click on it.

7. Click **OK** to close that dialog box, and **OK** again to return to the slide.

In this lesson, you learned how to add clip art images, pictures, sounds, and movies to your slides. In the next lesson, you will learn how to add a graph to a slide.

Adding a Graph

In this lesson, you will learn how to create a graph (or chart) and place it on a presentation slide.

Inserting a Graph

PowerPoint comes with a program called Microsoft Graph that transforms raw data into professional looking graphs. To create a graph, perform the following steps:

1. Display the slide to which you want to add the graph.

2. Click on the **Insert Graph** button on the Standard toolbar, or select **Insert**, **Microsoft Graph**. The Microsoft Graph window appears, as shown in Figure 15.1, with the Datasheet window up front.

Datasheet The *datasheet* is set up like a spreadsheet with rows, columns, and cells. Each rectangle in the datasheet is a *cell* that can hold text or numbers. Microsoft Graph converts the data you enter in the datasheet into a graph it displays in the Graph window.

3. First you change the datasheet values to your own figures. Click inside the cell that contains a label or value you want to change, and type your entry.

4. Click on the next cell you want to change, or use the arrow keys to move from cell to cell.

5. Repeat steps 3 and 4 until you enter all your data.

6. Click on the graph. The datasheet window disappears, and the graph appears.

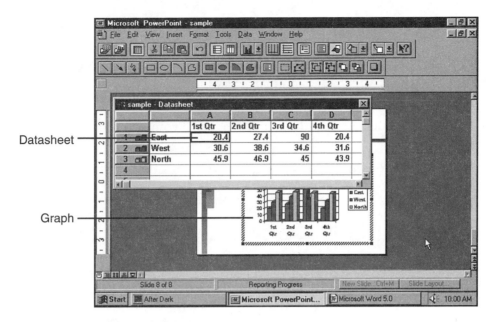

Datasheet

Graph

Figure 15.1   The Microsoft Graph Window

Redisplaying the Datasheet   If you need to make a change in the datasheet after you create it, see the next section, "Editing a Datasheet."

7. To leave Microsoft Graph and return to your slide in PowerPoint, click anywhere outside the graph.

Moving and Resizing the Graph   If the graph is too big or is in a bad location on the slide, you can resize and move it. Refer to Lesson 18 for details.

Editing the Datasheet

If you return to your slide and later decide that you want to edit the data that your graph is based on, perform the following steps:

1. Display the slide that contains the graph you want to edit.

431

2. Double-click anywhere inside the graph. PowerPoint starts Microsoft Graph and displays the graph.

3. If Microsoft Graph does not display the Datasheet window, select **View**, **Datasheet** or click the **View Datasheet** button in the Microsoft Graph toolbar. The Datasheet window appears.

4. Use the Tab key to go to the cell that contains the value you want to change, and type your change.

5. When you are done, click anywhere inside the graph window.

In addition to editing individual data entries, you can cut, copy, and paste cells; delete and insert rows and columns; and adjust column widths. This list gives you a quick overview of how to edit your datasheet:

Selecting Cells   To select one cell, click on it. To select several cells, drag the mouse pointer over the desired cells. To select a row or column, click on the letter above the column or the number to the left of the row. To select all the cells, click on the upper-leftmost square in the datasheet.

Clearing Cells   To erase the contents of cells, select the cells, and select **Edit**, **Clear**. Select **All** (to clear contents and formatting), **Contents** (to remove only the contents), or **Formats** (to remove only the formatting).

Cutting or Copying Cells   To cut cells, select the cells you want to cut. Then select **Edit**, **Cut**, or click on the **Cut** button. To copy cells, select the cells you want to copy. Then select **Edit**, **Copy,** or click on the **Copy** button.

Pasting Cells   To paste copied or cut cells into a datasheet, select the cell in the upper left corner of the area in which you want to paste the cut or copied cells. Select **Edit**, **Paste**, or click on the **Paste** button.

Inserting Blank Cells   To insert blank cells into your datasheet, select the row, column, or number of cells you want to insert. (Rows will be inserted above the current row. Columns will be inserted to the left of the current column.) Select **Insert**, **Cells**. If you select a row or column, PowerPoint inserts the row or column. If you select one or more cells, the Insert Cells dialog box appears, asking if you want to shift surrounding cells down or to the right. Select your preference, and click on the **OK** button.

Changing the Column Width   If you type entries that are too wide for a particular column, you may want to adjust the column width. Move the mouse pointer over the column letter at the top of the column with the width you want to change. Move the mouse pointer to the right until it turns into a double-headed arrow. Hold down the mouse button and drag the mouse until the column is the desired width.

Changing the Data Series

Say you create a graph that shows the sales figures for several salespersons over four quarters. You wanted each column in the graph to represent a salesperson, but instead, the columns represent quarters. To fix the graph, you can swap the data series by performing the following steps:

1. Open the **Data** menu.

2. Select **Series in Rows** or **Series in Columns**.

Quick Data Series Swap   To quickly swap data series, click on the **By Row** or **By Column** button on the Standard toolbar.

Changing the Graph Type

By default, Microsoft Graph creates a 3-dimensional column graph. If you want Microsoft Graph to display your data in a different type of graph, perform the following steps:

1. Select **Format, Chart Type**. The Chart Type dialog box appears, as shown in Figure 15.2.

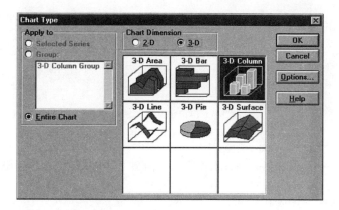

Figure 15.2 Pick the chart type you want.

2. In the Apply to area, make sure **Entire Chart** is selected.

3. In the Chart Dimension area, select **2-D** or **3-D**. The available graphs for the group you select appear.

4. Click on the desired chart type.

5. **(Optional)** For greater control, click the **Options** button and select other fine-tuning options for your graph.

6. Click on the **OK** button.

Selecting a Chart Design with AutoFormat

Microsoft Graph comes with several predesigned chart formats that you can apply to your graph. You select the design, and Microsoft Graph reformats your chart, giving it a professional look. Here's how you use AutoFormat to select a chart design:

1. Select **Format, AutoFormat**. The AutoFormat dialog box appears, as shown in Figure 15.3.

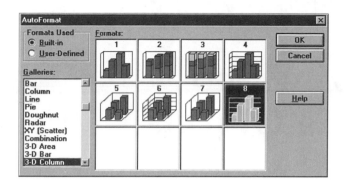

Figure 15.3   Select a chart design from the AutoFormat dialog box.

2. From the Galleries list, choose a chart type. In the Formats list, Microsoft Graph shows the available formats for the selected chart type.

3. Click on the desired chart type.

4. Click on the **OK** button. Microsoft Graph reformats the chart using the selected format.

In this lesson, you learned how to create and insert graphs on a slide, enter and edit graph data, and change graph types. In the next lesson, you will learn how to enhance graphs.

Moving and Sizing Objects

In this lesson, you will learn how to select, copy, move, and resize objects on a slide.

As you may have already discovered, *objects* are the building blocks you use to create slides in PowerPoint. Objects are the shapes you draw, the graphs you create, the pictures you import, and the text you type. In this and the next lesson, you will learn how to manipulate objects on your slides to create impressive presentations.

Selecting Objects

Before you can copy, move, or resize an object, you must first select the object. Change to Slide view, and perform one of the following steps to choose one or more objects:

- To select a single object, click on it. (If you click on text, a frame appears around the text. Click on the frame to select the text object.)

- To select more than one object, hold down the Shift key while clicking on each object. Handles appear around the selected objects, as shown in Figure 16.1.

- To deselect selected objects, click anywhere outside the selected objects.

TIP **Using the Selection Tool**   The Selection tool on the Drawing toolbar (the button with the mouse pointer on it) enables you to quickly select a group of objects. Click on the Selection tool and use the mouse pointer to drag a selection box around the objects you want to select. When you release the mouse button, PowerPoint selects the objects inside the box.

Selection tool

Selection handles

Figure 16.1   Handles indicate that objects are selected.

Working with Layers of Objects

As you place objects on-screen, they may start to overlap, making it difficult or impossible to select the objects in the lower layers. To move objects in layers, perform the following steps:

1. Click on the object you want to move up or down in the stack.

2. Open the **Draw** menu.

3. Select one of the following options:

   - **Bring to Front** brings the object to the top of the stack.

   - **Send to Back** sends the object to the bottom of the stack.

   - **Bring Forward** brings the object up one layer.

   - **Send Backward** sends the object back one layer.

Grouping and Ungrouping Objects

Each object you draw acts as an individual object. However, sometimes you want two or more objects to act as a group. For example, you may want to make the lines of several objects the same thickness, or move several objects together. If you want to treat two or more objects as a group, perform the following steps:

1. Select the objects you want to group.

2. Select **Draw**, **Group**.

3. To ungroup the objects, select any object in the group, and select **Draw**, **Ungroup**.

Drawing+ Toolbar For quick access to the Group, Ungroup, and layering commands, turn on the Drawing+ toolbar. (This is different from the regular Drawing toolbar.) To display the Drawing+ toolbar, right-click on any toolbar, and click on Drawing+.

Cutting, Copying, and Pasting Objects

You can cut, copy, and paste objects on a slide to rearrange the objects or to use the objects to create a picture. When you cut an object, PowerPoint removes the object from the slide and places it in a temporary holding area called the Windows Clipboard. When you copy an object, the original object remains on the slide, and PowerPoint places a copy of it on the Clipboard. In either case, you can then paste the object from the Clipboard onto the current slide or another slide. To cut or copy an object, perform the following steps:

1. Select the object(s) you want to cut, copy, or move.

2. Select **Edit**, **Cut** or **Edit**, **Copy**, or click the **Cut** or **Copy** button on the Standard toolbar.

3. Display the slide on which you want to place the cut or copied object(s). (You can also open a different Windows program, to paste into it, if you prefer.)

4. Select **Edit**, **Paste**, or click on the **Paste** button on the Standard toolbar. PowerPoint pastes the object(s) on the slide.

5. Move the mouse pointer over any of the pasted objects, hold down the mouse button, and drag the objects to where you want them.

6. Release the mouse button.

Deleting an Object   To remove an object without placing it on the Clipboard, select the object and then press the **Delete** key, or select **Edit**, **Clear.**

Dragging and Dropping Objects   The quickest way to copy or move objects is to drag and drop them. Select the objects you want to move, position the mouse pointer over any of the selected objects, hold down the mouse button, and drag the objects where you want them. To copy the objects, hold down the Ctrl key while dragging.

Resizing Objects

There may be times when an object you create or import is not the right size for your slide presentation. You can resize the object by performing these steps:

1. Select the object to resize.

2. Drag one of the handles (the black squares that surround the object) until the object is the desired size:

   • Drag a corner handle to change both the height and width of an object. PowerPoint retains the object's relative dimensions.

   • Drag a side, top, or bottom handle to change the height or width alone.

   • Hold down the **Ctrl** key while dragging to resize from the center of the picture.

3. Release the mouse button, and PowerPoint resizes the object (see Figure 16.2).

Drag a handle to resize an object.

Figure 16.2 Before and after resizing an object.

Cropping a Picture

In addition to resizing a picture, you can crop it. That is, you can trim a side or corner of the picture to remove an element from the picture or cut off some white space. To crop a picture, perform the following steps:

1. Click on the picture you want to crop.

2. Open the **Tools** menu, and select **Crop Picture**. The mouse pointer turns into a cropping tool. (See Figure 16.3.)

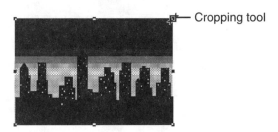

Cropping tool

Figure 16.3 Use the cropping tool to chop off a section of the picture.

3. Move the mouse pointer over one of the handles. (Use a corner handle to crop two sides at once. Use a side, top, or bottom handle to crop only one side.)

4. Hold down the mouse button, and drag the pointer until the crop lines are where you want them.

5. Release the mouse button. The cropped section disappears.

Uncropping   You can uncrop a picture immediately after cropping it by selecting **Edit**, **Undo**. You can also uncrop at any time, by performing the steps above and dragging the selected handle in the opposite direction you dragged it for cropping.

In this lesson, you learned how to select, copy, move, and resize an object on a slide. In the next lesson, you will learn how to use PowerPoint effects to change the look of an object.

Changing the Look of Objects

In this lesson, you will learn how to add borders, colors, patterns, and shadows to objects.

Framing an Object

You can frame an object (a picture, a text box, or whatever) by drawing a border around the object.

To add a border to an object, perform the following steps in Slide view:

1. Select the object you want to frame.

2. Select **Format**, **Colors and Lines**. The Colors and Lines dialog box appears, as shown in Figure 17.1.

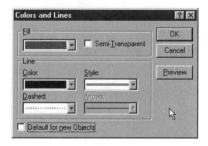

Figure 17.1 The Colors and Lines dialog box.

3. Open the **Color** drop-down list and choose a color for the line.

4. Open the **Style** drop-down list and choose a thickness and style for the line.

5. If you want the line to be dotted or dashed, open the **Dashed** drop-down list and choose a dash style.

6. Click on the **OK** button. The frame appears around the object.

More about Lines   Don't forget that there are buttons on the Drawing toolbar that control line thickness, color, and dash style, too.

Adding a Fill

A fill is a background color and shading combination that you can add to an object to make it stand out. To add a fill or change an existing fill, perform these steps:

1. Select the object(s) you want to fill.

2. Open the **Format** menu, and choose **Colors and Lines**. The Colors and Lines dialog box appears, as in Figure 17.1.

3. Open the **Fill** drop-down list and choose a fill color.

4. To make the color light enough so you can see through it, mark the **Semi-Transparent** check box.

5. Click **OK**.

Changing an Object's Color

If an object's color is the result of a simple fill, it's easy to change its color simply by changing the fill color (see the previous section). But if the object is a complex drawing with many colors, changing the fill color only changes the background color—it doesn't change the other colors of the drawing. To change the drawing's colors, you must use the Recolor feature. To recolor an object, follow these steps:

1. Select the object you want to recolor.

2. Select **Tools, Recolor**. The Recolor Picture dialog box appears, as shown in Figure 17.2.

3. Click on either **Fills** or **Colors**. Fills shows only the colors in backgrounds or fills, excluding line colors. Colors shows all the colors in the picture.

4. Select a color you want to change in the Original list. An X appears in the check box next to the color.

443

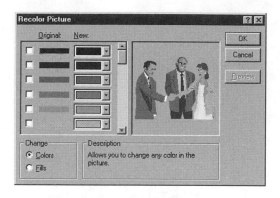

Figure 17.2 You can change each fill color.

All the Colors Aren't Shown At first, it may look like you have only six colors to work with. But notice that there's a scroll bar to the right of the colors. Use it to display all the other colors in the drawing.

5. Use the **New** drop-down menu to the right of the selected color to choose the color to which you want to change.

Using the Other Option At the bottom of each color's drop-down menu is the Other option. Select this option if you want to use a color that the menu doesn't list.

6. To view the effects of your changes, click on the **Preview** button.

7. Repeat steps 3 through 6 for each color you want to change.

8. Click on the **OK** button to put your changes into effect.

Adding a Shadow

A shadow gives a 3-D effect to an object, as shown in Figure 17.3. To add a shadow to an object, perform these steps:

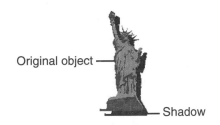

Original object ———

——— Shadow

Figure 17.3   The Statue of Liberty with a shadow effect.

1. Select the object to which you want to add a shadow.

2. Select **Format**, **Shadow**. The Shadow dialog box appears.

3. Open the **Color** drop-down list and click on the desired color for the shadow.

4. To change the position and thickness of the shadow, enter your settings in the Offset group.

Offset   To understand the offset options, think of the shadow as a silhouette of the original object that sits behind the object. You can move the silhouette behind the object in any direction, and move it out more from the object to make the shadow appear thicker.

5. Click on the **OK** button. PowerPoint applies the shadow to the object.

To remove the shadow, repeat the steps above, but select **No Shadow** from the Color drop-down list.

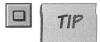

Quick Shadow   A quick way to apply or remove a shadow is to click the **Shadow** button on the Drawing toolbar.

Copying the Look of Another Object

If your presentation contains an object that has the frame, fill, and shadow you want to use for another object, you can pick up those design elements and apply them to another object. To do this, perform the following steps:

1. Click on the object with the style you want to copy.

2. Select **Format, Pick Up Object Style**. PowerPoint copies the style.

3. Click on the object to which you want to apply the style.

4. Select **Format, Apply Object Style**. The selected object takes on the look of the source object.

The style you pick up remains in a temporary holding area until you pick up another style, so you can apply the design elements to more than one object after you pick it up.

  Painting Styles You can bypass the Format menu by using the Format Painter button on the Standard toolbar. Select the object with the style you want to copy, and click on the **Format Painter** button. Select the object to which you want to copy the style.

In this lesson, you learned how to use borders, colors, patterns, and shadows to change the look of individual objects on a slide. You also learned how to copy design elements from object to object.

SCHEDULE+

Starting and Exiting Schedule+

In this lesson, you will learn how to start, logon, and exit Schedule+. You also learn how to change your logon password.

What Is Schedule+?

Schedule+ is a *Personal Information Manager*, or PIM. It's a lot like a 3-ring bound organizer that you might carry around during your business day, with various tabbed sections to help you organize particular parts of your daily life. Schedule+ comes with sections, too. Here's what you'll find in your Schedule+ program:

- **Appointment Book**   Use this feature to keep track of daily and weekly appointments, and set up reminders. You can even set up alarms that beep to remind you of an appointment.

- **To Do list**   Organize your daily or weekly tasks, or prioritize things you have to keep track of.

- **Contacts**   Enter your business contacts and keep a list of names, addresses, and phone numbers of people you need to reach often.

- **Planner**   Organize meetings and attendees with the Schedule+ Planner feature. The Planner's Meeting Wizard helps you coordinate meeting times.

- **Events**   Stay ahead of special occasions, including birthdays, anniversaries, conferences, and more, with the Events feature.

With Schedule+ you can keep track of daily appointments and meetings, prioritize your work, and a whole lot more.

Starting Schedule+

To begin working with Schedule+, you first have to start the program. To start Schedule+, follow these steps:

1. Click the **Start** button, then move the mouse pointer to Programs.

2. On the Programs menu, click **Microsoft Schedule+** to open the application (Figure 1.1).

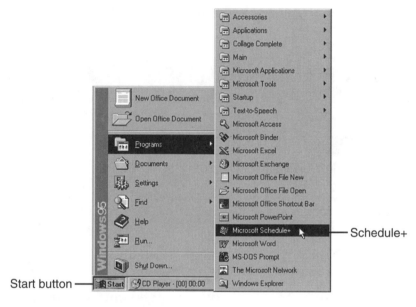

Figure 1.1   Use the Start button to open Schedule+.

 Quicker Ways to Open Schedule+   You can create a shortcut on your desktop from which to launch Schedule+ (see the Windows section of this book), or add an icon for Schedule+ to your Microsoft Office shortcut bar (see the Working Together section of the book).

Logging On with the Logon Box

You see a logon box every time you open Schedule+. Depending on whether you are on a network (connected to other computers) or not, your computer may show different logon boxes. If you're networked (and you share e-mail on the network with other users), you use a *group-enabled mode* box. If you're not connected to a computer network, you use a *stand-alone mode* box, as shown in Figure 1.2.

Figure 1.2   The Schedule+ Logon dialog box.

Logon names and passwords help you keep your data safe, especially if several people use the same computer. For example, if you use Schedule+ at home, other members of your family can set up and open their own schedules through the logon box.

Here are instructions for handling the logon modes:

- In group-enabled mode, type your name in the Profile name text box, type in your password (if assigned one), and click **OK**.

- In stand-alone mode, type your name in the User name text box, type in your password (if assigned one), and click **OK**.

The first time you create a schedule, the Schedule+ welcome box appears, as shown in Figure 1.3. (This box also appears when the program cannot find a schedule you previously created.)

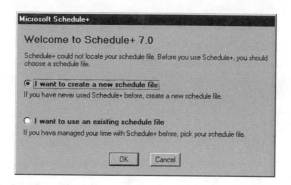

Figure 1.3 The welcome box has two options you can choose.

- To create a new schedule, select the **I want to create a new schedule file** option and click OK.

- To open a schedule, select the **I want to use an existing schedule file** option and click OK.

Either method opens the Select Local Schedule dialog box, shown in Figure 1.4. You use this dialog box to locate schedules, or to simply confirm information about your new schedule, such as its name and location.

Use this drop-down list to save your schedule in another folder.

Select Local Schedule	? ×
Look in: 🗀 Schedule ▼ 🔁 🖆 🏢 🏢	
🗐 Greg	
🗐 Melissa	
File name: *.scd;*.cal	**Open**
Files of type: Schedule+ [*.SCD;*.CAL] ▼	Cancel
	Help

Schedule+ files use a .SCD filename extension.

Figure 1.4 The Select Local Schedule dialog box.

- To confirm information about a new schedule, click on the **Save** button. If you want to save the schedule in another location, select a folder from the Save in drop-down list.

- To look for an existing schedule, use the Save in drop-down list to locate the folder containing the schedule. Once you find the schedule, select it and click on the **Open** button.

> **TIP**
>
> **How Do I Start a New Schedule?**   If you share your computer with other people, say family members, you probably want to know how to start new schedules for each user. To start a new schedule, you type a new logon name in the Schedule+ Logon dialog box. This sets up a schedule for the additional user that the new user can personally fill in.

Once you make it past the logon box and the startup procedure, your personal Schedule+ screen appears in full.

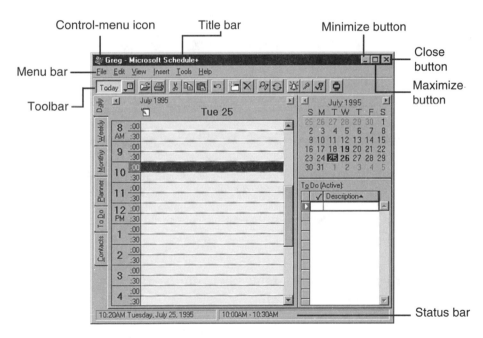

Figure 1.5   Welcome to Schedule+.

The Schedule+ screen contains all the familiar Windows elements you've worked with before in other Windows programs. (You'll learn all about the parts of the Schedule+ screen in the next lesson.)

Setting Up Passwords

Passwords help keep your data safe by allowing only users who know the password to access your files. You can set up a password for everyone who uses the Schedule+ program. If you use Schedule+ in a network environment, your network administrator may have already assigned you a password; however, you can change your password at any time.

To create or change a password for your Schedule+ program, perform the following steps:

1. Select **Tools**, **Change Password**.

2. In the Change Password dialog box, shown in Figure 1.6, type a password.

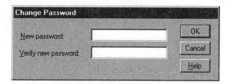

Figure 1.6 The Change Password dialog box.

3. Confirm the password by retyping it in the Verify new password text box.

4. Click **OK**. Schedule+ sets up the program with your new password.

You have to use the new password to log back onto the Schedule+ program. Be sure to remember your password, or write it down and keep it somewhere safe.

Exiting Schedule+

Although you're not ready to quit Schedule+ yet, you might as well learn how to exit it so you're ready when the time comes. To exit Schedule+, you can use any of these methods:

- Select **File**, **Exit**.
- Click on the **Close** button (X).
- Double-click on the program's Control-menu icon.
- Press **Alt+F4**.

Unlike with many other programs you use, you don't have to take steps to save your data with Schedule+. It automatically saves your data when you exit the program.

In this lesson, you learned how to start Schedule+, to use the logon box and set your password, and to exit the program. In the next lesson, you'll learn how to navigate the Schedule+ screen.

Navigating the Schedule+ Screen

In this lesson, you will learn how to move around and use the on-screen elements in Schedule+.

Looking Around the Schedule+ Screen

The whole Schedule+ program (see Figure 2.1) resembles one of those fancy personal organizer/planner books you buy at office stores, complete with tabs to separate your data. However, the pages of your organizer aren't held together by an expensive leather binder, and you don't have to lug it around with you. This organizer is all electronic, simple to use, and right by your side when you work on your computer.

The Schedule+ screen contains the same Windows 95 elements you use with other Windows 95 programs. Menus, toolbars, and scroll bars are in the familiar locations. But the Schedule+ program window looks a lot different than the other programs you use.

Here's a description of each of the on-screen elements:

- **Title bar**   Notice that the title bar displays your name. That's because it's your schedule. If someone else starts their own schedule on your computer, they see their name on the title bar when they logon.

- **Menu bar**   You find all of your Schedule+ commands on the various menus on the menu bar. To open a menu, simply click on its name.

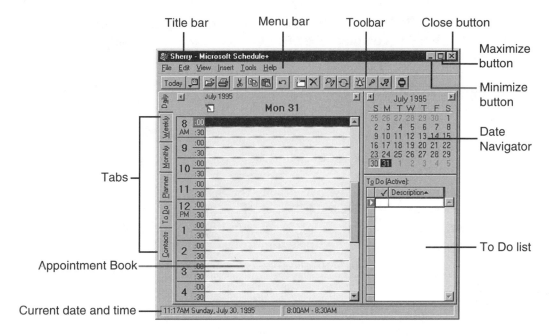

Title bar   Menu bar   Toolbar   Close button

Maximize button

Minimize button

Date Navigator

Tabs

To Do list

Appointment Book

Current date and time

Figure 2.1 The Schedule+ screen.

- **Toolbar**   A faster way to activate commands and tasks is to click on the corresponding toolbar buttons. Each button on the toolbar controls a specific task or command. To activate a button, click on it with your mouse pointer. (You learn more about the toolbar later in this lesson.)

- **Tabs**   The left side of your Schedule+ window holds vertical tabs. Each tab represents a different feature of the program. For example, the Daily view tab enables you to view your Appointment Book in daily view. To view a different tab on your screen, click on the tab name.

- **Appointment Book**   Use the Appointment Book to keep track of your daily schedule. You learn more about this feature in Lessons 4 and 5.

- **Date Navigator**   To change the Appointment Book to another date, you click on the date in the Date Navigator monthly calendar.

- **To Do list** Use this area to help you keep track of daily tasks you have to complete. (See Lesson 10 for more information.)

What Day Is It? If you suddenly forget what day it is, look at your Schedule+ status bar for help. It always displays the current date and time.

When you first start Schedule+ you may notice that it doesn't make full use of your whole monitor screen (see Figure 2.1). You can maximize the window by clicking the Schedule+ window's Maximize button (shown in Figure 2.1). If you minimize Schedule+, so you can use other programs while it's still running, click the **Minimize** button. You can open the Schedule+ window again when you need it by simply clicking on its button on the Taskbar.

Working with Schedule+ Tabs

There are six tabs along the left side of your screen, as shown in Figure 2.2. Each of these tabs enables you to use and view a specific Schedule+ feature. By default, Schedule+ is set up to open to the Daily view tab so that you can see the day's schedule of activities. However, you can open any tab by simply clicking on its name.

Here's a description of each tab and the feature it displays:

- **Daily** Click on this tab to view your daily schedule. You can quickly see your appointments and meetings arranged by times.

- **Weekly** Use the Weekly tab to view several consecutive days of your schedule at a glance.

- **Monthly** To see your schedule by month, like a calendar, click on the Monthly tab. This view enables you to see several weeks of your schedule at a time.

- **Planner** To see your schedule in blocks of busy and free times, use the Planner view. With this tab, you can also see the time blocks of other users on your network. See Lessons 16 and 17 for more on using Schedule+ on a network.

- **To Do**   Use this view to track and manage the tasks and projects that go along with your schedule. You can include a note to pick up the dry cleaning or write a grocery list, or you can list the complex project steps you must complete at work.

- **Contacts**   With Schedule+, you can compile a database of people you contact the most. You can keep an address book of clients, friends, and family, including names, addresses, phone numbers, and more.

You'll learn more about each of these tabs in the lessons to come.

These six tabs open specific Schedule+ features. —

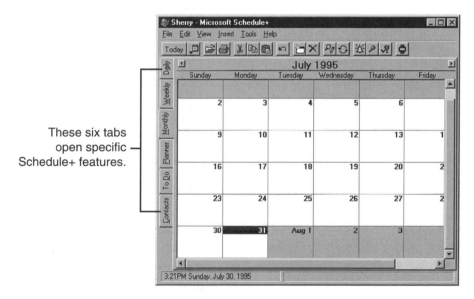

Figure 2.2   The Monthly view tab.

Using the Schedule+ Toolbar

The toolbar enables you to use shortcuts to common tasks, such as printing or copying. To use the toolbar tools, click on the button you want to activate. Many of these buttons are the same as other buttons on Microsoft programs, such as Cut, Copy, and Paste. However, there are plenty of new buttons on the toolbar as well.

Use this table to learn what each toolbar button does. (You'll learn more about these commands as we cover them in later lessons, but use this table as a reference.)

Table 2.1   Schedule+'s Toolbar Buttons

Button	*Name*	*Description*
Today	Select Today	Opens your Appointment Book to the current date's schedule.
	Go To Date	Enables you to open your Appointment Book to a specific date.
	Open	Opens another person's schedule file.
	Print	Opens the Print dialog box so you can select portions of your schedule to print out.
	Cut	Cuts the data you select and places it on the Windows Clipboard.
	Copy	Copies the data you select and places it on the Windows Clipboard.
	Paste	Pastes data from the Windows Clipboard into your schedule at the insertion point.
	Undo	Undoes your last action.
	Insert New Appointment	Opens a dialog box so you can insert an appointment into your schedule.
	Delete	Enables you to delete an appointment or task from your schedule.

Button	Name	Description
	Edit	Opens a dialog box so you can edit appointments.
	Recurring	Helps you set up an appointment as a recurring event on your schedule.
	Reminder	Adds a reminder icon to your appointment or task.
	Private	Adds a private icon to your appointment or task.
	Tentative	Schedules the appointment as a tentative item on your schedule.
	Meeting Wizard	Helps you cover the necessary steps for scheduling meetings on a network. (This button is only available in group-enabled mode.)
	Timex Watch Wizard	Enables you to upload schedule information onto your Timex Data Link watch.
	View Mail	Enables you to view your e-mail on the network mail system. (This button is only available in group-enabled mode.)

If you ever have any doubt about what a toolbar button does, you can always find out by moving your mouse pointer over the button, pausing while the mouse pointer touches the button, and reading the ToolTip name that appears.

In this lesson, you learned about the different elements of the Schedule+ screen, and how to use the toolbar buttons. In the next lesson, you'll learn how to find online help.

Getting Help

In this lesson, you will learn how to access Help to assist you with questions about Schedule+.

Working with the Help System

In case you ever get in a jam, you can call for help without dialing 911 by using Schedule+'s Help system.

All the Microsoft Office programs, including Schedule+, have very similar Help systems, and they all work almost exactly like the one in Windows 95 itself. Reread Lesson 5 in the Windows section of this book if you need a refresher.

As with any Microsoft Office program, to display the Help menu in Schedule+, click on the word **Help** on the menu bar. This action opens the Help menu, as shown in Figure 3.1.

Figure 3.1 The Help menu.

The Help menu has several options to choose from:

- **Microsoft Schedule+ Help Topics**   Opens a dialog box of Help topics.

- **Answer Wizard**   Opens a dialog box where you can type in a specific question, and the Answer Wizard answers it. Learn more about this later in this lesson.

- **Seven Habits Help Topics**   Schedule+ comes with helpful information from the book *The Seven Habits of Highly Effective People.*

- **The Microsoft Network**   If your computer has a modem, and you have an account with the Microsoft Network online service, you can use this feature to get help on Schedule+ via the Microsoft Network online service. Once you connect, you can access online help forums to assist you with any problems.

- **About Microsoft Schedule+**   Opens a window containing information about the program version and maker.

What's a Wizard?   Microsoft calls many of its automated features *wizards*. In short, a wizard is a step-by-step guide that leads you through a task or problem. When you select a wizard feature, such as the Answer Wizard, on-screen prompts appear asking you to choose from a variety of options.

Using the Help Topics Dialog Box

One way to access online Help is to use the Help Topics dialog box, shown in Figure 3.2. Within the dialog box are tabs with options for looking up online Help topics.

To open the Help Topics dialog box, follow these steps:

1. Open the **Help** menu and select **Microsoft Schedule+ Help Topics**.

2. The Help Topics dialog box opens, revealing its help options. To bring any tab to the front of the box, simply click on the tab name.

You have worked with these same tabs—Contents, Index, and Find—in every Microsoft Office application, and also in Windows itself, so I won't repeat all the steps here. Instead, refer to Lesson 5 of the Windows section in this book for complete coverage of these tabs.

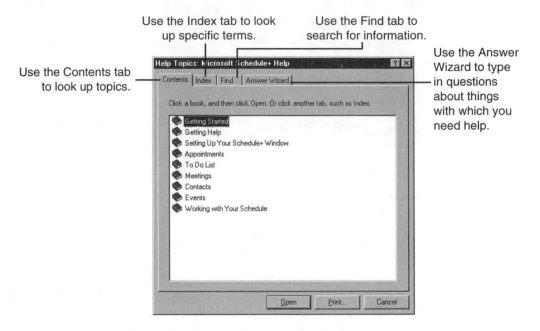

Use the Index tab to look up specific terms.

Use the Find tab to search for information.

Use the Contents tab to look up topics.

Use the Answer Wizard to type in questions about things with which you need help.

Figure 3.2 Help is on its way with the online Help system.

Using the Answer Wizard

By far, the most innovative part of the Help system is the Answer Wizard (shown in Figure 3.3). To open the Answer Wizard, you click on its tab in the Help Topics dialog box (which you open from the Help menu), or choose the Answer Wizard option directly from the Help menu.

Inside the Answer Wizard tab, all you do is type in your request, click on the **Search** button, and the list box displays the results. For example, if you're having trouble backing up a Schedule+ file, you can type in a question like "How do I backup a schedule?", and Answer Wizard answers you.

You can type in any kind of question, and Answer Wizard tries to respond to it. The Answer Wizard looks for key terms or words in the question and searches the online Help information for terms that meet the search criteria; then, the Answer Wizard supplies you with a list box of related topics, as shown in Figure 3.3.

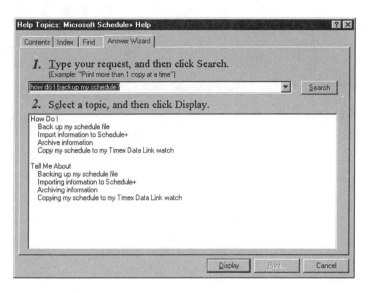

Figure 3.3   The Answer Wizard's answers.

When you see a list box appear after typing in your question, look through the topics. If you see something close to your request listed in the box, double-click on it to see detailed information about the subject matter.

To use the Answer Wizard, follow these steps:

1. Open the Answer Wizard tab. You can do this by selecting **Help**, **Answer Wizard** or clicking the **Answer Wizard** tab in the Help Topics dialog box.

2. Type in your question in the step 1 box and click on the **Search** button.

3. The results of the search appear in the step 2 box. To choose a topic, double-click on it.

4. To exit the dialog box, click on the **Cancel** button or the **Close** button.

Other Help Routes

Aside from the Help menu and Help Topics dialog box, there are other ways to find help. Another way to get help is to press **F1** on the keyboard. This opens the Help Topics dialog box directly. And speaking of dialog boxes, you can get help using them, too. Look for the help buttons (marked with a question mark icon) in the dialog boxes you work with to view more information about using the dialog box.

In this lesson, you learned how to access online Help. In the next lesson, you'll learn how to use the Daily view tab.

Using the Daily View Tab

In this lesson, you will learn use the Daily view tab and customize its appearance.

Parts of the Daily View Tab

By default, Schedule+ always opens to the Daily view tab so you can see your day's appointments at a glance. Take a look at the Daily view tab in the following figure.

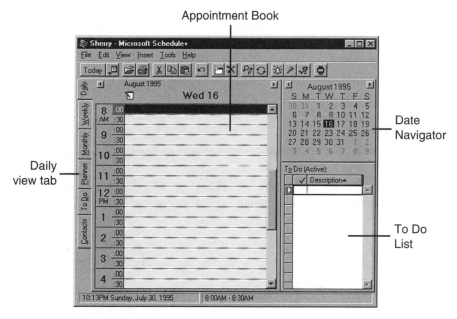

Figure 4.1 The Daily view tab.

There are several distinct parts of your Daily view tab. Three of them stand out in particular:

- The *Appointment Book* (the biggest part of your screen with all the times and lines in it) shows your daily schedule. You can use it to note appointments, meetings, and other items.

- Use the *Date Navigator* (the monthly calendar in the upper-right corner) to change the date in the Appointment Book.

- Use the *To Do list*, which appears right underneath the Date Navigator, to display a list of what you need to do on this date.

You can change the size of the display for the Appointment Book, Date Navigator, and To Do List by moving the lines that separate them. Follow these steps to resize the features:

1. Move your mouse pointer over any line between the Appointment Book, Date Navigator, or To Do list until the pointer becomes a double-headed arrow.

2. Hold down the left mouse button and drag the pointer to resize the screen items.

3. When you move the border to a new location, release the mouse button, and Schedule+ resizes the screen area.

Changing Dates in the Appointment Book

The Daily view tab always displays the current date on the Appointment Book when you first open Schedule+; to view other dates, you need to switch to other dates in your schedule. There are several ways to change the day that you view. Take a look at the Daily view tab screen again, shown in Figure 4.2.

Use the two tiny buttons with arrows on them at the top of Appointment Book area to move backward and forward in your schedule:

- A click on the left arrow button moves your schedule back one page to the previous date.

- A click on the right arrow button moves your schedule forward one page to the next date.

- Click on either the left or right arrow button and hold down your mouse button to speed through your schedule pages backward and forward, respectively.

Click here to display the next day's appointments.

Click here to
view the previous
day's appointments.

Month and year

Use the Date
Navigator calendar
to view other dates
in your schedule.

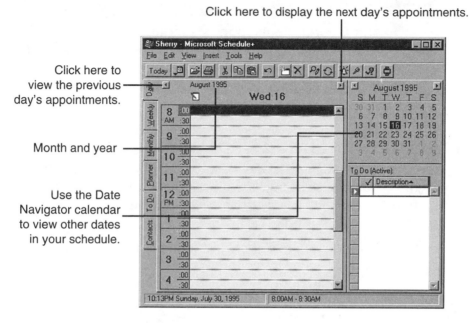

Figure 4.2   There are several ways to change the date you display in the Appointment Book.

   Back to Today   To quickly return to the current date, click on the **Today** button on the toolbar.

Another way to change dates fast is to use the Date Navigator calendar. You simply click on a date on the calendar, and Schedule+ displays it in the Appointment Book. Like the Appointment Book area, the Date Navigator has two arrow buttons on the top of the calendar that enable you to view previous or future months:

- Click on the left arrow button to display the previous month.

- Click on the right arrow button to view the next month.

- To shuffle quickly through the months in either directions, move your mouse pointer so it touches the appropriate arrow and hold down the left mouse button. Let go of the mouse button when you reach the month you're looking for.

Faster Calendar Selection You can also open a calendar quickly by clicking on the **Go To Date** button on the toolbar. When you click on this button, a calendar drops down from which you can select other dates to display.

Changing the Time Display

Not only can you change the days that you display in the Appointment Book, but you can also change the times. The scroll bar at the right of the Appointment Book enables you to scroll through the increments of time that appear in your daily schedule.

The Schedule+ program starts out with default settings for the time increments. The time frame the Appointment Book displays is set for typical use, and, for most of us, this setting works just fine. For example, the Appointment Book typically shows an 8:00 a.m. to 5:00 p.m. time frame broken down into 30-minute blocks in its window. However, you can always change this time frame to meet your own needs.

You change the time frame to suit the hours you keep using the Options dialog box. When you open this dialog box, you can use its four tabs to adjust settings for your schedule, screen display, and even reset your time zone.

Follow these steps to change the Appointment Book's time display:

1. Select **Tools, Options**.

2. Click on the **General** tab to bring the time controls to the front of the dialog box (see Figure 4.3).

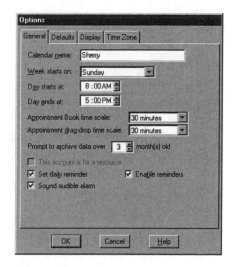

Figure 4.3   The Options dialog box.

3. To change what time the day display begins, set a time in the **Date starts at** drop-down list by clicking the up or down spinner buttons, or by clicking in the text box and typing a new time.

4. To change what time the day display ends, set a time in the **Day ends at** drop-down list the same way you set the start time in step 3.

5. To change how the Appointment Book displays minute increments, click on the drop-down list in the **Appointment Book time scale** text box and select a new increment.

6. Click **OK** to save your changes and exit the dialog box.

Changing the Time Zone

You can also use the Options dialog box to change the Appointment Book's time zone. For example, you might find it useful to view your schedule in another time zone if you do business across the country or across the world. You can even display a secondary time zone to help you as you arrange appointments with colleagues in other time zones.

To change the time zone, follow these steps:

1. Select **Tools**, **Options**.

2. Click on the **Time Zone** tab to bring it to the front of the dialog box, as shown in Figure 4.4.

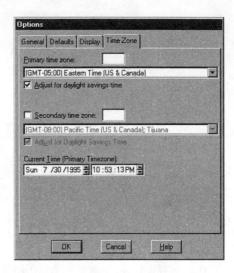

Figure 4.4   The Time Zone tab.

3. To change the time zone, click on the **Primary time zone** drop-down list and select a time zone for your Appointment Book. You can type in a description for the time zone, like EST, in the text box next to the Primary time zone drop-down list. This information then appears on your daily schedule.

4. Click **OK** to close the box.

Changing the Appointment Book's Appearance

You can also control how your Appointment Book looks with the Display tab in the Options dialog box, shown in Figure 4.5. You can change the background color of the daily schedule, and even change the point size of the text you use in the schedule.

Follow these steps to change the Appointment Book's appearance:

1. Select **Tools**, **Options**.

2. Click on the **Display** tab.

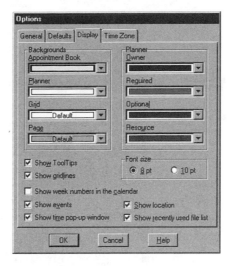

Figure 4.5 The Display tab.

3. To change the background, click on the **Appointment Book** drop-down list under the **Backgrounds** area and select a color.

4. To change font size for the appointment text (which you'll learn to enter in the next lesson), click on the **Font size** button you want to use.

5. Click **OK** to close the dialog box.

In this lesson, you learned how to understand and customize the Daily view tab. In the next lesson, you'll learn how to set up appointments in the Appointment Book.

Scheduling Appointments

In this lesson, you'll learn how to set appointments in your daily schedule.

Making an Appointment

Are you ready to start filling in your daily appointments? You can select any time slot in your Appointment Book and enter an appointment. Use the scroll arrows on the right side of the Appointment Book to move back and forth along your time schedule. (There are more hours than the typical 8:00 a.m. to 5:00 p.m.; scroll up and down to find them.) Take a look at Figure 5.1.

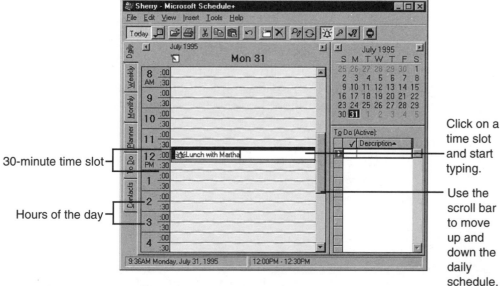

Figure 5.1 Entering appointments is easy.

To enter an appointment, perform these steps:

1. Click on the time slot into which you want to insert the appointment.

2. Type in a description of the appointment. If you type an exceptionally long description, you may not be able to see the whole description in the Appointment Book's time slot.

3. When you finish, click anywhere outside the time slot.

By default, Schedule+ assigns a reminder to the appointment, which appears as a bell icon at the front of the description. You'll learn more about reminders and other icons later in this lesson.

In many instances the appointments you're keeping track of require more time than 30 minutes. You can easily block out a longer time slot. To enter a longer appointment, follow these steps:

1. Click on the first time slot where the appointment starts.

2. Hold down the left mouse button, and drag to the ending time slot. This action highlights all the slots you select, as shown in Figure 5.2.

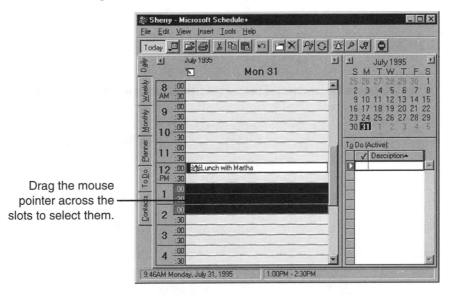

Drag the mouse pointer across the slots to select them.

Figure 5.2 You can easily select more than one time slot when you enter an appointment.

3. Release the mouse button. You can now type in your appointment's description, and Schedule+ sets the appointment in your Appointment Book (see Figure 5.3).

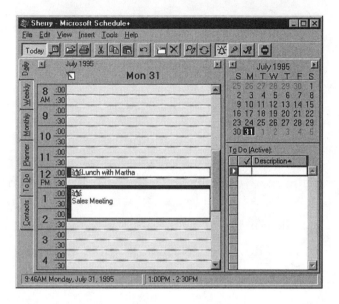

Figure 5.3 Here's an example of what a longer appointment looks like in the Appointment Book.

My Life Is Longer Than 30-Minute Increments! If you prefer to work with increments of time other than the default 30-minute time slots, you can do so. Turn back to Lesson 4 and follow the steps for changing your Appointment Book's time increments.

Once you enter an appointment, you can do all sorts of things to it:

- You can edit the appointment at any time. (See Lesson 7.)
- You can move it to another date or copy it. (See Lesson 7.)
- You can delete it. (See Lesson 7.)
- You can view it in weekly or monthly views. (See Lesson 9.)

- You can set up the appointment so that Schedule+ reminds you when the appointment time gets close. (This feature is turned on by default.) More on this in Lesson 6.

You'll learn how to do each of these things in the lessons to come. In the meantime, there's another way you can enter appointments into your schedule.

Quick Return to Today   You can return to the current date on your Appointment Book by clicking on the **Today** button on your toolbar.

Using the Appointment Dialog Box

Another route to entering more detailed appointments is to open the Appointment dialog box. To do this, double-click on a time slot. The Appointment dialog box appears on-screen, as shown in Figure 5.4.

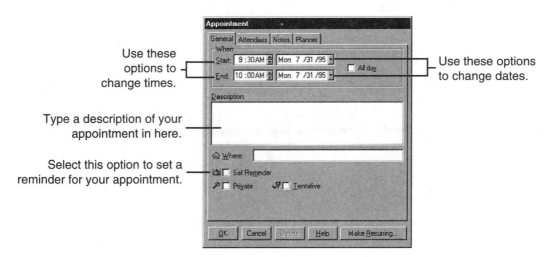

Use these options to change times.

Use these options to change dates.

Type a description of your appointment in here.

Select this option to set a reminder for your appointment.

Figure 5.4   The Appointment dialog box.

You can also access this dialog box by clicking on the **Insert New Appointment** button on the toolbar, or by opening the **Insert** menu and selecting **Appointment**.

The Appointment dialog box has four tabs for entering data. The General tab, shown in Figure 5.4, has options for setting up a new appointment. Here's an explanation of what each one of these options controls:

- **When**   This area shows the start and end times of your appointment. You can type in other times and dates as needed. The arrow buttons next to the times enable you to scroll through other hours. The drop-down arrows next to the dates enable you to view a monthly calendar to select a new date.

- **Description text box**   This text box is where you type in details about your appointment. For example, let's say you're entering your lunch date with Bob in your daily schedule. You can type **Lunch with Bob** in the description text box. When you close the Appointment box, this description appears in your daily schedule.

- **Where**   This option enables you to type in the location of the appointment.

- **Set Reminder**   If you want a reminder of your appointment beforehand with an on-screen message and an audible beep, select the **Set Reminder** option. When you select this option, additional controls appear for designating when the reminder message is to appear. (The message that appears is simply a dialog box telling you about your appointment.) For example, you can set it up to send you a reminder message fifteen minutes before your appointment. When you add a Reminder option to your appointment, a tiny bell icon appears next to the description in your schedule.

- **Private**   To keep your appointment descriptions away from the prying eyes of others, use the **Private** option. This option hides your appointments from other users on your computer network, but you can still see the appointments in your schedule. When you add the Private option, a tiny key icon appears next to your appointment description.

- **Tentative**   If your appointment is tentative, use the **Tentative** option. This keeps the appointment time from appearing as untouchable in your Planner feature. This is beneficial if you're networked and people are trying to set up meetings with you. (More about the Planner in Lesson 15.) When you select the Tentative option, a tiny check mark with a question mark icon appears next to the description in your schedule.

- **Command buttons** The command buttons at the bottom of the dialog box are standard. Use the **Delete** button to remove appointments, and the **Make Recurring** button to set up an appointment as a regular, recurring part of your schedule.

To set an appointment with the Appointment dialog box, follow these steps:

1. Double-click on any time slot in your daily schedule. This opens the Appointment dialog box.

2. Click on the **General** tab to bring its options to the front of the dialog box.

3. Set a specific time and date in the **Start** and **End** drop-down lists by clicking the up and down spinner buttons or clicking in the **Start** and **End** text boxes and typing a time and date. (By default, these boxes show the current date and the time of the time slot you double-clicked on in your schedule.)

4. Type a description of your appointment in the **Description** text box.

5. You can add any additional options, such as a reminder or a recurring appointment, by selecting those options now.

6. When you finish, click **OK**, and Schedule+ sets your appointment. The appointment now appears on your schedule.

Option Icons

When you assign an option, such as a reminder, to your appointment, an icon appears next to the description in your daily schedule. You need to learn to recognize the icons that appear in your Appointment Book and remember what they mean. Here's a handy table to help you out.

Table 5.1 The Appointment Book's Option Icons

Icon	Name	Description
🏠	Location	Indicates that there is a specific meeting place for the appointment.

continues

Table 5.1 Continued

Icon	Name	Description
	Reminder	Schedule+ reminds you about the upcoming appointment as it gets closer.
	Private	Schedule+ keeps other users on your network from seeing the appointment (if you're networked).
	Tentative	Schedule+ notes the appointment as a tentative item on the schedule to help you easily spot the time slot.

In Lesson 6, you'll find details about using each of these option icons in your own Appointment Book.

> **TIP**
>
> **Use Your Toolbar, Too!** You also find icons on the toolbar for the Reminder, Private, and Tentative options. When entering appointments directly without using the Appointment dialog box, click on the appropriate button on the toolbar to use any of these three options. You can turn the options on or off by clicking on the toolbar buttons.

Using the Other Appointment Dialog Box Tabs

There are some other things you can do in the Appointment dialog box besides set appointments. If you're networked, the other tabs in the Appointment box are useful for scheduling appointments.

Use the **Attendees** tab to view a list of people who are attending the appointment with you. (See Lesson 16 for more information.)

Use the **Notes** tab to create notes about your meeting, or type up a meeting agenda to distribute to the attendees. (See Lesson 7 for an explanation of how to use the Notes tab.)

Use the **Planner** tab, a miniaturized Planner feature that you'll learn about in Lesson 15, to view everyone's schedules to help you pick a free time for all. The **Auto-Pick** button helps you locate the first free time available among the attendees.

In this lesson, you learned how to add an appointment into your daily schedule. In the next lesson, you'll learn how to add the many appointment options to your appointments.

Setting Up Appointment Options

In this lesson, you will learn how to use the various appointment options to enhance your daily schedule.

Setting a Reminder

Do you have any pressing appointments that you can't possibly miss? Then the Reminder feature can really help you remember them. You already learned a little about inserting a reminder icon into your appointment in Lesson 5. When you set an appointment, a reminder icon that resembles a tiny bell appears in front of your appointment description, as shown in Figure 6.1.

Reminder icon ⸺

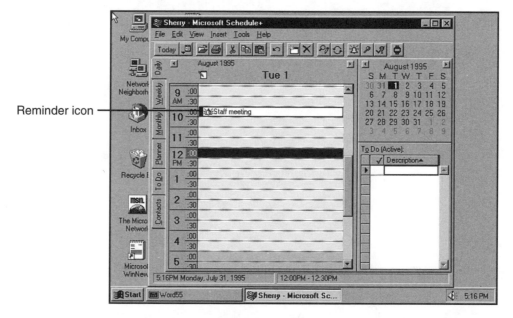

Figure 6.1   Reminder icons are easy to spot in your daily schedule.

By default, Schedule+ inserts a reminder icon whenever you type in a description in the daily schedule. You can also insert a reminder using the Appointment dialog box. To set a reminder with the Appointment dialog box, follow these steps:

It Didn't Remind Me!   If you set a reminder for a time setting that's already passed, the reminder can't alert you to the appointment. For example, if it's 3:00 and you add a 3:15 appointment to your schedule with a 20-minute prior warning, you never receive the reminder. That's because the reminder time has already passed.

1. Double-click on the appointment in the Appointment Book, or click on the **Insert New Appointment** button on the toolbar to add a new appointment to your schedule.

2. The Appointment dialog box appears on-screen. Make sure you select the **Set Reminder** check box. When you select this option, additional options appear in the dialog box, as shown in Figure 6.2.

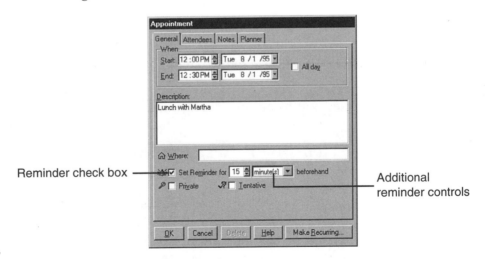

Reminder check box ——

Additional reminder controls

Figure 6.2   The Appointment dialog box.

3. Choose an advance time for the reminder. This option makes a reminder box appear on-screen when the appointment draws near.

483

4. To exit the dialog box, click **OK**.

Quick Reminders To quickly insert a reminder icon for an existing appointment, select the appointment and click on the **Reminder** button on the toolbar.

After setting a reminder, you won't be reminded about your appointment until it's time for the reminder to appear. (You learn all about the Reminder message box later in this section.) In order for the reminder to work, however, you must have your Schedule+ program open or minimized.

Turning Off the Default Reminder Setting

If you get tired of Schedule+ inserting a reminder icon every time you type in an appointment into the Appointment Book, you can turn off the default setting. To turn off reminders, follow these steps:

1. Select **Tools**, **Options**.

2. In the Options dialog box, click on the **Defaults** tab.

3. Deselect the **Set reminders for appointments automatically** check box.

4. Click **OK** to exit the Options dialog box.

To turn the default setting back on again, simply repeat the steps above, this time selecting the automatic reminder check box.

Using the Reminder Message Box

But when does the Reminder feature get around to reminding you? It depends. What advance time did you set? You can control when the Reminder feature reminds you of an appointment when you open the Appointment dialog box. You can select the Set Reminder check box to choose what time the Reminder feature calls your attention to the appointment. Fifteen minutes beforehand is a typical setting.

The catch to using this feature, however, is that you need to have your computer on, Schedule+ running (or minimized), and you need to be in the same room with your computer or you won't see or hear the reminder.

When your appointment nears, the Reminder message box pops up on your screen (depending on when you set it to appear), as shown in Figure 6.3. When the Reminder message box appears, you hear an audible beep and the message box suddenly interrupts what you were doing. The message box itself displays your appointment and its scheduled time.

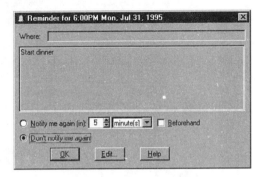

Figure 6.3 The Reminder box pops up on your screen to remind you about your appointment.

In the Reminder message box, you also see a description of the appointment and where your appointment is to take place (if you entered this information when you created the appointment). With the options at the bottom of the box, you can choose to remind yourself of the appointment again as the time for the appointment gets even closer.

- Click on the **Notify me again** option if you want another reminder before the appointment, and select a time for the reminder.

- If you don't need another reminder, select the **Don't notify me again** option.

- When you finish with the Reminder message box, click **OK** to exit.

Setting Recurring Appointments

Some of your appointments happen every week or every day, such as a weekly staff meeting or a daily car pool. Rather than typing these appointments over and over again in your schedule, use the Recurring option. The Recurring option is available on your toolbar, in your Insert menu, and even in the Appointment dialog box. Here's one way to set up a recurring appointment:

1. Select the appointment on your schedule.

2. Click the **Recurring** button on your toolbar. This opens the Appointment Series dialog box. (See Figure 6.4.)

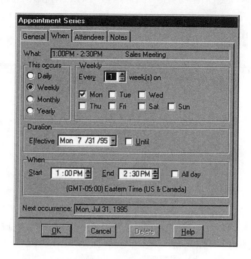

Figure 6.4 The Appointment Series dialog box.

3. Use the tabs to set up information about your recurring appointment. Click on the **When** tab to designate when the appointment occurs (daily, weekly, monthly, or yearly) and what day it falls on. You can also set the exact time of the meeting. Make your adjustments to the settings.

4. To set a reminder for the appointment, click on the **General** tab, which looks just like the Appointment dialog box. Use the **Set Reminder** option to add a reminder to the recurring appointment.

5. Click **OK** to exit the dialog box, and Schedule+ sets your recurring appointment.

A recurring appointment always appears with a circular icon beside it in your Appointment Book.

Setting Private and Tentative Appointments

If you're using Schedule+ on a network, you'll be happy to know about the Private option. This option enables you to keep appointments hidden from others who have access to your schedule on the network.

By assigning the Private icon to an appointment, you can keep others from viewing the details about the appointment. To assign a private icon to any appointment, simply click on the **Private** button on the toolbar.

Another way of keeping any important items on your schedule away from prying eyes is to use the Hide Text command. After you assign a private icon to your appointment, follow these steps:

1. Select **View, Hide Private Text**.

2. Click anywhere outside of the appointment, and Schedule+ hides the text description on your daily schedule. (See Figure 6.5.)

To see the text again, click inside the appointment, or turn off the Hide Private Text view.

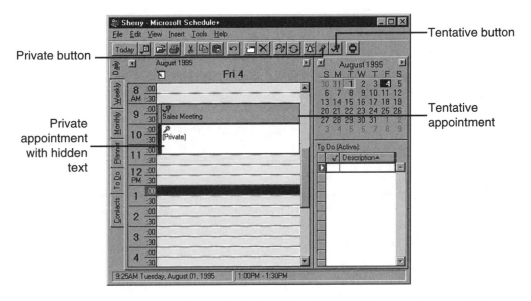

Figure 6.5   Here's an example of what a private icon and a tentative appointment look like.

The Tentative option enables you to set up the appointment in your daily schedule. Schedule+ applies shading to mark tentative appointments (refer to Figure 6.5). This shading clearly lets you know that the time slot can be made available for more pressing engagements as they come up. To make an appointment tentative, click on the appointment slot that holds the appointment, and click on the **Tentative** button on the toolbar.

In this lesson, you learned how to add appointment options to your daily schedule. In the next lesson, you'll learn how to edit and move appointments in the Appointment Book.

Juggling Appointments

In this lesson, you will learn how to edit and move your appointments.

Editing Appointments

There are several different ways to edit your scheduled appointments. You can use toolbar buttons or menu commands, or take a more direct approach. To make a change directly to an appointment as it appears in the Appointment Book, follow these steps:

1. Click inside the time slot (see Figure 7.1).

You can make edits directly to a selected appointment.

Use the toolbar buttons to help you edit your appointments, too.

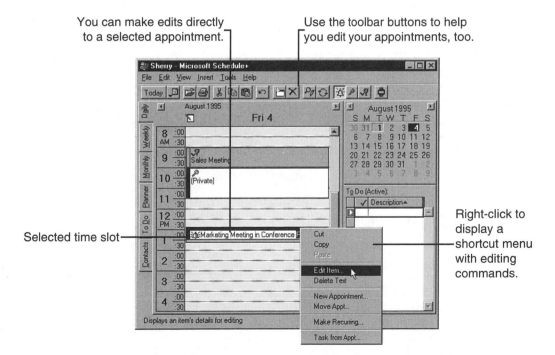

Selected time slot

Right-click to display a shortcut menu with editing commands.

Figure 7.1 Edits are a breeze in Schedule+.

2. You can edit the description text just like you edit text in a word processing program. You can delete characters, insert new words, and so on.

3. To turn appointment options on or off, simply click on the appropriate toolbar buttons. For example, to add a reminder to the appointment, click on the **Reminder** button.

4. When you finish with the edits, click anywhere outside the time slot.

Fast Edits   Right-click anywhere on your selected time slot to open a shortcut menu full of editing commands you can use.

Adding and Deleting Appointments

To add new appointments to your schedule, simply follow the steps you learned in Lesson 5. You can add new appointments directly onto your Appointment Book schedule, or your can add them with the Appointment dialog box. To add a new appointment to your schedule with the Appointment dialog box, double-click on the time slot where you want it to appear, or click on the **Insert New Appointment** button on the toolbar. This opens the Appointment dialog box that you fill in with details about the appointment.

It's very easy to remove appointments from your schedule. There are several procedures you can use. First, select the appointment you want to delete; then, follow any of these methods:

- Click on the **Delete** button on the toolbar.

- Double-click on the appointment to open the Appointment dialog box and click on the **Delete** button.

- Open the **Edit** menu and choose **Delete Item**.

- Press the **Delete** key on your keyboard.

- Right-click on the appointment to open a shortcut menu and select **Delete Item**.

Changing an Appointment's Time

You can increase or decrease the time allotted for your appointment by dragging its border to a new beginning time or ending time. Use these steps to change the appointment's time:

1. Move your mouse pointer over the bottom border of the selected time slot. The mouse pointer becomes a double-sided arrow, as shown in Figure 7.2.

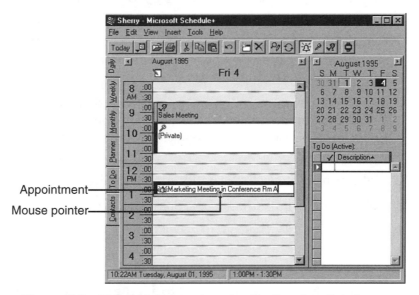

Figure 7.2   The first step in changing the time length is to move your mouse pointer over the border.

2. Hold down your left mouse button and drag the box to a new beginning or ending time.

Shorter Appointments?   If you have a short appointment that only lasts 15 minutes and your schedule is set up in 30 minute increments, you can't decrease the appointment to show less time than the time slot increments you set up. You'll need to change the time increment, as explained in Lesson 2.

3. Release the mouse button, and the appointment fills the new time slots.

491

Click and Hold   Any time you press and hold the left mouse button while you work in the daily schedule, a box detailing the date and time of the time slot appears on-screen next to your mouse pointer. Don't worry, the box is just an information box to help you.

Making Changes Using the Appointment Dialog Box

Another route to editing appointments is to open and edit them in the Appointment dialog box. To edit an appointment using the Appointment dialog box, follow these steps:

1. Select the appointment in the Appointment Book and click on the **Edit** button on the toolbar (or double-click on the appointment's time slot). This opens the Appointment dialog box containing the appointment's details.

2. Make your changes to the options in the dialog box.

3. Click **OK** to exit the dialog box. Schedule+ changes the appointment to match your edits.

Rescheduling Appointments

If you want to move the appointment to another time slot, you can drag it there with the mouse. Follow these steps to move an appointment in your daily schedule:

1. Move your mouse pointer over the left edge of the appointment that you want to relocate. The mouse pointer takes the shape of a four-sided arrow, as shown in Figure 7.3.

2. Hold down the left mouse button and drag the appointment to a new time slot. Notice that only the appointment's frame moves with the dragging motion (see Figure 7.4).

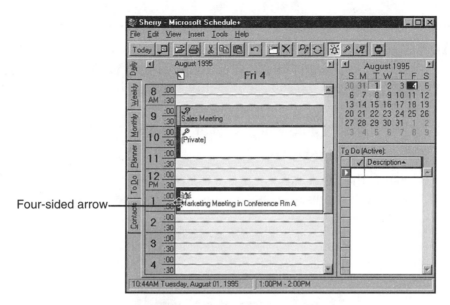

Four-sided arrow—

Figure 7.3 Click on the left border to select the appointment for moving.

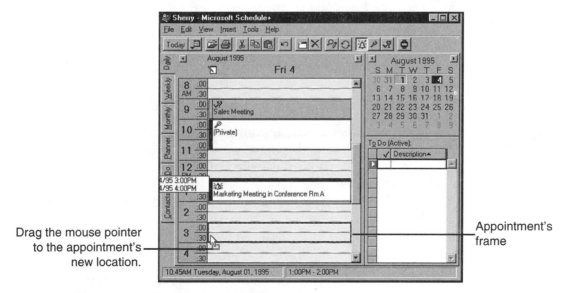

Drag the mouse pointer to the appointment's new location.

Appointment's frame

Figure 7.4 Moving the appointment.

3. Release the mouse button, and Schedule+ moves the appointment.

Moving Appointments with the Move Appointment Dialog Box

An even simpler way to move an appointment is with the Move Appointment dialog box, shown in Figure 7.5. Use these steps to activate the dialog box:

1. Select the appointment you want to move.

2. Select **Edit**, **Move Appt**.

3. When the Move Appointment dialog box appears, select a new time and date for the appointment. (See Figure 7.5.)

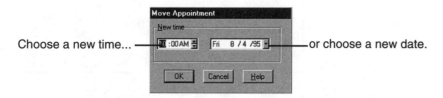

Choose a new time... ⎯⎯⎯⎯⎯⎯⎯⎯⎯ or choose a new date.

Figure 7.5   The Move Appointment dialog box.

4. Click **OK** to exit the dialog box. Schedule+ displays the appointment in its new date and time slot.

Moving Appointments with the Date Navigator

If you want to reschedule an appointment for a future date, use the Date Navigator (the calendar in the upper right corner). As you may recall from Lesson 2, you can use the Date Navigator to help you view other dates in your schedule. When you click on the appropriate date on the calendar, your Appointment Book turns to that date's schedule page. The tiny arrow buttons at the top of the Date Navigator enable you to move back and forth between months so you can view and select other dates on your schedule.

Aside from helping you view other dates, the Date Navigator also comes in handy when you want to move an appointment to another date. To move an appointment with the help of the Date Navigator, use these steps:

1. In the Date Navigator calendar, locate the month and date to which you want to move an appointment. (Use the Date Navigator arrow buttons to display the correct month.)

2. In the Appointment Book, select the appointment you want to move.

3. Hold down the left mouse button and drag the appointment over to the Date Navigator calendar to the new date.

4. Let go of your mouse button, and the appointment now appears in the other date's daily schedule.

Adding Notes to Appointments

With paper organizers, it's easy to add notes to your schedule: all you have to do is scribble your notes down. You can also add notes to your electronic schedule. You can create detailed notes along with any appointment you set. The notes don't appear in the daily schedule, but you can view your notes in the Appointment dialog box.

Follow these steps to add notes to an appointment:

1. Select the appointment to which you wish to add notes.

2. Click on the **Edit** button on the toolbar to open the Appointment dialog box.

3. Click on the **Notes** tab to bring this tab to the front of the dialog box.

4. In the empty text box that appears, you can type in all kinds of notes, jot down thoughts, etc.

5. To exit the dialog box, click **OK**.

To see the notes regarding the appointment, double-click on the appointment to open the Appointment dialog box again and click on the **Notes tab** to read them.

In this lesson, you learned how to edit and move appointments in your daily schedule. In the next lesson, you'll learn how to add events to the Appointment Book.

Adding Events to Your Schedule

In this lesson, you will learn how to add, reschedule, and edit events in your schedule with the Event Scheduler feature.

Using the Event Scheduler

Need to schedule a big event or an annual event on your busy calendar? Use the Event Scheduler to help you. Unlike appointments, events apply to the entire day, and appear at the top of your daily schedule. For instance, in Figure 8.1, today's event is Sales Recognition Day.

If you switch over to weekly view, which you'll learn about in Lesson 9, events appear at the top of the day of the week in which they occur.

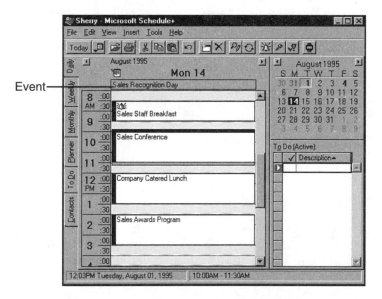

Figure 8.1 Schedule+ enables you to add events to your schedule.

What constitutes a big event? I consider my vacation to be a very big event, so I'm always trying to work it into my busy schedule. Other events might include out-of-town conferences or conventions, weddings, training classes, seminars, company trips, birthdays, and more. Events can be a one-day thing, or span days, weeks, or even months. With Schedule+, you can set recurring events so that they show up each week, month, or year. Recurring events are called Annual Events in Schedule+.

Birthday Events   Be sure to set up the birthdays of your friends and family members as events in your calendar. That way, you can spot them right away. If you set them up as recurring events, birthdays appear on your schedule every year!

Adding Events

Here's what you do to add an event to your schedule:

1. Click on the **Event** icon at the top of your schedule, as shown in Figure 8.2. A submenu appears with the options **Insert event** or **Insert annual event**.

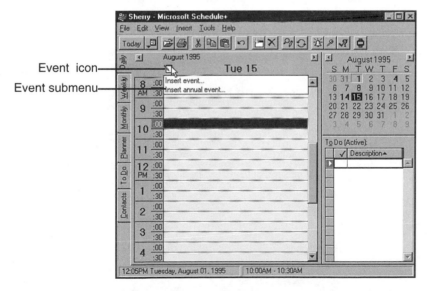

Figure 8.2   Add an event to your personal schedule with the Event feature.

2. From the submenu, choose the appropriate type of event you want to add. Either the Event or Annual Event dialog box appears on your screen (see Figure 8.3).

Set start and
end dates here.

Type in a
description
of the event.

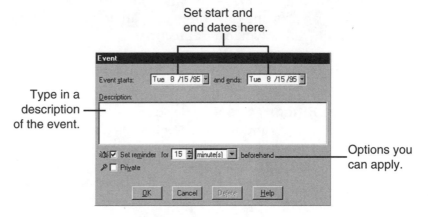

Options you
can apply.

Figure 8.3 The Event dialog box.

3. In the Event or Annual Event dialog box, choose the event start date and end date. You can use the arrow buttons next to the dates to choose other dates, or you can type in the dates you want.

Use the Menu Approach   You can also select **Insert**, **Event** to open the Event dialog box. If you're setting an annual event, select **Insert**, **Annual Event** to open the Annual Event dialog box.

4. Click in the **Description** text box and type in a description of the event.

5. Add any additional options, such as a reminder or a private icon.

6. Click **OK** to exit the dialog box. The event appears on your schedule as a heading at the top of the event day's column, as shown in Figure 8.4.

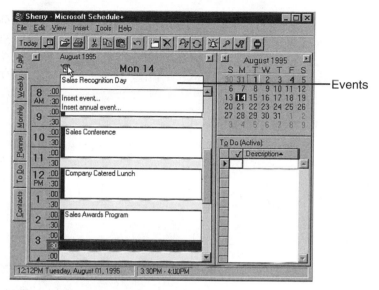

Figure 8.4   Here's an example of how events appear on your schedule.

When you set an event in your schedule, the Event icon that appears looks like it has writing on it. That's one way you can tell that you have planned an event that day. An event day also appears in bold type on the Date Navigator calendar.

Editing and Rescheduling Events

You can easily edit events at any time by reopening the Event or Annual Event dialog box and making your changes. To edit an event, follow the steps below:

1. Click on the **Event** icon; this time, your event's description appears in the submenu. You can also directly click on the Event description at the top of your daily schedule to view the submenu.

2. Double-click on the event's description in the submenu to open the Event or Annual Event dialog box.

3. Make your changes in the dialog box. For example, to change to the description, edit the description text. To edit any options, simply turn the option check boxes on or off.

4. Click **OK** to exit the dialog box.

Listing Events

Another way to edit your events, or to see a list of events, is to use the Edit menu. This is especially helpful when you want to edit events that do not appear on the current day in your schedule. To edit or list your events, use these steps:

1. Select **Edit, Edit List of**. Schedule+ displays a submenu.

2. From the submenu, select **Events** or **Annual Events**, depending on which type of event you want to edit.

3. An Events list box opens up, listing all of the events you scheduled with descriptions and start dates (see Figure 8.5).

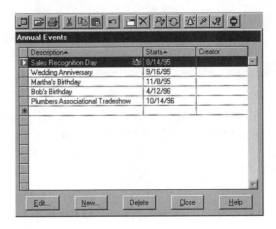

Figure 8.5 The Events list box.

4. To make changes to a specific event, select it and click on the **Edit** button. This opens the Event dialog box, shown previously in Figure 8.3. Make your edits to the event and click **OK**.

5. To add a new event to the list, click on the **New** button. This opens a new Event dialog box where you can enter detailed information about the event.

Delete It!   You can easily delete an event from the Events list by selecting it and clicking on the **Delete** button.

6. To exit the Events list box, click on the **Close** button.

To reschedule or move an event, you can open up the Events list box again and change the date by editing the event itself.

In this lesson, you learned how to add, reschedule, and edit events in your daily schedule. In the next lesson, you'll learn how to use the Weekly and Monthly view tabs.

Using the Weekly and Monthly Tabs

In this lesson, you will learn how to view your schedule with the Weekly and Monthly tabs.

Viewing Appointments with the Weekly Tab

It's time to switch views. How about looking at your busy schedule in a weekly format? You need to click on the **Weekly** tab. When you do this, your screen displays the Appointment Book in a slightly different view, as shown in Figure 9.1.

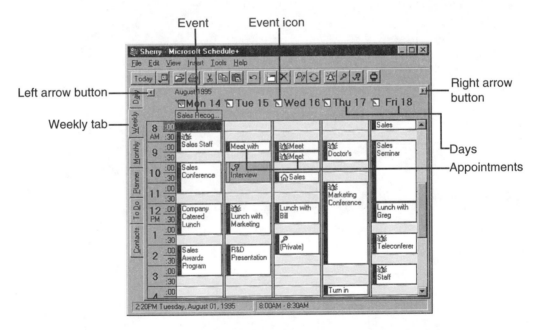

Figure 9.1 To change to the Weekly view, click on the Weekly tab.

By default, Schedule+ shows you five days of the week in Weekly view. You no longer see the Date Navigator or the To Do list. Your screen looks a little crowded in Weekly view, and some of your appointments may not fit completely into your weekly columns. You might want to maximize the Schedule+ window if it isn't so already.

I Can't See My Appointment!   If your appointment text is too long to fit in Weekly view, switch back to Daily view to read it all. You can also double-click on an appointment's border in Weekly view to open the Appointment dialog box and see details about the appointment.

The schedule you see in the Weekly view is the same as the schedule in Daily view—it's just a different look at it. You can perform the same functions in your Weekly view as in Daily view. The scroll bar at the far right side of the Weekly view screen enables you to scroll through the time slots on the schedule.

Viewing a Different Week

At the top of the Weekly view tab are two arrow buttons, shown in Figure 9.1, one on the left and one on the right. Like the arrow buttons in Daily view, you can use these arrow buttons to move your Weekly view back a week or forward a week.

To change weeks, use any of these methods:

- To move forward to the next week, click once on the right arrow button.

- To move back to the previous week, click once on the left arrow button.

- If you hold down your mouse button while selecting the arrow buttons, you move quickly through the weeks of the month.

Changing the Day Display

You can easily change the number of days that Schedule+ displays in the Weekly view tab. To change the day display, follow these steps:

1. Select **View**, **Number of Days** (see Figure 9.2).

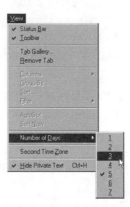

Figure 9.2 Use the View menu to change the day display. For example, to view all seven days of the week, choose 7 from the list.

2. In the submenu that appears, choose the number of days you want to display in the Weekly view tab.

3. The Weekly view changes to reflect the selection you made in the Number of Days submenu, as shown in Figure 9.3.

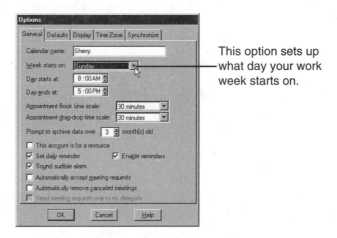

Figure 9.3 You can change the number of days Schedule+ displays using the View menu.

Specify Your Workweek and Work Hours

The General tab in the Options dialog box holds settings that affect when your schedule week starts, which days of the week are work days or non-work days, which hours are daily work hours and non-work hours, and what time increments displays, among other options. (You've already learned how to change the time increments back in Lesson 4.)

The day your workweek starts affects the display of days in the Date Navigator calendar and the days of the week that show in the Weekly view tab. The workdays and hours also affect the background colors of your schedule. As you may notice, the workweek appears in a brighter shade of color on the schedule, and non-work days and non-work hours appear in a darker shade.

Not everybody uses the same workdays and work hours, so you can adjust these settings to help you tailor the program to your situation. To change the settings for workweeks and workdays, you use the Options dialog box. To change what day of the week your workweek starts on, and what work hours you want to focus on, follow these steps:

1. Select **Tools, Options**.

2. Click on the **General** tab in the Options dialog box to bring it to the front and locate the **Week starts on** option. To change the day, click on the arrow in the drop-down list and select the appropriate day to start your workweek.

3. To change the hours that you designate as your work hours and non-work hours, change the settings in the **Day starts at** and **Day ends at** boxes.

4. To exit the dialog box and put the settings in effect, click **OK**.

Adding Schedule Items in Weekly View

You insert appointments, events, move items, delete items, and edit items in Weekly view just like you do in Daily view. The only difference is how you view the items on the daily schedule. You have a better picture of how busy your schedule is for any given week when you switch over to Weekly view.

Making Appointments on the Weekly Tab

You use the same methods for adding appointments to the Weekly view tab as you do in Daily view. You can insert appointments with the Insert New Appointment button on the toolbar, or you can add them directly to your schedule.

To add an appointment in Weekly view, follow these steps:

1. Double-click on the time slot where you want to add an appointment. This opens the Appointment dialog box. (You can also click on the **Insert New Appointment** button, or open the **Insert** menu and select **Appointment**.)

2. In the Appointment dialog box, set any start and ending times, type in a description of the appointment, and include any options.

3. Click **OK** to exit the dialog box.

You can edit appointments at any time from Weekly view. Use the same editing techniques that you apply to appointments when you edit in Daily view.

- Double-click on the appointment to open the Appointment dialog box. You use this dialog box to make changes to the appointment.

- Another way to open the Appointment dialog box is to select the appointment and click on the **Edit** button on the toolbar.

- You can also make changes directly to the appointment as it appears on the schedule. Just click on the appointment you want to edit and make your changes to the text.

- Use the toolbar buttons for options such as a reminder, private, or tentative to add these features to your appointments in Weekly view.

- You also find the editing commands and schedule options available on the Edit menu.

Adding Events in Weekly View

In Weekly view, each day has an Event icon at the top. You can use this icon just like the Event icon in Lesson 8. To insert an event into any day on your Weekly schedule, follow these steps:

1. Click on the **Event** icon at the top of the day you want to show an event.

2. In the submenu that appears, choose the appropriate type of event you want to add. This opens an event dialog box.

3. In the Event or Annual Event dialog box, choose the event start date and end date, type in a description, and add any other options you want to apply.

4. Click **OK** to exit the dialog box.

You can edit and add new events to the Weekly view tab at any time. (Turn back to Lesson 8 for tips on scheduling events.)

Viewing Your Schedule by Month

Want to see your entire month's worth of appointments? Switch over to Monthly view by clicking on the **Monthly** tab. Your screen opens and you see the entire month, as shown in Figure 9.4.

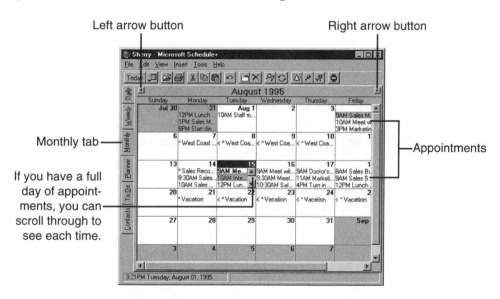

Figure 9.4   Use the Monthly tab to view an entire month's worth of appointments.

Mind you, things are a little crowded in Monthly view. If you want to see details about any appointment listed in your schedule from Monthly view, double-click on the appointment. This action opens the Appointment dialog box where you can see details about the appointment. If it's an event you want to see, double-click on it to open an event dialog box to view the details.

You can edit schedule items in Monthly view at any time; however, it's a little harder to see everything on-screen, so you're better off switching to Daily or Weekly view to make edits.

Changing Months

At the top of the Monthly view tab you see two arrow buttons (one on the left and one on the right), shown in Figure 9.5. Like the arrow buttons in Daily and Weekly view, you can use these to move your schedule view back a month or forward a month.

To change months, use any of these methods:

- To move forward to the next month, click once on the right arrow button.

- To move back to the previous month, click once on the left arrow button.

- If you hold down your mouse button while selecting the arrow buttons, you move quickly through the months of the year.

- Another way to move to the next month is to click anywhere on the shaded days or weeks that appear in Monthly view.

In this lesson, you learned how to view your schedule using the Weekly and Monthly tabs. In the next lesson, you'll learn how to use a To Do list.

Creating a To Do List

In this lesson, you will learn how to create a To Do list to help you manage the tasks you need to keep track of on your daily schedule.

Using the To Do List

The To Do list is a handy feature that helps you organize the things you need to accomplish. You can use it to enter, manage, and track tasks and projects that are important to the various dates and appointments on your schedule. With the To Do list, you can assemble lists of daily things you need to do, items you must work on to complete a project, and even compile a list of groceries you need to pick up on the way home. You can use the To Do list in all kinds of ways, but its main purpose is to help you keep track of things you need to do.

Task   Any item you list in the To Do list is a task. A task is something you need to take care of on a particular date, or something you need to do to complete a project.

Click on the **To Do** tab. This action opens a To Do list on-screen, as shown in Figure 10.1.

You've already seen the To Do list in smaller scale on the Daily view tab. (Flip back to Daily view to see the To Do list in the bottom right corner.) That particular list relates to the date you display on your Appointment Book schedule. It lists the tasks you need to complete that day, or any held-over tasks that you didn't complete the previous day. The To Do list in your To Do tab is the entire list of all the tasks you're tracking.

Task categories

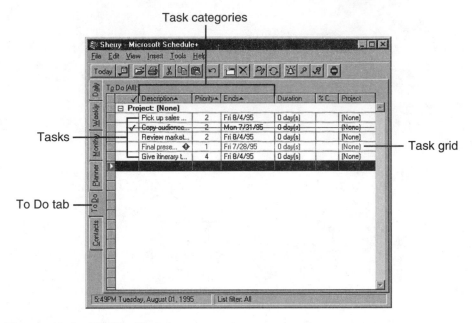

Tasks

To Do tab

Task grid

Figure 10.1   The To Do tab.

Working with Task Categories

As you can see from the previous figure, your big To Do list appears as a grid, and the more tasks you add, the bigger your grid gets. Schedule+ organizes the tasks into columns that represent categories (also called fields) such as task priority, end date, duration, and more. With these categories, and others you might assign, you can organize the tasks into group and projects. You can even filter and sort your tasks.

Changing the Grid Display

Schedule+ offers you several ways to control how it displays your To Do list grid. You can resize the columns to suit your needs. To change a column width, click on its border and drag it to a new location.

You can also change how the gridlines appear with the Options dialog box. Use these steps to turn the gridlines on or off:

1. Select **Tools**, **Options**. This opens the Options dialog box, shown in Figure 10.2.

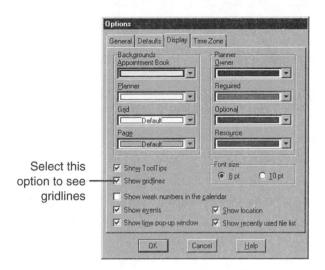

Select this
option to see
gridlines

Figure 10.2   The Options dialog box.

2. Click on the **Display** tab to bring this tab to the front of the dialog box.

3. Deselect the **Show gridlines** check box. (You remove the check mark from the box by selecting it.)

4. Click **OK** to exit the dialog box. The gridlines no longer show up in your To Do list.

5. To turn the gridlines on again, follow the same steps, but select the **Show gridlines** check box in step 3.

Changing Categories with the Columns Dialog Box

By default, Schedule+ shows several categories, or fields, that relate to the tasks you want to list. However, you can change the categories at any time. In the Columns dialog box, you can add and remove the task categories that appear on your grid.

If you don't like the task categories shown on the default grid, follow these steps to change the categories:

1. Select **View**, **Columns**, **Custom**. The Columns dialog box appears, as shown in Figure 10.3.

511

2. You can change the categories Schedule+ displays. The **Available fields** list box shows the remaining categories you can use. The **Show these columns** list box shows what categories Schedule+ currently displays in your grid.

Here's a list of other task categories you can use.

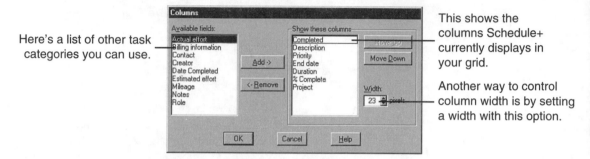

This shows the columns Schedule+ currently displays in your grid.

Another way to control column width is by setting a width with this option.

Figure 10.3 The Columns dialog box is where you can change the task categories Schedule+ displays.

3. To add a category to the Show these columns list, click on the category on the left and click on the **Add** button. To remove a category from the Show these columns list, select the category and click on the **Remove** button.

4. To change the order of the categories, select the category to move and click on the **Move Up** or **Move Down** buttons until the category is in the desired location.

5. To exit the dialog box and go back to your To Do list grid, click on the **OK** button. Schedule+ reflects any changes you made in the Columns dialog box on your To Do list grid.

Changing Categories with the Columns Command

For a faster change of your To Do list task categories, use the Columns submenu. Select **View**, **Columns**. In the submenu that appears you have several category options available:

- If you want to show all the possible task categories in your grid, select **All** from the submenu that appears.

- To show a limited number of task categories, choose **Few** from the submenu.

- To go back to the original task categories in the display, choose **Typical** from the submenu.

- If you don't want to see any additional categories at all, click on **Description** from the submenu. This option leaves you with just the Completed and Description task categories.

Reading the To Do List Grid

Take a look at the next figure to see what kinds of things the task grid tells you.

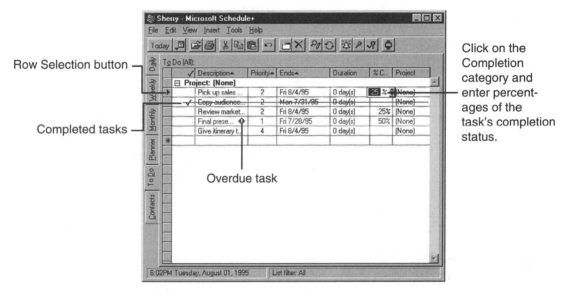

Figure 10.4   You can indicate on your task list how close you are to completing each task.

- Completed tasks appear with a line through them and a check mark in the Completed column.

- Any tasks you have not completed by the specified end date appear with an overdue symbol next to them. Also, the dates for these tasks are marked in red so you can't miss them.

- If you're viewing the To Do list in the Daily view tab, note that uncompleted tasks from the previous day or days are held-over and appear in red in the next day's To Do list.

513

- If you sort your tasks (which you'll learn to do in Lesson 11), you see an arrow next to the heading indicating which direction you sorted the tasks. An up arrow means you sorted the tasks in ascending order, and a down arrow means you sorted the tasks in descending order.

- You can group your tasks under project headings (see Lesson 11). The symbols in front (plus or minus signs) of the project heading enable you to hide or display the tasks related to the project. The project shown in Figure 10.4 has a minus sign next to its project heading, which means Schedule+ is displaying all the tasks.

- Some categories, when selected, open boxes for changing dates or percentages. These come in handy when you edit the progress and status information about your task.

- Use the **Row Selection** button to select an entire row.

Cells, Fields, and Records   Tables such as the one shown in the Schedule+ To Do list consist of intersecting columns and rows that form *cells*. Each row and column represents a *heading/entry* or *field/record*. In databases, which is what the To Do list is, each column is a field and each row is a record.

Adding Tasks

Time to start adding your own tasks to the list. A task can be any item you want to accomplish or track. To add a task to your own To Do list, follow these steps:

1. Click on the **To Do** tab to bring it to the front. Choose a row in which to start entering your task.

2. Click on the **Description** column and type in a description for your task.

3. Continue adding information in each category for the task until you fill in everything that's relevant, such as a due date for completing the task or a time range for how long you can work the task. (You can press the **Tab** key to advance to each category in the row, or you can click on the cells using your mouse.)

Using the Task Dialog Box

A second way to add tasks to your To Do list is with the Task dialog box. This dialog box enables you to add more detailed information about your task to the To Do list. Use these steps to add a task with the Task dialog box:

1. There are two ways to open the Task dialog box: you can double-click on the **Row Selection** button in front of the task (refer to Figure 10.4), or you can click on the **Insert New Task** button on your toolbar. Either method opens the Task dialog box, shown in Figure 10.5.

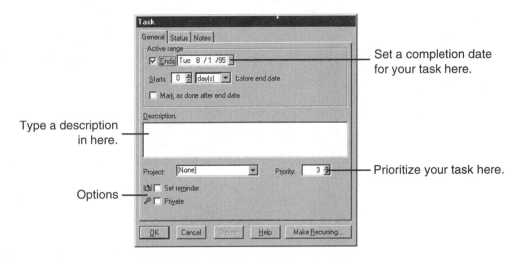

Set a completion date for your task here.

Type a description in here.

Prioritize your task here.

Options

Figure 10.5   The Task dialog box. It is very similar to the Appointment dialog box.

Task Shortcut   Another way to open the Task dialog box is to right-click on the grid and select **New Task**.

2. In the General tab, enter an ending date in the **Active range** area associated with the task, or select a date with the arrows in the drop-down list. You can also specify a starting date, which helps you track the duration of the task.

3. Use the **Mark as done after end date** check box to automatically mark the task when you complete it. By the way, this feature marks the tasks as completed after a period of time regardless of whether you remember to or not.

4. Type a description of your task in the **Description** text box.

5. If you want to associate the task with a specific project, type the project's name in the **Project** text box. (You learn more about projects in Lesson 11.)

6. If you want to prioritize the task, mark a priority rating in the **Priority** text box. By default, Schedule+ assigns a number 3, or normal, priority rating, but you can change this to another rating at any time.

7. If you need a reminder to alert you about a task, set one with the **Set Reminder** check box, and specify when you want the reminder to appear.

8. If you don't want anyone else viewing your task, click on the **Private** option.

9. Click **OK** to exit the dialog box and return to the To Do list; your new task appears on the grid.

You can use the Status tab and the Notes tab in the Task dialog box to add additional information about your task. You can also click on the **Make Recurring** button to turn a task into a recurring item.

In this lesson, you learned how to use and insert tasks in the To Do list. In the next lesson, you'll learn how to group tasks into projects and track the progress of projects.

Working with Tasks and Projects

In this lesson, you will learn how group tasks into projects and keep track of the projects in your schedule.

Turning Tasks into Projects

With Schedule+, you can group your tasks under a particular project name to help you organize the things you need to do. Let's say your boss put you in charge of creating a company brochure highlighting products and services. To accomplish a project like this, you have to complete many individual tasks, such as writing the copy to include inside the brochure, designing the layout, creating artwork, proofreading the material, and arranging to have the brochure printed by a professional printer.

Schedule+ can help you keep track of these various tasks with the To Do list. By organizing the tasks under one project name, you make it easier to locate, track, and see the tasks as you work on the project, as shown in Figure 11.1.

To create a project, follow this procedure:

1. Click the **To Do** tab to bring it to the front. Then select **Insert**, **Project**, or right-click to open the shortcut menu and select **New Project**.

2. The Project dialog box opens (see Figure 11.2). Type a name for your project in the **Name** text box.

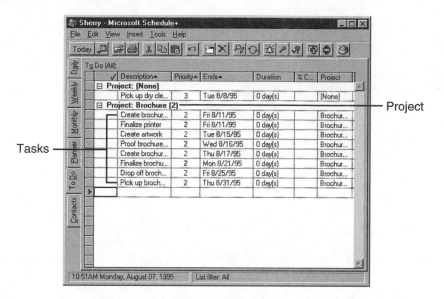

Figure 11.1 Schedule+ makes it easy to keep track of related tasks by listing them under project headings.

Figure 11.2 The Project dialog box.

3. You can prioritize your project with the **Priority** text box. Simply type in a priority assignment, or use the up and down arrows to set a different number.

4. If you want, you can turn the project into a private project using the Private check box. Click on the **Private** check box (a check mark indicates the feature is on) to hide the project.

5. Click **OK** to exit the dialog box. The project heading appears in the To Do list.

Once you have a project heading in place, you're ready to start adding tasks to it. To add tasks under the project heading, follow these steps:

1. To add new tasks to the project heading, select **Insert**, **Task**.

2. In the Task dialog box, type in information pertaining to the task, such as an end date and a task description.

3. To place the task under a project, click on the **Project** drop-down list, shown in Figure 11.3. Choose a project heading from the list.

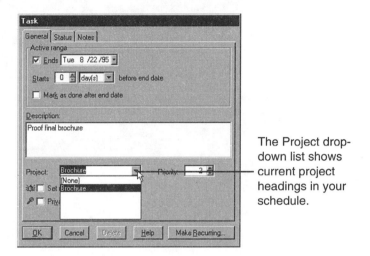

The Project drop-down list shows current project headings in your schedule.

Figure 11.3   Use the Task dialog box to assign new tasks to your project heading.

4. To exit the dialog box and add the task under the project heading, click **OK**.

If you have tasks in your To Do list, you can easily list them under project headings too. There are a couple ways to do this:

- Select the task by clicking on the **Row Selection** button (at the left of each task) and drag it under the appropriate project heading.

- Open the Task dialog box (by double-clicking on the task) and assign a project heading to the task from the **Project** drop-down list.

Displaying Projects and Related Tasks

When you have several projects on your To Do list, you can choose to list all the tasks under them, or hide the tasks. The tiny boxes in front of

519

the project heading enable you to turn your project task list on or off. A minus sign means all your tasks are visible (or expanded) under the project; a plus sign means the tasks are hidden (or collapsed) in the list. Take a look at Figure 11.4 to see what the boxes look like.

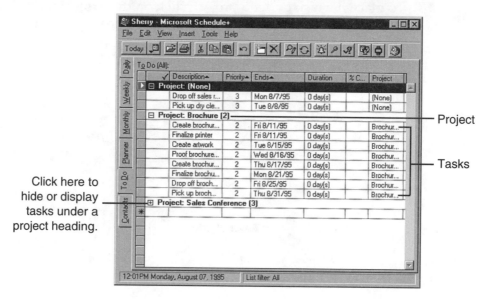

Click here to hide or display tasks under a project heading.

Figure 11.4 You can control how Schedule+ displays tasks under the project headings.

To hide the tasks under a project heading, click on the project heading box. This changes the minus sign to a plus sign. To display the tasks, click on the tiny box again.

Grouping Tasks

Not only can you control how projects and tasks appear on the To Do list (hidden or displayed), but also you can control how Schedule+ groups and lists the projects and tasks. For example, you can choose to list tasks by completion dates or by priority. You can determine the order in which Schedule+ lists your tasks under a project heading. You can list tasks in ascending or descending order and list the tasks based on information in your To Do list's categories.

The Group by dialog box enables you to group tasks in up to three levels or criteria. To group your tasks, follow these steps:

1. Double-click on the project heading, or select **View, Group by**. The Group by dialog box appears, as shown in Figure 11.5.

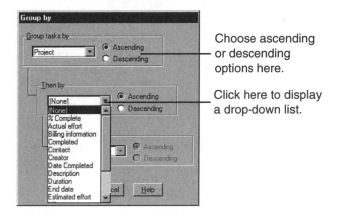

Choose ascending or descending options here.

Click here to display a drop-down list.

Figure 11.5   The Group by dialog box.

2. Select the first **Group tasks by** drop-down list. Choose a category by which you want to group the tasks in your list. For example, if you want to view your list by the End dates that you finish each task, select **End date** as the category you want to group by.

3. Next, select how you want to display the categories, either in ascending or descending order. Click on the appropriate option button to make this selection.

4. You can group your tasks by yet another level of information. To do this, select a second category in the **Then by** drop-down list and follow the same procedure as in step 2. Continue selecting the categories for grouping the tasks in your list.

5. When you finish selecting the category or categories by which to group your tasks, click **OK** to exit the dialog box. Schedule+ rearranges the tasks according to your selections.

Editing Tasks

There are all kinds of ways you can make changes to the tasks in your To Do list. Here are some methods you can use to edit tasks:

- You can double-click on the **Row Selection** button next to the task you want to edit, and make your changes in the Task dialog box.

- Or you can select a specific task field and make your changes directly into the individual parts of your task in the list.

TIP

Edit the Daily To Do List, Too!   You can apply the editing techniques listed here to your To Do list on the Daily view tab. You don't have to open the To Do tab every time to make changes.

- Depending on the column, additional controls appear when you click on a field. You can use the controls to set different percentages, dates, and so on. These controls are helpful in tracking the status of the tasks.

- You can right-click on your selected task to open a shortcut menu with more commands you can use to edit your task.

- To delete a task, select it and press the **Delete** key.

- To change your column headings (fields) open the **View** menu and select **Column**; then select **Custom**. This opens the Column dialog box where you can edit which columns appear in your list. (See Lesson 10.)

- To display more or fewer columns, open the **View** menu, select **Column**, and select the number of columns you want to display on your grid.

- To insert a new row onto your grid, select the row before which you want the new row to appear, open the **Insert** menu and choose **Row**.

TIP

Turning Tasks into Appointments   You can quickly turn a task into an appointment on your schedule. Select the task, right-click to display the shortcut menu, and select **Appt. from Task**. This opens the Appointment dialog box that you use to turn the task into an appointment.

Setting Task Reminders

You learned about setting reminders in your schedule in Lesson 6. You can also assign reminders to your tasks. If you add a reminder option to a task, you see a Daily Reminder box on your screen the day you need to work on a task. Task reminders work like the reminder message boxes you use with your daily appointments. However, task reminders appear at the beginning of the day, not at a specific time; Schedule+ associates task reminders with dates, not times.

For example, if you assign a specific date to a task, and set up a task reminder option for that date, you can expect to see a task reminder box appear on that date as soon as you start your Schedule+ program.

To add a reminder to any task, follow these steps:

1. Double-click on the task for which you want to set a reminder from the To Do list. This opens the Task dialog box (refer to Figure 11.3).

2. Click on the **Set Reminder** check box (the one with the bell icon) and set how many days before or after the task date that you want to receive a reminder about the task. For example, if you want to receive a reminder about a task three days before its end date, set your reminder for three days and select **End date** from the drop-down list.

3. Click **OK** to exit the dialog box. A reminder icon now appears beside the task description in the To Do list.

On the day you set for the reminder to alert of the task, the task reminder message box appears with an audible beep when you first start your Schedule+ program for the day. To close the message box, click **OK**. You can also choose to make changes, such as resetting the days, to the task reminder message box by clicking on the **Edit** button.

Tracking Tasks

Tracking tasks on your To Do list is fairly straightforward. When you complete a task, click on the **Completed** column (the column with a check mark at the top). This action places a check mark in front of your task, strikes through the task with a line, and the % Complete column shows 100% (if you use a % Complete category). Take a look at Figure 11.6 to see what a completed task looks like.

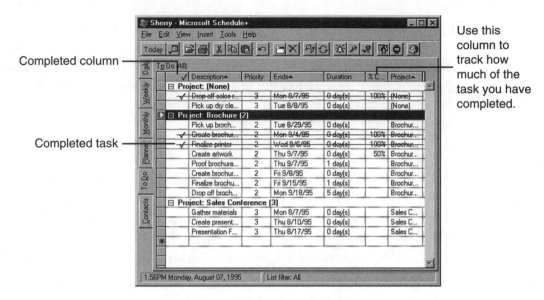

Completed column —

Use this column to track how much of the task you have completed.

Completed task —

Figure 11.6 Use the To Do list's tracking features to help you monitor a task's status.

There are lots of ways for you to use the To Do list's task categories to track a task's status. Here are a few things to remember when tracking your tasks:

- If a project or task is related to a specific date on your schedule, it shows up in the Daily view tab on the To Do list.

- Any tasks that are left over from the day before appear in red with an overdue symbol next to them on the To Do list.

- The % Complete column enables you to log in a percentage that indicates how much of the task is complete.

- The Priority column enables you to prioritize the tasks based on a number scale.

- The Ends column specifies when you are to complete the task.

There's a great deal of flexibility in the To Do list's tracking features that enables to you maintain a system that works best for you. Although Schedule+ helps you with reminders and overdue icons, it's still up to you to manage your To Do list and keep yourself on schedule.

In this lesson, you learned how to list tasks under project headings, to group the tasks in the To Do list, and to track tasks. In the next lesson, you'll learn how to build a database of contacts.

Building a
Contacts List

In this lesson, you will learn how to use Schedule+ to build a list of the people you contact the most.

Using the Contacts List

You use the Contacts tab to compile information about the people you contact the most, such as business associates, sales leads, and friends and neighbors. Once you complete your Contacts list, you can keep updating it and even use it to make appointments. You can also list birthdays or other special events associated with the contact so that the events appear on your schedule. If you use Schedule+ on a network, you can share your Contacts list with other users. Regardless of how you use it, you quickly find that the Contacts feature is an important part of your Schedule+ program.

The Contacts list that you build in Schedule+ is actually a database. A *database* is a collection of information that you can store, organize, and retrieve quickly. The information you store for each person is a *record*. The individual parts of the record, such as the name or address, are *fields*.

 Database   A database is computer program or feature designed to store, organize, and retrieve large collections of data.

You can use the names, addresses, and phone numbers from your Contacts list to create mailing lists, call up other computers (with a modem), and more. It's like having an electronic Rolodex at your fingertips.

To display the Contacts list, click on the **Contacts** tab on your
Schedule+ window. This action opens your program up to a screen
similar to the one shown in Figure 12.1.

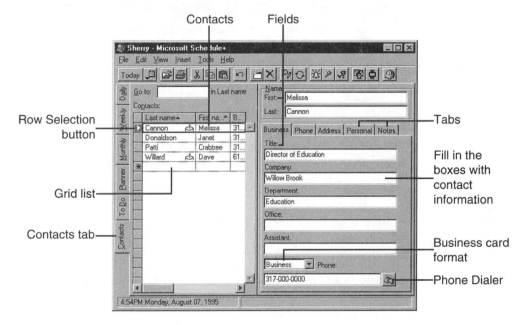

Figure 12.1 The Contacts tab.

As you look around the Contacts tab, you see a grid with a list of
contacts on the left and a business card type area for entering data on
the right. After you start a list of contacts, you can sort and group the
contacts.

Here's what each of the Contacts tab features can do:

- Use the **Go to** text box to quickly locate contacts in your database.
  Type in the name of the person you're looking for, and Schedule+
  highlights this person in your list.

- The **Contacts** area of the tab displays a grid list of your database
  names and fields.

- The **Name** area (in the business card area) displays a form in which you can enter information about your contact, such as the contact's name, business, phone, and address.

You'll learn more about using each of these features later in this lesson.

Entering Contacts

You might as well jump right in and start compiling your own list of contacts. Remember, a contact can be anybody you know or with whom you do business. Contacts can include friends, relatives, coworkers, business associates, vendors, and more. You can enter information about your contacts directly into the grid list, or you can use the business card area of tabs and fields. Here's one way you can enter a contact into the list:

1. Click on a **Row Selection** button in front of the row you want to enter your contact into, preferably an empty row. This action displays a blank Name form on the right side of your screen.

2. In the **Name** area, start typing in information into each field as necessary. For example, to enter a name, click inside the **First** text box and type a first name.

3. If necessary, click on the **Business** tab to bring it to the front. Start filling in the Business tab field. Click inside each text box, or field, to fill in related information. Keep in mind that you do not need to fill in every field, only the ones you use the most.

4. Click on the other business card tabs to enter in more details, such as other phone numbers and addresses.

5. To enter birthday or anniversary information about the contact, click on the **Personal** tab, shown in Figure 12.2, and set the date. When you enter personal information about a contact, such as a birthday, a birthday cake symbol appears in your contact grid.

6. When you finish with the contact information, click inside the grid area. Your entry now appears as a contact on the list, as shown in Figure 12.3.

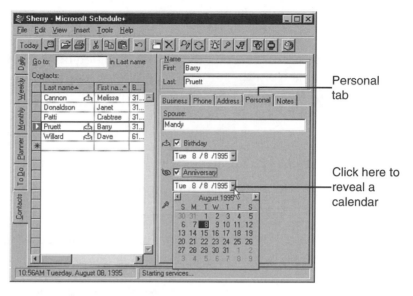

Figure 12.2   The Personal tab.

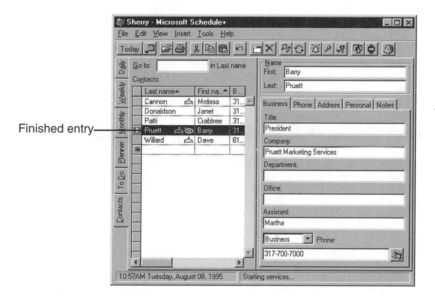

Figure 12.3   A finished entry appears in the Contacts grid.

You can repeat these steps to continue adding new contacts to your database.

529

Entering Contacts with the Contact Dialog Box

If you don't like the direct approach to building a Contacts list, you can use the Contact dialog box. This dialog box neatly displays similar fields from the form on the Contacts tab, but it places the information in a larger area. To open the Contact dialog box, choose one of these methods:

- Select **Insert**, **Contact**.
- Right-click to display the shortcut menu and select **New Contact**.
- Double-click on an empty row's **Row Selection** button.
- Click on the **Insert New Contact** button on your toolbar.

All of these methods open the Contact dialog box, shown in the next figure.

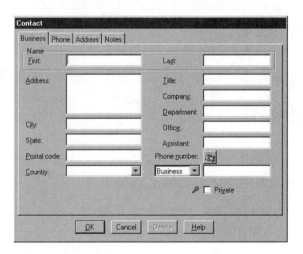

Figure 12.4   The Contact dialog box.

The dialog box looks like the business card area on your Contacts tab, only the information is spread out and arranged differently. However, you can't enter personal information about the contact in the Contact dialog box. You can only do this in the Personal tab back on the Contacts tab of the program. The Contact dialog box does not include fields for birthdays or anniversaries.

To use the Contact dialog box, fill in each field in the tabs for which you have information. If you want to keep certain listings in your Contacts tab private, click on the **Private** check box in the Contact dialog box. This keeps the information hidden from other users on your Schedule+ network. Click **OK** when you finish to return to the Contacts tab.

Editing Contacts

You can edit the records in your Contacts list at any time. You can make your edits directly into the grid list, in the business card area on the right, or with the Contact dialog box. You can also use the toolbar buttons and menus. Try any of these techniques to make changes to your own Contacts list:

- To edit records directly on your grid list, click inside the cell where you want to make changes. You use the scroll bars to move back and forth between the fields and records.

- To edit contact information directly in the business card area on the right side of the Contacts tab, select the record you want to change. This action displays the record's fields. Click inside any field on the right and make your changes to the information.

- Double-click on a row's **Row Selection** button to open the Contact dialog box and make changes.

- You can also display the Contact dialog box by right-clicking on the entry and choosing **Edit Item** from the shortcut menu, or by clicking on the **Edit** button on your toolbar.

As you work with your Contacts list over time, you may need to remove old contacts that you no longer need. To delete a contact, use any of these methods:

- Select the record by clicking on the record's **Row Selection** button (this highlights the entire record) and click on the **Delete** button on the toolbar.

- Double-click on the record's **Row Selection** button to open the Contact dialog box and click on the **Delete** button.

- Select the record using the **Row Selection** button, and press the **Delete** key on your keyboard.

- Select the record using the **Row Selection** button, open the **Edit** menu, and choose **Delete Item**.

- Right-click on the record to display a shortcut menu and select **Delete Item**.

In this lesson, you learned how to build and edit a Contacts list. In the next lesson, you'll learn how to sort and group your contacts.

Sorting and Grouping Contacts

In this lesson, you will learn how to group and sort information in your Contacts list, and how to insert your contacts into appointments and tasks.

Sort Through Your Contacts List

After you compile a list of contacts, you will want to be able to sort through the list, especially if it's a long list. When you perform a sort, Schedule+ looks through the database for specific records, fields, and common elements. You then can display those records that Schedule+ finds in a particular order.

There are several ways to sort your contacts. Let's start out with a simple sort in your Contacts grid. You can click on any of the column headings in your grid list to perform an immediate sort of data found in that column, or field, in ascending order. For example, if you click on the First name column heading, Schedule+ immediately sorts the database alphabetically by first names and displays the records in ascending order (As at the top of the list and Zs at the bottom). Take a look at Figure 13.1.

The up arrow on the column heading means that you sorted the selected column in ascending order. To sort in descending order (Z to A), press the **Ctrl** key while you click on the column heading. When you do this, Schedule+ sorts your list in descending order. Schedule+ determines the column headings that appear in your grid by the Group by settings, which you'll learn about later in this lesson.

That was an easy way to sort your information. There are a couple of other ways you can sort. If you want to sort new entries immediately after you enter them, use the AutoSort command. Select **View**, **AutoSort**. Any time you type in a contact, Schedule+ automatically sorts it as soon as you finish entering it. Yet another way you can sort data is with the Sort dialog box, which you'll learn about next.

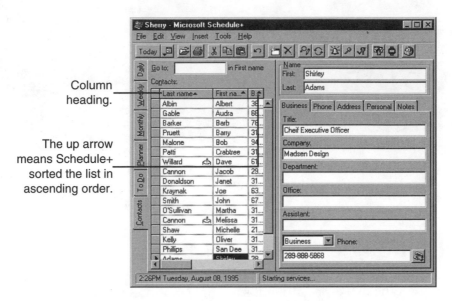

Column heading.

The up arrow means Schedule+ sorted the list in ascending order.

Figure 13.1 You can sort a Contacts list by first names.

Go To Don't forget about the Go to box at the top of your Contacts tab. It's a speedy route to the fields Schedule+ displays on your grid. (Remember, Schedule+ bases the columns it displays on the Group by specifications you make in the View menu. You'll learn about the Group by command later in this lesson.)

Ascending or Descending? When you sort, there has to be some type of order to the list that Schedule+ displays in your grid, either alphabetically or numerically. If you sort in ascending order, Schedule+ displays your records from A to Z, or from 1 to the greatest numerical value in your list. If you sort in descending order, Schedule+ reverses the order alphabetically or numerically.

Sorting with the Sort Dialog Box

Now try another sort, this time using more details. When you sort with the Sort dialog box, you have the option of sorting by three levels and by several categories. In addition to these options, you can choose to view the sort in ascending or descending order. In each level, you can click on the drop-down arrow to reveal the category by which you wish to conduct the sort.

All of the categories Schedule+ displays in the drop-down list are actually fields from your Contacts tab. The Sort feature enables you to choose to sort by any field available on the Contacts tab or the Contact dialog box.

You can use the Sort dialog box to be very specific about how Schedule+ displays your contacts in the grid list. For example, perhaps you want to sort your Contacts list by ZIP code (called *postal code* in Schedule+). In the Sort box drop-down lists, you have the choice of sorting by business address postal codes or home address postal codes. Schedule+ has a great deal of flexibility in its sorting capabilities.

To sort your contacts using the Sort dialog box, follow these steps:

1. Select **View**, **Sort**. This opens the Sort dialog box you use to determine how you want to arrange the list. You can sort your Contacts list using up to three different levels, shown in Figure 13.2.

2. Select the first sort level.

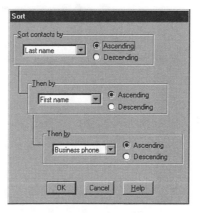

Figure 13.2   Start with the first sort level and select a category to sort you list by.

3. Click on the drop-down arrow in the **Sort Contacts by** drop-down list to display a list of sort categories and choose a category from the list.

4. Continue choosing other levels and categories from the **Then by** drop down lists to narrow your sort.

5. Click **OK** to exit the dialog box and perform the sort on your list.

Also on the View menu is a Sort Now command that immediately sorts your list based on specifications you set in the Sort dialog box.

Grouping Contacts

Do many of your contacts share the same information, such as phone numbers or departments? Another thing you can do with your list is group your contacts. For instance, because some of the people on your list work for the same company, or same industry, you can group them together. The Schedule+ grouping feature enables you to group contacts in a variety of categories and subgroups.

To group contacts, follow these steps:

1. Select **View**, **Group By**. This opens the Group by dialog box, shown in Figure 13.3.

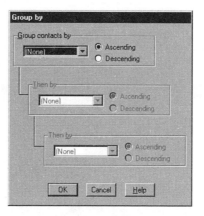

Figure 13.3 The Group by dialog box.

2. Open the **Group Contacts by** drop-down list by clicking the drop-down arrow and select a category by which you want to group your contacts. Schedule+ bases these categories on fields in your Contacts tab. The categories that you choose to group by in your list also determine which columns Schedule+ displays on the grid.

3. Choose additional categories to group by from the **Then by** drop down lists.

4. Choose ascending or descending order for each category you select.

5. Click **OK** to exit the dialog box and display your groups. The grid list now displays the groups that you specified, as shown in Figure 13.4. The group name appears in bold above each group of contacts on the list.

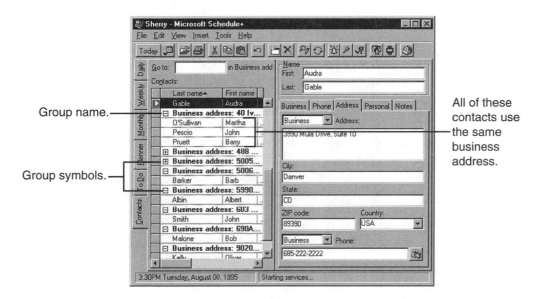

Figure 13.4 In this example, I grouped my contact list by business addresses.

6. You can expand or collapse the list in a group by clicking on the group symbol (the tiny box) in front of the group name. A minus sign in the tiny box in front of the group name means that every contact is visible, or expanded. A plus sign in the tiny box means that every contact pertaining to the group name is hidden, or

collapsed. Click on the plus or minus sign to hide or show contacts listed under the group name.

7. To ungroup your Contacts list, open the Group by dialog box again, this time select **None** for each group by category.

Using Contact Information in Appointments or Tasks

After compiling a list of contacts, you can use the Contacts list to schedule appointments or tasks to use with the other Schedule+ features. For example, you can select a contact from your list and use the information about the contact to create an appointment on your daily schedule. To use contact information to schedule an appointment, follow the steps below:

1. Select the contact with whom you want to schedule an appointment.

2. Right-click to open the shortcut menu and choose **Appt. from Contact**.

3. The Appointment dialog box appears on-screen, as shown in Figure 13.5. The **Description** box shows your contact's name and company. Set a time and date for the appointment.

Figure 13.5 The Appointment dialog box.

4. Click **OK** to exit the dialog box, and Schedule+ inserts the appointment in your schedule.

To use contact information in a task, follow these steps:

1. Select the contact about whom you need information for a task on your To Do list.

2. Right-click to open the shortcut menu and choose **Task from Contact**.

3. The Task dialog box appears on-screen, and its **Description** box shows your contact's name and company. Add any options you want to include in the task, such as an end date or reminder.

4. If the task is related to a specific project, identify that project heading with the **Project** drop-down list.

5. Click **OK** to exit the dialog box, and Schedule+ adds the contact information to the task on your To Do list.

Dial 'em Up!

You may notice a tiny phone icon in the Contacts tab or in the Contact dialog box. This is the Dial Phone button, and it's part of the Phone Dialer feature, a Windows 95 accessory program. The Dial Phone button enables you to use your computer modem to call your contact's modem or fax machine. You can use the little phone symbols that appear next to phone numbers to dial up your contacts. Just click on the **Dial Phone** button, and your computer starts dialing for you, as shown in Figure 13.6.

Your phone must be hooked up to a modem for this to work. You also need to make sure your modem is setup properly. (You can set up the modem settings in the Windows 95 Control Panel. Just click on the **Modems** icon to open the options.) To open the Windows 95 Phone Dialer feature, select **Start, Programs, Accessories, Phone Dialer**. You also can dial your contacts directly with the Phone Dialer window, too.

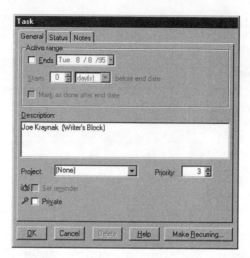

Figure 13.6 The Dial Phone button automatically starts dialing with your modem.

In this lesson, you learned how to work with your Contacts list, including grouping and sorting the list and using the Phone Dialer feature. In the next lesson, you'll learn how to print various portions of your schedule.

Printing Your Schedule

In this lesson, you will learn how to preview and print portions of your schedule, including appointments, To Do lists, and the Contacts list.

Printing with Schedule+

Being able to print out portions of your schedule is an important part of using Schedule+. There are times when you aren't sitting in front of your computer with your daily schedule ready to use. You may have to travel, or work at home, and you want a copy of your schedule on hand. Or perhaps you need to give a friend or coworker a copy of your To Do list or Contacts list.

Schedule+ offers you several ways to print portions of the various features. You find all the options listed in the Print dialog box, shown in Figure 14.1.

Let's go over the Print dialog box in more detail so you can learn how to use its options:

- At the top of the dialog box, you find a listing for your default printer. To change this to another printer, click on the **Setup** button and select another printer from the **Printer** drop-down list box.

- The Print layout list box lists all the available parts of your Schedule+ program that you can print out. Use the scroll bar to view different items in the list. More about this later in the lesson.

- The Paper format drop-down list box enables you to choose to print the selected item on paper, a Filofax page (a personal organizer), or on labels.

- The Schedule range options enable you to select the date(s) you print out for the selected item (when applicable). For example, if you're printing your weekly schedule, you can choose the exact week you want to print out.

The assigned printer appears here.

Choose the item you want to print from this list.

Controls print quality.

Click on this button to preview the selected item.

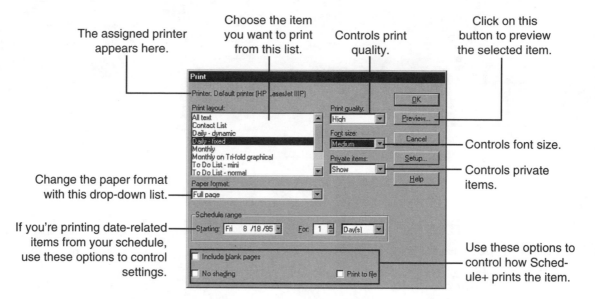

Change the paper format with this drop-down list.

Controls font size.

Controls private items.

If you're printing date-related items from your schedule, use these options to control settings.

Use these options to control how Schedule+ prints the item.

Figure 14.1   Each part of the Print dialog box controls how Schedule+ prints your item.

- The options at the bottom of the dialog box enable you to control how Schedule+ prints the item. For example, if you select the **No shading** check box, the top of your printout isn't shaded with the default design (which tends to use up a lot of your printer's ink).

- The three drop-down list boxes to the right of the Print layout list box enable you to control print quality, font size, and private items on your schedule.

- Use the **Preview** command button to preview how the select item looks before printing it out. (Learn more about this feature later in this lesson.)

Speedy Printing   By default, Schedule+ prints each item with shaded areas (sometimes these areas are located at the top of the page, or scattered on your page). To speed up printing, be sure to select the **No shading** check box. This keeps the printer from printing the shaded background, and you are able to read more clearly any text from the shaded areas.

Using the Print Layout List Box

The Print layout list box displays the parts of your Schedule+ program you can select for printing. Simply highlight the layout you want to print and click on the **OK** button to print it out. By default, the dialog box is setup to print a full page of the selected item on its current date.

Each of the items in the Print layout list box enables you to print certain portions of your Schedule+ features. To use these items effectively, you need to know what each item prints. The following table explains what kind of printout you receive after selecting the item for printing.

Table 14.1   Print Layout List Box Options

Option	Result
All text	Prints out all the text items in your daily schedule.
Contact List	Prints the entire list of contacts you have in the Contacts List.
Daily—dynamic	Prints the daily schedule in its most current state of change on your network.
Daily—fixed	Prints the daily schedule.
Monthly	Prints the monthly view of your schedule.
Monthly on Tri-fold graphical	Prints three elements on a single page, including the daily schedule, all 12 months, and the To Do list.
To Do List—mini	Prints the tasks associated with the selected date.
To Do List—normal	Prints the entire To Do list, including all the details associated with each task.
To Do List—text	Only prints the text descriptions of the tasks.
Weekly 5 day	Prints five days of the week on a single page.
Weekly 7 day	Prints seven days of the week on a single page.

There are a few additional details to keep in mind when printing the different layouts:

- All tentative appointments that you schedule appear in italic on the printout.

- If you scheduled lots of appointments in the daily schedule you print, the appointments may not fit in the designated space. If this happens, you find that Schedule+ carries the overflow of appointments into the Other Appointments box on the printout.

- If you print the To Do list or Contacts list, the printout reflects any sorts you performed on the columns.

Previewing Your Schedule

One of the best parts of the Print dialog box in Schedule+ is the Preview feature. It enables you to see what your information looks like in printed form before you actually go to the trouble of printing it out. The Print Preview window enables you to preview any of the layout items in the Print layout list box. Follow these steps to preview your layout:

1. Open the Print dialog box. (Click on the **Print** button on the toolbar, or select **File**, **Print**.)

2. In the **Print layout** list box, choose the item you want to print. Click on the layout to highlight the selection.

3. Choose any additional options you want to apply.

4. When you're ready to preview the layout, click on the **Preview** button.

5. The Print Preview window appears on-screen, as shown in Figure 14.2. Use the scroll bars to view different portions of the layout.

6. You can use the **First Page** and **Next Page** buttons at the top of the window to view other pages. Click on the **Zoom In** button to get a closer look, as shown in Figure 14.3.

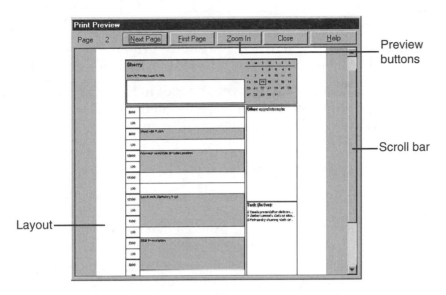

Preview buttons

Scroll bar

Layout

Figure 14.2 The Print Preview window.

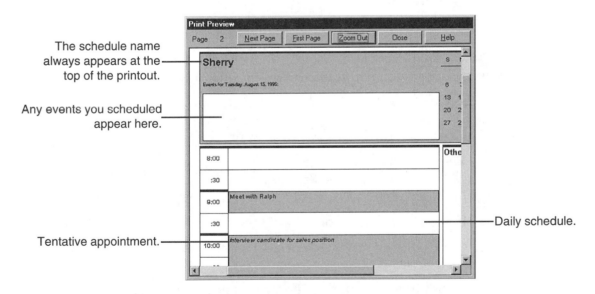

The schedule name always appears at the top of the printout.

Any events you scheduled appear here.

Tentative appointment.

Daily schedule.

Figure 14.3 You can get a better look at the layout's contents by using the zoom control.

7. To zoom back out again, click on the **Zoom Out** button.

8. When you're ready to exit the Print Preview window, click on the **Close** button to return to the Print dialog box.

Remember, the layout you see in the Print Preview window varies depending on the item you select in the Print layout list box. You can preview To Do lists, Contacts lists, and more.

Printing Your Schedule

Depending on what layout you select, your printout shows different elements and page orientation. You may be quite surprised at the professional-look of the printout that comes out of your printer. In the top-left corner of every page is the schedule name (usually your name, if that's the schedule you chose to print). At the very bottom of the printed page, you find a footer (text line) indicating when you printed the page, complete with date and time.

To print out a copy of your schedule or any other Schedule+ features, follow these steps:

Quick print   You can print using the default settings, and bypass the Print dialog box, by clicking on the **Print** button on the toolbar.

1. Open the Print dialog box by selecting **File, Print**.

2. The Print dialog box appears on your screen. Select the layout you want to print from the **Print layout** list box. (Click on the item to highlight it.)

3. If necessary, select from any of the other printing options.

4. Click **OK**, and Schedule+ prints the schedule layout you selected.

What's the Print to File Option For?   You can print other schedules besides the one you open in your program, such as another user's schedule on a network. Select the **Print to File** option; this action opens a dialog box that enables you to choose other schedules to print. You can also use this option to save your own schedule in another folder or file.

In this lesson, you learned how to print parts of your schedule and other items from Schedule+. In the next lesson, you'll learn how to work with the Planner.

Working with the Planner

In this lesson, you will learn how to use the Planner tab to view your schedule at a glance.

Using the Planner Tab

For a different perspective of your busy schedule, take a look at it in Planner view. Click on the **Planner** tab on the left side of your view area. This action opens your schedule in Planner view, as shown in Figure 15.1.

By default, the Planner view shows the schedule for several days as soon as you open it onto your screen. However, you can change what days and weeks are in view, and you can change the size of each date's space on-screen.

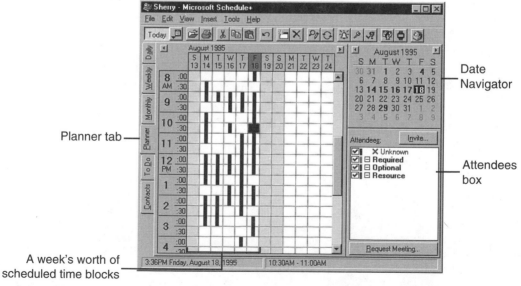

Figure 15.1 Planner view organizes your schedule into free and busy blocks of time.

The Planner shows you a graphical display of your schedule in chunks of time. This graphical depiction is called the *free/busy display*. Like the Daily and Weekly views, the Planner view shows your schedule with a vertical display of time increments. With the Planner view, you can easily examine your schedule over several days, and find available time blocks. If you're networked, you can view other users' Planner views to help you organize meetings for all attendees.

What Day Does It Show? If you open the Planner view tab after using any of the other scheduling tabs, the Planner displays the same time and dates as the previous view tab.

Also on your screen is the Date Navigator, which you recognize from the Daily view tab, and an Attendees box, which lists the other networked users that you invite to the meetings you schedule. You use the Attendees box only when you're networked with other Schedule+ users. (You learn more about using the Attendees box in Lesson 17.)

If you use the Planner view in group-enabled mode (on a network), you see the Invite and Request Meeting buttons, as shown in Figure 15.1. These buttons enable you to set up meetings with other network users. (You'll learn how to use these buttons in Lessons 16 and 17.)

If you use the Planner tab in stand-alone mode (not on a network), you don't see an Invite button, and, instead of the Request Meeting button, your screen shows a New Appointment button. You use the New Appointment button to schedule new appointments on your schedule. If you click on it, the New Appointment button opens the Appointment dialog box described in Lesson 5.

Hey, This Planner Looks Familiar If you already peeked at the Planner tab in the Appointment dialog box, you've seen this feature already. Of course, it was a scaled-down view, but it was still the Planner.

Changing the Planner Display

The Planner view shows the schedule for several days as soon as you open it onto your screen. However, you can change what days and weeks are in view, and you can also change the size of three main elements on-screen.

To change the dates in view on the Planner tab, use any of these methods:

- Click on the left arrow button to move the view back one week.

- Click on the right arrow button to move the view forward one week.

- To return your view to the current date, click on the **Today** button on the toolbar.

- Use the Date Navigator to select a specific date to view. Just click on the day you want to see in the Date Navigator's calendar. To change the month the Date Navigator displays, click on the left or right arrow buttons in the corners of the calendar.

- You can also view a day quickly with the **Go To Date** button on the toolbar. This button works the same way as the Date Navigator calendar.

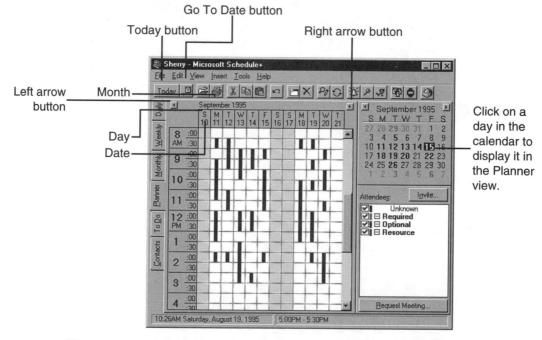

Figure 15.2 Schedule+ offers you many ways to change the dates that you see in the Planner view.

Shortcut Menu!   To quickly view dates in the Planner view, right-click on the **Date Navigator** calendar. When the shortcut menu appears, select the **Today** or **Go To** command.

Changing the Sizes of Planner Elements

You can enlarge the amount of space each of the three elements of the Planner view takes up. For example, if you want to see more of the schedule and less of the Date Navigator and Attendees box, you can use your mouse to drag the border separating the elements to a new dimension. Follow these steps to resize any of the elements:

1. Move your mouse pointer over the border separating the elements you want to enlarge or reduce. The mouse pointer turns into a double-headed arrow when you place it over a border, as shown in Figure 15.3.

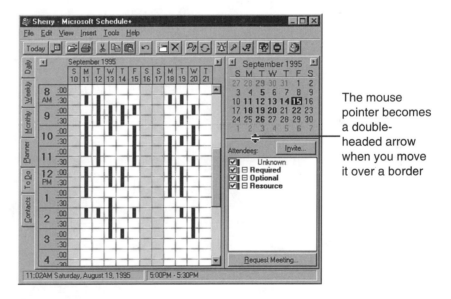

The mouse pointer becomes a double-headed arrow when you move it over a border

Figure 15.3   Drag the borders to resize the elements in the Planner view.

2. Hold down the left mouse button and drag the pointer in the direction you want to enlarge or reduce.

3. Let go of the mouse button, and Schedule+ resizes the elements.

Reading the Planner Schedule

Before you can use the Planner feature effectively, you need to know how to read the blocks of time it displays on-screen. Depending on your setup (networked or not networked), the Planner reveals different items on-screen. While the Planner is very helpful in stand-alone mode, it is even more useful in a network situation. For example, check these things out:

- The blue lines, called bars, extending up and down on the Planner schedule represent your appointments (see Figure 15.4). You can quickly see at a glance what times you are busy. (If you're networked, you see the display of other users' planner lines in other colors.)

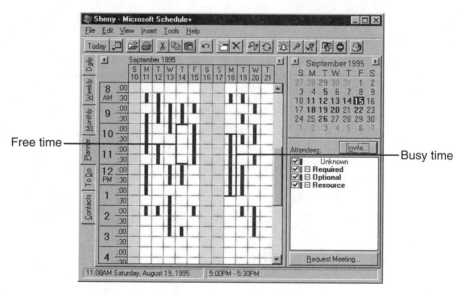

Figure 15.4 The blue bars represent your busy times.

- The vertical gaps between the blue bars represent open chunks of time that you did not set aside for appointments (free times). This view enables you to see when you're available for other appointments or commitments.

- To see the details about a particular appointment, double-click on one of the bars. This action reveals whose appointment it is. Click on the name to see details about the appointment.

- If you work in stand-alone mode (not connected to other computer users), your screen shows a New Appointment button. You can use the New Appointment button to quickly set another appointment on your already busy schedule.

- If you work in group-enabled mode (networked with other users), your screen shows a Request Meeting button. You can use this button to invite other networked users to your meetings.

- Also in group-enabled mode, you see little X's appear in the Attendees box if you happen to select a time slot in which that person is busy.

In this lesson, you learned how to use the Planner tab to view busy and free times on your schedule. In the next lesson, you'll learn how to use Schedule+ in a network environment.

Using Schedule+ on a Network

In this lesson, you will learn how to use Schedule+ on a network and set up access permissions for others to view your schedule.

Working with Access Permissions

The Planner tab, as described in Lesson 15, becomes extra useful when you're networked with other Schedule+ users. It enables you to see the busy schedules of others, coordinate meetings, and track responses of attendees. In this lesson, you learn to set up your schedule for viewing and accessing on a network.

Using Group-Enabled Mode   The very first time you open Schedule+, you have the option of using the program in group-enabled or stand-alone mode. If you're using Schedule+ on a network, be sure to select group-enabled mode. If you select the Don't ask me this question again check box, you won't be able to switch to another mode unless you reinstall Schedule+.

If you're using group-enabled mode, you can use the Planner view to check out the scheduled blocks of time of other users who publish their schedules on the network. You must have Read permission in order to see the schedules of other users, because, after all, they don't want just anybody knowing how busy or not-so-busy they are. The same goes for you—you probably don't want everyone on the network to have full access to your schedule. So the first step in viewing schedules on a network is establishing access permissions.

Viewing Access Permissions

Schedule+ enables you to use different levels of access permissions to view other users' schedules and let others view your schedule.

The level of access permission depends upon what role you assign to the user. Take a look at the various roles and levels available:

Table 16.1   Access Permissions

Role	Permissions
None	No viewing permissions.
Read	Ability to read all appointments, contacts, tasks, events, and appointment details.
Create	Ability to set up appointments, add to contacts, tasks, events.
Modify	Ability to make changes to appointments, contacts, tasks, and events.
Delegate	Ability to make changes to parts of schedule, except private items. Can also send and receive meeting messages on your behalf.
Owner	Ability to make changes to the schedule, plus view and change private items, and change users' permissions to access your schedule.
Delegate Owner	Same access as Owner, plus can send and receive meeting messages for you.
Custom	You specify what permissions you want to allow.

Obviously, you can control how much of your schedule others on the network can access. All of these roles for other users depend on your own network or office situation. For example, if you're a busy executive, you may want to assign your secretary the role of Delegate Owner in order to keep your schedule organized. In this role, your secretary can make changes to your schedule, coordinate meetings, and control the access permissions that others have to your schedule. On the other hand, another executive in another department may only want to assign his secretary to the role of Read when it comes to accessing his schedule. Or, a team of coworkers may want to grant each other equal or varying roles regarding each individual's schedule.

To view users' access permissions, follow these steps:

1. Select **Tools, Set Access Permissions**. This opens the Set Access Permissions dialog box, shown in Figure 16.1.

Figure 16.1 The Set Access Permissions dialog box.

2. To assign or view access permissions, click on the **Users** tab.

3. To add other users to your list, click on the **Add** button. This action opens the Add Users dialog box, shown in Figure 16.2.

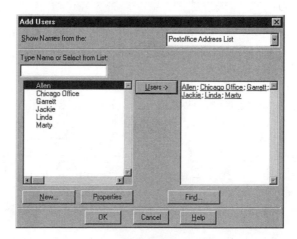

Figure 16.2 The Add Users dialog box enables you to add other network users' names to the Users list in the Set Access Permissions dialog box.

4. Choose the name you want to add from the list of users shown in the left column, or type in the user's name. To select names from a specific network post office, select the address list from the **Show Names** drop-down list and choose the specific user name you want to add.

5. Click on the **Users** button to add the name to the right column list. The right column shows the names of users whose schedules you can currently view in the Planner tab.

6. Continue following steps 4 and 5 to add more names. Click **OK** to exit the Add Users box and add the name(s) to the Users list in the Set Access Permissions dialog box.

7. The Set Access Permissions dialog box reflects your changes. Click **OK** to exit the dialog box.

Changing Access Permissions

You can change the access permissions that others have to your schedule at any time. Use these steps to change permissions:

1. Select **Tools, Set Access Permissions**.

2. This opens the Set Access Permissions dialog box (see Figure 16.3). To assign or change access permissions, click on the **Users** tab.

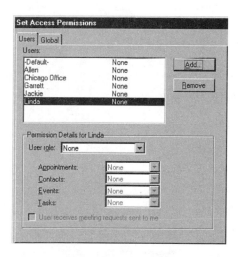

Figure 16.3   The Set Access Permissions dialog box lists users and their access permission status.

3. A list of users and their access permissions appears in the **Users** list box. Select the name of the person whose access you want to modify.

The User Name Isn't Shown! If the user's name doesn't appear in the list box, click on the **Add** button and choose the user's name from your network mail list. Then click **OK** to return to the dialog box.

4. To assign a new pre-defined role, click on the **User role** drop-down box, as shown in Figure 16.4. Select a role from the list.

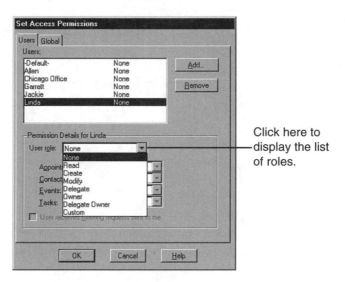

Click here to display the list of roles.

Figure 16.4 Select a new role from User role drop-down list.

5. Click on the **OK** button to exit the dialog box. (A warning box pops up on-screen telling you that Schedule+ is merging the changes you selected with the network's server.)

To customize the roles you assign, select the **Custom** role option in the **User role** drop-down list. Next, apply any of the permission options in the boxes that appear below the User role drop-down list:

- Click on the **Appointments** list box to select the level of access you want the person to have to your appointments.

- Click on the **Contacts** list box to select the kind of access you want the person to have to your contacts.

- Click on the **Events** list box to choose the access permission you want the person to have to your events.

- Click on the **Tasks** list box to assign the permission role you want the person to have regarding your To Do list.

Schedule Posting Options

To control which parts of your schedule you post on the network, use the **Global** tab of the Set Access Permissions dialog box. Here you can choose to allow overlapping appointments, recurring appointments, and designate how much of your schedule you want to publish on the network. Follow these steps to change global access to your schedule:

1. Open the **Tools** menu and select **Set Access Permissions**.

2. This opens the Set Access Permissions dialog box. Click on the **Global** tab to bring this tab to the front of the dialog box, as shown in Figure 16.5.

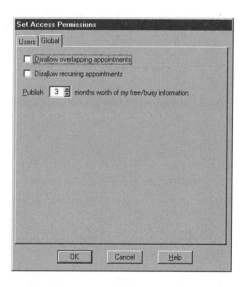

Figure 16.5   The Global tab of the Set Access Permissions box has options for displaying your schedule on the network.

3. If you prefer not to allow overlapping appointments in your schedule, click on the **Disallow overlapping appointments** check box.

4. If you prefer not to let others set up recurring appointments in your schedule, click on the **Disallow recurring appointments** check box.

5. You can control how many months of your schedule you post on the network with the **Publish** option. Choose 0 if you do not want to post your schedule at all.

6. Click **OK** to exit the dialog box and put the options into effect.

Opening Other Users' Schedules

If you have access, you can open another user's schedule. Depending on what kind of permission you have, the user may allow you to do more than just read the schedule. In many instances, you may be in charge of managing the user's schedule, or maintaining a task list or contact list. If you have the proper permissions, once you open the other person's schedule, you can make edits to it and add new items.

To open another schedule, besides your own, use these steps (these steps only apply to networked Schedule+ users):

1. Select **File**, **Open**. In the submenu that appears, choose **Other's Appointment Book**.

2. The Open Other's Appt. Book dialog box appears, as shown in Figure 16.6. Select the name of the person whose schedule you want open.

I Don't See the Person's Name in the List! If the name of the person whose schedule you want to open doesn't appear in the list box, click on the Show Names drop-down list and choose the address list containing the name of the person you want. You can also use the Find button to look up the name.

3. Click **OK** to exit the dialog box, and the schedule appears as a second opened program window in addition to your own schedule window. If it doesn't, you may not have the correct access role to open the other person's schedule.

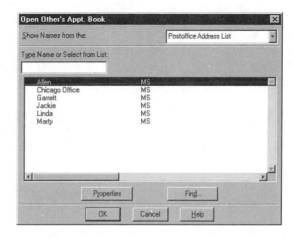

Figure 16.6 The Open Other's Appt. Book dialog box.

Once you open another user's schedule, you can read or make changes to it only if you have the proper access. You don't see items marked as private unless the user assigned you Owner or Delegate Owner access.

To close the schedule at any time, use the same methods you use to close your own Schedule+ program:

- Click on the **Close** button in the upper right corner.

- Select **File**, **Exit**.

- Double-click on the window's **Control-menu** icon (upper left corner).

In this lesson, you learned how to view and change access permissions as well as open other users' schedules. In the next lesson, you'll learn how to schedule meetings in a network environment.

Preparing to Schedule Meetings on a Network

In this lesson, you will learn the preparation steps you need to schedule a meeting on your network, including how to invite attendees and pick a time for the meeting.

Scheduling Group Meetings

When you use Schedule+ in a network environment, you can schedule meetings with other users on your network. It's easy and fast, plus you can coordinate the best possible meeting times, track responses to your meeting invitations, and reschedule appointments with minimal effort.

To actually invite someone to a meeting, you send the person an e-mail message describing the event and requesting attendance. You can even e-mail meeting invitations to people outside of your network environment, as long as they use Microsoft Exchange to receive and send e-mail messages (having Schedule+, although useful for automating the scheduling and tracking of meetings with attendees outside your network, is not required). For example, if you're setting up a seminar, and you want to invite colleagues from other companies, Schedule+ can help you arrange the event and send out e-mail invitations.

When you schedule a meeting, there are several steps you have to go through before you can finalize the meeting on every participant's schedule. Look at this overview of the procedures you need to follow to schedule network meetings. I'll go into more detail about each step later in this lesson.

1. Initially, you need to determine who needs to attend the meeting. After you do this, view the schedules of the people you want to attend the meeting using the **Invite** button on the Planner tab.

This button adds other users' schedules to your Planner view to enable you to see busy and free times.

2. Next, you need to check everybody's schedules for an available time in which you can all meet. When it comes to finding an appropriate meeting time, Schedule+ has several ways to help you. You can choose a meeting time by manually viewing schedules in the Planner view until you find a good time, or you can use the AutoPick feature that automatically coordinates an available time among all the attendees.

3. After you find a meeting time, you need to send out a Meeting Request. You use Schedule+'s Meeting Request form to send out request messages to everyone you want to attend the meeting. (More about this feature in Lesson 18.)

4. Finally, you can track everybody's responses to your request and find out who's attending the meeting and who's not (see Lesson 18).

One of the easiest ways to set up a meeting is to use Schedule+'s Meeting Wizard, a step-by-step approach to arranging a meeting from start to finish. (You learn more about this feature in Lesson 18.)

Using the Invite Button

The first step to preparing a meeting with other users on your network is to determine who needs to attend the meeting. You can use the Invite button on the Planner tab to view other users' free and busy times in the Planner view. The Invite button does not invite people to the meeting, it just enables you to see everybody's schedule at a glance.

There are three categories of attendees you can use when creating an attendance list for a meeting:

- **Required**   These are the people whom you require to attend the meeting, and who are essential for the meeting's success. When the attendee notes that you require attendance, it simply signals that you need the attendee's input.

- **Optional**   These are the people whose attendance is not absolutely necessary for the meeting, but you think these people may be interested in attending or participating.

- **Resource**   Use this category to indicate the meeting location or any special equipment you need for the meeting, such as a computer or video player. If you want to alert the person in charge of the location or equipment, you can select that person's name here.

Follow these steps to select attendees with the Invite button:

1. With Schedule+ open to the Planner view tab, click on the **Invite** button. (This button is only available if you're using group-enabled mode, see Lesson 1.) See Figure 17.1 to locate the Invite button.

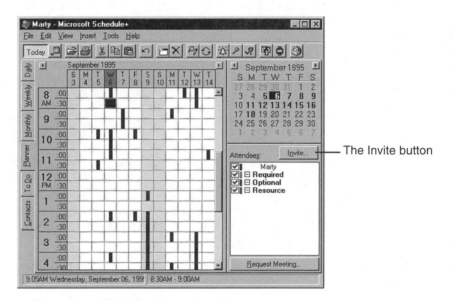

The Invite button

Figure 17.1   Locate the Invite button on the Planner view tab.

2. The Select Attendees dialog box appears, as shown in Figure 17.2. You may need to choose another address list from the **Show Names from the** drop-down list box. Then, select the name of a person you want to attend, or type in the name.

3. Next, click on the **Required**, **Optional**, or **Resource** button to assign the attendee to a category.

4. After you choose all of the meeting's participants, click on the **OK** button to return to the Planner view tab.

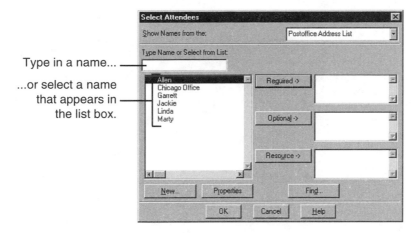

Figure 17.2   The Select Attendees dialog box.

A Step Ahead   By selecting categories in step 3, you can fill out a Meeting Request form to send out to the attendees more quickly. The names you assign as Required appear in the To line of the request form. The Optional names appear in the Cc line, and the Resource name appears in the Where line. You learn more about the Meeting Request form later in this lesson.

Viewing Free and Busy Times

There are several ways that you can view the schedules of the attendees. To see the attendees' busy times on the Planner as a group, you should view one attendee category at a time. For example, to see the busy times of the Required attendees, double-click on the Required heading in the Attendees box. A check box next to the category means that the attendees' schedules appear on the Planner. The busy times for all the attendees in that category appear highlighted by black borders on the Planner grid.

After viewing the busy times, click on the category heading to turn off the display for that category. To view all the attendees in each category, double-click on each heading, as shown in Figure 17.3.

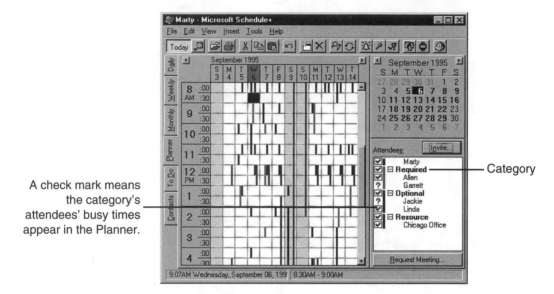

A check mark means the category's attendees' busy times appear in the Planner.

Category

Figure 17.3 Use the Attendees box to display the busy times of the people you want to attend your meeting.

- To view just one user's busy times, double-click on the person's name in the Attendees box. Black borders highlight the person's busy times on the Planner.

- Click anywhere in the Attendees box to clear the black borders from the Planner grid.

- To see the names of the people who are busy at a specific time on the Planner, double-click on the time slot, or right-click the mouse button.

- To see details about any particular user's schedule, double-click on the busy time slot and select the user's name from the list. If you have access to the user's schedule, you see the details about the user's previously scheduled appointment.

- Click on any time slot on the Planner grid and look over at the Attendees box to see who is busy and who is free. A check mark appears if that person's schedule is in the Planner. A question mark means that person's schedule is not available. An X indicates that the person has a prior commitment during the meeting time.

Reading Bars on a Network Planner

As you learned in Lesson 15, the blue bars in your Planner view are exclusive to your schedule. However, when you're networked, you see other colored bars on the Planner as well. When you publish your schedule on the network, it shows other users a colored bar representing the times you are busy. The colored bars help differentiate between users. Depending on what access permissions you assign, other users may or may not be able to see details about your schedule.

Here's how to read the colored bars in your Planner view:

- The gray bars on the Planner indicate the busy times of the required attendees at your meetings.

- The purple bars are busy times for the optional folks attending your meetings.

- The green bars represent busy times for the resource (meeting location or equipment).

Remember, you can double-click on a time block to see details about an attendee's appointments, as long as you have access to the attendee's schedule.

Selecting a Meeting Time

The next step in arranging a meeting is picking out an appropriate time. After you decide who should attend, and you view the free and busy times of the attendees, you're ready to select a meeting time.

Probably one of the best tools you can use when you schedule meetings is the AutoPick feature. You can use it to quickly locate free blocks of time for all attendees on the Planner. Here's what you do:

1. Select the time slot (one or more) in which you want to schedule the meeting—try to pick the earliest date or time you need.

2. Select **Tools**, **AutoPick**. Schedule+ goes to work and locates the earliest time available for all the attendees and highlights it on the Planner schedule.

3. If you like the time suggested, click on the **Request Meeting** button and send out your invitations. If you don't like the time suggested, open the AutoPick tool and do it again until you find a suitable time.

In this lesson, you learned how to prepare for meetings with other users on your network by determining who should attend and selecting a time for the meeting. In the next lesson, you'll learn how to send out Meeting Request Forms to invite people to the meeting.

Sending Meeting Requests on a Network

In this lesson, you will learn how to send out meeting invitations and manage responses to the requests on your network.

Calling a Meeting

Once you find an appropriate time to have the meeting (see Lesson 17), you're ready to invite the attendees. You need to use the Meeting Request form.

You Can't Invite Just _Anybody_...   Everybody you invite has to be hooked up to a mail server and the Microsoft Exchange system, in order to receive your invitation (including people you're inviting who are outside of your network environment, such as colleagues at other companies). Although it automates scheduling and tracking meetings, all attendees do not have to have Schedule+ to receive invitations to your meeting.

You can use Schedule+'s Meeting Wizard to help you call a meeting. You can also use the Request Meeting button on the Planner tab. When you set up a meeting, you must identify all the people whom you are inviting to attend, choose a meeting time, send out request messages, and receive responses to the messages. First, take a look at the Meeting Request form.

Sending Out Invitations with the Meeting Request Form

To invite the attendees yourself, you can fill out the Meeting Request form and e-mail it to the people you want to attend. Here's how to use this feature:

1. From the Planner view tab, click on the **Request Meeting** button in the Attendees box. The Meeting Request dialog box appears, as shown in Figure 18.1.

2. If you've already determined the names of the people attending and their appropriate categories, you notice that Schedule+ fills in the top portion of the form with this information. If not, you need to fill in the text blocks indicating where you are holding the meeting, and who needs to attend (fill in the **To** and **Cc** boxes).

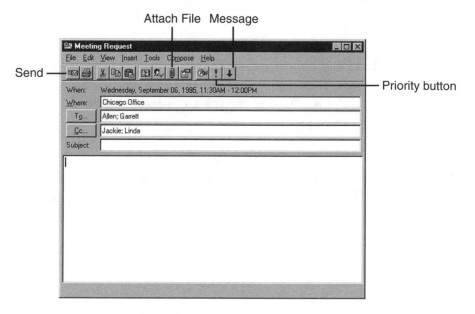

Figure 18.1   The Meeting Request form. (It looks just like a typical e-mail form.)

3. Next, click inside the **Subject** text box and type in a description of the meeting. This description appears in the schedules of the attendees.

4. Use the large text box to add any notes about the meeting, or to type up a meeting memo.

5. If you need to attach files to the message, or prioritize message importance, use the toolbar buttons to do so. (You use these same toolbar buttons on the network e-mail system.)

6. When you're ready to send the message, click on the **Send** button on the toolbar. This sends the e-mail request and exits the form.

Using the Meeting Wizard

An easier way to send invitations is with the Meeting Wizard. The Meeting Wizard button only appears on your Schedule+ screen if you're using group-enabled mode. Take a look at Figure 18.2 to find the button. To use it, click on the Meeting Wizard button on your toolbar and follow the prompts that appear. The Meeting Wizard leads you through all the steps and coordinates a time and date for the meeting. All you have to do is answer its questions and click on the Next buttons to proceed from dialog box to dialog box. Keep in mind that each wizard dialog box focuses on a particular aspect of the meeting, such as who to invite or where the meeting will be held.

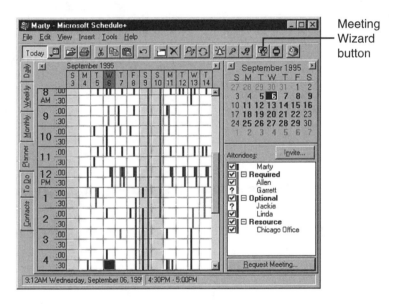

Meeting Wizard button

Figure 18.2   The Meeting Wizard button appears on your toolbar if you're using group-enabled mode.

To use the Meeting Wizard, follow these steps:

1. Click on the **Meeting Wizard** button on the toolbar (see Figure 18.2), or select **Tools, Make Meeting**.

2. The Meeting Wizard dialog box appears, as shown in Figure 18.3. Select the categories of people you want to attend and click on the **Next** button.

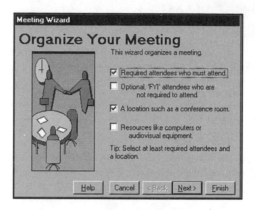

Figure 18.3   The first Meeting Wizard dialog box.

3. The second Meeting Wizard dialog box prompts you to select the names of your attendees. You can type them in directly, or select them from your network Address Book (click on the **Pick Attendees** button). After selecting names, click on the **Next** button to continue to yet another wizard dialog box.

4. The next wizard dialog box to appear gives you the option of selecting a location in which to hold your meeting. Make your selection and click on **Next** to continue to another wizard dialog box.

5. In the next Meeting Wizard dialog box you can select a duration time for the meeting. You can even factor in driving time if you are holding the meeting off-site. Make your selections, then click on **Next**.

6. The next wizard dialog box asks you to choose an acceptable time range and potential days for holding your meeting. Make your selections; then, click on **Next**.

Warning!   A warning box appears if Schedule+ cannot find information about a requested attendee. This only happens if you choose an attendee who is not using Schedule+ on your network, or if the person isn't using Schedule+ in group-enabled mode.

7. In the next wizard dialog box, you can see the available free and busy times of the attendees you're inviting, and Meeting Wizard enables you to find out which dates, times, and locations are good for all attendees. If you don't like the time the Meeting Wizard chooses, click on the **Pick Next Time** button to have Meeting Wizard locate another time. Click on **Next** to continue to another wizard dialog box.

8. When you make it through all of the Meeting Wizard's questions, it prompts you to send a meeting request form. Click on the **Finish** button, and the Meeting Request form appears on-screen (refer to Figure 18.1).

9. The Meeting Request form lists all the attendees whom you want to invite, and the time and location of the meeting. Fill in the rest of the form detailing the meeting and click on the **Send** button on the toolbar to send out the invitations.

Tracking Responses

As each attendee responds to your meeting request, the responses show up in your Inbox (part of your network e-mail system). You can easily identify the responses by the Schedule+ symbols.

If you happen to receive an invitation, open it up by double-clicking on the meeting request message; Schedule+ coordinates the request with your schedule and lets you know if you can make it or not. To automatically reply, click on the **Accept**, **Decline**, or **Tentatively Accept** buttons. This opens a mail window for responding to the originator.

Back on the receiving end, the originator of the meeting request can track responses to the invitations and find out who's coming to the meeting or not. If you're the one doing all the inviting, here's how to track the attendees responses:

1. Open your schedule to the Daily view tab; then, double-click on the meeting slot in your appointment book to open the Appointment dialog box.

2. Click on the **Attendees** tab to bring it to the front.

3. As each attendee responds to the request, their names appear in the list with symbols next to them. The symbols indicate the attendees' status regarding your meeting. (Table 18.1 shows what each symbol indicates.)

573

4. To close the dialog box, click **OK**.

Table 18.1 Identifying Responses to Meeting Invitations

Symbol	Indicates...
✓	Accepts invitation
✗	Declines invitation
✓?	Tentatively accepts invitation
☑	Accepts and includes a message response
☒	Declines and includes a message response
☑	Tentatively accepts and includes a message response
🖥	No response yet

Need Extra Help?   To learn more about using Schedule+ in a network environment, be sure to have your network administrator give you a few lessons.

In this lesson, you learned how to arrange meetings with other users on your network. In the next lesson, you'll learn how to customize your Schedule+ program.

ACCESS

What Is a Database?

In this lesson, you'll learn some basic database concepts and find out how Microsoft Access handles them.

What Are Databases Good For?

Strictly speaking, a *database* is any collection of information. Your local telephone book, for example, is a database, as is your Rolodex file and the card catalog at your local library. With a computerized database in Microsoft Access, you can store information, as with these three examples, but you can also do much more. For instance, if you keep a list of all your business customers in an Access database, you can:

- Print out a list of all customers who haven't bought anything in the last 60 days, along with their phone numbers, so you can call each one.

- Sort the customers by ZIP code and print out mailing labels in that order. (Some bulk-mailing services require you to presort by ZIP code to get the cheaper mailing rate.)

- Create a simple on-screen order entry form that even your most technically unskilled employee can use successfully.

These examples only scratch the surface. With Access, you can manipulate your data in almost any way you can dream up.

How Access Stores Your Data

In Access, the first thing you do is create a *database file*. That file holds everything you create for that database—not only all the information, but also the customized forms, reports, and indexes. If you have two or more businesses, you may want to create two or more separate databases, one for each business.

Tables

The heart of each database is its tables. A table is a lot like a spread-sheet. A *data table* (or just *table* for short) is shown in Figure 1.1.

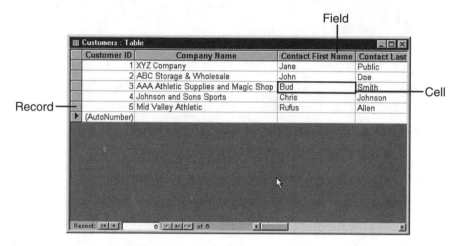

Figure 1.1   A typical table in Access.

Access stores each database entry (for example, each customer or each inventory item) in its own row; this is a *record*. For example, all the information about Mid Valley Athletic, including the contact person's first and last name, is a single record (see Figure 1.1).

Each type of detail is kept in its own column: a *field*. For example, **Contact First Name** is one field, and **Company Name** is another. All the Contact First Names in the entire table are collectively known as the Contact First Name field.

At the intersection of a field and a row is the individual bit of data for that particular record; this area is a *cell*. For example, in the cell where the **Contact First Name** column and **AAA Athletic Supplies and Magic Shop**'s record intersect, you'd find **Bud**.

You'll learn how to create tables in Lessons 7 and 8. Each database file can have many tables. For instance, you might have a table that lists all your customers and another table that lists information about the products you sell. A third table might keep track of your salespeople and their performance.

Forms

All the data you enter into your database ends up in a table, for storage. You can enter information directly into a table, but it's a little bit awkward to do so. Most people find it easier to create a special on-screen *form* in which to enter the data. A form resembles a fill-in-the-blanks sheet that you would complete by hand, such as a job application. You'll learn how to create a form in Lesson 13.

Access links the form to the table and stores the information you put into the form in the table. For instance, in Figure 1.2, Access will store the customer data I'm entering on this form in the table shown in Figure 1.1.

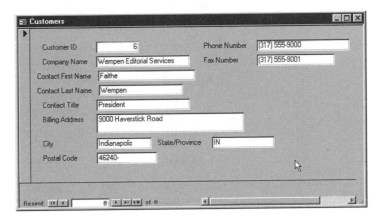

Figure 1.2   Forms make data entry more convenient.

   Multitable Forms   You can use a single form to enter data into several tables at once, as you'll learn in later lessons.

Reports

While forms are designed to be used on-screen, reports are designed to be printed. Reports are specially formatted collections of your data, organized in exactly the way you want. For instance, you might want to create a report of all customers who have ordered in the last year, including how many units they ordered and how much they spent, as shown in Figure 1.3.

579

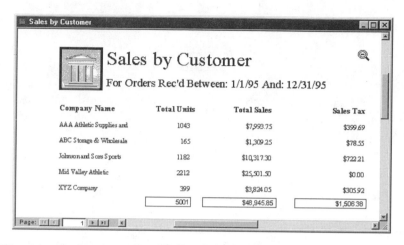

Figure 1.3 You can print this report and distribute it to key employees in the company.

 TIP

Print Preview Although you create reports so you can print them, you also can see them on-screen in Print Preview view, as in Figure 1.3. You'll learn how to view and print reports in Lesson 19.

Queries

A *query* is a way of weeding out the information you don't want to see, so you can see the information you do need more clearly. You can think of it as a sieve you dump your data into; the data you don't want falls through the holes in the sieve, leaving you holding only the data you're interested in.

Many people are afraid of queries because of the technical terms associated with them, such as values, criteria, and masks. But there's no need to be afraid, as you'll learn in Lesson 17 when you create and use a simple query.

How the Parts Fit Together

Even though you create tables, reports, forms, and queries in separate steps, they're all related. As I mentioned earlier, tables are the central focus of all activities—all the other objects do something to or with the table data. Reports summarize and organize the table data; forms help you enter info into the table; queries help you find information you want to use in the table. In future lessons, you'll learn one-by-one how each part relates to the whole database.

Access Wizards Make Databases Easy

Throughout this book, you will use Access's wizards. What's a *wizard*? It's a miniprogram that "interviews" you, asking you questions about what you want to accomplish. Then it takes your answers and creates the table, report, query, or whatever, according to your specifications. See a sample wizard screen in Figure 1.4.

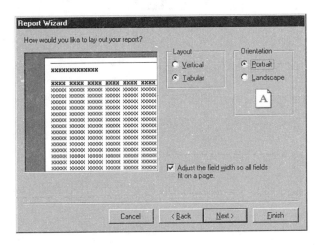

Figure 1.4   Wizards make it easy to create all kinds of database objects.

Each time you create a new object, such as a table or a form, you have the choice of creating it "from scratch" in a Design view, or using a wizard to help you along. I recommend that all beginners use wizards as much as possible—I use them because they're so convenient. Leave the tough stuff, the Design view creations, to those with lots of leisure time.

In this lesson, you learned some basic facts about databases and Access. In the next lesson, you'll learn some strategies for planning your database. Don't skip Lesson 2! Ten minutes worth of up-front planning can save you hours of backtracking later.

Planning Your Database

In this lesson, you'll learn some principles of good database design to help you plan your course of action.

Planning Is Important!

How many times have you dived enthusiastically into a new craft or skill without really knowing what you were doing? Your first attempt was probably pretty poor, whether it was pottery or computer programming. But as you worked, you probably made notes to yourself of what you'd do differently next time—and the next time you did better.

With something as important as your database, however, you can't afford to spend hours making mistakes and learning by doing. So in this lesson, I'll try to give you a crash course in all the database planning that most people learn the hard way.

Before you create your database, you should think about the following:

- *What data do I want to store, and how is the best way to organize it?* This determines what tables you need.

- *What data entry actions do I perform in the course of my business or hobby?* This determines the forms you need.

- *What information do I want to know about the status of the business or hobby?* This answer will tell you what reports you'll want.

Determining What Tables You Need

How many tables do you need? Technically, you only need one. That's the minimum a database can function with. However, the biggest mistake most people make with Access is to put too much information in one table. Access is a *relational* database program; that means unlike some simple database programs, it's meant to handle lots of tables and create relationships among them. Figure 2.1 shows a list of tables in an order processing database.

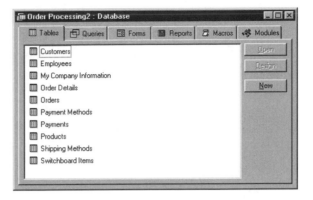

Figure 2.1   Access really shines when you take advantage of its capability to store many tables.

   **Plan Tables Now!**   You should plan your tables up front, before you create your database, because it's difficult to change a table's structure once it's filled with data.

Another big mistake people make in their tables is to try to make each table look like a stand-alone report. For instance, they might repeat a customer's name and address in all eight tables because they want that information readily available. This is a waste! You can easily create a report or form that includes this information whenever you need it; it needs to appear in only one table.

Normalizing Your Database

When a database suffers from poor table organization, experts say it's not *normalized*. There are rules that govern how a relational database should store its tables; these are the rules of *Data Normalization*.

Data Normalization   Making the tables as efficient and compact as possible to eliminate the possibility for confusion and error.

There are five normalization rules, but the latter ones are fairly complicated and used mostly by database professionals. In this lesson, I'll explain the first two normalization rules, which are all a beginner really needs to understand in order to avoid major mistakes.

 Normalized Wizards   Luckily, database professionals had a hand in creating Access's Database Wizard, so any tables you create using this feature (see Lesson 5) will be completely normalized with all rules.

Avoid Repeated Information

Let's say that you want to keep contact information on your customers and a record of each transaction you make with each customer. If you kept it all in one table, you would have to repeat the customer's full name, address, and phone number each time you entered a new transaction! It would also be a nightmare if the customer's address changed; you would have to make the change on every transaction.

Customer Name	Customer Address	Customer Phone	Order Date	Order Total
ABC Plumbing	201 W. 44th St.	(317) 555-2394	2/5/95	$155.90
ABC Plumbing	201 W. 44th St.	(317) 555-2394	5/14/95	$90.24
ABC Plumbing	201 W. 44th St.	(317) 555-2394	7/9/95	$224.50
Jack's Emporium	1155 Conner Ave.	(317) 555-4301	6/6/94	$1592.99
Jack's Emporium	1155 Conner Ave.	(317) 555-4301	7/26/95	$990.41
Millie's Pizza	108 Ponting St.	(317) 554-2349	8/29/95	$39.95

A better way would be to assign each customer an ID number. Include that ID number in a table that contains names and addresses; then include the same ID number as a link in a separate table that contains transactions.

Customers Table

Customer ID	Customer Name	Customer Address	Customer Phone
1	ABC Plumbing	201 W. 44th St.	(317) 555-2394
2	Jack's Emporium	1155 Connor Ave.	(317) 555-4301
3	Millie's Pizza	108 Ponting St.	(317) 554-2349

Orders Table

Customer ID	Order Date	Order Total
1	2/5/95	$155.90
1	5/14/95	$90.24
1	7/9/95	$224.50
2	6/6/94	$1592.99
2	7/26/95	$990.41
3	8/29/95	$39.95

But I Need to Use All the Data Together!   Don't worry. On reports, forms, and queries, you can easily use data from several tables at once. You can also link two tables together, as you'll learn in Lesson 21. Just because data is in its own table doesn't mean it is isolated.

Avoid Redundant Data

Let's say you want to keep track of which employees have attended certain training classes. There are lots of employees and lots of classes. One way would be to keep it all in a single Personnel table, like this:

Employee Name	Employee Address	Employee Phone	Training Date	Class Taken	Credit Hours	Passed?
Phil Sharp	211 W. 16th St.	(317) 555-4321	5/5/95	Leadership Skills	3	yes
Becky Rowan	40 Westfield Ct.	(317) 555-3905	5/5/95	Customer Service	2	yes
Nick Gianti	559 Ponting St.	(317) 555-7683	6/15/95	Public Speaking	9	yes
Martha Donato	720 E. Warren	(317) 555-2930	5/5/95	Public Speaking	9	no
Cynthia Hedges	108 Carroll St.	(317) 555-5990	6/15/95	Customer Service	2	yes
Andrea Mayfair	3094 110th St.	(317) 555-0293	6/15/95	Leadership Skills	3	yes

But what if an employee takes more than one class? You'd have to add a duplicate line in the table to list it, and then you have the problem described in the previous section—multiple records with virtually identical field entries. And what if the only employee who has taken a certain class leaves the company? When you delete that employee's record, you delete the information about the class's credit hours, too.

A better way would be to create separate tables for Employees, Classes, and Training Done, like so:

Employee Table

Employee ID	Employee Name	Employee Address	Employee Phone
1	Phil Sharp	211 W. 16th St.	(317) 555-4321
2	Becky Rowan	40 Westfield Ct.	(317) 555-3905
3	Nick Gianti	559 Ponting St.	(317) 555-7683
4	Martha Domato	720 E. Warren	(317) 555-2930
5	Cynthia Hedges	108 Carroll St.	(317) 555-5990
6	Andrea Mayfair	3094 110th St.	(317) 555-0293

Class Table

Class ID	Class	Credits
C1	Leadership Skills	3
C2	Customer Service	2
C3	Public Speaking	9

Training Table

Employee ID	Date	Class	Passed?
1	5/5/95	C1	Yes
2	5/5/95	C2	Yes
3	6/16/95	C3	Yes
4	5/5/95	C3	No
5	6/15/95	C2	Yes
6	6/15/95	C1	Yes

Summary: Designing Your Tables

Don't be overwhelmed by all this information about database normalization; good table organization boils down to a few simple principles:

- Each table should have a theme, for instance, Employee Contact Information or Customer Transactions. Don't try to have more than one theme per table.

- If you see that you might end up repeating data in a table in the future, plan now to split the information that will be repeated into its own table.

- If there is a list of reference information you want to preserve (such as the names and credit hours for classes), put it in its own table.

- Wherever possible, use ID numbers, as they'll help you link tables together later and help you avoid typing errors that come from repeating long text strings (such as names) over and over.

What Forms Will You Use?

As explained in Lesson 1, forms are data entry tools. You can arrange fields from several tables on a form and easily enter data into those fields on a single screen. For instance, your order entry form might contain fields from the Customers, Employees, Payment Methods, Products, and Shipping Methods tables, since an order brings together all these factors. Figure 2.2 shows a form that combines customer and product information.

When thinking about what forms you need, the question is really "what actions do I perform?" Perhaps some of these:

- Hiring employees (and entering their information in the database)
- Selling goods or services
- Making purchases
- Collecting the names and contact information for volunteers
- Keeping track of inventory

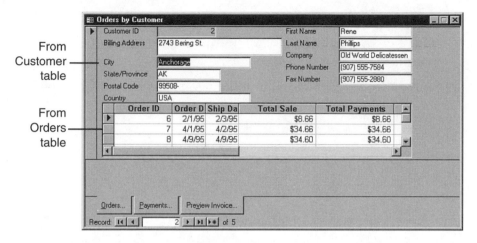

From Customer table

From Orders table

Figure 2.2 A form can be the link between several tables.

I Can't Predict What Forms I'll Need! Although it's important to have effective forms, you can make changes to forms at any time fairly easily (unlike tables), so you don't have to know exactly what forms you want before you start. You'll learn to create forms in Lesson 13.

What Reports Will You Want to Produce?

A report satisfies your need for information about your data. It's usually printed (unlike tables and forms, which are usually used on-screen only). For instance, you may want a report of all people who have not paid their membership dues, or all accounts with a balance owed of more than $1,000.00. (You can find this information with a Query, too, as you'll learn in Lesson 17.)

A report is usually for the benefit of other people who aren't sitting with you at your computer. You might print a report to hand out to your board of directors, for instance, to encourage them to keep you on as CEO! A report can pull data from many tables at once, perform calculations on the data (such as summing or averaging), and present you with neatly formatted results. Here are some things you can do with reports:

- Print a list of all your personal possessions with a replacement value of over $50, for insurance purposes.

- Show a listing of all club members who have not paid their dues.

- Calculate and show the present depreciated value of all capital equipment.

- List the commissions paid to each of your top 50 salespeople in the last quarter, compared to the company-wide average.

You can create new reports at any time; you do not have to decide on all of them before you create your database. However, if you know you want a certain report, you might be able to design your tables more effectively for that report's use.

Bringing It All Together   Before you begin creating your database, you might want to draw a diagram of the various components you'll create and how they'll fit together.

In this lesson, you planned your database tables, forms, and reports. In the next lessons, you'll learn to start and exit Access.

Starting and Exiting Access

In this lesson, you'll learn to start and exit Microsoft Access.

Starting Access

There may be several ways you can start Access, depending on how you've installed it. The most straightforward way is to use the Start button. Follow these steps:

1. Click the **Start** button. A menu appears.

2. Highlight or point to **Programs**. A list of your program groups appear.

3. Click on **Microsoft Access**. Access starts.

Moving Programs Around on the Start Menu If you would prefer for Access to be in a different program group, right-click the **Start** button, and select **Explore**. Then use the Explorer to find and move the Microsoft Access shortcut to a different program group. See the Windows section of this book for more information about the Explorer.

Other Ways to Start Access

Here are some other ways to start Access. Some of these require more knowledge of Windows 95 and Microsoft Office—if you're confused by them, stick with the primary method explained in the preceding section.

- You can create a shortcut icon for Access to sit on your desktop, and start Access by double-clicking it. See the Windows section of this book to learn how to create a shortcut in Windows 95.

- When you're browsing files in Windows 95's Explorer program, you can double-click on any Access data file to start Access and open that data file. Access data files have an MDB extension on them, and a little icon next to them that resembles the icon next to Microsoft Access on the Programs menu.

- If you can't find Access, you can search for it. Click the **Start** button, select **Find**; then select **Files or Folders**. In the Named box, type **msaccess.exe**. Open the **Look in** list and select **My Computer.** Then select **Find Now**. When the file appears on the list below, double-click on it to start Access.

When you start Access, the first thing you'll see is a dialog box asking if you want to create a new database or open an existing one (Figure 3.1). For now, click **Cancel**. (We won't be working with any particular database in this lesson.

Figure 3.1   This Microsoft Access dialog box appears each time you start Access.

Parts of the Screen

Access is much like any other Windows program: it contains menus, toolbars, a status bar, and so on. Figure 3.2 points out these landmarks. Notice that in Figure 3.2, many of the toolbar buttons are grayed out (unavailable,which means you can't use them right now) and there are only a few menus. There's also nothing in the work area. That's because no database file is open. The Access screen will become a much busier

591

place in later lessons when we begin working with a database. There will be more menus, the buttons will become available, and your database will appear in the work area.

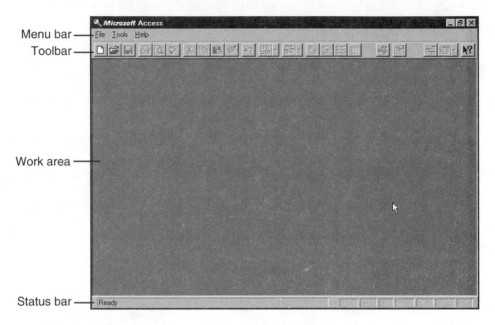

Menu bar

Toolbar

Work area

Status bar

Figure 3.2 Access has all the same interface landmarks as any Windows program.

Understanding Access Toolbars

If you have used Windows programs before, you are probably familiar with toolbars. They're rows of buttons that represent common commands you can issue. Toolbar buttons are often shortcuts for menu commands.

The toolbar changes depending on which object you're working with at the time (Table, Form, and so on) and what you're doing to it. More toolbars sometimes appear when you're doing special activities, such as drawing. To find out what a toolbar button does, point at it with your mouse pointer. Its name appears next to the pointer, and a description of the tool appears in the status bar (see Figure 3.3). This feature is a *ToolTip*; you can use ToolTips even when a button is unavailable for use.

Button name ——

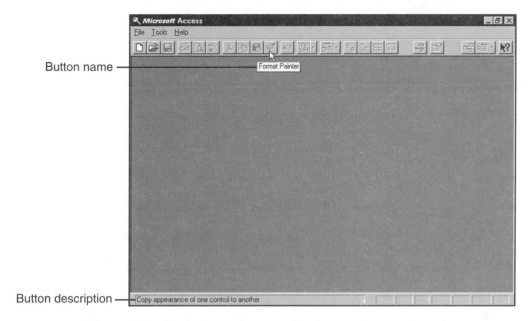

Button description ——

Figure 3.3 To find out what a toolbar button does, point at it.

 Customizing Toolbars You can choose which toolbars you'll view at any time, and even add and remove buttons from a toolbar. Right-click on any toolbar, and a shortcut menu appears. You can select a toolbar for viewing from that list, or click **Customize** to open a dialog box where you can customize any toolbar.

Exiting Access

When you finish working with Access, you should exit to free up your computer's memory for other tasks. There are several ways to exit Access:

- Press **Alt+F4**.
- Select **File**, **Exit**.
- Click the Access window's **Close** (**X**) button (see Figure 3.3).

If you have made changes to a database that you haven't saved yet, you will be asked whether you want to save your changes. Click **Yes** or **No** in answer, and Access will finish closing. However, at this point, we haven't created any databases yet, so you won't see this query.

In this lesson, you learned to start and exit Access, and you learned about the main parts of the screen, including the toolbar buttons. In the next lesson, you'll learn how to use Access's Help system.

Getting Help

In this lesson, you'll learn about the various types of help available to you in Access.

Help: What's Available?

Because every person is different, Access offers many different ways to get help with the program. You can:

- Click the **Help** button on the toolbar; then click on the on-screen object you need help with.

- Choose what you're interested in learning about from a series of Help Topics.

- Use the **Answer Wizard** to enter your question in plain English and see a demonstration how to use a feature.

- Press **F1** to get *context-sensitive help* (information about the action you are currently performing.)

Getting Help with Screen Elements

If you wonder about the function of a particular button or tool on the screen, wonder no more. Just follow these steps:

1. Click the **Help** button in the toolbar.

2. Click on the screen element for which you want help. A box appears explaining the element, as shown in Figure 4.1.

... and then click on whatever you want to know about.

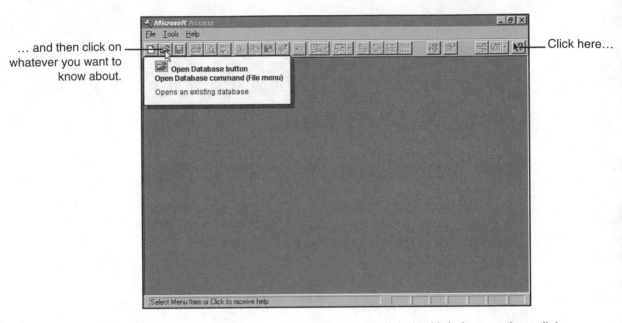

Click here...

Figure 4.1 To get help on a screen element, click the Help button; then click the element.

ToolTips, Too As you learned in Lesson 3, you can find out what a toolbar button does by pointing at it with the mouse pointer. Its name appears next to it, and its description appears in the status bar.

Using the Access Help Topics

A more conventional way to get help is through the *Help menu*. When you open the Access Help system, you move through the topics listed to find the topic you're interested in.

There are several tabs in the Help system, so you can use Help the way you want it. To access the Help system:

1. Select **Help**, **Microsoft Access Help Topics**.

2. Click on the tab for the type of help you want.

3. Click on the topic you're interested in, if there's a list, or type in your topic and press **Enter**.

The tabs that appear in the Help Topics dialog box are the same as the ones that appear in Windows itself, except for one: the Answer Wizard. Check out the Windows section of this book for complete details about each tab: Contents, Index, and Find. The following explains the remaining tab, the Answer Wizard.

The Answer Wizard

The *Answer Wizard* is a tab in the Help Topics dialog box, but you can also access it in other ways; you can select it directly from the **Help** menu, or you can press **F1** (as explained in the next section). The Answer Wizard provides help based on plain-English questions you type in. You enter a question, and then the Answer Wizard actually shows you how to perform the task.

To use the Answer Wizard:

1. Select **Help**, **Microsoft Access Help topics**.

2. Click on the **Answer Wizard** tab.

3. Type what you want to do in the top box (**1**), and click the **Search** button.

4. Double-click on the topic that appears in the bottom box (**2**) that matches your interest (see Figure 4.2).

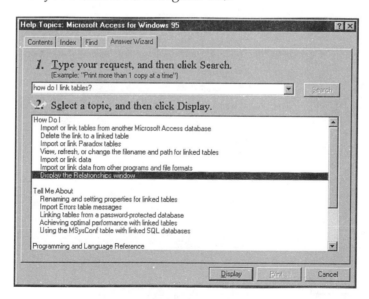

Figure 4.2   The Answer Wizard lets you ask questions in everyday English.

5. Depending on the topic, normal help text may appear, or a dialog box may appear telling you that the Answer Wizard will show you how to perform the procedure. If you get a dialog box, click **Next**.

6. Watch as the Answer Wizard shows you how to perform the task.

When the Answer Wizard is showing you something (step 6), it'll be like someone else is controlling your mouse and keyboard; menus will open, commands will execute, and so on. Just watch and learn.

F1 for Help

Pressing **F1** for help is an old tradition in Windows programs, and it still works. When you press **F1**, the Answer Wizard appears with what it thinks you're doing already typed in as a question. You can modify the question if it's not exactly what you want to ask, or just click **Search** to accept it. See the information about the Answer Wizard in the preceding section for more information.

In this lesson, you learned about the many ways that Access offers help. In the next lesson, you'll learn to create a new database.

Creating a New Database

In this lesson, you'll learn how to create a new, blank database. You'll also learn how to create a database with pre-made tables, reports, and forms using the Database Wizard.

Choosing The Right Way to Create Your Database

Before you create your database, you have an important decision to make: should you create a blank database from scratch, and then manually create all the tables, reports, and forms you'll need, or should you use a Database Wizard, which does all that for you?

Database Wizard   Access comes with several Database Wizards. These are mini-programs that interview you regarding your needs, and then create a database structure that matches them. (You enter the actual data yourself.)

The answer depends on how well the available wizards match your needs. If there is a Database Wizard that is close to what you want, it's quickest to use it to create your database, and then modify it as needed. (Of course, you won't know what wizards are available until you open the list of them, later in this lesson.) If you're in a hurry, using a wizard can save you lots of time.

On the other hand, if you want a special-purpose database that isn't similar to any of the wizards, or if you're creating the database primarily as a training exercise for yourself, you should create the blank database.

Creating a Blank Database

Creating a blank database is very simple, because you're just creating an outer shell at this point, without any tables, forms, etc. Just do one of the following:

If you just started Access, and the Microsoft Access dialog box is still displayed (see Figure 5.1), follow these steps:

1. Click **Blank Database**.

2. Click the **OK** button.

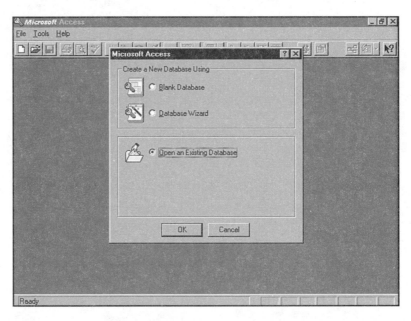

Figure 5.1 When you first start Access, you can start a new database quickly from the Microsoft Access dialog box.

If the dialog box is gone, you can't get it back until you exit from Access and restart it. But you don't need that dialog box—you can start a new database at any time by following these steps:

1. Select **File, New,** or click the New button on the toolbar. The New dialog box appears (see Figure 5.2).

2. Double-click the **Blank Database** icon. The File New Database dialog box appears.

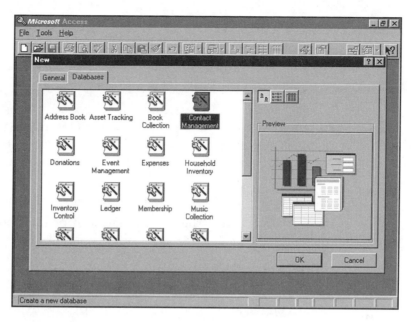

Figure 5.2   The New dialog box.

3. Type a name for your new database (preferably something descriptive) in the File name box. For example, I typed Kennel Records. Then click Create. Access creates the new database, as shown in Figure 5.3.

Your database is completely blank at this point. You can click on any of the tabs in the database window (see Figure 5.3), and you won't find anything listed on any of them. Later, you'll learn to create tables (Lessons 7 and 8), forms (Lesson 13), queries (Lesson 17), and reports (Lesson 19) to fill these tabbed windows.

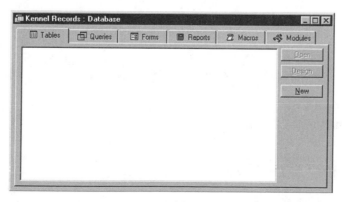

Figure 5.3   A new, blank database window.

601

Creating a Database with Database Wizard

A Database Wizard can create almost all the tables, forms, and reports you will ever need, automatically! The only trick is choosing the right wizard to suit your purpose. Follow these steps:

1. If you just started Access, and the Microsoft Access dialog box is still onscreen (refer to Figure 5.1), click **Database Wizard**, then click **OK**. Or, if you've already closed the dialog box, select **File**, **New Database**. Either way, the New dialog box appears (refer to Figure 5.2).

2. Click on one of the Database Wizards. (They're the icons with the magic wands across them.) A preview appears in the Preview area.

3. When you've found the wizard you want, click **OK**. The File New Database dialog box appears.

4. Type a name for the database, then click **Create** to continue. The wizard starts, and some information appears explaining what the wizard will do.

5. Click **Next** to continue. A list of the tables to be created appears (see Figure 5.4). The tables appear on the left, and the selected table's fields on the right.

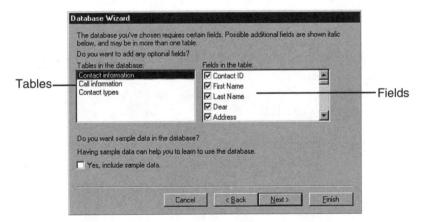

Figure 5.4 These are the tables and fields that this wizard will create automatically for you.

6. Click on a table and examine its list of fields. Optional fields are in italics. To include an optional field, click on it to place a check mark next to it.

I Don't Want All These Tables and Fields!   Sorry, that's the price you pay for going with a prefabricated wizard. You can't deselect any fields except the optional (italicized) ones. But you can delete the tables and fields you don't want later. See Lesson 9 to learn how to delete individual fields or an entire table.

Nothing Looks Right!   If the tables and fields appear totally inappropriate, perhaps you are using the wrong wizard for your needs—click **Cancel**, and try another.

7. (Optional) If you are creating this database as a learning experience only, click the **Yes, include sample data** check box. This tells Access to enter some dummy records into the database, so you can see how they will work in the database.

8. Click **Next** to continue. The wizard asks you what kind of screen display style you want.

9. Click on a display style on the list, and examine the preview of that style that appears. When you have decided on a style, click on it, then click **Next**. The wizard asks you for a style for printer reports.

10. Click on a report style, and examine the preview of it. When you have decided on a style, click on it, then click **Next**.

11. The wizard asks what title you want for the database. The title will appear on reports. It can be different from the filename. Enter a title (see Figure 5.5).

12. (Optional) If you want to include a picture on your forms and reports (for example, your company's logo), click the **Yes, include a picture** check box. Then click the **Picture** button, choose a graphics file, and click **Open** to return to the Wizard.

13. Click **Next** to continue. Then, at the Finish screen, click **Finish** to open the new database. The wizard goes to work creating your database. (It may take several minutes.)

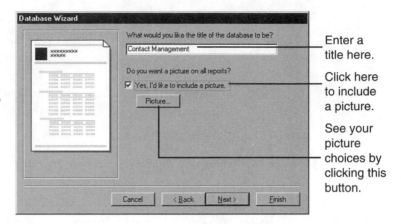

Enter a
title here.

Click here
to include
a picture.

See your
picture
choices by
clicking this
button.

Figure 5.5 Enter a title for the database, and optionally, choose a graphic to use for a logo.

When the database is finished, a Switchboard window appears (see Figure 5.6). The Switchboard will open automatically whenever you open the database. All of the databases created by a Database Wizard include the Switchboard.

The Switchboard is nothing more than a fancy report with some programming built in. It lets you perform common tasks with the database by clicking a button. We won't be working with the Switchboard, so just click the Switchboard window's Close button to get rid of it.

I Hate That Switchboard!   To prevent the Switchboard from opening when you open the database, select **Tools, Startup**. Open the **Display Form** drop-down list, and select **[None]**. Click OK. The Switchboard won't bother you anymore.

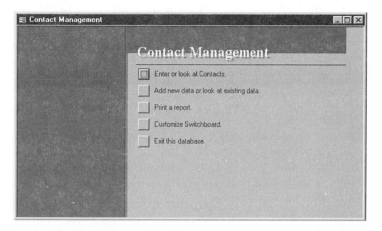

Figure 5.6   The Switchboard window is an extra bonus provided by the Database Wizards.

Once you close the Switchboard window, you see the database window. If it's minimized, double-click on its title bar (bottom left corner of the screen) to open it again. Click on the Tables tab, and you see that several tables have been created for you. Click on the other tabs to see the other objects created as well. You're well on your way!

Even though you may have all the tables, reports, and forms you need, you may still want to continue through the lessons in this book in chronological order, to learn about creating and modifying these objects. If you're in a hurry to enter your data, though, skip directly to Lesson 10, where you'll learn how to enter data in a table, or the end of Lesson 13, where you'll learn about data entry on a form.

In this lesson, you learned to create a database from scratch and using a Database Wizard. In the next lesson, you'll learn how to save, close, and open a database.

Saving, Closing, and Opening a Database

In this lesson, you'll learn to save your database, close it, and reopen it. You'll also learn how to find a database file that you may have misplaced.

Saving a Database

So that you don't lose anything you've typed after you turn off the computer, you need to save your work. When you created the database, you saved it when you named it. Then, when you enter each record, Access automatically saves your work. (You'll learn to enter records in Lesson 10.) There's no need to save your work before closing your database.

When you change the structure of a table, form, or other object, however, Access will not let you close that object or close the database without confirming whether or not you want to save your changes. You'll see a dialog box like the one in Figure 6.1; just click **Yes** to save your changes.

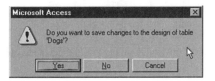

Figure 6.1 When you make changes to an object's structure, Access asks whether it should save your changes. When you enter data, it saves it automatically.

Notice that the Save and Save As commands on the File menu aren't even available most of the time; they're grayed out. When you have a particular object highlighted in the Database window, such as a table, the Save As/Export command is available. You can use this command to save your table in a different format that another program (such as Excel) can read.

Using Tables in Other Programs   Another way to copy a table to another application, or another database, is with the Copy and Paste commands. Highlight the table in the Database window and select **Edit, Copy**. Then open a different database or another application and select **Edit, Paste**.

Closing a Database

When you finish working with a database, you should close it. If you're done using Access, just exit the program (see Lesson 3), and the database closes along with the program. However, if you want to close the database and then open another, do any of the following to close a database:

- Double-click the **Control-menu** icon (in the top left corner) for the database (see Figure 6.2).

- Click on the database window's **Close** (**X**) button (the top right corner).

- Select **File, Close**.

- Press **Ctrl+F4**.

- Press **Ctrl+W**.

Can't I Have More Than One Database Open?   Sure, you can. In fact, you may want several open, so you can transfer data among them. However, if your computer is short on memory (less than 16 megabytes), you'll find that Access runs faster when you close all files that you're not using.

Select Close from the File menu.

Double-click here.

Click here.

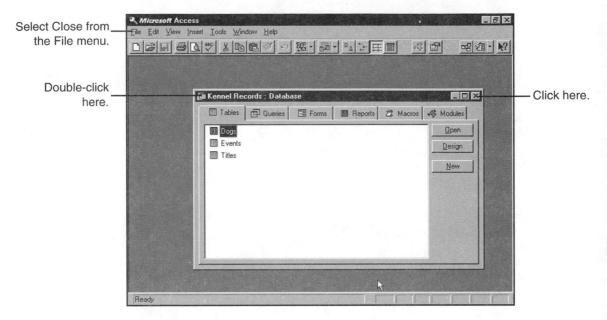

Figure 6.2 There are several ways to close a database.

Opening a Database

When you start Access the next time you want to use your database, you won't create a new one from scratch, of course, as you did in Lesson 5. You'll open your existing one.

The easiest way to open a database you've recently used is to select it from the File menu. Follow these steps:

1. Open the **File** menu. You see up to four databases you've recently used listed at the bottom of the menu.

2. Click on the database you want to open.

If the database you want to open isn't listed, you'll need to use the following procedure instead:

 1. Select **File**, **Open** or click the **Open** button on the toolbar. The Open dialog box appears (see Figure 6.3).

Folder names ⎯

File names ⎯

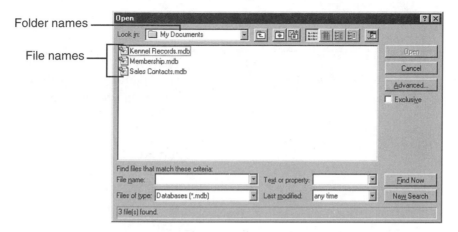

Figure 6.3 Open a different database file with this dialog box.

2. If the file isn't in the currently displayed folder, change drives and folders. Refer to the next section, "Changing the Drive or Folder."

3. Double-click on the file to open it.

Changing the Drive or Folder

Windows 95 applications provide a different dialog box for opening files than you may be used to with Windows 3.1 applications. It takes a bit of getting used to. Figure 6.3 shows the dialog box; Table 6.1 explains the buttons you see in it.

Table 6.1 Buttons Available for Changing Drives and Folders in Windows 95 Dialog Boxes

Button	Purpose
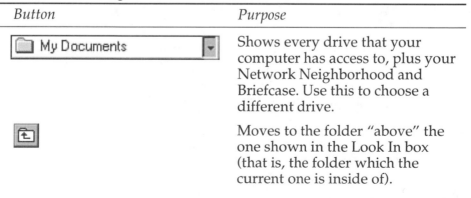	Shows every drive that your computer has access to, plus your Network Neighborhood and Briefcase. Use this to choose a different drive.
	Moves to the folder "above" the one shown in the Look In box (that is, the folder which the current one is inside of).

continues

609

Table 6.1   Continued

Button	Purpose
![button icon]	Shows the C:\WINDOWS\FAVORITES folder, no matter which folder was displayed before.
![button icon]	Adds a shortcut to the currently displayed folder to the C:\WINDOWS\FAVORITES folder.
![button icon]	Shows the folders and files in the currently displayed folder in a list.
![button icon]	Shows details about each file and folder.
![button icon]	Shows the properties of the selected file.
![button icon]	Shows a preview (if available) of the selected file.
![button icon]	Opens a shortcut menu of settings you can change that affect the way the dialog box shows you the files, or that affect the selected file.

 Network Neighborhood and Briefcase   These are two special locations that you may have available on the list of folders. Network Neighborhood gives you access to computers on your local area network, and Briefcase manages files between your laptop and your main computer. Most people will probably never use either of these.

Finding a Database File

If you're having trouble locating your file, Access can help you look. Follow these steps:

1. Select **File, Open Database** if the File Open dialog box is not on-screen.

2. In the **File name** box at the bottom of the dialog box, type the name of the file you're looking for. (Refer back to Figure 6.3).

Wild Cards   You can use wild cards if you don't know the entire name of the file you're looking for. A * means "any characters" and a **?** means "any single character." For instance, if you know the file begins with P, you could use P*.mdb to find all Access files that begin with P.

3. (Optional) If desired, enter other search criteria:

   - If you're looking for a different file type, choose it from the **Files of type** drop-down list.

   - If you're looking for a file containing certain text, type it in the **Text or property** box.

   - If you know when you last modified the file, choose the time interval from the **Last modified** drop-down list.

4. Click the **Advanced** button. The Advanced Find dialog box appears (see Figure 6.4).

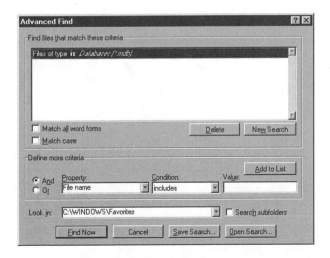

Figure 6.4   Use the Advanced Find dialog box to select which folders and drives to look in.

611

5. In the **Look in** section at the bottom of the Advanced Find dialog box, narrow down the search area as much as possible:

- If you are sure the file is in a certain folder, type that folder's path in the **Look in** box, for example, C:\WINDOWS.

- If you are sure the file is on a certain drive, select it from the **Look in** drop-down list.

- If you don't know which drive contains the file, select **My Computer** from the **Look in** drop-down list.

6. Make sure to select the **Search Subfolders** check box.

7. Click the **Find Now** button. The Open dialog box reappears, and the files that were found appear for your selection.

8. Double-click on the desired file to open it.

More Search Options As you may have noticed in Figure 6.4, there are many more complex search options available to you—too many to cover here. See your Access documentation for details.

In this lesson, you learned how to save, close, and open a database. In the next lesson, you will learn how to create a table using Table Wizard.

Creating a Table with the Table Wizard

In this lesson, you'll learn to create a table using Table Wizard. (You'll learn about creating a table from scratch in Lesson 8.)

Why Create a Table?

Tables are the basis for the whole database. Tables hold your data. Everything else is just dress-up. If you created an empty database in Lesson 5, you'll need to create tables now, following the plan you developed in Lesson 2. If you used the Database Wizard to create your tables, you can create new tables here to augment them, or you can skip to Lesson 9, where you'll learn to modify and customize the tables.

When you create a table, you can create it "from scratch," or you can use the Table Wizard. This lesson covers the Table Wizard, and Lesson 8 covers the less-automated method.

The Table Wizard can save you lots of time by creating and formatting all the right fields for a certain purpose. Access comes with dozens of premade business and personal tables from which to choose. You can pick and choose among all the fields in all the premade tables, constructing a table that's right for your needs. Even if you can't find all the fields you need in premade tables, you may want to use the Table Wizard to save some time up-front, and then you can add the missing fields later (see Lesson 9).

How Can I Know Beforehand? You won't know exactly what premade fields Access offers until you start the Table Wizard and see the listings; if you find that there are no tables that meet your needs, you can click **Cancel** at any time and go to Lesson 8.

Creating a Table Using Table Wizard

If the fields you want to create are similar to any of Access's dozens of premade ones, the Table Wizard can save you a lot of time and effort. With the Table Wizard, you can copy fields from any of the dozens of sample tables.

To create a table using Table Wizard, follow these steps:

1. Select **Insert**, **Table** from the menu bar along the top of the screen. Or in the Database window, click the **Tables** tab and click **New**. The New Table dialog box appears (Figure 7.1).

Figure 7.1 Choose how you want to create the new table from the New Table dialog box.

 Quick! A New Object! Instead of step 1, you can click the down arrow next to the New Object button on the toolbar. A drop-down list of the available object types appears. Select **New Table** from that list.

2. Click **Table Wizard** and click **OK**. The Table Wizard window appears (see Figure 7.2).

3. Click on a table in the **Sample Tables** list; its fields appear in the **Sample Fields** list.

Business or Pleasure? There are two separate lists of tables. By default, you see the Business list. To see the Personal list, click the **Personal** button below the **Sample Tables** list (shown in Figure 7.2).

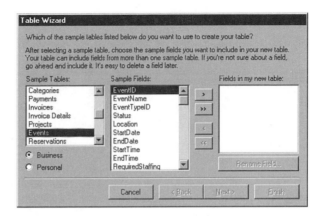

Figure 7.2 Choose your table's fields from those that come with any of the premade tables.

4. If you see a field that you want to include in your new table, select it from the **Sample Fields** list; then click the **>** button to move it to the **Fields in my new table** list. To move the entire contents of the selected Sample Table to your list, click the **>>** button.

TIP

Name Change! If you see a field that is close to what you want, but you would prefer a different name for it, add it to your list (steps 3 and 4). Then click the field name to select it; click the **Rename Field** button, type a new name, and click **OK**. This renames the field on your list only, not on the original.

5. Repeat steps 3 and 4 to select more fields from more sample tables until your list of fields in your new table is complete. Then click **Next** to continue.

6. Next, you're asked for a name for the table. Type a name to replace the default one. (The default is **Table 1**, **Table 2**, and so on.)

7. Click **Yes, set a primary key for me** to have the wizard choose your primary key field, or **No, I'll set the primary key** to do it yourself. (To follow along with me, choose **No ...** and click **Next**; otherwise skip to Step 10.)

Primary Key Field   The designated field for which every record must have a unique entry. This is usually an ID number, since most other fields could conceivably be the same for more than one record (for instance, two people might have the same first name).

8. A dialog box appears (see Figure 7.3) asking which field will be the primary key. Open the drop-down list and select the field.

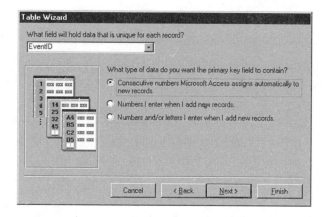

Figure 7.3   You can set your own primary key for the table.

9. Choose a data type for the primary key field:

   - **Consecutive numbers Microsoft Access assigns automatically to new records.** Choose this if your primary key field is a simple record number, that is, if you're numbering the records you enter consecutively as you enter them.

   - **Numbers I enter when I add new records.** Pick this to enter your own numbers. Access will not allow you to enter any letters. This choice works well for unique ID numbers such as drivers' licenses.

   - **Numbers and/or letters I enter when I add new records.** Pick this if you want to include both numbers and letters in the field. For instance, if your primary key field is a vehicle identification number for the cars in your fleet, you will need to enter both numbers and letters.

10. Click **Next** to continue.

11. The next screen asks about relationship between tables. Just click **Next** to move past it for now; you'll learn about relationships later.

12. At the Finish screen, click one of the following options:

- **Modify the table design.** This takes you into Table Design view, the same as if you had created all those fields yourself. Choose this if you have some changes you want to make to the table before you use it.

- **Enter data directly into the table.** This takes you to Table Datasheet view, where you can enter records into the rows of the table. Choose this if the table's design seems perfect to you as-is.

- **Enter data into the table using a form the wizard creates for me.** This jumps you ahead a bit in this book; it leads you right into the Form Wizard covered in Lesson 13. Leave this one alone for now if you want to continue following along with the lessons in this book in order.

13. Click **Finish** to move where you indicated you wanted to go in step 12.

If you decide you don't want to work with this table anymore right now (no matter what you selected in step 12), just click the **Close** (**X**) button for the window that appears. (Remember, it's the **X** in the top right corner of the window.)

Now you have a table. In the Database window, when you click the **Table** tab, you can see your table on the list (see Figure 7.4).

Figure 7.4 Now you have a table on your Tables tab.

Now What?

From here, there are a number of places you can go:

- To learn how to create a table from scratch, go on to Lesson 8, "Creating a Table Without a Wizard."

- To modify the table you just created, jump to Lesson 9, "Modifying a Table."

- To enter data into your table, skip to Lesson 10, "Entering Data into a Table."

- To create a data entry form for easier data entry, check out Lesson 13, "Creating a Simple Form." (Don't do this yet if there are still modifications you'd like to make to your table.)

In this lesson, you learned to create a new table using the Table Wizard. In the next lesson, you'll learn how to create a table without the wizard.

Creating a Table Without a Wizard

In this lesson, you'll learn to create a table in Table Design view.

Why Not Use a Wizard?

Access's wizards are very useful, but they do not offer as much flexibility as performing the equivalent tasks "from scratch." For instance, if you want to create a table that contains special fields not available in a wizard, you are better off creating that table in *Table Design view*. You'll learn how in this lesson.

Creating a Table in Table Design View

To create a table in Table Design view, follow these steps:

1. Select **Insert**, **Table**, or from the Database window, click the **Table** tab and click the **New** button. The New Table dialog box appears (Figure 8.1).

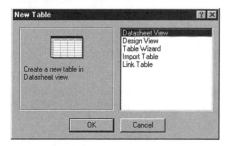

Figure 8.1 Start your new table in Design View from here.

Quick! A New Object!   Instead of step 1, you can click the down arrow next to the New Object button on the toolbar. A drop-down list appears of the available object types. Select **New Table** from that list.

2. Click **Design View** and click **OK**. Table Design view opens, as shown in Figure 8.2.

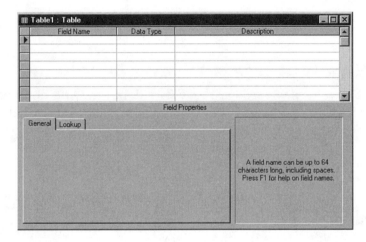

Figure 8.2   From Table Design view, you have full control over the table creation process.

3. Type a field name on the first empty line of the **Field Name** column. Then press **Tab** to move to the **Data Type** column.

Field Naming Rules   Field names, and all other objects in Access for that matter, can be up to 64 characters and can contain spaces if you like, and any symbols except period (.), exclamation mark (!), grave symbol (`), or square brackets ([]).

4. When you move to the **Data Type** column, an arrow appears for a drop-down list there. Open the **Data Type** drop-down list and select a field type. See the section "Understanding Field Types and Formats" later in this lesson if you need help deciding which field type to use.

5. Press **Tab** to move to the **Description** column, and type a description of the field. (This is optional; the table will work fine without it.)

6. In the bottom half of the dialog box, you see **Field Properties** for the field type you selected (see Figure 8.3). Make any changes desired to them. See "Understanding Field Types and Formats" later in this lesson for help.

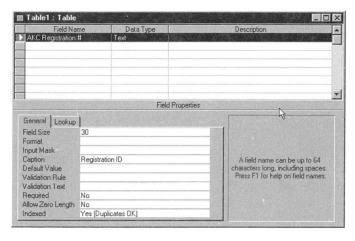

Figure 8.3 The Field Properties change depending on the field type.

Switching Between Views   At any time after you've entered the first field, you can switch to Datasheet view to see how your table is going to look. Just select **View, Datasheet**. You may be asked to save your work before you enter Datasheet view; if so, click **Yes**, enter a name, and then click **OK**.

7. If you have more fields to enter, repeat steps 3 through 6.

No Primary Key!   When you close Table Design view, you may get a message that no primary key has been assigned. See the "Setting the Primary Key" section later in this lesson to learn about this.

Understanding Data Types and Formats

Each field must have a type, so Access will know how to handle its contents. Here are the types you can choose from:

Text Plain, ordinary typing, which can include numbers, letters, and symbols. A Text field can contain up to 255 characters.

Memo More plain, ordinary text, except you don't set a maximum field length, so you can type an infinite amount of text.

Number A plain, ordinary number (not currency or a date). Access won't allow any text.

Date/Time Self-explanatory: a date or a time.

Currency A number formatted as an amount of money.

AutoNumber Access fills in a consecutive number for each record automatically.

Yes/No The answer to a true/false question.

OLE Object A link to another database or file. This is an advanced feature which we won't cover in this book.

Lookup Wizard Lets you create a list to choose a value from for each record. Another advanced feature that we won't cover here.

In addition to a field type, each field has formatting options you can set. They appear in the bottom half of the dialog box, in the **Field Properties** area. The formatting options change depending on the field type, and there are too many to list here, but here are some of the most important ones you'll encounter:

Field Size The maximum number of characters a user can input in that field.

Format A drop-down list of the available formats for that field type.

Default Value If a field is usually going to contain a certain value (for instance, a certain ZIP code for almost everyone), you can enter it here to save time. It will always appear, and you can type over it in the rare instances when it doesn't apply.

Decimal Places   For number fields, you can set the default number of decimal places a number will show.

Required   Choose **Yes** or **No** to tell Access whether a user should be allowed to leave this field blank when entering a new record.

Setting the Primary Key

Every table must have at least one field that has a unique value for each record. For instance, in a table of the dogs your kennel owns, you might assign an ID number to each dog, and have an ID # field in your table. Or you might choose to use each dog's AKC registration number. This identifier field is known as the *Primary Key field*.

You must tell Access which field you are going to use as the Primary Key, so it can prevent you from accidentally entering the same value for more than one record in that field. To set a primary key, follow these steps:

1. In Table Design view, select the field that you want for the primary key.

2. Select **Edit, Primary Key**. A key symbol appears to the left of the field name, as shown in Figure 8.4.

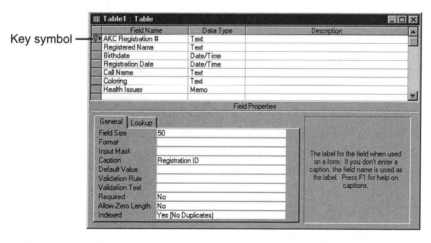

Figure 8.4   The primary key field is marked by a key symbol.

Primary Key Field The designated field for which every record must have a unique entry. This is usually an ID number, since most other fields could conceivably be the same for more than one record (for instance, two people might have the same first name).

Switching Between Design and Datasheet Views

When working with tables, there are two views available: Design and Datasheet. To switch between views, follow these steps:

1. Open the **View** menu.

2. Select **Table Design** or **Datasheet**, depending on which view you are currently in.

3. If you're moving from Table Design to Datasheet view, you may be asked to save your work. If so, click **Yes**.

4. If you're asked for a name for the table, type one and click **OK**.

Switching Views with the Toolbar You can bypass the View menu by clicking on the down arrow next to the View button on the toolbar. A list of available views appears. Choose the view you want from the list.

Creating a Table in Datasheet View

Some people prefer to create their table in Datasheet view. Access designed Datasheet view for data entry and viewing, not for table structure changes, however, so I do not recommend creating the table this way.

To create a table in Datasheet view, follow these steps:

1. Select **Insert**, **Table**.

2. Click **Datasheet View** and click **OK**. A blank table opens, as shown in Figure 8.5.

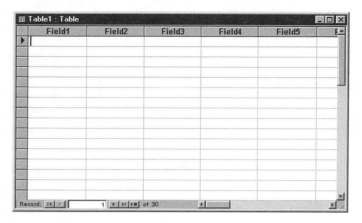

Figure 8.5 Creating a new table in Datasheet view gives you a quick, generic table.

How Do I Set the Field Names? When you create a table in Datasheet view, the fields have generic names such as **Field1**. To change a field name, click on the present name to select the column. Then select **Format**, **Rename Column**, type the new name and press **Enter**.

3. Make changes to the design of the table (as explained in Lesson 9, "Modifying a Table").

4. Close the table by clicking its **Close (X)** button. Access asks if you want to save the design changes.

5. Click **Yes**. Access asks for a name for the table. Type one and click **OK**.

In this lesson, you learned to create a table without the help of a wizard. Before you enter data into your table, you should make sure it's exactly the way you want it. In the next lesson, you'll learn how to make any changes needed to your table.

Modifying a Table

In this lesson, you'll learn how to change your table by adding and removing fields and hiding columns.

Now that you've created a table, you may be eager to begin entering records into it. You'll learn to do that in Lesson 10, "Entering Data into a Table." Before you begin, you should make certain that your table is structured exactly as you want it, so you don't have to backtrack later.

Editing Fields and Their Properties

No matter how you create your table (either with or without the Table Wizard), you can modify it using Table Design view. If you create the table without Table Wizard, Table Design view will look very familiar to you.

To enter Table Design view, do one of the following:

- From the Database window, click the **Table** tab, select the table you want to work with, and click the **Design** button.

- If the table appears in Datasheet view, select **View**, **Table Design**.

Quick View Changes   Don't forget, you can quickly change views with the **View** button at the far left end of the standard toolbar. Click the down arrow next to the button, and select a view from the list that appears.

Once you're in Table Design view (see Figure 9.1), you can edit any field, as you learned in Lesson 8, "Creating a Table Without a Wizard." Here is the general procedure:

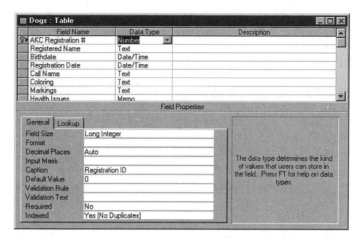

Figure 9.1   In Table Design view, you can modify the attributes of any field.

1. Click on any field name in the **Field Name** list.

2. If desired, click in its **Data Type** area and select a new data type from the drop-down list.

3. In the **Field Properties** area (the bottom half of the Table Design screen), click in any text box to change its value. Some text boxes have drop-down lists, which you can activate by clicking in the box.

4. Repeat steps 1–3 for each field you want to change.

I Need More Help!   For those who created their table without a wizard (Lesson 8), the above steps will be self-explanatory. However, if you used Table Wizard, you may be a little lost right now. Review Lesson 8 to get up to speed.

Adding Fields

Before you enter data into your table (see Lesson 10), you should make very sure that you have included all the fields you'll need. Why? Because if you add a field later, you'll have to go back and enter a value for that field for each record that you already entered.

You can add a field in either Table Design or Datasheet view. Let's try it in Table Design view first, since we're already there:

1. Select the field *before which* you want the new field to appear.

2. Click the **Insert Row** button on the toolbar, or select **Insert**, **Row**. A blank row appears in the **Field Name** list.

3. Enter a name, type, description, and so on for the new field. (Refer back to Lesson 8 as needed.)

Deleting Fields

If you realize that you don't need one or more fields that you created, now is the time to get rid of them. Otherwise, you'll needlessly enter information into each record that you will never use.

Don't Remove Important Fields! Be very careful about deleting fields once you start entering records in your table. Once you delete a field, all the information stored for each record in that field is gone, too. The best time to experiment with deleting fields is now, before you enter any records.

You can do the deed in either Table Design or Datasheet view. To delete a field in Table Design view, follow these steps:

1. Switch to Table Design view if you're not already there.

2. Select a field.

3. Do any of the following:

   • Press the **Delete** key on your keyboard.

   • Click the **Delete Row** button on the toolbar.

   • Select **Edit**, **Delete Row**.

If you prefer, you can delete the field in Datasheet view. Unlike adding fields, where there's an advantage to using Table Design view, you can accomplish a field deletion equally easily in either view. Follow these steps to delete a field in Datasheet view.

1. Switch to Datasheet view if you're not already there.

2. Select the entire column for the field you want to delete.

3. Select **Edit**, **Delete Column**.

Hiding a Field

If there's a field that you don't want to use at the moment, but you will want it later, you may want to hide it instead of deleting it. There are two advantages to hiding a field:

- If you have entered any records, you can preserve any data you entered into that field.

- The Field Properties you set when you created the field will remain intact, so you don't have to re-enter them later.

You must hide a field using Datasheet view; you cannot hide it using Table Design view. Follow these steps:

1. Switch to Datasheet view, if you aren't there already.

2. Select the field(s) you want to hide.

3. Select **Format**, **Hide Columns**. The columns disappear.

   To unhide the column(s) later, follow these steps:

1. Select **Format**, **Unhide Columns**. The Unhide Columns dialog box appears (Figure 9.2). Fields with a check mark beside them are unhidden; fields without a check mark are hidden.

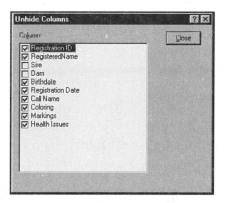

Figure 9.2   You can either unhide or hide fields with the Unhide Columns dialog box.

2. Click on the check box of any field that you want to change. Clicking toggles between hidden and unhidden status.

3. Click **Close**.

They're Still There   Hidden fields are still very much a part of your database. As proof of that, you'll still see them in Table Design view, along with all the other fields.

Hiding with the Unhide Dialog Box   As you can see in Figure 9.2, the Unhide dialog box lets you hide fields as well as unhide them. To hide a field from there, just click to remove the check mark from its check box.

Deleting a Table

Now that you've created a table and worked with it a bit, you may discover that you made so many mistakes in creating it that it would be easier to start over. (Don't feel bad; that's what happened to me the first time.) Or you may have several tables by now and find that you don't need all of them. Whatever the reason, it's easy to delete a table. Follow these steps:

1. From the Database window, click the **Tables** tab.

2. Select the table you want to delete.

3. Select **Edit**, **Delete**, or press the **Delete** key on your keyboard.

4. A message will appear asking if you are sure you want to do this. Click **Yes**.

Cut Versus Delete   You can also cut a table. Cutting is different from deleting, because the table isn't gone forever; it moves to the Clipboard. From there, you can paste it into a different database, or into some other application. However, since the Clipboard holds only one item at a time, you will lose the table if you don't paste the table elsewhere before you cut or copy something else.

In this lesson, you learned how to modify your table by adding and removing fields, hiding fields, and editing the information about each field. In the next lesson, you'll begin entering data into a table.

Entering Data into a Table

In this lesson, you'll learn how to add records to a table, print the table, and close it.

At this point, you have created your table structure, and you've fine-tuned it with the exact settings you want. It's finally time to enter records! So let's open the table and start.

 Other Ways to Enter Records Entering records directly into a table, which you'll learn in this lesson, is not the best way to enter records. It's more efficient to create a form in which to do your data entry. You'll learn to create a form in Lesson 13.

Entering a Record

If you read Lessons 1 and 2 (I hope you did!), you know that a *record* is a row in your table. It contains information about a specific person, place, event, or whatever. You enter a value for each record into each field (column) in your table.

First, you must open the table. Remember, to open a table, you double-click on it in the Database window, or click once on it and then click **Open**. Then follow these steps to enter a record:

 **There's a Number in the First Column!** If you've set up the first field to be automatically entered (for instance, a sequentially numbered field), start with the second field instead.

1. Click in the first empty cell in the first empty column.

Cell   The intersection of a row and a column. It's where you enter the data for a particular field for a particular record. Sometimes, the word *field* is used to mean the entry in a field for an individual record, but "field" really refers to the entire column. Cell is the more proper name for an individual block.

2. Type the value for that field.

3. Press **Tab** to move to the next field and type its value.

4. Continue pressing **Tab** until you get to the last field. When you press **Tab** in the last field, the insertion point moves to the first field in the next line, where you can start a new record.

Insertion Point   When you click in a field, you see a blinking vertical line, called an *insertion point*, which tells you that's where anything you type will appear.

5. Continue entering records until you've entered them all.

Some Data Entry Tricks

You can enter all your data with nothing more than the **Tab** key and some typing, but here are a few keyboard tricks that will make the job easier:

- To insert the current date, press **Ctrl+;** (semicolon). To insert the current time, press **Ctrl+:** (colon).

- If you have defined a default value for a field (in Table Design view), you can insert it by pressing **Ctrl+Alt+Spacebar**.

- To repeat the value from the same field in the previous record, press **Ctrl+'** (apostrophe).

Moving Around in a Table

In the preceding steps, you pressed **Tab** to move from field to field in the table, but there are other ways to move around that you might find even more convenient. For instance, you can click in any field at any time to move the insertion point there.

There are many keyboard shortcuts for moving around in a table; they're summarized in Table 10.1.

Table 10.1   Table movement keys.

To Move To	*Press*
Next field	**Tab**
Previous field	**Shift+Tab**
Last field in the record	**End**
First field in the record	**Home**
Same field in the next record	**Down arrow**
Same field in the previous record	**Up arrow**
Same field in the last record	**Ctrl+down arrow**
Same field in the first record	**Ctrl+up arrow**
Last field in the last record	**Ctrl+End**
First field in the first record	**Ctrl+Home**

Printing a Table

Normally, you will not want to print a table—it won't look very pretty. A table is just a plain grid of rows and columns. Instead, you'll want to create and print a report that contains exactly the data you want (see Lesson 19).

However, sometimes, you may want a quick printout of the raw data in the table, and in that case, follow these steps:

1. Open the table.

2. Click the **Print** button on the toolbar. The table prints.

More Printing Control You can set some printing options before you print if you want. Instead of clicking the **Print** toolbar button, select **File**, **Print** and choose your printing options from the Print dialog box. Then click **OK** to print.

Closing a Table

By now you have probably discovered that a table is just another window; to close it you simply click its **Close** button (**X**) or double-click its **Control-menu** box (see Figure 10.1).

Control-menu icon

Close button

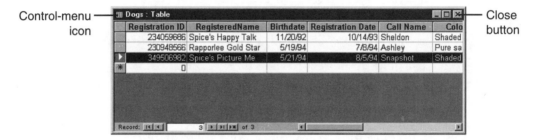

Figure 10.1 Close a table the same way you close any window.

In this lesson, you learned to enter records into a table, to print the table, and to close it. In the next lesson, you'll learn to edit your table data.

Editing Data in a Table

In this lesson, you'll learn how to change information in a field, select records, and insert and delete records.

Very few things are perfectly done the first time around. As you're entering records into your table, you may find you need to make some changes. This lesson shows you how.

Changing a Cell's Content

Editing a cell's content is easy. You can either replace the old content completely or edit it. Which is better? It depends on how much you need to change; you make the call.

Replacing a Cell's Content

If the old content is completely wrong, it's best to enter new data from scratch. To replace the old content in a field:

1. Select the cell. Do this by moving to it with the keyboard (see Table 10.1 in Lesson 10) or by clicking on it.

   If you are going to select the cell by clicking on it, position the mouse pointer at the left edge of the field so the mouse pointer becomes a plus sign (see Figure 11.1); then click. That way you select the entire content.

2. Type the new data. The new data replaces the old data.

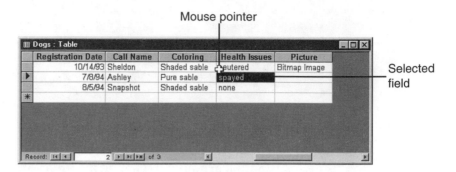

Figure 11.1 To select a field's entire content, make sure the mouse pointer is a plus sign when you click.

Editing a Cell's Content

If you have a small change to make to a cell's content, there's no reason to completely retype it; just edit the content. Follow these steps:

1. Position the mouse pointer in the cell, so the mouse pointer looks like an I-beam (see Figure 11.2).

2. Click. An insertion point appears in the cell (shown in Figure 11.2).

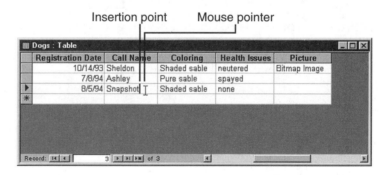

Figure 11.2 Click in the cell to place the insertion point in it.

3. Move to the location in the cell where you want to start editing (see Table 11.1).

4. Press **Backspace** to remove the character to the left of the insertion point, or press **Delete** to remove the character to the right of it. Then type your change.

Table 11.1   Moving around within a cell.

To Move	*Press*
One character to the right	**Right arrow**
One character to the left	**Left arrow**
One word to the right	**Ctrl+right arrow**
One word to the left	**Ctrl+left arrow**
To the end of the line	**End**
To the end of the field	**Ctrl+End**
To the beginning of the line	**Home**
To the beginning of the field	**Ctrl+Home**

Selecting Records

In addition to editing individual cells in a record, you may want to work with an entire record. To do this, click in the gray square to the left of the record (the *record selection area*). The entire record appears highlighted (white letters on black), as shown in Figure 11.3.

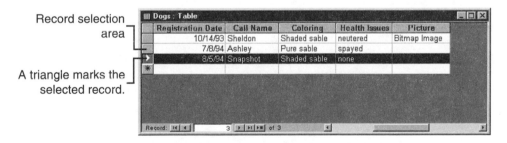

Record selection area

A triangle marks the selected record.

Figure 11.3   The highlighted selected record.

You can select several records as a group; select the first one and hold down **Shift** while you select the others. You can only select contiguous groups of records; you can't pick them from all over the list.

Selecting All Records   There are several quick ways to select all the records at once. Click the blank box at the intersection of the row and column headings or press **Ctrl+A**. Or choose **Edit, Select All Records** from the menu bar at the top of the window.

Understanding Record Selection Symbols

When you select a record, a triangle appears in the record selection area (refer to Figure 11.3). There are two other symbols you might see in this area, too:

   Being entered or edited

   Blank

Only One Triangle   If you select several records, only the first one you click on will have the triangle symbol beside it. That doesn't matter, though; they're all equally selected.

Inserting New Records

New records are inserted automatically. When you start to type a record, a new line appears below it, waiting for another record, as shown in Figure 11.3. You can't insert new records between existing ones. You must always insert new records at the end of the table.

What If I Want the Records in a Different Order?   It's easy to sort your records in any order you like. You'll learn how to sort in Lesson 16, "Sorting and Filtering Data."

Deleting Records

If you find that one or more records is out of date or doesn't belong in the table, you can easily delete it. You can even delete several records at a time. Follow these steps:

   1. Select the record(s) you want to delete.

2. Do any of the following:

- Click the **Delete Records** button on the toolbar.

- Press the **Delete** key on the keyboard.

- Select **Edit, Delete**.

- Select **Edit, Delete Record**.

Delete Versus Delete Record   If you select the entire record, there's no difference between these two commands. If you don't select the entire record, though, **Delete** removes only the selected text, while **Delete Record** removes the entire record.

Moving and Copying Data

As with any Windows program, you can use the Cut, Copy, and Paste commands to copy and move data. Follow these steps:

1. Select the field(s), record(s), cell(s), or text that you want to move or copy.

2. Open the **Edit** menu and select **Cut** (to move) or **Copy** (to copy). Or click the **Cut** or **Copy** button on the toolbar.

3. Position the insertion point where you want to insert the cut or copied material.

4. Select **Edit, Paste** or click the **Paste** button on the toolbar.

Moving and Copying Entire Tables   You can move and copy entire objects, not just individual fields and records. From the Database window, select the table, report, query, and so on you want to move or copy; then issue the **Cut** or **Copy** command. Move where you want the object to go (for example, in a different database) and issue the **Paste** command.

In this lesson, you learned to edit data in a field, to insert and delete fields, and to copy and move data from place to place. In the next lesson, you'll learn about table formatting.

Formatting a Table

In this lesson, you'll learn to improve the look of a table by adjusting the row and column sizes, changing the font, and choosing a different alignment.

Why Format a Table?

Most people don't spend a lot of time and effort formatting Access tables, because they don't have to look at or print their tables. They use data entry forms (Lesson 13) to see the records on-screen and reports (Lesson 19) to print their records. The tables are merely holding tanks for raw data.

However, creating forms and reports can be a lot of work, and may be more than you want to tackle right now. For instance, if your database is very simple, consisting of one small table, you may want to add enough formatting to your table to make it look fairly attractive; then you can use it for all your viewing and printing, foregoing the fancier forms and reports.

Even if you decide later to use a form or report, you might still want to add a bit of formatting to your table, so it will be readable if you ever need to look at it.

Changing Column Width and Row Height

One of the most common problems in a table is that you can't see the complete contents of the fields. Most fields can hold more data than will fit across a column's width, so the data in your table appears truncated, or cut off.

There are two ways to fix this problem: make the column wider, so it can display more data, or make the row taller, so it can display more than one line of data.

Changing Column Width

Access offers many different ways to adjust column width in a table, so you can choose the method you like best.

One of the easiest ways to adjust column width is to simply drag the column headings. Follow these steps:

1. Position the mouse pointer between two field names (column headings), so the mouse pointer turns into a vertical line with left and right-pointing arrows (see Figure 12.1). You'll be adjusting the column on the left; the column on the right will move to accommodate it.

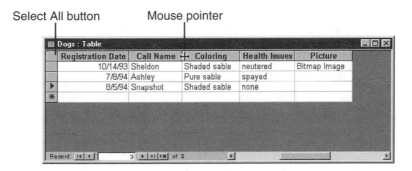

Figure 12.1   Position the mouse pointer between two column headings.

2. Click and hold down the mouse button, and drag the column to the right or left to increase or decrease the width.

3. Release the mouse button when the column is the desired width.

Another, more precise way to adjust column width is with the Column Width dialog box. Follow these steps:

1. Select the column(s) you want to adjust the width for. If you want to adjust all columns, select them all by clicking the **Select All** button (shown in Figure 12.1).

2. Select **Format, Column Width**. The Column Width dialog box appears (Figure 12.2).

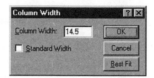

Figure 12.2   Adjust column width precisely here.

3. Do one of the following to set the column width:

   - Adjust the column to exactly the width needed for the longest entry in it by clicking **Best Fit**.

   - Set the width to a precise number of field characters by typing it in the **Column Width** text box.

   - Reset the column width to its default value by selecting the **Standard Width** check box.

4. Click **OK** to apply the changes.

Column Width Shortcut   Instead of selecting **Format, Column Width**, you can right-click on the column and select **Column Width** from the shortcut menu that appears.

Changing Row Height

If you don't want to make a column wider but still want to see more of its contents, you can make the rows taller.

Which Rows Should I Adjust?   It doesn't matter which row you've selected; the height you set applies to all rows. You can't adjust the height of individual rows.

One way to make rows taller is to drag one of them, just as you dragged a column in the preceding section. Position the mouse pointer between two rows in the row selection area; then drag up or down.

Another way is with the Row Height dialog box. It works the same as the Column Width dialog box except there's no Best Fit option. Select **Format**, **Row Height**, enter the new height, and click **OK**.

Changing the Font

Unlike in other Access views (like Report and Form), you can't format individual fields or entries differently from the rest. You can choose a different font for the display, but it automatically applies to all the text in the table, including the column headings.

Font changes you make in Datasheet view will not appear in your reports, queries, or forms; they're for Datasheet view only.

 Why Would I Change the Table Font? You might want to make the font smaller so you can see more of the field contents on-screen without bothering to adjust column width. Or you might make the font larger so you can see the table more clearly.

To choose a different font, follow these steps:

1. Select **Format**, **Font**. The Font dialog box appears (Figure 12.3).

2. Choose a font from the **Font** list box.

3. Choose a style from the **Font style** list box.

4. Choose a size from the **Size** list box.

5. Choose a color from the **Color** drop-down list.

6. (Optional) Click the **Underline** check box if you want underlined text.

7. You can see a sample of your changes in the Sample area. When you're happy with the look of the sample text, click **OK**.

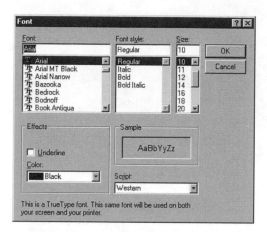

Figure 12.3   The Font dialog box lets you set one font for the entire table.

More Cell Appearance Changes   Another way you can change the look of your table is with the Cells Effects dialog box. Select **Format**, **Cells** to see it. You can change the background color, the color of the divider lines between each row and column, and whether the lines show or not.

In this lesson, you learned how to format a table. In the next lesson, you'll learn how to create a simple data entry form.

Creating a Simple Form

In this lesson, you'll learn to create a form, both with and without the Form Wizard.

Why Create Forms?

As you saw in Lessons 10 and 11, it's possible to do all your data entry and editing in a table, but that's not the best way. For one thing, unless you set your field widths very wide (see Lesson 12), you probably won't be able to see everything you type in the field. For another, if you have data you want to enter into several tables, you have to open each table individually.

A better data entry method is to create a *form*. With a form, you can allot as much space as needed for each field, and you can enter information into several tables at once. You also avoid the headaches of trying to figure out which record you're working with on the table; each form shows only one record at a time.

There are three ways to create a form:

- AutoForm is great when you want an extremely quick, generic form that contains all the fields in a single table.

- Form Wizard provides a compromise between speed and control; you can create a form by following a series of dialog boxes and choose which fields it will contain.

- Creating a form from scratch is the most difficult way, but the method that provides the most control.

Each of these is explained in this lesson.

Creating a Form with AutoForm

The easiest way to create a form is with *AutoForm*. AutoForm simply plunks down the fields from a single table into a form; it's the least flexible way to create a form but it's very quick. Follow these steps:

1. From the Database window, click the **Forms** tab.

2. Click the **New** button. The New Form dialog box appears (Figure 13.1).

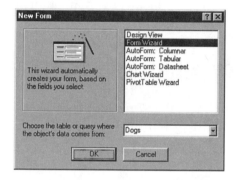

Figure 13.1 Choose how you want to create your form here.

3. Click **AutoForm: Columnar** to create a columnar form (the most popular kind); click **AutoForm: Tabular** or **AutoForm: Datasheet** instead.

4. Open the drop-down list at the bottom of the dialog box and choose the table this form will be associated with.

5. Click **OK**. The form appears, ready for data entry.

If the form created by AutoForm is not what you want, delete it and try again with the Form Wizard, explained in the next section. To delete the form, close it, and answer **No** when asked if you want to save your changes.

Creating a Form with Form Wizard

The *Form Wizard* offers a good compromise between the automation of AutoForm and the control provided by creating your form from scratch. Follow these steps to use the Form Wizard:

1. From the Database window, click the **Forms** tab.

2. Click the **New** button. The New Form dialog box appears (Figure 13.1).

3. Click **Form Wizard**.

Don't I Have to Pick a Table?   You don't have to choose a table from the drop-down list in the New Form dialog box because you'll choose it in step 5.

4. Click **OK** to begin the Form Wizard (Figure 13.2).

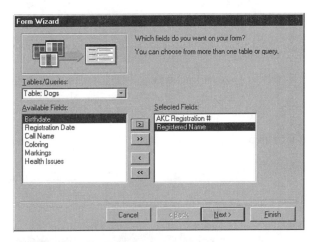

Figure 13.2   The Form Wizard lets you choose which fields you want to include, from as many different tables as you like.

5. Open the **Tables/Queries** drop-down list and choose a table from which to select fields.

6. Click on a field in the **Available Fields** list that you want to include on the form, and then click the **>** button to move it to the **Selected Fields** list.

7. Repeat step 6 until you've selected all the fields you want to include from that table. If you want to include fields from another table, go back to step 5 and choose another table.

Relationships?   If you use two or more tables, they must have at least one field in common and have a relationship set up. Don't worry—it's not as bad as it sounds.

Selecting All Fields   You can quickly move all the fields from the **Available Fields** list to the **Selected Fields** list by clicking the **>>** button. If you make a mistake, you can remove a field from the **Selected Fields** list by clicking on it and clicking the **<** button.

8. Click **Next** to continue. You'll be asked to choose a layout: **Columnar**, **Tabular**, or **Datasheet**. Click on each of the buttons to see a preview of that type. (Columnar is the most common.) Then click on the one you want and click **Next**.

9. Next you're asked to choose a style. Click on each of the styles listed to see a preview of it; click **Next** when you've chosen the one you want.

10. Enter a title for the form in the **Form** text box (see Figure 13.3).

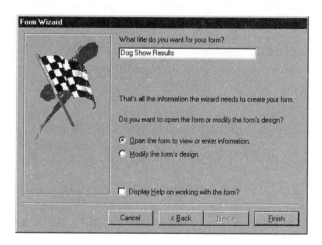

Figure 13.3   Enter a title for your form, and you're almost done.

11. Click the **Finish** button. The form appears, ready for data entry.

Creating a Form from Scratch

The most powerful—and difficult—way to create a form is using *Form Design*. In Form Design view, you decide exactly where to place each field and how to format it.

The following steps start you using Form Design view; you'll learn more about this view in Lesson 14.

1. From the Database window, click the **Forms** tab.

2. Click the **New** button. The New Form dialog box appears (Figure 13.1).

3. Click **Design View**.

4. Select a table or query from the drop-down list at the bottom of the dialog box. This is important! You won't have the opportunity to select this later in the process.

Only One Table Per Form Design Form   One thing you can't do with Form Design view that you can do with Form Wizard is create a form containing fields from more than one table. However, you can trick Form Design into doing this by basing the form on a query that references multiple tables. You'll learn about queries in Lesson 17.

5. Click **OK**. A Form Design screen appears, as shown in Figure 13.4. You're ready to create your form.

Toolbox and Field List   You'll want to use the Form Design toolbox and the Field List shown in Figure 13.4. If they're not visible, click the **Toolbox** button and/or the **Field List** button in the toolbar.

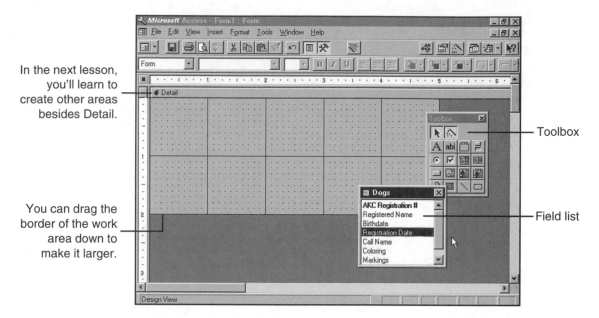

In the next lesson, you'll learn to create other areas besides Detail.

Toolbox

You can drag the border of the work area down to make it larger.

Field list

Figure 13.4 Form Design view presents a blank canvas on which to design your form.

Adding Fields to a Form

The basic idea of the Form Design screen is simple: it's like a light table or pasteup board where you place the elements of your form. The fields you add to a form will appear in the **Detail** area of the form. The **Detail** area is the only area visible at first; you'll learn to add other areas later in the next lesson.

To add a field to the form, follow these steps:

1. Display the **Field List** if it's not showing. Click the **Field List** button or select **View**, **Field List** to do so.

2. Drag a field from the **Field List** onto the **Detail** area of the form (see Figure 13.5).

3. Repeat step 2 to add as many fields as you like to the form.

Don't worry about crowded labels; you'll fix that in the next lesson.

The mouse cursor changes to show a field is being placed.

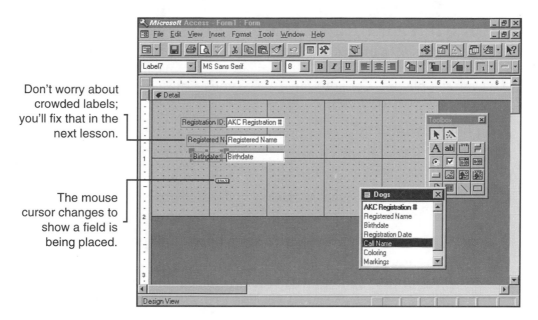

Figure 13.5   Drag fields from the Field List to the grid.

You can drag more than one field to the form at once. In step 2, instead of clicking on a single field and then dragging it, do one of the following before dragging:

- To select a block of fields, click on the first one you want, and hold down **Shift** while you click on the last one.

- To select nonadjacent fields, hold down **Ctrl** as you click on each one you want.

- To select all the fields on the list, double-click the **Field List** title bar.

You can move objects around on a form after you've initially placed them; you'll learn how to do this in Lesson 14. Don't worry if your form doesn't look very professional at this point. In the next several lessons, you'll learn how to modify and improve your form.

Using Snap to Grid   If you find it hard to align the fields neatly, select **Format, Snap to Grid** to place a check mark next to that command. If you want to align the fields on your own, select it again to turn it off.

Entering Data in a Form

The whole point of creating a form is so you can enter data more easily into your tables. The form acts as an attractive "mask" that shields you from the plainness of your table. Once you create a form, follow these steps to enter data into it:

1. Open the form:

   - If your form appears in Form Design view, select **View, Form** to enter Form view.

   - If the form isn't open at all, click the **Form** tab in the Database window and double-click on the form's name.

2. Click in the field you want to begin with and type the data.

3. Press **Tab** to move to the next field. If you need to go back, you can press **Shift+Tab** to move to the previous field. When you reach the last field, pressing **Tab** moves you to the first field in a new, blank record.

4. Repeat steps 2 and 3 to enter all the records you like. They're saved automatically as you enter them.

Data Entry Shortcuts   See the "Some Data Entry Tricks" section in Lesson 10 for some shortcut ideas. They work equally well in forms and tables.

In this lesson, you created a simple form and added data to it. In the next lesson, you'll learn how to make changes to your form to make it better suit your needs.

Modifying Your Form

In this lesson, you'll learn to modify a form. You can use any form, created in any of the ways you learned in Lesson 13.

This lesson is about making changes to *forms*. You might have a very rough form at this point, which you created from scratch, or you might have a polished, good-looking form that the Form Wizard created for you. The steps are the same no matter what you're starting with. (The examples in this lesson use a form from Form Wizard.)

Moving Fields

The most common change to a form is to move a field around. You might want to move several fields down to make room so you can insert a new field, or just rearrange how the fields appear. From Form Design view, Follow these steps:

1. Click on a field's name to select it. Selection handles appear around it (see Figure 14.1). You can select several fields by holding down **Shift** as you click on each one.

2. Position the mouse pointer so the pointer becomes a hand (see Figure 14.1). If you're moving more than one field, you can position the mouse pointer on any of the selected fields.

3. Click and hold down the left mouse button as you drag the field to a different location.

4. Release the mouse button when the field is at the desired new location.

Selection handles ───  ─── Mouse pointer

Figure 14.1 To move a field, first select it. Then drag it when the mouse pointer is a hand.

Adding Text

The next thing that most people want to do is add text to the form: titles, subtitles, explanatory text, and so on. Just follow these steps:

1. If the Toolbox is not displayed, select **View**, **Toolbox**.

2. Click the **Text** tool in the toolbox (the one with the capital letter **A** on it). The mouse pointer changes to a capital **A** with a plus sign next to it (see Figure 14.2).

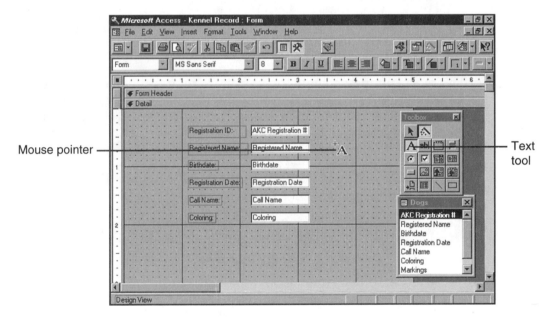

Figure 14.2 Select the Text tool in the toolbox.

3. Click anywhere on the form where you want to create the new text. A tiny box appears. (The box will expand to hold the text as you type.)

4. Type the text.

5. Click anywhere outside of the text's area to finish.

Text Dragging   Don't worry about positioning the text as you create it. You can move text in the same way that you move fields. Just click on it, position the mouse pointer so the hand appears, and then drag it to where you want it to go.

Viewing Headers and Footers

The area that you have been working with so far on your form has been the Detail area, but there are other areas you can use, too, as shown in Figure 14.3.

Form header and footer contain text you want repeated on each on-screen form.

Page header and footer contain text you want repeated on every page when you print the form.

Detail contains fields that will change with every record.

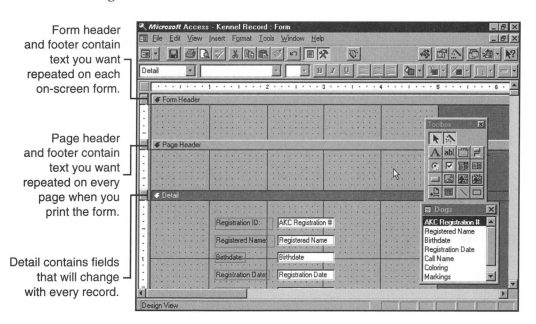

Figure 14.3   Each form can have several areas.

To display these areas, follow these steps:

1. To view the Page Header/Footer, select **View, Page Header/ Footer**.

2. To view the Form Header/Footer, select **View**, **Form Header/ Footer**.

3. To turn either one off again, select it again.

Once you display any of these headers and footers, you can add text to them, the same way that you learned to add text in the preceding section.

Changing Field Lengths

As you can see in Figure 14.3, the **Registration ID** field looks like it can display about 10 characters in the field entry area. That's fine, but what if you have a longer ID number? You just drag the field entry area to make it longer so more characters will show. Follow these steps:

1. Click on the field entry area to select it. Selection handles appear around it.

2. Position the mouse pointer at the right edge of the field entry area so the mouse pointer turns into a double-headed arrow (see Figure 14.4).

3. Drag the field to its new length, then release the mouse button.

Selection handles —— Registration ID · · · AKC Regist —— Mouse pointer

Figure 14.4   You can change the size of the field entry area by dragging it.

Formatting Text on a Form

Once you place all your information on the form (that is, the fields you want to include and any titles or explanatory text), the next step is to dress the form up and make it look more appealing.

All the formatting tools you need are on the Formatting toolbar (the second toolbar from the top in Form Design view). Table 14.1 shows the controls. To use a control, just select the element you want to format, then issue the command to apply the control.

Some controls, like the font and size, are drop-down lists. You click the down-arrow next to the control, and then select from the list. Other controls are simple toggles such as Bold and Italic. Still other controls such as the coloring and border buttons are a combination of a button and a drop-down list. If you click on the button, it applies the current value. You can click the down arrow next to the button to change the value.

Table 14.1   Controls on the Formatting Toolbar

Button	*Purpose*
Call Name	Lists the fields in the table you are using
MS Sans Serif	Lists the available fonts
8	Lists the available sizes for the selected font
B	Toggles Bold on/off
I	Toggles Italics on/off
U	Toggles Underline on/off
≣	Left-aligns text
≣	Centers text
≣	Right-aligns text
	Fills the selected box with the selected color
	Colors the text in the selected box
	Colors the outline of the selected box

continues

Table 14.1 Continued

Button	Purpose
	Adds a border to the selected box
	Adds a special effect to the selected box

Changing the Background Color You can change the color of the background on which the form sits, too. Just click the header for the section you want to change (for instance, Detail) to select the entire section. Then use the background color control to change the color.

AutoFormat A shortcut for formatting your form. If you created the form with Form Wizard, you already saw AutoFormat at work. To see it again, select **Format**, **AutoFormat**. You'll be asked to choose from among several premade color and formatting schemes.

Changing Tab Order

When you enter data on a form, you press Tab to move from field to field, in the order they're shown in the form. The progression from field to field is the *tab order*. When you first create a form, the tab order runs from top to bottom.

When you move and rearrange fields, the tab order doesn't change automatically. For instance, if you had 10 fields arranged in a column, and you rearranged them so that the 10th one was at the beginning, the tab order would still show that field in 10th position, even though it's now at the top of the form. This makes it more difficult to fill in the form, so you'll want to adjust the tab order to reflect the new structure of the form.

Tab Order Improvements   You may want to change the tab order to be different from the obvious top-to-bottom structure, to make data entry easier. For instance, if 90% of the records you enter skip several fields, you may want to put those fields last in the tab order, so you can skip over them easily.

Follow these steps to adjust the tab order:

1. Select **View**, **Tab Order**. The Tab Order dialog box appears (see Figure 14.5).

2. The fields appear in their tab order. To change the order, click on a field, and then drag it up or down on the list.

3. To quickly set the tab order based on the fields' current positions in the form (top-to-bottom), click the **Auto Order** button.

4. Click **OK**.

Figure 14.5   Use the Tab Order dialog box to decide what tab order will be used on your form.

In this lesson, you learned to improve a form by moving fields, adding text, adding formatting, and adjusting the tab order. In the next lesson, you'll learn to search for data.

Searching for Data

In this lesson, you'll learn the most basic ways to search for data in a database: with the Find and Replace features.

Using the Find Feature

The *Find* feature is useful for locating a particular record that you have previously entered. For instance, if you keep a database of customers, you might want to find a particular customer's record quickly when he is ready to make a purchase, so you can verify his address. Or in the Kennel example we've been using, you could quickly find the record for the dog with the call name of Sheldon, to look up his birth date.

Finding More Than One Record   If you need to find several records at once, Find is not the best tool. It only finds one record at a time. A better tool for finding multiple records is a *Filter*, discussed in Lesson 16.

To find a particular record, follow these steps:

1. Switch to either Datasheet view or Form view. Either one supports the Find feature.

2. Click in the field that contains the data you want to find, if you know which field it is. For instance, if you're going to look for a customer based on his last name, click in the **Name** field.

3. Select **Edit, Find**. Or click the **Find** tool in the toolbar or press **Ctrl+F**. The Find dialog box appears (see Figure 15.1).

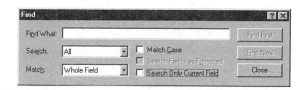

Figure 15.1   Use the Find dialog box to find data in a record.

4. Type the text or numbers that you want to find into the **Find What** text box.

5. Open the **Match** drop-down list and select one of the following:

   Whole Field   Finds fields where the specified text is the only thing in that field. For instance, "Smith" would not find "Smithsonian."

   Start of Field   Finds fields that begin with the specified text. For instance, "Smith" would find "Smith" and "Smithsonian," but not "Joe Smith."

   Any Part of Field   Finds fields that contain the specified text in any way. "Smith" would find "Smith," "Smithsonian," and "Joe Smith."

6. If you want to search only forward from the current record, open the **Search** drop-down list and select **Down**. If you want to search only backward, select **Up**. The default is **All**, which searches all records.

7. To limit the match to only entries that are the same case (upper and/or lower), select the **Match Case** check box. After doing this, "Smith" would not find "SMITH" or "smith."

8. To find only fields with the same formatting as the text you type, select **Search Fields as Formatted**. With this option on, "12/12/95" would not find "12-12-95," even though they are the same date, because they're formatted differently.

TIP   **Don't Slow Down**   Don't use the Search Fields as Formatted option unless you specifically need it, because it makes your search go more slowly.

Option Not Available! The Search Fields as Formatted option is available only if you select Search Only Current Field.

9. To limit the search to the field where you clicked when you started this procedure, select the **Search Only Current Field** check box. (Do this whenever possible, because it makes the search faster.) If you don't know what field the data is in, leave this unmarked.

10. Click **Find First** to find the first match for your search.

11. If needed, move the Find dialog box out of the way by dragging its title bar so you can see the record it found. Access highlights the field entry containing the found text (see Figure 15.2).

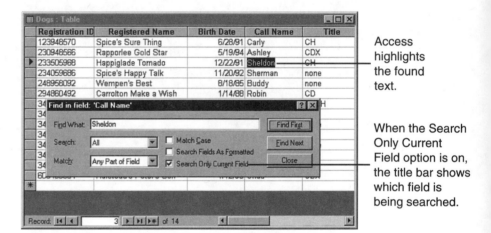

Access highlights the found text.

When the Search Only Current Field option is on, the title bar shows which field is being searched.

Figure 15.2 Access finds records that contain the selected text, one instance at a time.

12. To find the next occurrence, click **Find Next**. If Access cannot find any more occurrences, it tells you **The search item was not found**. Click **OK** to clear that message.

13. When you finish finding your data, click **Close** to close the Find dialog box.

Using the Replace Feature

Replacing is a lot like finding; it finds the specified text, too. But then as an extra bonus, it replaces the found text with other text that you specify. For instance, if you found that you misspelled a brand name in your inventory list (perhaps you used Train instead of Trane?), you could replace the word Train with Trane. Or in our dog kennel example, you could find the dog named Sheldon and change his name to Sherman, if his new owners changed his name.

To find and replace data, follow these steps:

1. Select **Edit**, **Replace** or press **Ctrl+H**. The Replace dialog box appears (see Figure 15.3).

Type the text you want to find here. ⌐

Type the text you want to replace it with here. ⌐

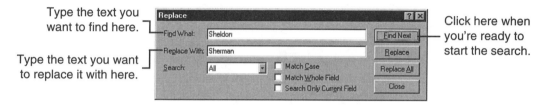

Click here when you're ready to start the search.

Figure 15.3   You can find specific text and replace it with different text.

2. Type the text you want to find in the **Find What** text box.

3. Type the text you want to replace it with in the **Replace With** text box.

4. Select any options you want, as you learned to do with the Find dialog box in the previous section.

There's No Match   The one thing that the Replace dialog box lacks from the Find dialog box is the Match drop-down list. The Replace feature always uses the **Any Part of Field** option for matching.

5. Click **Find Next**. Access finds the first occurrence of the text.

6. Drag the title bar of the Replace dialog box to move the box if needed to see the text that was found.

7. Click the **Replace** button to replace the text.

8. Click **Find Next** to find other occurrences if desired, and replace them by clicking the **Replace** button.

Replace All   If you are certain you want to replace every instance of the text in the entire table, click **Replace All**. It's quicker than alternating between **Find Next** and **Replace** many times. Be careful, though! You may not realize all the instances that may be changed—for instance, you wouldn't want to change "will" to "would" only to find that "willfully" has been changed to "wouldfully," for instance.

9. When you finish replacing, click **Close**.

Other Ways to Find Data

The Find and Replace features work well on individual records, but there are several more sophisticated ways of locating data in your database, as you'll earn in upcoming lessons. They include:

- **Sorting**   Rearranging the data on-screen so it's easier to skim through the list to find what you want. See Lesson 16.

- **Filtering**   Narrowing down the list to eliminate the data you know you don't want to see. See Lesson 16.

- **Querying**   Creating a more formal filter with complex criteria that you can save and apply again and again. See Lessons 17–18.

- **Reporting**   Creating a printed report containing only the records and fields that you're interested in. See Lessons 19–20.

In this lesson, you learned to find and replace data in a database. In the next lesson, you'll learn about two other ways of locating the data you want: sorting and filtering.

Sorting and Filtering Data

In this lesson, you'll learn how to find data by sorting and filtering.

Access has many ways of finding and organizing data, and each is good for a certain situation. As you learned in Lesson 15, Find and Replace are great features when you're working with individual instances of a particular value, for example, finding Mr. Smith's record quickly. This chapter explains two other ways of finding what you need.

Sorting Data

Even though you enter your records into the database in some sort of logical order, at some point, you'll want them in a different order. For instance, if we entered the dogs in our kennel according to registration number, we might later want to look at the list according to the dogs' birth dates, from oldest to youngest.

The *Sort* command is the perfect solution to this problem. With Sort, you can rearrange the records according to any field you like. You can sort in either ascending (A to Z, 1 to 10) or descending (Z to A, 10 to 1) order.

Which View? You can sort in either Form or Datasheet view, but I prefer Datasheet view because it shows many records at once. Use Sort to locate a record in relation to others (for example, to look for the oldest dog).

Follow these steps to sort records:

1. Click anywhere in the field on which you want to sort.

2. Click the **Sort Ascending** button or **Sort Descending** button on the toolbar. Or if you prefer, select **Records**, **Sort**, and then choose **Ascending** or **Descending** from the submenu. Figure 16.1 shows our table of dogs sorted in Ascending order by birth date.

Access sorted the table by this column.

Registration ID	Registered Name	Birth Date	Call Name	Title
248958092	Wempen's Best	8/18/85	Buddy	none
294860492	Carrolton Make a Wish	1/14/88	Robin	CD
340968690	Roanoke Old Times	2/9/88	Leeza	OTCH
349586760	Elfstone Watch Me GO	5/5/89	Butch	CD
349586029	Sheltie Joy III	2/4/90	Shep	CD
348572983	Homestead Star	9/9/90	Emmy	CH
123948570	Spice's Sure Thing	6/28/91	Carly	CH
233505968	Happiglade Tornado	12/22/91	Sheldon	CH
234059686	Spice's Happy Talk	11/20/92	Sherman	none
606433884	Halstead's Peter's Son	1/12/93	Chad	CDX
230948566	Rapporlee Gold Star	5/19/94	Ashley	CDX
349506982	Spice's Picture Me	5/21/94	Snapshot	none
349283049	Ripley Beauregard	3/15/95	Rooster	UD
349205986	Wileys Last Chance	5/18/95	Scotty	none

Record: |◀| ◀ | 7 | ▶ | ▶| | ▶* | of 14

Figure 16.1 Access sorted this table in Ascending order by the Birth Date column.

3. If you want to restore the records to their presorted order, select **Records, Remove Filter/Sort**.

TERM

What Is Presorted Order? If you defined a Primary Key field when you created your database (see Lesson 7), the records appear sorted in ascending order according to that field by default. This is the order they revert to when you remove a sort (as in step 3).

Filtering Data

Filtering is for those times when you want to get many of the records out of the way, so you can see the few that you're interested in. Filtering temporarily narrows the number of records that appear, according to criteria you select.

Filters versus Queries Queries also narrow down the records displayed, as you'll learn in Lesson 17. A filter is easier and quicker to use than a query, but a filter can't be saved for later use. (However, you can save a filter as a query, as you'll learn later in this lesson.)

There are three ways to apply a filter: Filter by Selection, Filter by Form, and Advanced Filter/Sort. The first two are the most common for casual users, so we will cover them in the following sections. The third method is for advanced users only.

Sorting and Filtering Neither of the filtering methods you'll learn in this lesson allow you to sort at the same time that you filter. However, it's easy enough to sort the filtered records, using the same sorting process you learned earlier in this lesson.

Filter by Selection

Filtering by selection is the easiest method of filtering, but before you can use it, you have to locate an instance of the value you want the filtered records to contain. For example, if you want to find all the dogs in your table that have earned the title of CD (companion dog), you must first locate a record that meets that criteria. Then you'll base the rest of the filter on that record.

To filter by selection, follow these steps:

1. In a field, find one instance of the value you want all filtered records to contain.

2. Select the value, as follows:

    • To find all records where the field value is identical to the selected value, select the entire field entry.

    • To find all records where the field begins with the selected value, select part of the field entry beginning with the first character.

> • To find all records where the field contains the selected value at any point, select part of the field entry beginning after the first character.

3. Click the **Filter by Selection** button on the toolbar, or select **Records, Filter, Filter by Selection.** The records that match the criterion you selected appear.

Figure 16.2 shows the Dogs table filtered to show only dogs that have earned the CD title.

Access filters the table by this column.

Figure 16.2 The result of a filter; only the records which match the criterion appear.

Filtering by More Than One Criterion With Filter by Selection, you can filter by only one criterion at a time. However, you can apply successive filters after the first one to further narrow the list of matching records.

You can also filter for records that don't contain the selected value. After selecting the value, right-click on it; then select **Filter Excluding Selection**.

You can cancel a filter by selecting **Records, Remove Filter/Sort**, or by clicking the **Remove Filter** button (the same as the Apply Filter button).

Filter by Form

Filtering by form is a more powerful filtering method than filtering by selection. With filter by form, you can filter by more than one criterion at a time. You can also set up "or" filters, which find records in which any one of several criteria is matched. You can even enter logical expressions (such as "greater than a certain value").

To filter by form, follow these steps:

1. In Datasheet or Form view, click the **Filter by Form** button on the toolbar or select **Records, Filter, Filter by Form.** A blank form appears, looking like an empty datasheet with a single record line.

2. Click in the field you want to set a criterion for, and a down-arrow appears for a drop-down list. Click on the arrow, and select the value you want from the list. Or you can type the value directly into the field if you prefer.

3. Enter as many criteria as you like in various fields. Figure 16.3 shows two criteria, including a criteria that uses a less-than sign, a mathematical operator (explained in Lesson 17).

4. If you want to set up an "or" condition, click the **Or** tab at the bottom of the Filter by Form window, and enter the alternate criteria into that form. Notice that another Or tab appears when you fill this one, so you can add multiple "or" conditions.

 5. After you enter your criteria, click the **Apply Filter** button on the toolbar. Your filtered data appears.

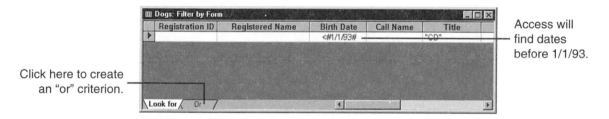

Click here to create an "or" criterion.

Access will find dates before 1/1/93.

Figure 16.3   Filter by Form lets you set more than one criterion.

 Special Symbols   Notice in Figure 16.3 that there are # signs around numbers, and quotation marks ("") around text. Access enters those for you, so you don't have to type them.

   As with Filter by Selection, you can undo a filter by selecting **Records, Remove Filter/Sort**, or by clicking the **Filter** button again.

Saving Your Filtered Data as a Query

Filters are a convenient alternative to creating a simple query from scratch. You can save a filter as a query, and use it just as you would use a query; it even appears on your Queries list in the Database window. (You'll learn more about working with queries in Lesson 17.)

To save a filter as a query, follow these steps:

1. Display the filter in Query by Form view.

2. Select **File**, **Save As Query** or click the **Save** button on the toolbar. Access asks for a name for the new query.

3. Type a name and click **OK**. Access saves the filter.

In this lesson, you learned how to sort and filter your database. In the next lesson, you'll begin learning about queries, a more sophisticated way of isolating and organizing the information you want to see.

Creating a Query

In this lesson, you'll learn how a query can help you find the information you need, and you'll learn to create a simple one using the Simple Query Wizard. You'll also learn how to save and print any query's results, and you'll learn about other Query Wizards that Access provides for special situations.

What Is a Query?

As you learned in Lesson 16, Access offers many ways to help you narrow down the information you're looking at, including sorting and filtering. A *query* is simply a more formal way to sort and filter.

Queries enable you to specify:

- Which fields you want to see

- In what order the fields should appear

- Filter criteria for each field (see Lesson 16)

- The order in which you want each field sorted (see Lesson 16)

Saving a Filter When the primary purpose of the query is to filter, you may find it easier to create a filter and save it as a query. See Lesson 16 for details.

In this lesson, you'll create a very simple query, which may not do everything you want it to do. But in the next lesson (Lesson 18), you'll learn how to modify it to make it more powerful.

Creating a Simple Query Using Query Wizard

The easiest way to create a query is with a Query Wizard, and the easiest Query Wizard is the Simple Query Wizard. (The other Query Wizards are "special-use" ones that you'll probably never need; they're described later in this lesson.)

The Simple Query Wizard lets you select the fields you want to display—that's all. You don't get to set criteria for including individual records, or specify a sort order. (You'll learn to do those things in Lesson 18.) This kind of simple query is useful when you want to weed out extraneous fields, but you still want to see every record.

 Select Query The query that the Simple Query Wizard creates is a very basic version of a Select query. The Select query is the most common query type. With a Select query, you can select records, sort them, filter them, and perform simple calculations on the results (such as counting and averaging.)

To create a simple Select query with the Simple Query Wizard, follow these steps:

1. Open the database you want to work with, and click on the **Queries** tab.

2. Click the **New** button. The New Query dialog box appears.

3. Click on **Simple Query Wizard**; then click **OK**. The first box of the Simple Query Wizard appears, as shown in Figure 17.1. This screen may look familiar; it's similar to the first screen of the Form Wizard, described in Chapter 13.

4. Choose the table from which you want to select fields from the **Tables/Queries** drop-down list. For example, I'm going to use Dogs.

5. Click on a field name in the **Available Fields** list; then click on the → button to move it to the **Selected Fields** list. Repeat to move all the fields you want.

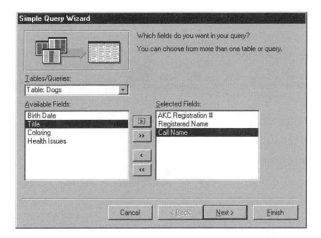

Figure 17.1   The Simple Query Wizard first asks what fields you want to include.

6. Select another table or query from the **Tables/Queries** list and add some of its fields to the **Selected Fields** list if you like. When you finish adding fields, click **Next**, and the next dialog box appears (Figure 17.2).

Figure 17.2   Next, enter a title for your query.

7. Enter a title for the query in the **What title do you want for your query?** text box. I'm going to call mine Dog Names.

673

8. Click **Finish** to view the query results. Figure 17.3 shows my results.

Registration ID	Registered Name	Call Name
123948570	Spice's Sure Thing	Carly
230948566	Rapporlee Gold Star	Ashley
233505968	Happiglade Tornado	Sheldon
234059686	Spice's Happy Talk	Sherman
248958092	Wempen's Best	Buddy
294860492	Carrolton Make a Wish	Robin
340968690	Roanoke Old Times	Leeza
348572983	Homestead Star	Emmy
349205986	Wileys Last Chance	Scotty
349283049	Ripley Beauregard	Rooster
349506982	Spice's Picture Me	Snapshot
349586029	Sheltie Joy III	Shep
349586760	Elfstone Watch Me GO	Butch
606433884	Halstead's Peter's Son	Chad

Record: 1 of 14

Figure 17.3   Here are the results of my simple query.

This simple query is too simple; it has limited usefulness and doesn't show off any of Access's powerful query features. You could get the same results by hiding certain columns in datasheet view! Luckily, the Select query is much more powerful than the Simple Query Wizard makes it appear, as you'll see in the next lesson. But before you go there, take a look at a few basics that apply to any query.

Saving a Query

When you create a query, Access saves it automatically. You don't need to do anything special to save it. Just close the query window, and look on the Queries tab of the database window. You'll see the query on the list.

Close the Query?   Close a query window the same way you close any window, by clicking its **Close** button (the **X** in the top-right corner).

Redisplaying a Query

At any time, you can redisplay the results of your query. If the data has changed since the last time you ran the query, the changes will be reflected.

To redisplay a query, follow these steps:

1. Open the database containing the query.

2. Click on the **Queries** tab in the Database window.

3. Double-click on the query you want to redisplay, or click once on it and then click the **Open** button (see Figure 17.4).

Double-click here to open the Dog Names query.

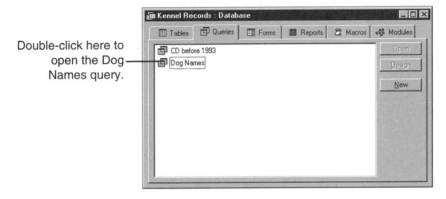

Figure 17.4   Redisplay any query by opening it from the Queries tab.

Working with Query Results

Query results appear in Datasheet view, as shown in Figure 17.3. You can do anything to the records that you can do in a normal Datasheet view (see Lesson 11), including copy and delete records and change field entries.

For example, let's say you wanted to update a sales database to change the Last Contacted field (a date) to today for every record. From your query results window, you could make that change. Or perhaps you want to delete all records for customers who haven't made a purchase in the last two years. You could delete the records from the query results window, and they would disappear from the table too.

Of course, with the latter example, it would be easier if the records were sorted according to the field in question, and the Simple Query Wizard you learned about in this lesson won't let you sort. However, in Lesson 18, you'll learn about some other, more powerful Query Wizards that let you choose more options.

Printing Query Results

The query results window not only edits like a datasheet, but also prints like one. To print the query results, do the following:

1. Make sure the query results window is active.

2. Select **File**, **Print**, or press **Ctrl+P**. The Print dialog box appears.

3. Select any print options you want (refer to Lesson 11); then click **OK**.

Other Query Wizards

Access's query features are very powerful; they can do amazingly complicated calculations and comparisons on many tables at once. You can create queries with their own dialog boxes for custom entry of special criteria, link a query to external databases (databases in other programs), and much more. Access's query capabilities are top-notch.

Unfortunately, the process for creating much of these powerful queries is quite complicated. It's enough to give ordinary, casual users quite a headache. That's why in this book, we stick to the basic Select type of query, which does almost everything an average user needs to do.

However, Access does come with a few other Query Wizards that will help you experiment with more complex query types without causing too much stress. Each of these Query Wizards appears on the list when you click the **New** button from the **Queries** tab. We won't cover any of them in this book, but you may want to try them out yourself:

- **Crosstab Query Wizard** Displays summarized values, such as sums, counts, and averages, from one field, and groups them by one set of facts listed down the left side of the datasheet as row headings and another set of facts listed across the top of the datasheet as column headings.

- **Find Unmatched Query Wizard**   Compares two tables and finds all records that do not appear in both tables (based on comparing certain fields).

- **Find Duplicates Query Wizard**   The opposite of Find Unmatched. It compares two tables and finds all records that appear in both.

- **Archive Query Wizard**   Copies all the records from one table into another table.

In this lesson, you learned to create a simple query, and to save, edit, and print query results. In the next lesson, you'll learn how to modify the query you created.

Modifying a Query

In this lesson, you'll learn how to modify the simple query you created in Lesson 17 using Query Design view.

Introducing Query Design View

In Lesson 17, you created a very simple query using the Simple Query Wizard. That query selected and displayed fields from a table. There's a lot more you can do with your query, but to do it, you need to enter Query Design view.

Query Design view is much like Table Design view and Form Design view, both of which you've encountered earlier in this book. In Query Design view, you can change the rules that govern your query results.

Opening a Query in Query Design View

To open an existing query in Query Design view, follow these steps:

1. Open the database that contains the query you want to edit.

2. Click the **Queries** tab.

3. Click the query you want to edit; then click the **Design** button.

The query created in Lesson 17 is shown in Query Design view in Figure 18.1. You'll learn how to edit it in this lesson.

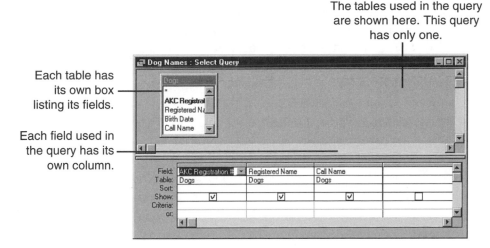

The tables used in the query are shown here. This query has only one.

Each table has its own box listing its fields.

Each field used in the query has its own column.

Figure 18.1   In Query Design view, you can edit a query you've created.

Starting a New Query in Query Design View

Instead of using the Simple Query Wizard to begin your query, as you did in Lesson 17, you can begin a query from scratch in Query Design view. As you become more familiar with Access queries, you may find that this is faster and easier than using a wizard.

To begin a new query in Query Design view, follow these steps:

1. Open the database in which you want the query.

2. Click the **Queries** tab in the Database window.

3. Click the **New** button.

4. Click **New Query** and click **OK**. The Show Table dialog box appears, listing all the tables in the database.

5. Click on a table to choose which table you want to work with; then click **Add**. To choose more than one table, hold down **Shift** as you click on several tables.

6. Click **Close** when you finish adding tables. The Query Design view window opens, as in Figure 18.1, except there won't be any fields selected yet.

Adding Fields to a Query

If you created your query from scratch (as in the preceding set of steps), the first thing you need to do is add the fields you want to work with. You can also use this same procedure to add additional fields to an existing query.

Adding More Tables   You can add additional tables to your query at any time. Just select **Query, Show-Table** or click the **Show Table** button on the toolbar. Then select the table(s) you want and click **Add.** Click **Close** to return to your query design.

There are two ways to add a field to a query. Both methods are easy; try both, to see which one you prefer. Here's the first method:

Only One Table?   If you are using only one table in the query, you can skip the first two steps in this procedure.

1. Click in the **Table** row of the first blank column. A down-arrow button appears, indicating a drop-down list is available.

2. Open the drop-down list and select a table. The tables available on the list are the same as the table windows that appear at the top of the query design window.

3. Click in the **Field** row directly above the table name you just chose. A down-arrow button appears, indicating a drop-down list is available.

4. Open the drop-down list and select a field. The fields listed come from the tables you chose for the query. The field's name appears in the Field row, in the column where you selected it.

Here's the other method of adding a field:

1. Scroll through the list of fields in the desired table window at the top of the Query Design box, until you find the field you want to add.

2. Click on the field name, and drag it into the **Field** row of the first empty column. The field's name appears where you dragged it.

Deleting a Field

There are two ways to delete a field from your query:

- Click anywhere in the column, and select **Edit, Delete Column**.

- Position the mouse pointer directly above the column, so the pointer turns into a down-pointing black arrow. Then click to select the entire column, and press the **Delete** key; or click the **Cut** button on the toolbar.

Cut Versus Delete   If you cut the column, rather than deleting it, you can paste it back into the query. Just select the column where you want it, and then choose **Edit, Paste** or click the **Paste** button on the toolbar. Be careful, though, the pasted column replaces the selected one. The selected column doesn't move over to make room for it. Select an empty column if you don't want to replace an existing one.

Adding Criteria

Criteria will be familiar to you if you read Lesson 16, which deals with filters. *Criteria* let you choose which records will appear in your query results. For example, I could limit my list of dogs to those whose birth dates were before 8/5/94.

Filters Versus Queries   If the primary reason for creating the query is to filter, you may want to create the filter part first using one of the procedures in Lesson 16, and then you can save the filter as a query. You can open that query in Query Design view and fine-tune it as needed.

To set criteria for a field that you've added to your query, follow these steps:

1. In Query Design view, click in the **Criteria** row in the desired field's column.

2. Type the criterion you want to use, as shown in Figure 18.2. Table 18.1 provides some examples you could have entered in Figure 18.2, and the results you would have gotten.

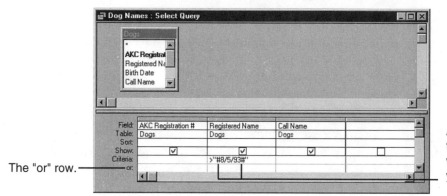

The "or" row.

Access adds these # symbols when you type your criteria.

Figure 18.2 Enter criteria into the Criteria row in the appropriate field's column.

Table 18.1 Sample Criteria for Queries

Enter This	To Get Records Where This Value Is
8/5/93	Exactly 8/5/93
<8/5/93	Before 8/5/93
>8/5/93	After 8/5/93
>=8/5/93	8/5/93 or after
<=8/5/93	8/5/93 or before
Not <8/5/93	Not before 8/5/93
Not >8/5/93	Not after 8/5/93

Text, Too   You can also enter text as a criteria. The < and > (before and after) operators apply to alphabetical order with text. For instance, <C finds text that begins with A or B.

Did you notice the **or** row under the **Criteria** row (see Figure 18.1)? You can enter more criteria using that line. The query will find records where any of the criteria is true. When you enter criteria into the **or** row, another **or** row appears, so you can enter more.

What About "And"?   When you have two criteria that must both be true, you can put them both together in a single Criteria row, with the word "**And**." For instance, you might want birth dates that were between 12/1/93 and 12/1/95. It would all be in a single Criteria row, like this: **>12/1/93 And <12/1/95**.

Sorting a Field in a Query

After all this complicated criteria discussion, you will be happy to know that Sorting is fairly straightforward. To sort any field, just follow these steps from the query results window:

1. Click in the Sort row for the field you want to sort. A down-arrow for a drop-down list appears.

2. Open the drop-down list and select **Ascending** or **Descending**.

Later, if you want to cancel sorting for this field, repeat these steps, but select **(not sorted)**. Refer back to Lesson 16 for more information about sorting.

Showing or Hiding a Field

Some fields are included in your query only so you can filter or sort based on them. You may not necessarily be interested in seeing that field in the query results. For instance, you may want to limit your query to all dogs born before 8/5/93, but you don't want each dog's birth date to appear in the query.

To exclude a field from appearing in the query results, just deselect the check box in the Show row. To include it again, select the check box again.

Viewing Query Results

When you're ready to see the results of your query, select **Query**, **Run**, or click the **Run** button on the toolbar. Your results appear in a window that resembles a datasheet (see Figure 18.3).

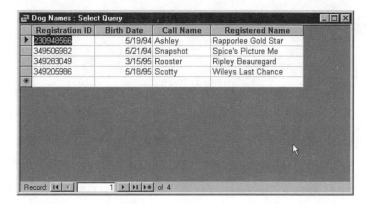

Figure 18.3   The results of a kennel query based on birth dates.

In this lesson, you learned to modify and strengthen your queries. In the next lesson, you'll learn how to create a simple, attractive report suitable for printing and sharing with others.

Creating a Simple Report

In this lesson, you'll learn how to create reports in Access using AutoReport and Report Wizard.

Why Create Reports?

So far in this book, you've learned many ways to organize and view your data, but they've all focused on on-screen use. Forms help with data entry on-screen, and queries help you find information and display the results on-screen.

You can print any table, form, or query, but the results will be less than professional looking. Why? Because those tools are not designed to be printed. Reports, on the other hand, are designed specifically to be printed and shared with other people. With a report, you can generate professional-quality results that you can be proud of.

There are several ways to create a report, ranging from easy-but-limited (AutoReport) to difficult-but-very-flexible (Report Design view). In the middle is Report Wizard, which offers some flexibility along with a fairly easy procedure.

Using AutoReport to Create a Report

If you want a plain, no-frills report based on a single table or query, *AutoReport* is for you. You can go back and improve its appearance later, when you learn about customizing reports in Lesson 20.

You can create either a Tabular or a Columnar report. A tabular report resembles a datasheet, and a columnar report resembles a form. Both are equally easy to create.

To create a report with AutoReport, follow these steps:

1. Open the database containing the table or query on which you want to report.

2. Click the **Reports** tab in the Database window, and click the **New** button. The New Report dialog box appears (see Figure 19.1).

3. Click on **AutoReport: Columnar** or **AutoReport: Tabular**, whichever you want.

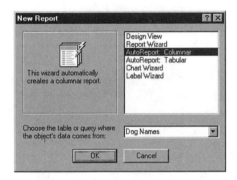

Figure 19.1   Choose one of the AutoReports from this window.

4. In the drop-down list at the bottom of the dialog box, select the table or query on which you want to base the report.

Multiple Tables?   AutoReports can use only one table or query. If you want to create an AutoReport that uses several tables, first create a query based on those tables, and then base the AutoReport on the query.

5. Click **OK**. The report appears in Print Preview. See the "Working with Reports in Print Preview" section later in this lesson to learn what to do next.

The AutoReports' output is not much better than a raw printout from a table or form, as you can see in Print Preview. If you want a better looking report, try Report Wizard, as explained in the following section.

Creating a Report with Report Wizard

The Report Wizard offers a good compromise between ease of use and flexibility. With Report Wizard, you can use multiple tables and queries and choose a layout and format for your report.

Follow these steps to create a report with Report Wizard:

1. Open the database containing the table or query on which you want to report.

2. Click the **Reports** tab in the Database window, and click the **New** button. The New Report dialog box appears (see Figure 19.1).

3. Click **Report Wizard**, and click **OK**. The Report Wizard starts (see Figure 19.2).

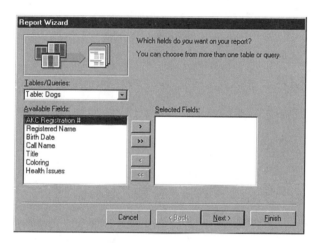

Figure 19.2 The first Report Wizard screen.

Multiple Tables/Queries Allowed You don't need to select a table or query from the drop-down list in the New Report dialog box in step 3, because you'll be selecting tables and queries in step 4 instead, as part of the wizard.

4. Open the **Tables/Queries** drop-down list, and select one of the tables or queries from which you want to include fields.

687

5. Click on a field in the **Available Fields** list, and then click the >
   button to move it to the **Selected Fields** list. Repeat to select all the
   fields you want.

6. If desired, select another table or query from the **Tables/Queries**
   list and repeat step 5. When you finish selecting fields, click **Next**.
   The next screen of the wizard appears (Figure 19.3).

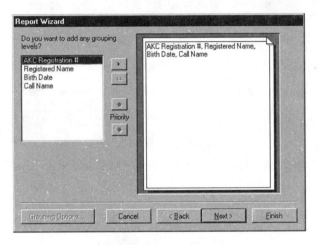

Figure 19.3 Set your report's grouping.

7. If you want the records grouped by any of the fields you selected,
   click on the field, and click the > button. You can select several
   grouping levels; select them in the order you want them. Then
   click **Next** to move on.

Grouping? The instructions on the screen are a bit cryptic.
By default, there are no groups. You have to select a field and
click the > button to create a grouping. For instance, I could
group my dogs by age by grouping by the Birth Date field.
Grouping sets of each group on the report.

TIP **Sorting Versus Grouping** In Report Wizard, you can't sort unless you group. What if you don't want groups? For instance, what if you don't have any fields that have any common information? Just set up the first field you want to sort by as a "group." Each group will consist of a single record, and it will be just as if you had sorted them.

8. If you created a grouping, you'll be asked what sort order you want to use within the groups (Figure 19.4). If you want sorted records, open the top drop-down list and select a field to sort by. Select up to four sorts from the drop-down lists; then click **Next**.

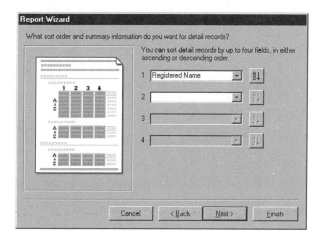

Figure 19.4 Set the sort order.

 TIP **Ascending or Descending?** By default, the sort is in ascending order (A–Z). Click the **AZ** button next to the box to change the sort order to descending (Z–A) if you like. See Lesson 16 for more information about sorting.

9. In the next dialog box (see Figure 19.5), choose a layout option from the **Layout** area. When you click on an option button, the sample in the box changes to show you what you selected.

689

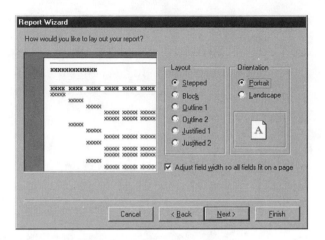

Figure 19.5 Choose the layout of your report.

Where Are All the Layouts? If you didn't choose any grouping in your report, your layout choices will be confined to two: Vertical and Tabular. The other layouts shown in Figure 19.5 are unique to grouped reports.

10. Choose which orientation your printed report will have: **Portrait** (across the narrow edge of the paper) or **Landscape** (across the wide edge of the paper). Then click **Next** to continue.

11. In the next Wizard dialog box, you're asked to choose a report style. Several are listed; click on one to see a sample of it; then click **Next** when you're satisfied with your choice.

12. Finally, you're asked for a report title. Enter one in the **Report** text box, and click **Finish** to see your report in Print Preview (see Figure 19.6).

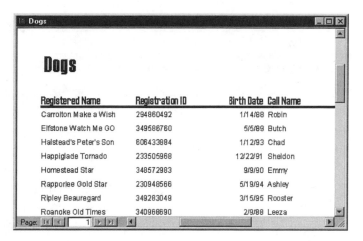

Figure 19.6   Here's a very simple report, with no sorting or grouping.

Viewing and Printing Reports in Print Preview

When you finish a report with either Report Wizard or AutoReport, the report appears in Print Preview (as shown in Figure 19.6). From here, you can print the report, if you're happy with it, or you can go to Report Design view to make changes if you aren't, as you'll learn in Lesson 20.

If you want to print the report and specify any print options (such as number of copies), open the **File** menu and select **Print**. If you want a quick hard copy, click the **Print** button on the toolbar. Table 19.1 shows the complete set of toolbar buttons offered in Print Preview.

Table 19.1   The Print Preview Toolbar

Button	Purpose
🖨	Prints immediately
🔍	Zooms in to see the report more closely
🗎	Shows the report in single full-page view

continues

691

Table 19.1 Continued

Button	Purpose
⬜	Shows the report in two-page view
100% ▾	A drop-down list where you can set the zoom magnification
Close	Closes Print Preview
⬜ ▾	OfficeLinks (if you have the full Microsoft Office suite of programs); see the note following this table.
⬜	Returns to the database window
⬜ ▾	Creates a new object (use the drop-down list to select which kind)
▶?	Help; click on it, then click on the object you need help with.

Click on the button appropriate to what you want to do. To go to Report Design view, click **Close**. (Report Design view is actually open; it's just obscured by the Print Preview window.)

OfficeLinks This feature enables you to quickly import what you're working on into another Microsoft Office program. Open the drop-down list on the **OfficeLinks** button to see your choices. For instance, with the report I created, I had the choices of **Publish It with MS Word** or **Analyze It with MS Excel**. A third choice, **MS Merge**, was unavailable.

In this lesson, you learned to create and print a simple report. In the next lesson, you'll learn how to work in Report Design view to customize your report.

Customizing a Report

In this lesson, you'll learn to use Report Design view to make your report more attractive.

Entering Report Design View

When you finish previewing a report you've created, just close Print Preview and you're automatically in Report Design view.

If you want to come back to Report Design view later, from the Database window, perform these steps:

1. Click the **Reports** tab.

2. Click the report you want to modify.

3. Click the **Design** button. The report appears in Design view, as shown in Figure 20.1.

Report Design view may seem familiar to you; it looks a lot like Form Design view. Almost everything you learned about editing forms in Lessons 14 applies also to reports. Just like Form Design view, there is a toolbox of common editing tools.

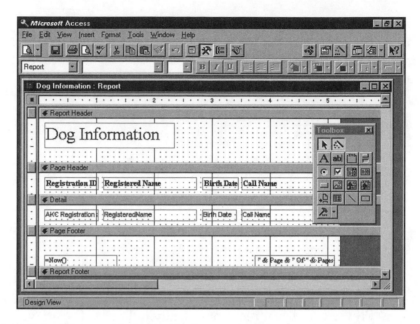

Figure 20.1   The report created in the previous lesson, in Design view.

Working with Objects on Your Report

Working with report objects in Report Design view is exactly the same as working with objects in Form Design view. An object is any control, such as a field name or a title. Turn back to Lesson 14 for the full story, or follow the brief review here:

Selecting objects   Just like in Form Design view, you select an object on your report by clicking on it. Selection handles appear around it (little squares in the corners). See Chapter 14 for more details.

Moving objects   To move an object, first select it. Then position the mouse pointer over a border so the pointer turns into an open black hand. Then click and drag the object to a new location.

Resizing objects   First, select the object. Then position the mouse pointer over one of the selection handles, and drag the handle to resize the object.

Formatting text objects Use the **Font** and **Font Size** drop-down lists on the toolbar to choose fonts; then use the **Bold**, **Italic**, and **Underline** toolbar buttons to set special attributes.

Adding and Removing Fields

You can add more fields to your report at any time. Follow these steps to add a field to your report:

1. If you don't see the Field List, select **View**, **Field List** or click the **Field List** button on the toolbar. A floating box appears listing all the fields in the table you're using.

2. Drag any field from the Field List into the report. Place it anywhere in the **Detail** area that you want.

To delete a field, select it by clicking on it, and press the **Delete** key. This deletes the reference to the field from the report, but it remains in the table from which it came.

Arranging Your New Fields

When you add a field to your report, you're actually adding two things: a *label* and a *text box*. These two elements are bound together: the label describes the text box, and the text box represents the actual field that will be used (see Figure 20.2). You can change the label without affecting the text box; for instance, you could change the label on the Coloring field to Dog Color without affecting the contents. To change a label, just click on it, and then retype.

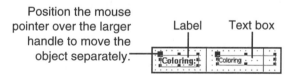

Figure 20.2 The text box and its label.

By default, when you move the text box, the label follows. When you position the mouse pointer over the border of the text box, and the pointer changes to an open hand, that's your signal that the label will follow the text box when you drag it.

695

However, you can also move the text box and the label separately. Notice that in the upper-left corner of each, there is a selection handle (square) that's bigger than the others. When you position the mouse pointer over that handle, the cursor becomes a pointing hand. That's your signal that you can click-and-drag the object separately from the other.

Moving the label separately can come in handy when you don't want the label to appear in its default position (to the left of the text box). For instance, you may want the label to appear above the text box.

Adding Labels

In the preceding section, you saw how to add a field: a text box plus a label, both bound together. But you can also add labels by themselves, with extra text in them that is not necessarily associated with a particular field—for instance, an informational note about the report in general. Just click on **Label** button in the toolbox. Then click anywhere on the report and start typing. When you finish, click anywhere outside the label.

Adding a Calculated Text Box

The most common thing that text boxes hold is references to fields, as you have seen in this lesson. However, text boxes have another purpose; they can also hold calculations based on values in different fields.

Creating a calculated text box is a bit complicated; first you have to create an unbound text box (that is, one that's not associated with any particular field). Then you have to enter the calculation into the text box. Follow these steps:

1. Click the **Text Box** tool in the toolbox, and click-and-drag on the report to create a text box.

2. Change the label to reflect what's going to go into that box. For instance, if it's going to be Sales Tax, change it to that. Position the label where you want it.

3. Click in the text box, and type the formula you want calculated. (See the following section for guidance.)

4. Click anywhere outside the text box when you finish.

Rules for Creating Calculations

The formulas you enter into your calculated text box use standard mathematical controls:

+   Add
-     Subtract
*   Multiply
/   Divide

All formulas begin with an equals sign (=), and all field names are in parentheses. Here are some examples:

To calculate a total price by multiplying the value in the Quantity field by the value in the Price field, enter **=(Quantity)*(Price)**.

To calculate a 25% discount off the value in the Cost field, enter **=(Cost)*.075**.

To add the total of the values in three fields, enter **(Field1)+(Field2)+(Field3)**.

More Room If you run out of room in the text box when typing your formula, press **Shift+F2** to open a Zoom box, where there's more room.

In this lesson, you learned to customize your report by adding and removing objects, moving them around, and creating calculations. In the next lesson, you'll learn how to create a chart based on a table or query in your database.

Creating Relationships Between Tables

In this lesson, you'll learn how to link two or more tables together so you can work with them as you would a single table.

Why Create Relationships?

Earlier in the book, in Lesson 2, I encouraged you to make separate tables for information that was not directly related. As you've learned along the way, when you create forms, queries, and reports, you can pull information from more than one table easily. But this works best when there is a well-defined relationship between the tables.

Let's say, for instance, that I have two tables containing information about my customers. One table, Customers, contains their names and addresses, and the other, Orders, contains their orders. The two tables have a common field: Customer ID#. All records in the Orders table correspond to a record in the Customers table. (This is called a *"many-to-one" relationship* because there could be many orders for one customer.)

As another example, in my kennel database, I have several tables describing my dogs and their activities. I have a table listing all the different colorings a dog can have. I can create a relationship between the Dogs table and the Coloring table, matching up each dog's coloring field with one of the accepted colors listed in the Coloring table. This would ensure that I didn't record any dog's coloring as a type that's not allowed.

More Complicated   Relationships can be extremely complicated. I'm showing you only simple examples in this lesson, because they're probably all you'll need to get started. For more information on relationships, see your Access documentation.

Creating a Relationship Between Tables

To create a relationship between tables, you open the Relationships window and add relationships from there. Follow these steps:

1. From anywhere in the database select **Tools, Relationships**. The Relationships window opens.

2. Open the **Relationships** menu and select **Show Table**. The Show Table dialog box appears (see Figure 21.1).

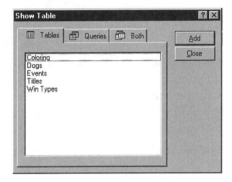

Figure 21.1   Add tables to your Relationships window using this dialog box.

3. Click on a table that you want to use for a relationship; then click the **Add** button.

4. Repeat step 3 until you've selected all the tables you want to work with, and click **Close**. Each table appears in its own box on the Relationships window, as shown in Figure 21.2.

Make It Bigger   If you can't clearly see all the fields in a table's list, drag the border of its box to make it large enough to see everything. I've done that in Figure 21.2 to make the Dogs table completely visible.

5. Click on a field in one table that you want to link to another table. For instance, I'm going to link the Coloring field in my Dogs table to the Coloring field in my Coloring table.

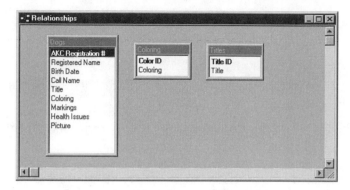

Figure 21.2 I've added three tables to my Relationships window, for this example.

6. Hold down the mouse button and drag away from the selected field. Your mouse pointer will turn into a little rectangle. Drop the little rectangle onto the destination field. The Relationships dialog box appears (see Figure 21.3).

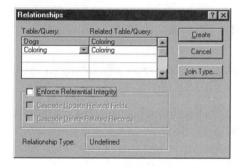

Figure 21.3 The Relationships dialog box asks you to define the relationship you're creating.

7. Choose any Referential Integrity options you want (see the following section), then click **Create**. If all goes well, a relationship will be created, and you'll see a line between the two fields in the Relationships window (see Figure 21.4).

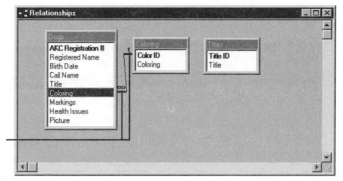

You will see a plain line here instead if you didn't choose Enforce Referential Integrity.

Figure 21.4   The line represents a relationship between the two fields.

I Got an Error Message!   If you checked the Envorce Referential Integrity check box, and an error message appeared when you tried to create the relationship, check out the latter part of this lesson to learn why, and how you can fix it.

Relationship Symbols   Notice in Figure 21.4 that next to the Dogs table there's an infinity sign (looks like a sideways 8), and next to the Coloring table there's a **1**. These symbols appear in relationships where Enforce Referential Integrity is turned on. The infinity sign means "many." That means many records in this table can match a single record (hence the **1** sign) in the related Coloring table.

What Is Referential Integrity?

Referential Integrity keeps you from making data entry mistakes. It says, essentially, that all the information in the two fields should match. If there is an entry in one table in the linked field that doesn't exist in the other, it's a problem.

An example will make this clearer. In the Coloring field in my Dogs database, I have a number that matches up with the Color ID field

701

in the Coloring table. The Coloring table lists all the allowable colors for the breed of dog. I don't want my clerks to be able to accidentally enter a number in the Dogs table that doesn't match up with any of the colors in the Coloring table, so I chose to Enforce Referential Integrity. Now Access won't let anyone enter anything in the Coloring field of the Dogs table except one of the numbers contained in the Color ID field in the Coloring table.

What happens if someone tries? It depends on which of the other two check boxes shown in Figure 21.3 you marked.

- **Neither marked** Access gives an error message and won't let you make the entry.

- **Cascade Update Related Fields** If you mark this check box and you make a change to the related table (in our example, the Coloring table), Access makes the change in the other table, too (the Dogs table). For instance, if I decided to make a certain coloring number 8 instead of 7, and I made the change in the Coloring table, all the 7s in the Dog table would change to 8s.

- **Cascade Delete Related Fields** If you mark this check box and you make a change to the primary table (Dogs) so that the entry in the related table isn't valid anymore, Access will delete the entry. For instance, if I deleted all the dogs from my Dogs table that had coloring number 3, Access would delete the record in the Coloring table for Coloring ID number 3.

If you try to use Referential Integrity, you will likely get an error message the first time you try, because there is usually some condition that prevents it from working, as Murphy's Law goes. For instance, when I first created the relationship shown in Figure 21.4, with Enforce Referential Integrity marked, Access wouldn't allow it because the field type for the Coloring field in the Dogs table was set to Text while the Color ID field in the Coloring table was a number. (It didn't matter that I had entered only numbers in the Coloring field in the Dogs table.)

Editing a Relationship

Once you create a relationship, you can edit it by redisplaying the Relationships dialog box. To do so, double-click on the line between the two tables. Then make changes as you learned to do earlier in this chapter.

Removing a Relationship

To delete a relationship, just click on it in the Relationships window, then press the **Delete** key. Access will ask for confirmation; click **Yes**, and the relationship disappears.

In this lesson, you learned how to create, edit, and delete relationships between tables.

WORKING TOGETHER

Understanding
Object Linking
and Embedding

In this lesson, you'll learn some important OLE terms and learn the difference between pasting, linking, and embedding.

What Is Object Linking and Embedding (OLE)?

OLE (pronounced "oh-LAY") stands for *Object Linking and Embedding*. It is a Windows feature that enables the Windows applications that employ it to transparently share information.

OLE 2.0 The current version of OLE is 2.0, and many applications will brag that they are OLE 2.0 compatible. Don't worry about version numbers with Microsoft Office for Windows 95—it's all OLE 2.0 compatible.

For example, you might create a quarterly report in Microsoft Word that contains an Excel Chart and a list of employees created in an Access database. Each quarter, the Excel data in the chart and the employee list changes. When it comes time to generate the next quarterly report, you could try to find the most up-to-date version of the Excel chart and the employee list, copy and paste them into the report, or you could use OLE's linking and embedding features to automatically update the report with the changes made in each supporting document.

To understand how to use OLE you'll need to learn the terms listed below.

Object Pieces of data that you either link to, or embed in, another document. An object can be any size, from a small snippet of text to an entire multi-page spreadsheet. Examples include: a range of

Excel cells containing numeric data, a company logo created in a drawing application, a sound clip created in Microsoft Sound Recorder.

Container File (also called **Compound Document** or **Destination Document**) A document that contains links to other Windows documents. The linked parts are called objects. For example, a Word document containing a pie chart from Excel (an object) is a container file.

Source File The document that contains the object you are linking. For example, if you are placing an Excel chart into a PowerPoint presentation, the Excel worksheet that contains the desired chart is the source file.

Client Application The client application is the application in which you're assembling the container file. The client application receives objects created in other applications and places them in the container file. For example, if you create a Quarterly Report in Microsoft Word that contains linked objects from Access and Excel, Word is the client application.

Server Application A server application is a Windows application that created an object being linked to a container file. For example, if you create a presentation in PowerPoint that contains an object created in Excel, Excel is the server application (and PowerPoint is the client application).

What Is Linking?

Now that you understand some of the terms associated with OLE, let's look at what linking (the "L" in OLE) entails, and examine some examples.

When a linked object is placed in a container file, any changes you make to the object in its native application (the server application) are automatically made to the copy of the object in the container file.

For example, let's revisit the quarterly report mentioned earlier in the lesson. In quarter 1, when the report is first created in Word, spreadsheet data from Excel and database data from Access are placed as linked objects in the report. Over the course of the quarter, changes are made in Excel and Access to the data. When it is time to assemble the report for quarter 2, the user simply opens the report in Word. The object links are still there, and the changed data from Excel and Access is automatically updated in the report. Figure 1.1 shows an example of some Excel data in a Word report.

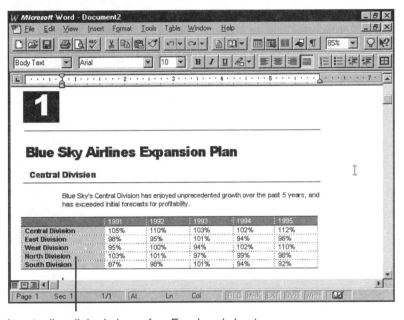

This table is actually a linked piece of an Excel worksheet.

Figure 1.1   An example of a container file containing linked objects.

One way to create links such as just described is with the Paste Special command on the Edit menu. It works a little differently from the regular Paste command on the Edit menu.

When an object is pasted into a document with the regular Paste command, the object is simply dropped in, with no information about its origin. In contrast, when an object is pasted into a document with Paste Special, several pieces of information about the object are stored as part of the container file, including the source file's name and location, the server application, and the location of the object within the source file. This extra information is what makes it possible for the object to be updated whenever the source file is updated.

You'll learn the specifics about how to link objects in lessons that follow.

What Is Embedding?

When you embed an object, you insert a copy of it into your document, like the regular Paste command does. A link to the source file is not maintained. However, embedding does offer something that regular pasting does not. When you embed an object into a document, a link is maintained to the client application, so you can double-click on that object at any time to open the server application and edit the object.

A good example of an embedded object is a company logo created in Microsoft WordArt, embedded as part of a letterhead document created in Word. The logo is not likely to change very often, nor is it maintained as part of another regularly updated graphic file, so linking is not necessary. When you do need to change the logo, you double-click on it to open WordArt and edit the logo. Figure 1.2 shows an example of an embedded object in a Word document.

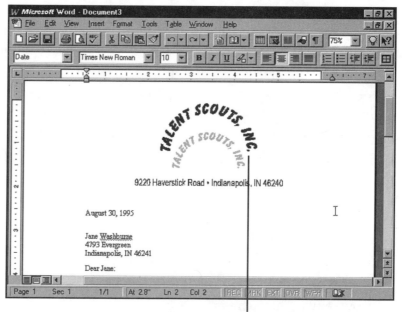

This logo is embedded.

Figure 1.2   An embedded WordArt graphic in Microsoft Word.

As an embedded object, all the information about the logo is maintained in the letterhead document, so you do not have to worry about managing or locating a separate file for the logo.

The Paste Special command can also be used to embed as well as to link. You choose linking versus embedding by making the choice in the Paste Special dialog box. The Insert Object command can be used to link or embed an existing file, or to create a new embedded file from scratch. You'll learn more about these commands in later lessons.

In this lesson, you learned some important terminology you'll see repeatedly in the following lessons. In the next lesson, you'll learn the difference between Paste Special and Insert Object, two methods of linking and embedding.

Paste Special and Insert Object

In this lesson, you'll be introduced to two ways to create an OLE link: the Paste Special command and the Insert Object command.

Linking and Embedding with Paste Special

As you've learned in other sections of this book, Windows offers a simple cut-and-paste feature that enables you to cut or copy from any Windows program and paste your selection into any other Windows program. This is accomplished with the Cut or Copy command on the Edit menu and then the Paste command (on the same menu).

To link or embed, you also can use the Copy command, but instead of choosing Paste, you select Paste Special. This opens the Paste Special dialog box, which is used to inform Windows how you want the special linking or embedding to occur.

Exploring the Paste Special Dialog Box

After you've Copied the desired object to the Clipboard, the Paste Special command on the Edit menu becomes available. When you select **Paste Special**, the Paste Special dialog box appears. Figure 2.1 shows the Paste Special dialog box for Word. The following list explains the options found there.

Source   This is the name and location of the object currently in the Windows Clipboard. It's information-only; you can't edit it.

Paste   Pastes the contents of the Window Clipboard into the document at the location of the insertion point. The link is not maintained, but you can double-click on the pasted material to edit it. (This is *embedding*.)

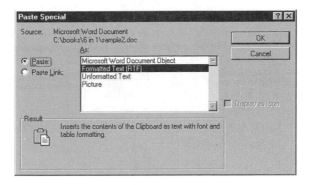

Figure 2.1 The Paste Special dialog box.

Paste Link This option is available if the contents of the Clipboard can be linked to the container file. With this option selected, a link is created between the source file and the container file. If you have not saved the source file, the Paste Link option is not available.

As This section of the dialog box lists the possible formats the object in the Clipboard can be pasted as. The formats listed change depending on the object type. Some formats you might see include:

> *...Object* A type that ends with the word Object is a recognized OLE-capable format that you can either link or embed. If you want to embed, you should choose a data type that ends with the word "object." For example, in Figure 2.1, you would choose Microsoft Word Document Object.

> *Formatted Text (RTF)* This data type formats text as it is formatted in the source file. If the text is formatted as bold italic, it is pasted as bold italic. This format does not support embedding.

> *Unformatted Text* No formatting is applied to the object when this data type is selected. This format does not support embedding.

> *Picture* This data type formats the object as a Window metafile picture, but does not support embedding.

Bitmap This data type formats the object as a bitmap picture, such as a Windows Paintbrush image. It does not support embedding.

Display As Icon Selecting this option displays the pasted object as an icon of the object, rather than the object data. This option is only available if you have selected Paste Link. This is useful for pasting Sounds and MediaClips, because you can double-click on them to play them later.

Result The Result section of the dialog box gives a description of the outcome of the options you've selected in the dialog box.

Some Hints for Linking and Embedding

When deciding which options to select in the Paste Special dialog box, pay close attention to the notes that appear in the Result area. These notes tell you what will happen if you choose **OK** with the present set of options.

The type of linking, embedding, or pasting that is done depends both on your choice of **Paste** or **Paste Link** and your choice of type in the **As** list. Here's an example for a Bitmap picture cropped from Paintbrush:

Paste/Paste Link	Data type	Result
Paste	Paintbrush Picture Object	Embeds but does not link
Paste	Bitmap	Neither embeds nor links
Paste Link	Paintbrush Picture Object	Links and embeds
Paste Link	Bitmap	Links and embeds

Edit It When you double-click on a Paintbrush image in Word that is not embedded, instead of Paintbrush opening to edit it, Microsoft Draw opens (a simple drawing program that comes with Word).

Linking and Embedding with Insert Object

Another method of linking and embedding objects in a document is to use the **Object** command on the **Insert** menu. This command is useful if you have not yet created the object in the source application, or if you want to insert an entire document as your object (rather than a cut or copied piece of one). You can't use Insert Object to link a portion of a file; it must be the entire file.

Exploring the Object Dialog Box

There are two tabs on the Object dialog box: Create New and Create from File. Click on the **Create New** tab to view the options for creating a new object if you have not yet created the object you want to embed or link into your document. Figure 2.2 shows the Create New portion of the Object dialog box. The following list explains the options found there.

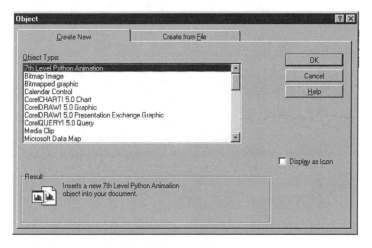

Figure 2.2   The Object dialog box.

Create New   This file folder-like tab of the dialog box displays the options for creating a new object to embed into the container file.

Object Type   This is a list of all the OLE-compatible applications installed on your computer. Selecting an object type of Microsoft Excel Chart, for example, will start Excel so you can create a chart.

Display as Icon   Selecting this option causes the embedded object to be displayed as an icon when embedded, rather than the object itself.

Result   The Result section of the dialog box describes the results of the options you choose in the dialog box.

Click on the **Create from File** tab if you want to insert an existing file as the object to be linked or embedded. Figure 2.3 shows the Create from File portion of the Object dialog box.

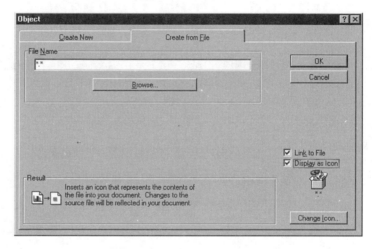

Figure 2.3   The Object dialog box with Create from File options.

Create from File   This tab changes the options in the dialog box so you can locate and select a file to embed in, or link to, the document you're working in.

File Name   This list box displays the file name you've entered. By default it's *.*, but you can change this.

.   This is another way of saying "all files." The asterisks are wild cards which represent any characters. *.doc means all files with a .doc extension; read.* means all files named read, no matter what the extension is. *.* means all files, period.

Browse   Click here to locate the file name you want. You can browse through all the folders and drives on your computer.

Link to File   This option creates a link between the inserted file and the document you're working in.

Display as Icon   Selecting this option causes the embedded or linked object to be displayed as an icon, rather than the object itself.

Change Icon   If you choose Display as Icon, this button appears to enable you to choose which icon is displayed.

Result   The Result section of the dialog box describes the results of the options you choose in the dialog box.

Don't worry if you don't understand all these options immediately; they're covered in greater detail in lessons to come.

In this lesson, you learned about the various options available in the Paste Special and Insert Object dialog boxes. In the next lesson, we'll walk through the steps of creating a link.

Creating an OLE Link

In this lesson, you'll learn to create an OLE link.

One of the primary benefits of creating an OLE link is the ability to edit the linked object at its source (that is, in the original application and document it was created in) and have all of the container files that contain the linked object updated automatically. This lesson shows you, step by step, how to create a link between two OLE applications, using both the Paste Special and the Insert Object methods that you learned about in Lesson 2.

Linking with the Paste Special Command

Creating a link between two applications with Paste Special is quite similar to using the Windowscut and paste procedure, with a few additional options at the paste step. Paste Special is used when you want to link or embed a piece of a file, but not the entire file.

What Are My Options?   The menu options for creating links between documents vary among Windows applications, or may not be available at all. Be sure to check your application's documentation if you find variances in the location or names of the menu options.

To create a link with **Edit, Paste Special**, start with the server application (the application in which the object to be linked was originally created). For example, to link an Excel chart to a Word document, start in Excel. Here are the steps:

1. Start the server application, and create or open the source file (the document that contains the object).

2. If you create a new document in the server application, be sure to use **File, Save** to save your document. You cannot link from a document that has not been saved.

3. Create the object to be linked if it does not already exist.

4. Select the object. The object may be text, a range of cells, a graphic, or database records.

5. Select **Edit, Copy**. The object you selected is copied to the Windows Clipboard.

6. Minimize the server application, and start the client application (the application into which you want to paste the object). Or if the client application is already open, simply switch to it by clicking on its name in the Taskbar.

7. If it is not already open, open the container file (the document to receive the pasted object) in the client application.

8. In the container file, position the cursor where you want the pasted (linked) object to appear.

9. Choose **Edit, Paste Special**. A dialog box appears (Figure 3.1) showing the Data Types list of different formats in which the object can appear.

It's Not There!   Some applications use slightly different wording for commands. If the Paste Special command does not appear on the Edit menu, use **Paste Links** instead.

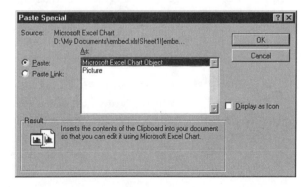

Figure 3.1   The Paste Special dialog box.

10. From the As list, select the data form in which you want the object to appear. Consult Lesson 2 to review the Object type options.

11. Click on the **Paste Link** button. Notice that the Result section of the dialog box describes the result of the options you are choosing in the dialog box.

12. Click on **OK** to paste the linked object into your document. The object is pasted into the container file, and Windows creates an automatically updating link between the object and its source file.

Now, each time you update the information in the source file, the changes you make can be reflected in the container file. The links you create can be updated automatically or manually. In the next lesson, you'll learn how to set the manual and automatic update options.

Linking with Insert Object

If you want to link an entire file to your document, such as a entire Excel spreadsheet, you can use the Insert Object command. It appears in the Edit menu of most Window's applications.

Unlike with Edit Paste, you do not have to open the source file to retrieve the object. You can perform the entire procedure without leaving the client application. Follow these steps:

1. Start the client application (the one to receive the object), and create or open the container file. We'll use Microsoft Word as the client application in this example.

2. Select **Insert, Object**. The Object dialog appears (Figure 3.2), listing the OLE application Object types that can be inserted.

3. Click on the **Create from File** tab at the top of the dialog box. The dialog box changes to show a file name list box (Figure 3.3).

4. Click the **Browse** button, and select the name of the file you want to insert and link to the container file. We'll use an Excel work-sheet in this example. Navigate through the directories and subdirectories to locate the file if it does not appear in the current directory. When you locate the file, double-click on it.

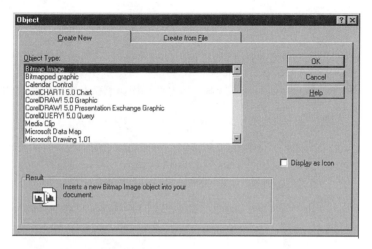

Figure 3.2 The Object dialog box.

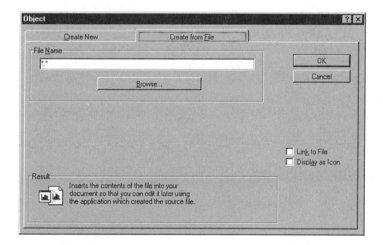

Figure 3.3 The Create from File options.

5. Click on the **Link to File** check box. This will create an active link between the source file and the destination file. Notice that the Result section of the dialog box describe the results of the option you choose in the dialog box.

6. Select **OK**. The dialog box closes, and the source file is inserted into the container file.

721

Whole Files Only   Remember that using the Insert Object command to create a linked file links an entire file to the container file. You cannot use this command to link an individual object, such as a range of Excel cells, to the container file. Use the steps for Linking with the Paste Special command for that.

Now, the next time you update the source file that contains the data you linked, the file can be automatically or manually updated with the changes you make.

In this lesson, you learned how to create a link between applications. In the next lesson, you'll learn how to edit and manage your links between applications.

Managing OLE Links

In the lesson, you will learn how to edit, break, restore, lock, and unlock OLE links.

Editing Linked Objects

Once you have created a linked object, you may want to edit and update the information in the object. At this stage, you'll realize the full benefit of an OLE link, because you can edit the object one time and it will be updated in every document that it is linked to.

There are two ways to edit a linked object. The first is to start at the source file, using the server application to make changes to the object. The second is to start at the container file and let the link information lead you to the correct source file and server application. With the second method, you do not have to remember the name of the source file or even what server application created it. Follow the steps below to learn how to edit objects using these two methods.

Editing from the Source File

To edit a linked object starting from the source file:

1. Start the server application, and open the source file that contains the object you want to edit.

2. Edit and make changes to the object.

3. Save the document and close the server application.

4. Switch to (or start) the client application, and open the container file. The changes should automatically be reflected in the container file.

If the changes are not reflected, the document may not be set up to automatically update links. Skip to "Managing a Link's Update Settings" later in this lesson to learn how to update the links.

Now You See It, Now You Don't   Some client applications let you edit or make changes directly to the object that is linked to the container file without starting the server application. This can cause problems because the source file is not being changed, only the image of the object. The changes you make to the image will be wiped out when the object is updated via the source file. You will not have this problem with Microsoft Office products, but it may occur with other, non-Microsoft applications.

Editing from the Container File

Editing from the container file is quick and easy, because you do not have to find and open the server application manually. To edit a linked object from the container file:

1. From the container file, double-click on the linked object you want to update. The server application starts and displays the source file. Figure 4.1 shows a linked Excel range ready to be edited in a Word document.

2. Edit the object in the source file. You can make as many changes to the object as like.

3. Choose **File, Save** in the server application.

4. Choose **File, Exit** in the server application. You're returned to the container file, which reflects the changes you made to the linked object.

If double-clicking on the object does not start the server application, open the Links list dialog box by choosing **Links** from the **Edit** menu. Select the link you want to edit, and click on the **Open Source** button (see Figure 4.2). The server application will start and display the source file.

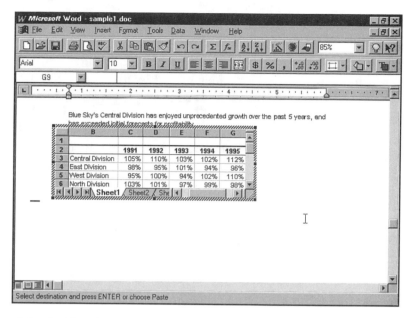

Figure 4.1   An Excel range linked to a Word document.

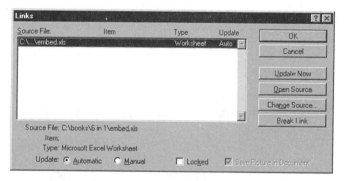

Figure 4.2   Another way to edit the object is to select it from the Links dialog box and click on the Open Source button.

Managing a Link's Update Settings

Once you have created a linked object, you can control when changes to the source file are reflected in the container file(s). You can update a link manually or automatically. If a link is set to be updated manually, you must remember to follow the update steps each time you change the source file that contains the linked object.

With the automatic setting enabled (the default update setting), the changes you make to the source file are automatically updated each time you open the container file.

To set a linked object to be manually updated, follow these steps:

1. Open the container file that contains the object link you want to update.

2. Choose **Edit, Links**. The Links dialog box appears (Figure 4.2). For the linked objects in your document, the list indicates the Link name, the path name of the source file, and whether the link is set to update automatically or manually.

3. Select the link you want to update.

4. Change the Update setting to **Manual**.

5. Update the link by clicking on the **Update Now** button in the Link list dialog box. The object is then updated with any changes that were made to the source file.

6. Click on **OK** to close the dialog box.

7. Choose **Save** from the **File** menu to save the document and changes to the link settings.

With the link set for manual update, you must repeat step 5 of this procedure each time you want the linked object to reflect changes made in the source file.

Locking and Unlocking Links

In addition to setting link update options to manual and automatic, you can lock a link to prevent the link from being updated when the source file is changed.

To lock and unlock a link, follow these steps:

1. Open the document containing the linked object.

2. Choose **Edit, Links**. The Links dialog box appears.

3. Select the link that you want to lock.

4. To lock the link, select the **Locked** check box. To unlock the link, make sure the check box is empty.

5. Click on **OK** to close the dialog box.

A locked link will not be updated until it is unlocked.

Breaking Links

If at some point, you decide that you want a linked object in your document to remain fixed and no longer be updated by its source file, you can break (or cancel) the link. This does not delete or alter the object, it merely removes the background information that directly ties the object to its source file. The object becomes like any other object that was placed by Window's Copy and Paste operation.

To break or cancel a linked object, follow these steps:

1. Open the container file that contains the object whose link you want to break.

2. Select **Edit, Links** (or **Link Options** in some applications). The Links list dialog box appears (Figure 4.2), showing linked object information.

3. Select the link name of the object you want to break.

4. Choose **Break Link** (or **Delete** in some applications). A warning box may appear cautioning that you are breaking a link. Click on **OK** or **Yes** to confirm your choice.

Restoring a Broken Link

It is possible to accidentally break a link to an object. If you move the source file from the directory in which it was saved when the link was created, or if you change the name of the source file, Windows will not be able to find it and the link is effectively broken. If this happens, and the link is set to automatically update, a warning dialog box appears telling you that the source file is missing or corrupted. To re-establish the broken link you must move the source file back to its original location, or tell Windows where to find the document in its new location.

To re-establish a broken link, follow these steps:

1. Open the container file containing the object with the broken link. If you received an alert dialog box warning of the broken link, you have already completed this step.

2. Choose **Edit, Links**. The Links list dialog box appears, listing the objects in the container file that are linked.

3. Select the object whose link is broken.

4. Click on the **Change Source** button. A dialog box appears showing the location of the linked object (Figure 4.3).

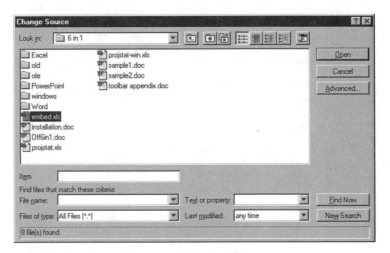

Figure 4.3   The Change Link dialog box.

5. Choose a different location or file name to reflect the new location or name of the source file.

6. Click on **OK** to complete the restoration of the link. The link is now re-established between the source and container files.

In this lesson, you learned how to share and dynamically update your documents. In the next lesson, you'll learn how to embed objects in OLE applications.

Embedding Objects in Windows Applications

In this lesson, you'll learn the difference between linking and embedding, how to embed an object in a Windows document, and how to edit an embedded object.

Understanding OLE Embedding

As you learned in Lessons 1 and 2, the procedure for embedding objects into your documents is essentially the same as that for linking objects, but the resulting connection between the source file and destination document is quite different.

Embedded objects are not linked to a source file. If you update the source file, any object in that document that is embedded in another document is not changed. The primary advantage of using embedded objects is the ease of editing the parts of a container file. Use embedding instead of linking if automatic updating of objects is not required.

Embedded objects can be edited easily because they provide quick access to the application that created them. If you double-click on an embedded object, the application that created the object starts, allowing you to edit the object. When you're finished editing the object, you exit the application by choosing **Update** from the **File** menu. The application closes and you see the updated object back where you started.

Creating Embedded Objects

There are two ways to embed an object in a document. You can create the object in the server application and embed it in the destination document using the **Paste Special** command, or you can start at the destination document and choose **Object** on the **Insert** menu to launch the server application, create the object, and embed the object in the destination document.

Embedding with the Paste Special Command

The Paste Special command is useful to embed a portion of a document into another document. For example, you might want to embed a few cells from a large Excel worksheet into a Word document. (If you wanted to embed the entire worksheet, you would use the Insert Object command instead, which is covered in the next section.)

To embed an object with the Paste Special command, follow these steps:

1. Start the server application, and either open or create the document that contains the object you want to embed.

2. Select the object to be embedded.

3. Choose **Edit, Copy**. The object is copied to the Windows Clipboard.

4. Start or switch to the client application, and open or create the destination document.

5. Place the insertion point where you want the object to appear.

6. Choose **Edit, Paste Special**. A dialog box appears (Figure 5.1) enabling you to select the data type of the object to be embedded.

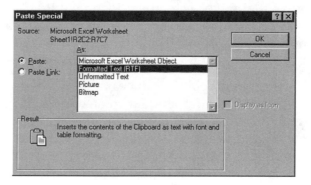

Figure 5.1 The Paste Special dialog box.

A Different Command   The Paste Special command's name varies slightly in some Windows applications. Be sure the command you choose allows you to select the data type of the object, and be sure *not* to select the Paste Link option.

7. Select the **Object** data type from the As list box (Microsoft Excel 5.0 Worksheet Object in this example).

8. Click on **OK.** The object is inserted at the insertion point and embedded in the destination document. Figure 5.2 shows the embedded object in the destination document.

9. Save the destination document. You can switch to the server application and either save or discard the source file. The destination document does not need the source file to maintain the embedded object (unlike a linked destination document that needs the source file containing the linked object.

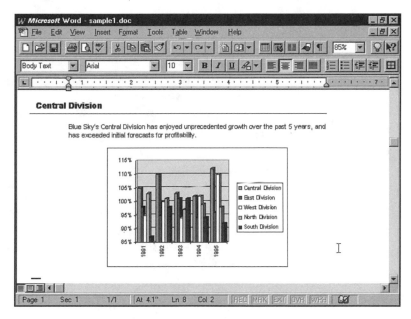

Figure 5.2   An embedded Excel 5 Graph in a Word document.

Embedding with Insert Object

If you have yet to create the object to be embedded, or if you want to embed an entire file, the Insert Object command is your best choice.

To create a new object, follow these steps:

1. Start the client application, and open the destination document. This is the document that you will place the embedded object into.

2. Choose **Insert, Object**. A dialog box appears listing the server applications and object types that can be embedded in your document (Figure 5.3).

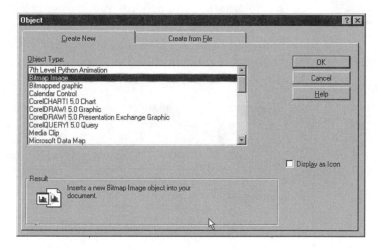

Figure 5.3 The Object dialog box.

3. Choose the server application you want to use, and click on **OK**. A special version server application starts, with the destination document still displayed on the screen. Figure 5.4 shows Microsoft Excel in a Word document.

4. Create the object using the server application's tools and commands. Notice that some of the menus and toolbar icons on the menu bar at the top of the application window have changed to those of the Server application's.

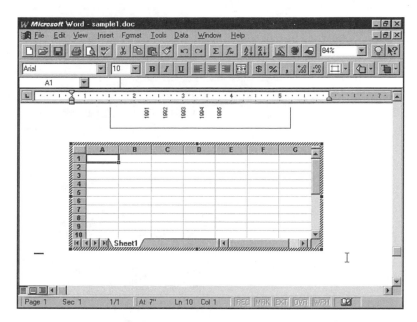

Figure 5.4 Microsoft Excel ready to create an object to embed in Word.

5. Once you've created the data, click on a portion of the destination document window. The server application closes, and the embedded object appears in the destination document. In some cases, you might need to manually exit the server application to return to the destination document.

6. Save the destination document.

If you want to embed a file that you've already created, click on the **Create from File** tab at the top of the Insert dialog box. The dialog box changes to a file list box, where you can locate the file to be embedded. Click on **OK** to insert the existing file in the destination document. Note that this option will only embed an entire file, not a individual object.

Editing Embedded Objects

Editing an embedded object is where the greatest advantage of embedding comes into play. You do not have to remember the name and location of the source file that you used to create the embedded object. You simply double-click on the object and the source application starts, allowing you to edit the object.

Follow these steps to edit an embedded object:

1. Start the client application and destination document containing the embedded object you want to edit.

2. Double-click on the object. The server application of the embedded object starts and displays the object (Figure 5.5). You can also choose **Edit, Object** to open the server application of the embedded object.

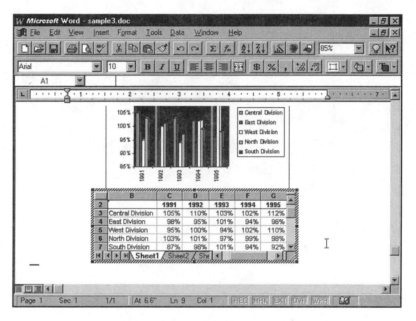

Figure 5.5 An Excel worksheet embedded as an editable object.

Modified Launch   Some objects perform a function or action when you double-click on them. For example, Windows Sound recorder objects play a sound when double-clicked on. To edit objects like this, hold down the **Alt** key while double-clicking the object.

3. Edit the object using the server application's tools and commands.

4. Click on a portion of the destination document. The server application closes, and you are returned to the destination document. The

embedded object reflects the changes you made. In some cases, you might have to select the **Exit** command to close the server application.

Converting the File Format of an Embedded Object

There may be a time when you need to edit a container file containing embedded objects, but you do not have the same applications that created the embedded objects installed on your PC. For example, you receive a container file from a co-worker that contains an embedded Excel object, but you do not have Excel on your PC, you use Lotus 1-2-3. Fortunately, you can change the server application of the embedded object. (You can't convert a linked object.)

To convert an embedded object to a different file format, follow these steps:

1. Open the document containing the object whose source application you want to convert to.

2. Select the embedded object.

3. Select the last command on the **Edit** menu, **Worksheet Object** in this example. This command name changes, depending on the object type you selected in step 2. A submenu appears (see Figure 5.6).

Figure 5.6 The Object Edit menu option on the Edit menu.

4. Choose **Convert** from the submenu. The Convert dialog box appears (Figure 5.7), displaying the possible Object types to convert the object to.

5. Select the Object type you want to convert the object to.

6. Choose **Convert To** to permanently change the object to the file format you selected in step 5. Choose **Activate As** to temporarily change all of the objects of the type selected to the file format you specified in step 5.

7. Click on **OK** to complete the conversion of the object.

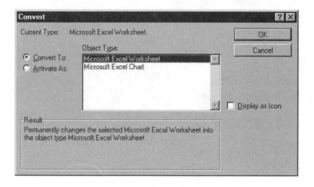

Figure 5.7 The Convert dialog box.

The next time you double-click the object to edit it, the application that you converted to will open so you can edit the object.

Update 'em Now If you install a new version of an application that was used to create embedded objects, you might have to use the Convert procedures in this section to update the objects to the new version of software.

In this lesson, you learned how to use OLE embedding to create a container file that provides easy access and editing of objects created in different Windows OLE applications. In the next lesson, you'll learn to use the shortcut bar.

Using the Shortcut Bar

In this lesson, you'll learn about the Microsoft Office shortcut bar. You'll see how to display or hide it, and how to use it to start Office programs.

What Is the Shortcut Bar?

You may have noticed that when you installed Microsoft Office, a bar of small icons appeared at the top of your Windows 95 screen. That's the shortcut bar, and it can save you time and effort.

The buttons that appear on the shortcut bar vary somewhat depending on which Office components you have installed, but it probably looks something like the one in Figure 7.1.

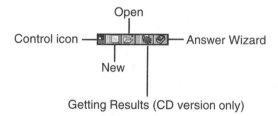

Figure 7.1 The Office Shortcut Bar gives you some quick ways to use Office programs.

Opening a New Document with the Shortcut Bar

You can start a new document in any Microsoft Office program with the shortcut bar. It's much faster to start a new document this way than to open the program and then issue the New command. Follow these steps:

1. Click the **New** button on the shortcut bar. A large New dialog box appears, with many tabs, as shown in Figure 7.2.

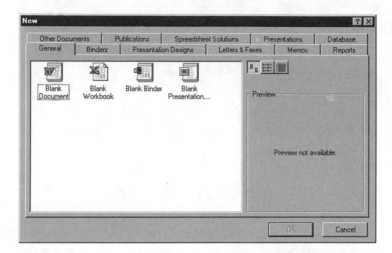

Figure 7.2 This dialog box enables you to open any kind of Microsoft Office document.

2. If you want to create a new blank document, click on one of the icons on the General tab, which is displayed by default (see Figure 7.2). For instance, to create a new spreadsheet, click on the **Blank Workbook** icon.

Or, if you want to create a document based on a template, click one of the other tabs in the New dialog box, and select one of the template icons. For instance, click the **Reports** tab, then click on **Professional Report**.

3. Click **OK,** and the application opens and starts the new document you selected.

 Starting a Blank Database To start a new database, you must click the **Database** tab; a blank database icon does not appear on the general tab along with all the other Office document types.

Opening a Document with the Shortcut Bar

Just as you can easily create a new document with the shortcut bar, you can also open existing ones. It's much faster and easier than opening the application and then opening the file.

Follow these steps to open a document:

1. Click the **Open** button on the shortcut bar. An Open dialog box appears (Figure 7.3).

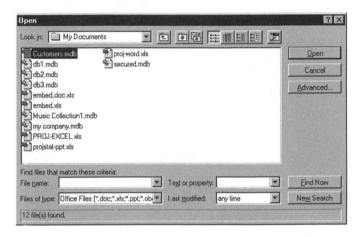

Figure 7.3   This Open dialog box works like the ones in the individual applications.

2. All Office data files are shown; if you want to narrow down the list to a specific type, select it from the **Files of type** drop-down list.

3. Change the drive and/or folder if desired, just as you would when opening a file in any of the applications.

4. Click **Open**. The application starts and the file opens.

Getting Help with the Shortcut Bar

You may have noticed that there are two Help buttons on the shortcut bar shown in Figure 7.1: Getting Results and Answer Wizard. Getting Results is a tutorial that comes with the CD version of Office; the Answer Wizard is the same Answer Wizard that you have encountered in each application. Click on either button to activate the feature.

Adding Icons to the Shortcut Bar

In addition to the icons that are displayed by default, you can display a variety of other icons on the shortcut bar. For instance, you can display icons for each of the Office applications, and start each application by clicking on its buttons.

Follow these steps to change the icons that appear on the shortcut bar:

1. Click the control icon at the far left end of the shortcut bar (shown in Figure 7.1). A menu opens.

2. Select **Customize** from the menu.

3. In the Customize dialog box that appears, click the **Buttons** tab. The dialog box will look something like Figure 7.4.

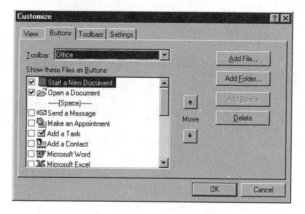

Figure 7.4 You can choose which icons appear on your shortcut bar from here.

4. To add an icon to the shortcut bar, click on the check box next to it to select it. (A check mark appears in the box.) For instance, to display an icon for Microsoft Word on the shortcut bar, click on the check box next to Microsoft Word.

5. To remove an icon from the shortcut bar, click on its check box to remove the check mark.

6. To move an icon to a different location on the shortcut bar, select it, then click the ↑ or ↓ buttons to move that icon to a different location on the list.

7. To add a space on the toolbar, select the icon before which the space should occur, then click the **Add Space** button. To delete a space, select the (Space) marker, then click **Delete**.

8. When you are finished, click **OK**.

Changing Which Icons Appear on the List

If the program or document you want to add to the shortcut bar doesn't appear on the list (refer to Figure 7.4), you can add it. From the Customize dialog box's Buttons tab:

1. Click **Add File**.

2. In the Add File dialog box, change the folder and/or drive if needed to locate the file you want.

3. Click on the file you want to add to the shortcut bar, then click the **Add** button.

Your file now appears on the list in the Customize dialog box, and you can select and deselect it to appear just as you do any of the other files on the list.

You can delete an icon from the list in the Customize dialog box even more easily—just select it and click the **Delete** button. Answer **Yes** to the warning that appears. Don't worry that you're deleting the program file—you're not. You're just deleting the shortcut copy of it.

Drag Icons to the Shortcut Bar One easy way to add an icon to the shortcut bar is to drag it there. You can drag it from any Explorer or My Computer window, or from the desktop itself.

In this lesson, you learned how to use the Office shortcut bar and to modify which icons appear on it.

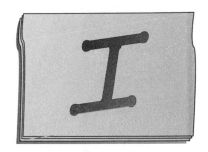

INDEX

W-X

Y-Z

GET CONNECTED
to the ultimate source of computer information!

The MCP Forum on CompuServe

Go online with the world's leading computer book publisher! Macmillan Computer Publishing offers everything you need for computer success!

Find the books that are right for you!
A complete online catalog, plus sample chapters and tables of contents give you an in-depth look at all our books. The best way to shop or browse!

➤ Get fast answers and technical support for MCP books and software

➤ Join discussion groups on major computer subjects

➤ Interact with our expert authors via e-mail and conferences

➤ Download software from our immense library:

 ▷ Source code from books
 ▷ Demos of hot software
 ▷ The best shareware and freeware
 ▷ Graphics files

Join now and get a free CompuServe Starter Kit!

To receive your free CompuServe Introductory Membership, call **1-800-848-8199** and ask for representative #597.

The Starter Kit includes:
➤ Personal ID number and password
➤ $15 credit on the system
➤ Subscription to *CompuServe Magazine*

Once on the CompuServe System, type:

GO MACMILLAN

for the most computer information anywhere!

MACMILLAN
COMPUTER
PUBLISHING

 **CompuServe**

Complete and Return this Card for a *FREE* Computer Book Catalog

Thank you for purchasing this book! You have purchased a superior computer book written expressly for your needs. To continue to provide the kind of up-to-date, pertinent coverage you've come to expect from us, we need to hear from you. Please take a minute to complete and return this self-addressed, postage-paid form. In return, we'll send you a free catalog of all our computer books on topics ranging from word processing to programming and the internet.

Mr. ☐ Mrs. ☐ Ms. ☐ Dr. ☐

Name (first) [_____] (M.I.) ☐ (last) [_____]

Address [_____]
[_____]

City [_____] State ☐☐ Zip [____][___]

Phone [___][_____][_____] Fax [___][_____][_____]

Company Name [_____]

E-mail address [_____]

1. Please check at least (3) influencing factors for purchasing this book.

Front or back cover information on book .... ☐
Special approach to the content .... ☐
Completeness of content .... ☐
Author's reputation .... ☐
Publisher's reputation .... ☐
Book cover design or layout .... ☐
Index or table of contents of book .... ☐
Price of book .... ☐
Special effects, graphics, illustrations .... ☐
Other (Please specify): _____ ☐

2. How did you first learn about this book?

Saw in Macmillan Computer Publishing catalog .... ☐
Recommended by store personnel .... ☐
Saw the book on bookshelf at store .... ☐
Recommended by a friend .... ☐
Received advertisement in the mail .... ☐
Saw an advertisement in: _____ ☐
Read book review in: _____ ☐
Other (Please specify): _____ ☐

3. How many computer books have you purchased in the last six months?

This book only .... ☐   3 to 5 books .... ☐
2 books .... ☐   More than 5 .... ☐

4. Where did you purchase this book?

Bookstore .... ☐
Computer Store .... ☐
Consumer Electronics Store .... ☐
Department Store .... ☐
Office Club .... ☐
Warehouse Club .... ☐
Mail Order .... ☐
Direct from Publisher .... ☐
Internet site .... ☐
Other (Please specify): _____ ☐

5. How long have you been using a computer?

☐ Less than 6 months   ☐ 6 months to a year
☐ 1 to 3 years   ☐ More than 3 years

6. What is your level of experience with personal computers and with the subject of this book?

	With PCs	With subject of book
New	☐	☐
Casual	☐	☐
Accomplished	☐	☐
Expert	☐	☐

Source Code ISBN: 0-7897-0559-1

7. Which of the following best describes your job title?

Administrative Assistant ☐
Coordinator ☐
Manager/Supervisor ☐
Director ☐
Vice President ☐
President/CEO/COO ☐
Lawyer/Doctor/Medical Professional ☐
Teacher/Educator/Trainer ☐
Engineer/Technician ☐
Consultant ☐
Not employed/Student/Retired ☐
Other (Please specify): _____ ☐

8. Which of the following best describes the area of the company your job title falls under?

Accounting ☐
Engineering ☐
Manufacturing ☐
Operations ☐
Marketing ☐
Sales ☐
Other (Please specify): _____ ☐

Comments: _____
_____
_____

9. What is your age?

Under 20 ☐
21-29 ☐
30-39 ☐
40-49 ☐
50-59 ☐
60-over ☐

10. Are you:

Male ☐
Female ☐

11. Which computer publications do you read regularly? (Please list)

_____
_____
_____
_____
_____
_____
_____
_____
_____
_____

Fold here and scotch-tape to mail.